The Political Economy of the

In recent years, the persecution of the Kurds in the Middle East under ISIS in Iraq and Syria has drawn increasing attention from the international media. In this book, Veli Yadirgi analyses the socioeconomic and political structures and transformations of the Kurdish people from the Ottoman era through to the modern Turkish Republic, arguing that there is a symbiotic relationship between the Kurdish question and the de-development of the predominantly Kurdish domains, making an ideal read for historians of the region and those studying the sociopolitical and economic evolution of the Kurds. First outlining theoretical perspectives on Kurdish identity, socioeconomic development and the Kurdish question, Yadirgi then explores the social, economic and political origins of Ottoman Kurdistan following its annexation by the Ottomans in 1514. Finally, he deals with the collapse of the empire, and the subsequent foundation and evolution of the Kurdish question in the new Turkish Republic.

Veli Yadirgi is a Research Associate and a Teaching Fellow in the Department of Development Studies at the School of Oriental and African Studies (SOAS), University of London. He has previously worked as a political correspondent and an editor in a variety of European media companies, and is a member of the London Middle East Institute, the Centre for Ottoman Studies, and Neoliberalism, Globalisation and States (all at SOAS).

The Political Economy of the Kurds of Turkey

From the Ottoman Empire to the Turkish Republic

Veli Yadirgi

School of Oriental and African Studies (SOAS), University of London

CAMBRIDGE
UNIVERSITY PRESS

CAMBRIDGE
UNIVERSITY PRESS

University Printing House, Cambridge CB2 8BS, United Kingdom

One Liberty Plaza, 20th Floor, New York, NY 10006, USA

477 Williamstown Road, Port Melbourne, VIC 3207, Australia

4843/24, 2nd Floor, Ansari Road, Daryaganj, Delhi – 110002, India

79 Anson Road, #06–04/06, Singapore 079906

Cambridge University Press is part of the University of Cambridge.

It furthers the University's mission by disseminating knowledge in the pursuit of education, learning, and research at the highest international levels of excellence.

www.cambridge.org
Information on this title: www.cambridge.org/9781107181236
DOI: 10.1017/9781316848579

First published 2017

Printed in the United Kingdom by Clays, St Ives plc

A catalogue record for this publication is available from the British Library.

Library of Congress Cataloging-in-Publication Data
Names: Yadirgi, Veli, author.
Title: The political economy of the Kurds of Turkey : from the Ottoman Empire to the Turkish Republic / Veli Yadirgi.
Description: Cambridge, United Kingdom : Cambridge University Press, 2017. | Includes bibliographical references and index.
Identifiers: LCCN 2017026039| ISBN 9781107181236 (hardback) | ISBN 9781316632499 (paperback)
Subjects: LCSH: Kurds – Turkey – Economic conditions. | Kurds – Turkey – Politics and government. | Kurds – Turkey – Social conditions. | Kurdistan – Economic conditions. | Kurdistan – Politics and government. | Kurdistan – Social conditions.
Classification: LCC DR435.K87 Y326 2017 | DDC 330.9561/008991597–dc23
LC record available at https://lccn.loc.gov/2017026039

ISBN 978-1-107-18123-6 Hardback
ISBN 978-1-316-63249-9 Paperback

To My Parents

Contents

Figures and Tables

Figures

Tables

Maps

Preface

This book examines the linkages between economic development in the predominantly Kurdish provinces in Eastern and Southeastern Anatolia (ESA) and Turkey's Kurdish question. In so doing, it adopts a historical, structural and political-economic approach, which entails that socioeconomic and political developments, structures and transformations in ESA are analysed in juxtaposition with those of other domains within the context of the larger geographical area and political entity of which these territories have constituted a part: the Ottoman Empire and the Turkish Republic.

This study is comprised of three main parts. The first part discusses the key theoretical foundations of the research: theories on Kurdish identity; theoretical perspectives on the Kurdish question in Turkey; and theoretical approaches to socioeconomic development in ESA. The second part explores the social, economic and political alterations, formations and events in Ottoman Kurdistan after 1514 when the bulk of the Kurdish territories largely located in ESA came under the administration of the Ottoman Empire. The final part deals with issues pertaining to the collapse of the Ottoman Empire and the subsequent foundation and evolution of the Turkish Republic and Turkey's Kurdish question.

The central argument of this book is that there is a symbiotic relationship between the Kurdish question in Turkey and the peculiar form of underdevelopment witnessed in ESA, which is accurately captured by the notion of de-development. De-development is an economic process generated by a hegemonic power to ensure that there will be no economic base to support an independent indigenous existence (Roy, 1995). Underlying de-development in ESA as well as Turkey's Kurdish question is the Turkish elite's paramount political-national objective of maintaining Turkey's national unity and territorial integrity.

Acknowledgements

It took nearly six years to complete this book. Indubitably, it was an extensive, incredible journey – by far the greatest task, as well as the most exciting and educative process I have hitherto experienced. I was fortunate enough to begin this voyage surrounded by many altruistic and encouraging people, and to meet many more along the way. I am unable to acknowledge everyone, but must mention those who have played the most central roles.

I would never have been able to write this thesis without the constant support of my family, especially my mother, Maviş, my father, Hüseyin, my brother, Güney and my partner, Devrim, who has been a true helpmeet. I felt their unwavering and inexhaustible support throughout this journey.

I am also especially grateful to my supervisor, Prof. Gilbert Achcar, whose guidance and experience has played a defining role in the completion of this study. Additionally, I would like to thank Prof. Şevket Pamuk for his very helpful and instructive suggestions in the early stages of this journey. I cannot pass without expressing gratitude to my PhD examiners, Prof. Hamit Bozarslan and Prof. Özlem Onaran, for their enlightening, constructive and supportive comments during and after my viva. I should be most ungracious if I were to omit expressing my appreciation of Maria Marsh, Commissioning Editor, for her instrumental guidance, time and labour.

I also wish to thank individually (in alphabetical order) Chloe Barget, Çiğdem Esin, Cengiz Gunes, Roman (Pach) Pawar, Haldun Sonkaynar, and Kahraman Yadirgi, as they all contributed, in different ways, to the development and completion of this project. I finally would like to acknowledge all the selfless, edifying and exemplary people (unfortunately too many to mention here one by one) whom I met during my fieldwork. Thank you for your time, labour, knowledge, hospitality and assistance.

Abbreviations

A&P:	Great Britain: Parliamentary Papers, Account Papers
AKP:	Justice and Development Party (Adalet ve Kalkınma Partisi)
AMMU:	General Directorate for Tribes and Immigrants (Aşair ve Muhacirin Müdüriyet-i Umûmiyesi)
ANAP:	The Motherland Party (Anavatan Partisi)
AP:	Justice Party (Adalet Partisi)
BDP:	Peace and Democracy Party (Barış ve Demokrasi Partisi)
ÇATOM:	Multi-purpose Community Centres (Çok Amaçlı Toplum Merkezi)
CHP:	Republican People's Party (Cumhuriyet Halk Partisi)
CKMP:	Republican Peasants' Nation Party (Cumhuriyetçi Köylü Millet Partisi)
CUP	Ottoman Committee of Union and Progress
DDKO:	Revolutionary Eastern Cultural Hearths (Devrimci Doğu Kültür Ocakları)
DEHAP:	Democratic People's Party (Demokratik Halk Partisi)
DEP:	Democracy Party (Demokrasi Partisi)
Dev-Genç:	Federation of the Revolutionary Youth of Turkey
DİSK:	Confederation of Revolutionary Trade Unions of Turkey (Türkiye Devrimci İşçi Sendikalar Konfederasyonu)
DP:	Democrat Party (Demokrat Parti)
DSİ:	Directorate of State Hydraulic Works (Devlet Su İşleri)
DTP:	Democratic Society Party (Demokratik Toplum Partisi)
EC:	European Council
ERP:	Economic Recovery Plan

ESA:	Eastern and Southeastern Anatolia
EU:	European Union
FO:	Great Britain, Foreign Office
FYP:	Five-Year Plan
GAP:	Project of Southeastern Anatolia (Güneydoğu Anadolu Project)
GAP-GIDEM:	GAP-Entrepreneur Support and Guidance Centres (GAP-Girişimci Destekleme Merkezi)
GAP-RDA:	Project of Southeastern Anatolia-Regional Development Administration
GDP:	Gross Domestic Product
GNAT:	Grand National Assembly of Turkey
GNI:	Gross National Income
GNP:	Gross National Product
HCPP:	Great Britain, House of Commons Parliamentary Papers
HDI:	Human Development Index
HDP:	Peoples' Democratic Party (Halkların Demokrasi Partisi)
HEP:	Peoples' Labour Party (Halkın Emek Partisi)
İAMM:	Directorate for the Settlement of Tribes and Immigrants (İskân-ı Aşâir Muhacirîn Müdüriyeti)
IDPs:	Internally Displaced Peoples
IEA:	International Energy Agency
İHD:	Human Rights Association (İnsan Halkları Derneği)
ILO:	International Labour Organisation
IMF:	International Monetary Fund
ISI:	Import Substitution Industrialisation
ISIL:	Islamic State of Iraq and the Levant
Kawa:	Kurdish mythical figure and name of a Kurdish political party
KDP:	Kurdistan Democratic Party (Partiya Demokrat a Kurdistanê)
KHRP:	Kurdish Human Rights Project
KRG:	Kurdistan Regional Government (Iraq)
MBK:	National Unity Committee (Milli Birlik Komitesi)
MGK:	National Security Council (Milli Güvenlik Kurulu)
MHP:	Nationalist Action Party (Milliyetçi Hareket Partisi)
NAPP:	National Programme for Adopting the Acquis Communautaire
NF:	National Front Coalition Governments
NGOs:	Non-governmental Organisations

OECD:	Organisation for Economic Co-operation and Development
OHAL:	State of Emergency (Olağanüstü Hal)
PDRs:	Priority Development Regions (Kakınmada Öncelikli Yöreler)
PKK:	Kurdistan Workers' Party (Partiya Karkarên Kurdistan)
PSK:	Kurdistan Socialist Party (Partiya Sosyalista Kurdistan)
PYD:	Democratic Union Party (Partiya Yekîtiya Demokrat)
SEEs:	State Economic Enterprises
SHP:	Social Democratic Populist Party (Sosyaldemokrat Halkçı Partisi)
SPO:	State Planning Organisation (Devlet Planlama Teşkilatı)
TBB:	Association of Banks of Turkey (Türkiye Bankalar Birliği)
TCBIUM:	The Maiden Turkish Statistical Institute (Türkiye Cumhuriyeti Başvekalet İstatistik Umum Müdürlüğü)
TESEV:	Turkish Economic and Social Studies Foundation
TİP:	Workers' Party of Turkey (Türkiye İşçi Partisi)
TKAE:	Research Institute on Turkish Culture (Türk Kültürünü Araştırma Enstitüsü)
TKP	Turkish Communist Party (Türkiye Komünist Partisi)
TMMOB:	Union of Chambers of Turkish Engineers and Architects (Türkiye Mühendis ve Mimar Odalar Birliği)
TOBB:	Union of Chambers and Commodity Exchange of Turkey (Türkiye Odalar ve Borsalar Birliği)
TPAO:	Turkish Petroleum Corporation (Türkiye Petrolleri Anonim Ortaklığı)
TR:	Turkish Lira
TRL:	Old Turkish Lira
TRT:	Turkish Radio and Television Corporation (Türkiye Radyo Televizyon Kurulu)
TRY:	New Turkish Lira
TMO:	Office for Soil Products (Toprak Mahsulleri Ofisi)
TÜİK:	Turkish Statistical Institute (Türkiye İstatistik Kurumu)

TÜSİAD:	Turkish Industrialist and Businessmen's Association (Türk Sanayicileri ve İşadamları Derneği)
UNDP:	United Nations Development Programme
US:	United States
USARM:	Union of Southeastern Anatolia Region Municipalities (Güneydoğu Anadolu Bölgesi Belediyeleri Birliği)
VAT:	Value-Added Tax
WB:	World Bank
YTP:	New Turkey Party (Yeni Türkiye Partisi)

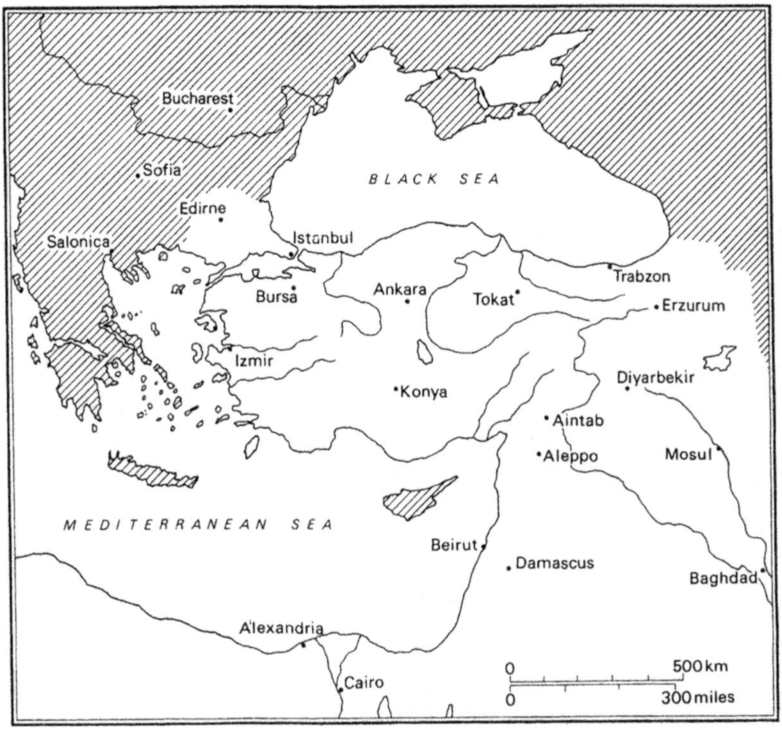

Map 1 Map of the Ottoman Middle East, ca. 1914.

Map 2 Map of Turkey

Introduction

This book is concerned with the role and impact of economic development in the predominantly Kurdish provinces in Eastern and Southeastern Anatolia (ESA) on the rise and evolution of Turkey's Kurdish question. As background to the exploration of these domains after the proclamation of the Turkish Republic in 1923, this study traces the political and economic history of ESA. Thus, although the study focuses mainly on events that materialised after the establishment of the Republic, it also deals rather extensively with broader historical issues germane to the subject matter of this investigation.

The guiding research questions in this study will be the following: How developed or underdeveloped was ESA during the Ottoman period? What were the economic and social impacts of the institution and the suppression of the Kurdish polities in Ottoman Kurdistan? Is the relatively worse-off position of the predominantly Kurdish provinces a by-product of uneven capitalist development in Turkey? Or is it attributable to the lack of transformation in the inimical social structures in these domains? Alternatively, can the economic, social and political actualities of these regions be imputed to the discriminatory policies the Turkish state implemented against Turkey's Kurds? How has Turkey's exposure to the forces and features of neoliberal capitalism influenced the Turkish state's preoccupation with the Kurdish question and the issue of socio-economic development in ESA?

The concepts, theoretical debates and methodology utilised in this study stem in large measure from the nature of the subject and the motivation to examine Turkey's Kurdish question in the context of economic development and political change in the Ottoman Empire and modern-day Turkey. The relevant central concepts, theories and methodology for this thesis will be delineated and adumbrated in the succeeding chapter, but it is worth elaborating at this stage what the key issues are and clarifying how some of the central concepts will be mobilised by this investigation.

In this study, *development* denotes a qualitative process of widespread structural transformation at all levels of society: economic, social, cultural and political. Development, therefore, necessitates augmenting the productive performance of the economy to meet essential human needs just as much as it requires enhancing political liberties and the range of human choices via the abolition of suppression and dependence. Nonetheless, owing to the lack of longitudinal assessments of economic changes in ESA, and the implications of economic issues for sociopolitical manifestations and alterations in these domains, development – as measured by the degree of structural change – will be analysed *largely* through an economic lens.

Similarly, this book emphasises the multidimensional context of the Kurdish question. This issue is examined as a corollary of rather complex interactions, including concurrent and sequential operations of a diverse array of interacting social, economic, cultural and political factors. The socioeconomic disparities between the ESA regions and the rest of Turkey, the negation of the collective rights of the Kurds in Turkey, the popular mobilisation of the Kurds against the imposed Turkish identity and authoritarian political system with the desire for political pluralism and/or autonomy, and the Kurdish insurgency post-1984 are all constitutive aspects of the Kurdish question in Turkey.

Following Steven Metz and Raymond Millen (2004: 2), *insurgency* in this study connotes the following:

> [A] strategy adopted by groups which cannot attain their political objectives through conventional means or by quick seizure of power ... characterised by protracted, asymmetrical violence and ambiguity, the use of complex terrain (jungles, mountains, [and] urban areas), psychological warfare, and political mobilization – all designed to protect the insurgents and eventually alter the balance of power in their favour. Insurgents may attempt to seize power and replace the existing government (revolutionary insurgency) or they may have more limited aims such as separation, autonomy, or alteration of a particular policy.

Even though it became a central theme of political debate in Turkey only after 1984 with the emergence of the Kurdish insurgency conducted by the Kurdistan Workers' Party (Partiya Karkarên Kurdistan, PKK), the Kurdish question has been a persistent feature of Turkish politics throughout the twentieth century. The protracted armed struggle waged by the PKK is only the most recent and most prolonged in a series of Kurdish rebellions instigated against state authorities. Hence, in order to apprehend comprehensively the roots and trajectory of this issue, some analysis of the relevant events and policies that have surfaced pre-1980s is in order.

The transfiguration of a multinational (Ottoman) empire into a (Turkish) nation state involved a nation-state–building process that necessitated economic, social and political reforms implemented by a Turkish nationalist elite bent on creating a 'homogenous', 'secular' and 'Westernised' Turkish nation. Nation-state building in the post-Ottoman political space, as was the case in Europe, North America, Latin America, Asia and Africa, describes a twin process, where 'nation-building' implicated 'the process whereby a sense of shared identity, patriotism, and loyalty to homeland develops', while the notion 'state-building' entailed 'the construction of governmental and political institutions' (Bill and Springboard, 1990: 40). Moreover, as rightly observed by James A. Bill and Robert Springboard, '[t]he more the artificial the country, the more difficult are the challenges of nation- and state-building' (ibid.).

The delimitation of the national identity as solely Turkish and such that it outlawed the public countenance of minority cultural differences, as well as the construction of a unitary and authoritarian political system in Turkey, were offshoots of this process. As conveyed by the following unreserved speech by İsmet İnönü, Turkey's second president, in 1925:

> We are frankly [n]ationalists . . . and [n]ationalism is our only factor of cohesion. In the face of a Turkish majority, other elements have no kind of influence. We must turkify the inhabitants of our land at any price, and we will annihilate those who oppose the Turks or 'le turquisme' [Turkism]. (Barkey and Fuller, 1998: 10)

The birth of the authoritarian Turkish nation-state ensued the economic peripheralisation, territorial losses and demographic changes that befell the Ottoman Empire during the nineteenth and early twentieth centuries. These vicissitudes were, to a large extent, repercussions of the growing influence of Europe in the Ottoman Empire and the reactions it occasioned in the Ottoman state and society. The European influence on Ottoman polity and people was felt in three different but interrelated spheres. First, the incorporation of the Ottoman lands into the capitalist world system, which began in the late eighteenth century and gathered pace in the first quarter of the nineteenth century. Second, the expansion of the influence of the Great Powers of Europe (such as Great Britain, France, Austria, and Russia), as evinced by the British economic and political hegemony, as per their provision of both trade and loans to the Empire after the imposition of the free-trade regime in 1838. Third, the impact of European ideologies of nationalism, liberalism, secularism and positivism.

Following the conclusion of the war between the Ottoman Empire and Russia in 1812, Sultan Mahmut II (1785–1839), the Ottoman Sultan from 1808 to 1839, began to implement Westernisation and centralisation reforms, which were continued by his successors. Full-scale Ottoman restructuring was unleashed by the Imperial Rescript of 1839, which went on to determine the nature of the policies in the *Tanzimat* period (1839–76). This Rescript set out the following modifications: (i) 'an orderly system of taxation to replace the system of tax-farming'; (ii) 'the establishment of guarantees for the life, honour and property of the sultan's subjects'; (iii) 'a system of conscription for the army'; and (iv) 'equality before the law of all subjects, whatever their religion (although this was formulated somewhat ambiguously in the document)' (Zürcher, 1994: 53). These reorganisations were designed in order to modify the Ottoman political, administrative and social structure in line with the prerequisites of the international capitalist system on the one hand, and as part of the central authorities' strategy to recapture control over provinces and attenuate fiscal resources of the Empire on the other.

The administrative, social and political arrangements aimed at centralising the Empire and absorbing the Christian and non-Turkish populaces initiated the obliteration of local autonomy. Unsurprisingly, the fusion of centralist reforms and the spread of nationalism in the Empire set in motion a series of rebellions in Serbian, Greek and Lebanese Christian communities, as well as among Muslims in Ottoman Kurdistan who had been accustomed to varying degrees of self-rule (Celil, 1992; Özoğlu, 2004). Thus the promise – even if on paper – of equality with the Muslim majority did not inhibit the proliferation of ethno-nationalism particularly among the Christian communities, leading to the birth and sharpening of what came to be termed among foreign diplomats the 'Eastern Question' – that is, the question of how to satiate vying Balkan nationalisms and the imperialist objectives of the major powers without engendering the demise of the Ottoman Empire or, if its destruction was inescapable, to dismember it without disturbing the balance of power in Europe and triggering a general war. In addition, the economic privileges granted to Europeans in order to maintain the flow of urgently needed loans were often extended to their non-Muslim partners too, and consequently the Empire's Christian bourgeoisie gained the most from Ottoman trade with Europe in the nineteenth century (Keyder, 1987; Kasaba, 1988).

These occurrences alienated the Muslim communities in the Empire and fostered trepidations amidst the Ottoman political leaders about how to maintain the Empire's position and preserve its political and territorial integrity. The amalgamation of these consternations laid the groundwork for two significant phenomena on the eve of the twentieth century: the emergence of nationalism among the Muslim populace, and the formation of the Ottoman Committee of Union and Progress (CUP) in 1889. The CUP led the Young Turk Revolution of 1908 under the banner of 'Liberty, Equality, Fraternity and Justice' and thus promised political pluralism and establishment of constitutional order. However, soon after the Revolution – for reasons discussed at length in Chapter 4 – the CUP reneged on both of these assurances and adopted an aggressive and exclusionist form of Turkish nationalism. This ignited successive Kurdish revolts in the Ottoman Kurdish emirates, some of which, like the Baban, Bitlis and Barzan revolts, were organised with pro-self-rule demands, and others were solely mobilised against the perceived injustices in the policies of the CUP administration explicated in Chapter 4.

The belligerent pan-Turkist policies of the CUP, coupled with the destructive ramifications of the First World War, transformed ESA from imperial borderlands into imperial shatter zones. The widespread devastation that the Armenian and Greek communities experienced during and after the war substantially altered the demographic landscape of the Ottoman Empire. As a consequence of not attaining the autonomy promised to them by the European victors of the Great War in the Treaty of Sèvres – signed on 10 August 1920 between the Allies and the Ottoman government – which decreed independence to Armenia and administrative autonomy to Kurdistan, the Kurds were the only non-Turkish ethno-national community at the birth of the new Republic. Article 62 of the Treaty of Sèvres stated the following:

> A Commission sitting at Constantinople and composed of three members appointed by the British, French and Italian Governments respectively shall draft within six months from into force of the present Treaty a scheme of local autonomy for the predominantly Kurdish areas lying east of the Euphrates, south of the southern boundary of Armenia as it may be hereafter determined, and north of the frontier of Turkey with Syria and Mesopotamia, as defined in Article 27, II (2) and (3). (McDowall, 2000: 464)

Although the Treaty of Lausanne, which formally established the currently existing borders and sovereignty of Turkey, superseded this Treaty on 24 July 1923 as a result of the successful rebellion led by Mustafa Kemal (Atatürk), the fret of Kurdish autonomy always weighed heavily on the minds of the rulers of the Turkish Republic. Put differently, at a time when a new regional system, based on two independent states

(Iran and Turkey) and two mandatory states (Iraq and Syria) had been established, the autonomy promised to Kurds in the former Treaty ostensibly engendered a new 'Eastern Question' for the rulers of the Turkish Republic. Ever since, there has been a tendency to assess the demands of the Kurds in Turkey along conspirative lines with persistent reference to the 'Eastern Question' and the Treaty of Sèvres.

After the proclamation of the Turkish Republic, Turkish republican nationalism or *Kemalism*, named after the founder and maiden president of the Republic, Mustafa Kemal, became the official state ideology and the source of an array of social, political and economic reforms. The social engineering projects implemented by the Republican People's Party (Cumhuriyet Halk Partisi, CHP) during the single-party period (1923–45) as expounded in Chapter 4, prompted the conflictual ties between the Kurds and the Turkish state and wrought socioeconomic destruction to the ESA regions. The Kemalist centralist authorities had obdurately defended the doctrine of the unity and indivisibility of the Turkish state, its territory and its people. This dogma became the established reason for suppressing the linguistic, cultural and collective rights demanded by the Kurds because these demands were perceived as a threat to the unitary and uniform structure of the nation and the state.

The freedoms, albeit limited, granted by the 1961 constitution enabled Kurds to raise their demands and address some of their grievances through legitimate channels, as evinced by the 'Eastern Meetings' of the 1960s. The 'Eastern Meetings' were the pinnacle of Kurdish activism in that decade. Commencing on 13 August 1967 in Silvan, a sequential series of protests was held against the underdevelopment in ESA in Diyarbakir on 3 September 1967, Siverek (Urfa) on 24 September 1967, Batman on 8 October 1967, Tunceli (Dersim) on 15 October 1967, Ağrı on 22 October 1967, and the finale took place in Ankara on 18 November 1967 (Beşikçi, 1992). These robust protests were directed against the traditional policies of the Turkish state and the excessive power of the Kurdish clientele rural elite in ESA, and thereby threatened the rule of both the former and the latter in these domains.

The political activism of the Kurds in the 1960s and 1970s enabled pro-Kurdish campaigners to make significant electoral gains. For example, in the 1977 municipal elections, Mehdi Zana, a supporter of the Kurdish left-wing Kurdistan Socialist Party (Partiya Sosyalista Kurdistan, PSK), won the mayoralty of Diyarbakir, considered the Kurdish cultural and political centre. However, with the arrival of the *coup d'état* in 1980, all of the gains, activism and organisations of the progressive left-wing movements – of which Kurdish activists constituted an important part – were supressed, leading Kurdish campaigners to seek other avenues to address their demands.

The most vital and violent expression of this search has been the guerrilla warfare the PKK waged in 1984. Thus, as Hamit Bozarslan rightly indicated, '1980 is a turning point in Kurdish history in Turkey: all nationalist activity was suspended following the military coup, and the subsequent return to civil administration has been marked above all by a continuing guerrilla warfare' (2003b: 15). The war between the PKK and the Turkish state has had colossal political, social and economic consequences, which will be elucidated in Chapters 4 and 5.

Unsurprisingly, the emergence of the armed conflict between the PKK and the Turkish army and the surge in the Kurdish nationalist movement in the Middle East from the 1980s onwards witnessed a parallel increase in scholarly studies and research on the Kurds. Overall, these works attempt to account for a multifarious range of issues and concentrate on varying periods and aspects of Kurdish society and politics. Nearly all of these scholarships either analyse the genesis and evolution of Kurdish nationalism in the Middle East[1] or examine Kurdish nationalism and the political history of the conflict in Turkey.[2] In comparison to the conflict analyses and political history literature, there are relatively miniscule studies synthetically investigating the economic and political history of the predominantly Kurdish areas of ESA.[3]

The conflict analyses and political history literatures readily accept that ESA constituted one of the least-developed areas of the Ottoman Empire. In postulating causal explanations for the existence of the conflictual ties between the Turkish state and its Kurdish citizens, these studies, on the one hand, emphasise the role of socio-economic inequality and regional underdevelopment in fostering Kurdish discord in Turkey and on the other, highlight the significance of Kurdish society's urbanisation, migration, and contact with the wider world during the 1960s and 1970s in the political expression of Kurdish discontent (Gunter, 1990; Kirişçi and Winrow, 1997; Barkey and Fuller, 1998; Ibrahim and Gürbey, 2000; McDowall, 2000; van

[1] Olson (1989); Entessar (1992); Hassanpour (1992); Kreyenbroek and Sperl, eds. (1992); van Bruinessen (1992, 2000); Chaliand, ed. (1993); McDowall (2000); Vali, ed. (2003); Natali (2005); Romano (2006); MacDonald and O'Leary, eds. (2007).

[2] Gunter (1990, 2011b); Olson, ed. (1996); Kirişçi and Winrow (1997); Barkey, and Fuller (1998); Ibrahim and Gürbey (2000); White (2000, 2015); Taşpınar (2005); Özcan (2006); Marcus (2007); Gunes (2012); Gunes and Zeydanlıoğlu, eds. (2014).

[3] Mehmet Emin Bozarslan ([1966] 2002); Beşikçi ([1969] 1992); Jafar (1976); Aydın (1986); Sönmez ([1990] 1992).

Bruinessen, 2000; White, 2000; Taşpınar, 2005). However, none of these studies systematically analyses the economic history of ESA and/or the economic aspects of the Kurdish question.

Studies focusing on the economic features of ESA provide fragmentary accounts of the economic history of these territories and only study the years prior to the armed conflict between the PKK and the state (M. E. Bozarslan, [1966] 2002; Beşikçi, [1969] 1992; Jafar, 1976) or years just after the armed conflict (Z. Aydın, 1986; Sönmez, [1990] 1992). Relatedly, a methodical investigation incorporating the political and economic experiences of Eastern and Southeastern Anatolian societies during the Ottoman and contemporary eras is a desideratum. This is precisely why this study has decided to examine Turkey's Kurdish question and the issue of economic development in ESA within a historical framework.

Research Motivations and Contributions

Evidently, this research agenda can be addressed in different forms and with manifold purposes. This research topic is of interest for a trinity of reasons. First, although there are fragmentary accounts of the economy of the primarily Kurdish provinces in ESA, there has been no comprehensive and longitudinal investigation of this complex subject. This has resulted in political transformations within these regions being studied largely without a detailed analysis of the pivotal economic changes. The paucity of research on economic activities, relations and transformations in the predominantly Kurdish domains is due to a combination of data-related issues, like the existence of miniscule historical archival resources, and profounder ontological (i.e. how the Kurds are defined), methodological (i.e. how the Kurds are studied) and epistemological (i.e. how knowledge about the Kurds is produced) issues.

As expounded in Chapters 3 and 4, because of the minimal quantitative historical information presently available on the economy of Ottoman Kurdistan, economic life in this Ottoman borderland is the *terra incognita* on the Ottoman history map. David McDowall in the foreword to his highly influential study on the Kurds, *A Modern History of the Kurds*, highlights the lack of coverage in the historical archives of the economy of this Ottoman frontier region, and the resultant void it has left in the study of this area, with the noteworthy observation that:

> [P]erhaps the most important [void was] the processes of economic and social change. I cannot help feeling that if these were better documented and understood, many of the events we do know about in Kurdistan would undergo re-evaluation. (2000: xii)

Yet the lack of historical archives on the economy of these regions is not the sole reason for the aforementioned lacuna. The long-standing failure of the academic studies on the Ottoman Empire to aptly analyse Ottoman Kurdistan and the Kurds, coupled with the tendency of recent investigations on this domain to make *political relations* between the Kurdish rulers and the Ottoman state the sole locus of their analysis (O. Kılıç, 1999; Öz, 2003; Sinclair, 2003; Özoğlu, 2004), have further contributed to the absence of a systematic examination of the economy of the primarily Kurdish provinces in ESA.

Mainstream academic research on the history and legacy of the Ottoman Empire often does not properly account for the incorporation of the Kurdish emirates into the Ottoman Empire and/or address the legacies of the Ottoman period in the remnants of Ottoman Kurdistan in contemporary Turkey. As pointed out by the erudite Armenian scholar Stephan H. Astourian, up until very recently, 'Kurds, for their part, [were] simply left out of Ottoman historiography altogether, although they constituted a plurality in the eastern provinces' (Kaiser, 1998: ix). To cite a few examples will, no doubt, illustrate this case. In spite of the momentous events that occurred during and after the disintegration of the Ottoman Empire involving the Armenians and the Kurds inhabiting the ethnically heterogeneous Eastern provinces, L. Carl Brown, in the introduction to the oft-quoted *Imperial Legacy: The Ottoman Imprint on the Balkans and the Middle East*, glosses over the legacy of Ottoman rule in ESA. More staggeringly, in the detailed list of 'Dates and Duration of Ottoman Rule by Country or Region' outlined by the author, Ottoman Kurdistan is unstipulated (Brown, 1996: xiv–xvi). In *The Shaping of the Modern Middle East*, Bernard Lewis states that the Kurds are one of the remaining linguistic and ethnic minorities of any importance surviving in the central lands of the Middle East. Besides that, the Kurds are only alluded to very briefly as an obstacle to Arabism in Iraq (1994: 19, 94–5).

In other publications such as *An Introduction to the Historical Geography of Anatolia* (*Anadolu'nun Tarihi Çoğrafyasına Giriş*) authored by Prof. Tuncer Baykara, and published by the Research Institute on Turkish Culture (Türk Kültürünü Araştırma Enstitüsü, TKAE),[4] the very existence of Ottoman Kurdistan is openly negated, and the Kurds are defined simply as *Turkish people who live in the mountainous regions of Turkey* (Baykara, 1988: 26). Baykara's study is emblematic of the plethora of

[4] TKAE was established in 1961 by President Cemal Gürses. This institution publishes journals and books exploring Turkish culture and history from a pan-Turkist perspective. For a systematic analysis of the TKAE, see Landau (1995).

'scientific works' produced by mainstream academics in Turkey from the 1930s onwards, demonstrating the 'Turkish' origins of the Kurds or, to employ the official definition ascribed to Kurds in Turkey up until the late twentieth-century, '*mountain Turks*'. These Turkist studies attained their theoretical nourishment from the Kemalist *mythomoteur* of pre-Islamic Turkic civilisations as the source of all civilisations and languages, which came to prominence after the First Historical Congress of 1932 organised in Ankara under Atatürk's direction.[5]

All of these stated lacunae are inextricably linked to how knowledge about the Kurds and Kurdish-dominated regions have been produced by conventional Middle Eastern studies and the academic and research circles in Turkey. As accurately postulated by Colin Williams in *Minority Nationalist Historiography*, historical and geographical accounts of a region or state are customarily analysed by the use of materials written in the languages of the dominant nations, rather than minority languages; thus the minorities' ideas are meagrely represented, if at all, in scholarly literature. Put differently, historical accounts of an area or polity regularly '*tell it from the victor's angle*' (1988: 203–4). The Kurds, until very recently, were marginalised in all their host countries, so their account of or role in history has largely been covered or represented defectively by mainstream researchers of the Middle East.

With restricted freedom of thought and expression, steeped in Turkish nationalism, academic science in Turkey has been made to conform to the ideological interests and policies of the state.[6] Research produced about the Kurds within academic circles in Turkey is often aimed at producing applied knowledge. That is to say, knowledge on the principally Kurdish regions and their populations has been formed with the aims of buttressing the official discourse or state ideology on Kurds, and laying the foundations for state interventions in these regions via theorising on issues of population policies, modernisation and territorial integration.

On the other hand, studies that fell into conflict with the hegemonic ideology on Kurds were vilified within academic circles, and scholars that undertook heterodox research on predominantly Kurdish-inhabited

[5] This congress approved of the 'Turkish Historical Thesis', according to which Turks had been forced to migrate from Central Asia due to severe climatic conditions and thus with time this process created the world's great civilisations in the Middle East, such as the Hittites and the Sumerians. Congruently, the 'Sun-Language Theory' supported the thesis that all languages derived originally from one primal language, to which Turkish was the closest before its contamination by Arabic and Persian. For a detailed analysis of these theses, see Beşikçi (1977) and Ersanlı-Behar (1992).

[6] For a detailed study of Turkish nationalism and its relationship with higher educational institutions in Turkey, see A. Arslan (2004: 58–159).

areas were removed from their academic positions. This was exemplified with İsmail Beşikçi's academic profession coming to a swift expiration after authoring *The Order of East Anatolia: Socio-economic and Ethnic Foundations* (*Doğu Anadolu'nun Düzeni: Sosyo-Ekonomik ve Etnik Temeller*) – first published in 1969 – wherein he committed an academic crime by formulating the unspeakable: the ethnic dimension of the predominantly Kurdish ESA regions.[7]

The practice of producing, reinforcing and disseminating the official discourse about the Kurds began during the late Ottoman period. In accordance with the instructions of Talaat Pasha to investigate Anatolia after the 1913 Unionist Coup, Turkist missionary ethnologists and sociologists such as Mehmed Ziya Gökalp[8] (1876–1924) studied the Kurds and Kurdish tribes with the purpose of assimilating them into the Turkish culture (Dündar, 2002; Üngör, 2011). Throughout the single-party period too, social engineering specialists were sent to ESA to collate information and, in turn, to produce reports about the social organisation, economic wealth and relations and ethnic characteristics of the indigenous population. These field studies in east and south-east Turkey formed the basis of the plan of 'Reform of the East' in the 1920s (Bayrak, 1994).

Similarly, in the multi-party period, the 'East Group' within the State Planning Organisation (SPO) produced policy-oriented reports like *The Principles of the State Development Programmes in Eastern and Southeastern Anatolia*, which was prepared in 1961. The common theme in these state-sanctioned reports was that the native tribal social structure fostered the 'backward' nature of the Kurdish-majority regions and thus necessitated state intervention in these areas in order to transform the 'primitive' autochthonous structures and people. State interference in these domains involved 'turkification' of the local populace and deportation of the members of the disobedient Kurdish tribes, a subject matter fully discussed in Chapter 5.

Analogous studies on the primordial loyalties and structures in ESA continued from the 1980s on, this time under the aegis of the state-led Project of Southeastern Anatolia (Güneydoğu Anadolu Project, GAP).

[7] For a concise exploration of the academic life, works and investigations of İsmail Beşikçi, see van Bruinessen (2003–4: 19–34).

[8] Ziya Gökalp was a sociologist, poet and probably the most prominent ideologue of the CUP. He was born in Çermik, Diyarbekir, of a Kurdish mother and a Turkish father. Gökalp published inestimable articles in journals, founded the CUP branch in Diyarbekir and rapidly rose to become a member of the Central Committee of the CUP. He pragmatically reinterpreted Emile Durkheim's theories into a distinct set of ideas that laid the ideological bases of modern Turkish nationalism. For an expanded political biography of Gökalp, see Hyed (1979).

Institutes working on the GAP were founded within universities. The academic research and surveys conducted by GAP research and practice centres established in the Middle East Technical University and Dicle University in Diyarbakir in the 1990s unswervingly highlighted the severity of the tribal structures and the pivotal role state initiatives employed under the GAP could adopt in order to resolve this issue and to nurture modernisation and development. All of these reports at no time mention the ethnic component of the Kurdish question or the armed conflict between the state and the PKK (Özok-Gündoğan, 2005; Scalbert-Yücel and Le Ray, 2006).

These studies made the autochthonic tribes in ESA the central focus of their research and thereby postulated them as *explanans* (that which contains the explanation) for underdevelopment in the predominantly Kurdish-populated ESA regions. This approach renders the tribal organisation as the determinate source of attaining knowledge about the Kurds and the principally Kurdish provinces, and as immutable and fixed entities as though they are a fact of nature that unequivocally determines the behaviour of Kurds. In other words, the aforementioned state-sponsored studies fail to account for the specific social, economic and political conditions that mould and transform tribal identity and organisation, and, owing to the rural-centred analysis, overlook structures, activities and developments in predominantly Kurdish cities in ESA.

Owing to this approach, mainstream ethnographic and sociological studies in Turkey have precipitated three pitfalls, which have hitherto devalued and obfuscated the undertaking of a longitudinal analysis of the economy of the principally Kurdish regions of Turkey: (i) depriving Kurds of their proper national and socioeconomic characteristics; (ii) analysing Kurds without a diachronic and holistic perspective of their social, political, economic and territorial interactions, organisations and activities; and (iii) depicting the largely Kurdish regions as static 'primitive regions' on account of the persevering regressive social structures that are not conducive to economic development. For the purposes of systematically analysing the linkages between economic development in ESA and Turkey's Kurdish question – free from the long-standing drawbacks of the dominant traditions of scholarship summarised earlier – one of the overriding aims and contributions of this study will be to provide a detailed account of the political and economic structures, relations and changes in these domains pre- and post-1923.

The second reason for the pursuit of this research project is pertinent to the diminutive significance that scholars – particularly economic historians – have ascribed to the ramifications of a chilling series of violent events in ESA during and after the First World War on the economy of these regions in the years subsequent to the institution of the Turkish Republic. For instance, the economic historian Zvi Yehuda Herschlag in his widely cited *Turkey: An Economy in Transition* hypothesises that after the Great War private enterprise in Turkey was too weak, and the state had to act as the locomotive of economic life in the eastern provinces (1958: 39–40). Herschlag's oft-quoted postulation is made without any consideration of the issue of dispossession and uprooting of the indigenous entrepreneurs, especially – but not exclusively – Armenian and Kurdish, as part of the nationalist demographic policies implemented in ESA during the CUP period (1913–18) and after the establishment of the Turkish Republic. Correspondingly, more contemporary researchers of the eastern economy such as Servet Mutlu in *The Roots of the Eastern Question: An Economic Perspective* (*Doğu Sorunun Kökenleri: Ekonomik Açıdan*) study the continuity of ESA's underdevelopment with minimal engagement with the wars, ethnocide and forced deportations experienced by the autochthonous inhabitants, as though these events never happened and the concomitant economic impoverishment was inexorable.

In this study, the notion of *demographic engineering* will be used synonymously with social engineering and population politics to denote 'a series of coercive state measures in pursuit of population homogeneity' (Bloxham, 2008: 101). As laboriously outlined by Milica Zarkovic Bookman (1997), states attempt to obtain homogenisation by means of implementing six different social engineering policies:

(1) manipulation of the censuses; (2) natality policies that aim to obtain the numerical superiority of the dominant national core or group at the expense of minorities; (3) border alterations to attain total overlap between ethnic and political boundaries; (4) dragooning of the minority groups into the dominant cultural identity; (5) forced deportation to decrease the populace of undesirable sections of society in a particular area; and (6) economic and/or political incentives and pressures to leave the country.

This study will concentrate on the latter three policies in illuminating how Turkist demographic policies implemented in the ethnically diverse ESA have shaped the economic decline of these territories.

The failure of scholars to overlook the repercussions of the pre-1923 violent encounters and actions on the eastern economy runs the risk of producing an ahistorical economic analysis of these regions by rejecting all prior (Ottoman) history. This approach to the history of these regions is analogous to the Kemalist interpretation of Turkish history lucidly summarised with the following words of Mustafa Kemal

(Atatürk): 'The new Turkey has no relationship to the old. The Ottoman Empire has passed into history. A new Turkey is born' (Timur, 1987: 5). The epistemic value of assessments of the Kurds and the predominantly Kurdish regions that do not exhaustively scrutinise events, processes and state practices in the pre-Kemalist period are dubitable. This is because, as pointed out by Andrew Mango, '[t]he ideology which has shaped the policy of the government of the Turkish republic towards its Kurdish citizens antedates Atatürk' (1999: 10). Thus, the precondition of obtaining an accurate understanding of the evolution of political, economic and social structures and processes in ESA is to review the occurrences prior to 1923 in these regions.

One of the initial scholars to study the nationalist population policies was İsmail Beşikçi, who analysed the 1934 Settlement Act and explained the deportations orchestrated by the Kemalist rulers (Beşikçi, 1991). Despite shedding much-needed light on a hitherto understudied area and instigating further research on the field of social engineering in Turkey, Beşikçi's approach had two drawbacks. First, he began his periodisation in 1923 and resultantly glossed over the CUP deportations during the First World War. Second, he gave minimal importance to the economic ramifications of these forced displacement policies. Other researchers have investigated this matter further, contributing immensely to the widening of knowledge about demographic engineering policies. However, they have researched nationalist population policies either only during the CUP period (Dündar, 2002; Akçam, 2012) or until the end of the Republican period (1923–50) (Çağaptay, 2006; Üngör, 2011), and resultantly the social engineering programmes actuated after 1950 have not been deliberated. Considering that in the second half of the twentieth century – according to official figures – around 1 million Kurds had been forcibly displaced from their ancestral lands, it is of vast importance for any study dealing with the socioeconomic and political history of principally Kurdish regions to assess the deportation policies executed after the single-party period in Turkey.

The third and final motivation for this study stems from a strong element of dissatisfaction with the prevailing development paradigm concerning ESA, that is, underdevelopment. In light of the longitudinal data prepared for and analysed in this study, it is highly desirable to revaluate this age-old and readily accepted heuristic device of regional underdevelopment. Put differently, the novel empirical facts germane to the Kurdish-majority regions of Anatolia attained by this study necessitate a rethinking of the underlying assumptions of this prevailing theoretical approach. These are that the predominantly

Kurdish provinces of pre- and post-1923 Anatolia have been underdeveloped areas not conducive to capitalist development on account of several regional features: the dominance of feudal social relations, the lack of modern infrastructure, and ESA's geopolitical position – far afield from both the former imperial capital, Istanbul, and the contemporary political capital, Ankara.

Structure of the Chapters

This book is divided into five chapters. Chapter 1 presents a detailed critical examination of the main theoretical perspectives concerning the Kurds, the Kurdish question in Turkey and socioeconomic development in ESA, as well as outlining methodological resources that this study draws on in conducting this research. Chapters 2–3 paint a picture of political, social and economic life in Ottoman Kurdistan. Chapter 2 looks at the political and economic events and changes in this Ottoman borderland in the years 1514–1800. That is, the period from the time when the Kurdish principalities were incorporated into the Ottoman Empire and the semiautonomous Kurdish regimes were established, until the dawn of the suppression of these polities. Chapter 3 investigates the political and economic history of Ottoman Kurdistan in the years 1800–1914: the era during which all semiautonomous regimes in Ottoman Kurdistan had been overthrown, the penetration of world capitalism into the Ottoman Anatolia had deepened and the First World War began. The structures and changes in this region during these three centuries will be compared with those of the bordering Ottoman territories, which today constitute modern-day Turkey.

Chapter 4 deals with issues pertaining to the collapse of the Ottoman Empire and the subsequent formation and evolution of the Turkish Republic and Turkey's Kurdish question. In this chapter, socioeconomic and political developments, structures and transformations in ESA will be juxtaposed with those of other regions within the context of the larger geographical area and political entity of which it is a part: the Turkish Republic. There will be four separate sections dealing with three successive periods under the following headings:

- The Collapse of the Empire, Rise of the 'National Economy' and the Implementation of the Nationalist Population Policies (1914–18)
- From the Mudros Armistice of 1918 to the Lausanne Treaty of 1923
- Society, Economic and Politics in the Republican People's Party Era (1923–50)
- Transition to a Turbulent Democracy and 'Incorporation' of ESA (1950–80)

Chapter 5 assesses how the neoliberal restructuring of the Turkish polity and economy from 1980 to the 2010s has influenced Turkey's Kurdish question and socioeconomic development in ESA. Finally, a conclusion outlines the findings of this study and discusses the possible political and economic steps that could be taken to resolve the Kurdish question in Turkey and overcome the barriers to socioeconomic development in ESA.

1 The Kurds, the Kurdish Question in Turkey and Economic Development in ESA: An Exploration of the Central Theoretical Debates and Outline of the Methodological Resources

1.1 Defining the Kurds

Kurdish ancestry, ethno-genesis, native land and language are matters of persistent scholarly debate. Different theories exist concerning the ancestry of the Kurds. Certain scholars claim that they were the people of 'Gutium' in ancient Sumeria (Izady, 1988, 1992). The most prominent hypothesis, particularly among Kurds, is that the Kurds descended from the ancient Indo-European people, the Medes, who established the Median Empire (728–550 BC) in the current areas of south eastern Turkey, northern Iraq and western Iran (Wahby, 1982; Kendal, 1996). Another line of thought conceives that the modern Kurds, while possibly descending from some or all of these ancestries imputed to them, were formed as an amalgamation into a novel, ethnically distinct people (Bois, 1966). Other researchers, in the same vein as the aforementioned TKAE-affiliated Turkish nationalist scholars, vehemently dispute all of these views and instead maintain that the Kurds are a branch of the Turkic people, negating that the Kurds are a distinct people (Kırzıoğlu, 1963; Türkdoğan, 1997).

However, what may be the least controversial definition is the degree of consciousness among Kurds in Iraq, Iran, Turkey and Syria that they constitute one people. They brand themselves Kurds, even with the dissimilarities in their economic activities, political and economic development and modern history. Kurds and most researchers attempting to define them approve of this postulation.

Nonetheless, the causality of this consciousness has been a source of controversy. Broadly speaking, there are two main streams of thought on this interminable debate: the primordialist or essentialist and the constructivist. The former argues that the nation is a natural and perennial entity that has existed since time immemorial and predates nationalism (Geertz, 1973; Armstrong, 1982). Thus according to the primordialist, the source of modern national awareness is the old and acutely felt ethnic, linguistic, religious and cultural differences. In that vein, the Harvard academic of Kurdish origin Mehrad R. Izady posits that the period from the fifth century BC through to the sixth century AD 'marks the homogenization and consolidation of the modern Kurdish national identity. The ethnic designator Kurd is established finally, and applied to all segments of the nation' (1992: 23). The Kurdish linguist Jamal Nabaz postulates a classic example of the primordial conceptualisation of the Kurdish identity and nationalism. Nabaz contends that the '*Kurdayetî* [Kurdish nationalist] movement, as we see it, is not the construction of any class or group ... *Kurdayetî* is a natural, dynamic, and perpetual movement' (Sheyholislami, 2011: 52). As Abbas Vali correctly observed, '[T]he mainstream Kurdish nationalist ... is "primordialist." For him/her the Kurdish nation is a primordial entity, a natural formation rooted in the nature of every Kurd defining the identity of people and community history' (2003b: 59). Therefore, studies or individuals influenced by this dominant approach overlook the modern character of the Kurdish identity and the socially constructed nature of its features.

The constructivists argue that nations are relatively recent and contingent entities generated over the past two centuries by the development of modern economic, social and political conditions. Within constructivism, there is a wide range of different approaches. Ernest Gellner (1992) emphasises the importance of industrialisation and the shift from premodern village communities. Benedict Anderson (1983) stresses the development of print culture or 'print capitalism' and of people who are conscious of a common identity. Marxist writers like Eric Hobsbawm (1990) analyse the rise of national economies and social classes as the basis of nations and nationalism.

Anthony Smith, who highlights that the premodern basis of nations permits modernist change but on grounds of historic continuities, espouses a 'third way' stance between primordialist and constructivist approaches. Smith hypothesises that nation is the advanced version of ethnicity and the main difference between the two is that the latter does not have a common polity. Ethnic community or *ethnie*, according to Smith, is a historically specific segment of a country's population that shares the following six features: a collective name, a common myth of descent (or *mythomoteur*), a shared history, a distinctive shared culture, an affiliation with a specific territory and a sense of solidarity (1986: 22–32).

This study perceives the construction of Kurdish identity and nationalism from a constructivist perspective and recognises the vital role played by historical, international, socioeconomic and political factors in the construction of national identities and nationalist movements. As Fred Halliday cogently contends, the constructivist approach 'need not rest on a narrow, industrial-society model: rather, starting from the rise of modern industrial society in Europe and the USA, it seeks to show how the impact of this society was felt throughout the world, in economic change and industrialisation certainly, but also in the political, social and ideological changes that accompanied the subjugation to this model of the world, in the two centuries 1800–2000' (2006: 15). Relatedly, Halliday proposes a constructivist framework for studying the history of Kurdish nationalism and the basis of Kurdish identity formation, applying four extensive processes of modernism: 'war and conflict', 'nationalism and state building', 'ideology' and 'socio-economic transformation' (ibid.: 15–18).

The concepts of the nation and nationalism as the sole and supreme focus of one's loyalty are relatively new, having only commenced in the latter part of the eighteenth century and specifically during the 1789 French Revolution. After 1789, the nation became a way of legitimising the political domination of social classes of people by the new capitalist class – the bourgeoisie – and had fundamental ramifications for the process of state-building. Skirmishes for participation in the state occasioned confrontations between the feudal aristocracy and the bourgeoisie; the latter's interests were often represented by a parliament. The bourgeoisie claimed to be the advocates of 'the nation' and in opposition to the former insisted they were the true espousers and defenders of 'national liberties'.

During the nineteenth and twentieth centuries, moreover, the concept acquired a cultural meaning, referring to a unique people with a distinct identity. This change in meaning was a result of the cultural understandings of community and power undergoing alterations following economic changes, social and scientific innovations and expansion of communication, initially in Western Europe and subsequently elsewhere, after the nineteenth century. In other words, the concurrent expansion of capitalism, means of communication (particularly print materials) and the development of vernacular languages beside Latin played a pivotal role in large groups of people perceiving themselves as distinct communities (Anderson, 1983). Hence, the idea of the nation came to denote a community of people shaped by common descent, culture, language, aspirations and history. Nationalism as both a modern ideology and a social or political movement aims at the formation and upkeep of self-government and/or the creation and reconstruction of collective cultural/national identity for a group who believes itself to be a nation or proto-nation.

The percolation of the concepts of nation and nationalism in the minds of the Kurds, when compared to European nations, is newer. As posited by Van Bruinessen (2000, 2003), H. Bozarslan (2003a) and Vali (2003a), the construction of Kurdish national identity and the birth of Kurdish nationalism are recent phenomena, dating back to the beginning of the past century. Van Bruinessen rightly observes that under Ottoman rule, Kurds, analogous to other people in the multi-religious and multiethnic Ottoman Empire, despite being aware of their Kurdishness, did not categorise themselves as an ethnic group or nation in the way they do today, because tribes were the main collective with which Kurds identified (2003: 43–5). Similarly, Denise Natali espouses the view that 'in both the Ottoman and Qajar [Persian] Empires the absence of an exclusive official nationalist project based on ethnicity prevented Kurdayetî from becoming salient or highly ethnicized' (2005: 24). In other words, in the pre-twentieth century, there were neither political nor socioeconomic prerequisites in Kurdistan for the existence of any notion of the nation. Despite the Ottoman Empire's centralisation policies and the infiltration of capitalism into Ottoman Anatolia after the 1830s arousing nationalist proclivities amidst Ottoman Kurds, most of the Kurdish movements were Ottomanist in outlook (H. Bozarslan, 2003a: 165–72) and this was a restricted process, encompassing exclusively the Kurdish elite (Van Bruinessen, 2003: 55–6).

The politicisation of the Kurdish identity and Kurdish national mobilisation was largely catalysed by four different factors. The first of these is the assimilationist policies stemming from Arab, Persian and Turkish official nationalisms (Van Bruinessen, 2000; Natali, 2005; Vali, 2006). That is to say, the exclusionary policies and monolithic understanding of society and state by the states that host Kurds impelled them to conserve their distinct identities, and thereby initiated a symbiotic development of Kurdish and Arab/Persian/Turkish nationalisms.

The second factor that fostered Kurdish identity and nationalism is the uneven socioeconomic and political development commonly experienced by the Kurdish societies in the modern Middle East. As Tom Nairn rightly noted, nationalism has commonly 'arisen in societies confronting a dilemma of uneven development ... where a conscious, middle-class elite has sought massive popular mobilization to right the balance' (1977: 41–2). Michael Hechter also makes a similar and pertinent observation: 'to the extent that social stratification in the periphery is based on observable cultural difference, there exists the probability that the disadvantaged group will, in time, reactively assert its own culture as equal or superior to that of the relatively advantaged core. This may help it conceive of itself as a separate "nation" and seek independence' (1975: 10). As these valuable annotations highlight, nationalism neither emerges erratically in the history of a populace, nor is it a perennial or romantic phenomenon; it is a contingent phenomenon rooted in the socioeconomic actualities of the modern age.

The spread of war between the Kurdish armed organisations and the states that host the Kurds after 1960 – i.e. Iraq: intermittently from 1960 to 2003; Iran: intermittently from 1980 to present; Turkey: intermittently from 1984 to present – has amplified the shared socioeconomic and political problems experienced by Kurds, and thereby nurtured national awareness among Kurds, even with their territorial, linguistic and political fragmentations. These wars have engendered a constant movement of Kurdish populations – often to similar destinations, such as the metropolises of the hosting states or the megalopolises of Western Europe – enabling them to share experiences of struggle, displacement, poverty and homelessness.

The final and most contemporary factor empowering the politicisation of the Kurdish identity and the Kurdish national movement is imputable to sequential momentous events and transformations in the Kurdish-inhabited countries in the Middle East from 2010 on, namely the Arab uprisings after December 2010 and the rise of the so-called Islamic State of Iraq and the Levant (ISIL) after 2014. The transformative impact of the former was employed by the people in the Middle East to develop a new discourse on changing the balances and political situations in the region. The stout desire for more democratic, pluralistic and decentralised governments and broader civil/political rights that appeared during the uprisings strengthened this discourse. Relatedly, the Arab uprisings have given a lot of momentum to the movements and struggles of the non-Arab indigenous peoples by holding out the hope of socioeconomic and political change via toppling or severely weakening oppressive regimes reviled by Kurds, as evinced in the case of Syria's Kurds.

On 19 July 2012, Syria's long repressed Kurds – largely under the leadership of the Democratic Union Party (Partiya Yekîtiya Demokrat, PYD), the PKK's sister organisation in Syria – took control of the local administration in major Kurdish-populated areas in Afrin, Jazira and Kobanê, now collectively designated as Rojava. This de facto Kurdish autonomy came on the back of government troops abruptly pulling out of the major Kurdish areas in an attempt to consolidate their increasingly desperate position in mid-July 2012. The autonomous structure in Rojava encouraged the Kurds, not only in other parts of Syria but also in Turkey, as showcased by declarations of autonomy in ESA towns, such as Cizre and Doğubeyazıt, by PKK-affiliated local political structures in the summer of 2015.

The genocidal campaign ISIL unleashed against Kurds in Iraq and Syria consolidated the political ties between Kurds, despite their differing political perspectives. This was deftly demonstrated with two successive events. The PKK militants from the Qandil Mountains in northern Iraq, the KRG Peshmerga and the PYD/PKK fighters from Rojava cooperated to save Yezidi Kurds threatened by ISIL in August 2014. And the Kurds across ESA – and all over the world – rose up in late 2014 against Turkey's indolent policy towards the then ISIL-besieged Kobanê. Consequently, Kobanê today is for Syria's Kurds and Turkey's Kurds what the Halabja chemical-weapons attack in 1988 was for Iraqi Kurds – a stepping-stone for national mobilisation – and it has immensely strengthened Kurdishness.

The emergence of the modern nation-state coincided with the rise of capitalism, a novel type of economic structure, ideology and political structure in contrast to that existing under feudalism.[1] Under feudalism in Europe, for instance, political domination had been legitimised by reference to the divine right of the kings to rule. Theoretically, under capitalism, notions of 'popular sovereignty' or 'common will' define the nature of political authority in the constitution of the nation-states. A chain of bourgeois revolutions gave an end to the feudal aristocracy's rule and gave birth to the nation-states. The classic example of this is the aforementioned French Revolution.

The existential and core principle of the nation-state is that all its citizens are members of a single political unit, regardless of their ideational dissimilarities. This principle habitually assumes an organic link between the dominant nation and the state. The construction of the nation-states in Turkey, Iran, Iraq and Syria, which began soon after the First World War, shared this ethos. Often, the cement of this unison is a form of national myth, which unites and defines the features specific to each nation. Put differently, most fellow-members of a nation will never know each other, but they will entertain the identical national myth.

[1] *Feudalism* in this book will denote a social and economic arrangement, characterised by an obligation laid on the producers by force and independently of their own volition to fulfil certain economic demands of an overlord, that is, the feudal superior, whether these demands take the form of services to be performed or of dues to be paid in money or in kind. This coercive force may be that of military strength, possessed by the feudal superior, or of custom backed by a juridical procedure or the imposition of law.

Thus the nation has been perceived as an 'imagined community', since the 'image of their communion' is instilled in the minds of each member of any given nation (Anderson, 1983: 6), unlike in pre-capitalist or traditional societies, where most members of society know each other. Kurds have also employed appeals to 'imagined community' in mobilising nationalist sentiment.

The construction and deployment of a myth of origin tracing the origins of the Kurds to the first millennium BC to an ancient people, the Medes, and the Newroz myth[2] in the political discourse of the Kurdish national movement have been highly influential in the awareness by Kurds that they constitute one people (Gunes, 2012; D. Aydın, 2014). As McDowall asserts, these myths 'are valuable tools in nation building, however dubious historically, because they offer a common mystical identity, exclusive to the Kurdish people' (2000: 4). To sum up, real socioeconomic and political problems commonly experienced by Kurds in the modern Middle East combined with the fictitious or constructive factors have shaped the process of national identity formation among Kurds.

The amalgamation and culmination of the fictive and real factors at the turn of this century, as Van Bruinessen observed in the mid-1990s, 'have strengthened contact between the Kurds; there is now a stronger awareness of belonging together than there was in the past' (2000: 62). However, these developments do not implicate that Kurds have transformed into a unitary, collective actor with common purposes and resultantly done away with all divisions. There still exists diverse political agendas amidst Kurdish political actors, as exhibited with the two competing visions for Rojava offered by the PKK-affiliated and the Kurdistan Democratic Party–oriented (Partiya Demokrat a Kurdistanê, KDP) political formations in this region.[3] Yet what these contemporary political events germane to the Kurds accentuate is that, drawing on Miroslav Hroch's model of nation-building,[4] the majority of the Kurds

[2] The myth of Newroz narrates the toppling of the Assyrian King Dehak by a mass uprising led by Kawa the Blacksmith (Kawayi Hesinkar), who, on 21 March 612 BC, initiated an uprising by the Medes, defeated the Assyrian Empire, annihilated Dehak and liberated the Medes (the supposed ancestors of Kurds) from years of oppression and tyranny. Kurdish nationalists construct the myth of origin around the Newroz festival (traditionally celebrated across the Middle East on 21 March, which coincides with the spring equinox, as a New Year festival) as a national festival date.

[3] For a comprehensive analysis of the vying political visions for Rojava amidst Kurdish political actors, see Gunes and Lowe (2015).

[4] This model distinguishes between a maiden phase where activists commit themselves to erudite inquiry into the cultural, historical and linguistic features of their ethnic group; a penultimate stage where a new range of activists emerges, trying to gain the support of as many of their compatriots as feasible for the project of creating a nation; and a final period

have reached the final phase of nation-building and national consciousness has become the concern of the majority of the Kurdish population.

Nevertheless, by virtue of multifarious and complex international, historical, political and economic factors explored in the subsequent sections of this study, and even with the recent Kurdish regimes[5] established by Kurds in the twenty-first century, they have been unable to institute an independent state. Accordingly, the Kurds claim the status of the largest nation without a state of its own.

Language

The Kurds speak an Indo-European language, Kurdish, which is a branch of the Iranian language family. There are a number of dialects and subdialects of the Kurdish language. Kurmanji is the most widely spoken dialect by northern Kurds (in Turkey) and by western Kurds (in Syria) as well as by Kurds in former Soviet Republics (Armenia, Georgia, Azerbaijan). Kurds living in Iraq, or southern Kurds, mostly speak Sorani. Sub-dialects or local dialects include those mostly used by Kurdish-inhabited areas of Iran (eastern Kurds) of Kirmanshani, Gurani (Gorani) and Leki (Laki). A minority of northern Kurds also speak Zaza. There is disagreement however, about whether Zaza is actually a Kurdish language, because it is noticeably different from, though not completely dissimilar to, other Kurdish dialects, except Gurani (Gorani) (McDowall, 2000: 10). An additional problem is the different written scripts of the Kurdish language. It is written in the Arabic, the Latin and, in the case of Kurmanji in Armenia, Georgia and the Azerbaijan republics, in the Cyrillic alphabets.[6]

Religion

The Kurds are overwhelmingly Muslim. The majority of the Kurds are Sunni Muslims who are a part of the Shafi'i school of Islam, unlike their Arab and Turkish Sunni neighbours, who mainly adhere to the Hanafi school, and their Azeri and Persian neighbours, who are Shi'ites. Most of the eastern Kurds living in the provinces of Kermanshah and Ilam are

when the national consciousness becomes the concern of the majority of the population (Hroch, 1993: 3–20).

5 The formalisation of the semi-independent Kurdish administrative unit in Iraq following the US-led invasion of this country in 2003, and in 2014 Kurds gaining control of the de facto autonomous region in northern and northeast Syria.

6 For detailed and differing explorations of the Kurdish language, see Minorsky (1927: 1151–5); MacKenzie (1961: 68–86); and Kreyenbroek (1992: 68–83).

Shi'ite. Other Kurds observe heterodox and syncretistic sects 'with beliefs and rituals that are clearly influenced by Islam but owe more to other religions, notably old Iranian religions' (Van Bruinessen, 1991: 7). Such sects include the Ahl-i Haqq ('People of Truth or the Kaka'is), the Alevis (otherwise known as the Qizilbash) and the Yezidis. There are small communities of Kurdish Baha'is, Christians and Jews.[7]

Land

It is generally agreed that the Kurds have lived in a geographical entity, namely, Kurdistan (literally, the land of the Kurds). However, owing to the various political, economic and social vicissitudes, the geographical extent of Kurdistan has varied significantly over the centuries and its territorial confines have been a matter of contention among its researchers. Indubitably, the following four core characteristics of Kurdistan have fuelled this debate (O'Shea, 2004):

(i) it is not, and never has been, recognised as an independent state;
(ii) it does not constitute an economically distinct area;
(iii) it is not, and at no time has it been, entirely ethnically, linguistically or religiously cohesive as a region;
(iv) it lies on the major overland trade routes between Asia, Europe, Russia and the Arab Middle East, as well as being home to rich oil and water resources, prompting outside powers to become involved in its fate.

The amalgamation of the aforementioned factors engendered the elasticity and the degeneration of the notion of Kurdistan over centuries.

In the eleventh century, the geographer Al Qashgari produced a stylised map of what he titled *States of the East*, which built in, along with all the 'races' acknowledged in the East, the land of the Kurds. This perhaps is the first map to include Kurdistan (O'Shea, 2004: 230). During the tenth and eleventh centuries, whilst part of the Arab Caliphate (seventh–eleventh centuries), a number of Kurdish dynasties – the Shaddadids (951–1174, Transcaucasia), Hasanwaydhids (959–1095, Dinawar), Marwanids (990–1096, Diyarbakir) and Annazids (991–1117, Hulwan) – took control of their local matters, but were wiped out by the invasions of the Seljuk Turks (eleventh–twelfth centuries) (Hassanpour, 1992: 50; McDowall, 2000: 21–4). In the year 1150, the Seljuk Sultan Sanjar

[7] For in-depth analysis of religion in Kurdistan, see Van Bruinessen (1991: 5–27) and Kreyenbroek (1996: 85–110; 1998: 163–84).

created a province of Kurdistan, with the town of Bahar as its capital, and it comprised areas that are presently located in the predominantly Kurdish regions of contemporary Iraq and Iran, namely, the provinces of Dinawer, Kermanshah, Shahrazur and Sincar (Kendal, 1996: 10). Yet it was not until the sixteenth century that the geographical expression *Kurdistan* came into common usage to denote a system of Kurdish fiefs generally, and not merely the Seljuk-designated province.

The geographical extent of this definition grew immensely during the next three centuries owing to the instigation of a few interrelated processes from 1514 onwards: the incorporation of nearly all of the Kurdish principalities in or around eastern Asia Minor into the Ottoman Empire, and the migratory movements of the Kurds. The aggrandisement of the territorial scope of Ottoman Kurdistan becomes apparent when the investigations of nineteenth-century contemporaries on its territorial confines are surveyed. Probably the most detailed account of it is delineated in a little-known study of the Ottoman military scholar, Ahmed Cemal.

In 1895, Cemal, after having graduated from the Ottoman Imperial War Academy in 1892, with the blessing of the Council of Military Education (Meclis-i Maarif-i Askerriye) published a geography textbook titled *Ottoman Geography* (*Çoğrafya-yi Osmânî*) in an attempt to acquaint senior high school students with the topography of the empire. It was republished in 1900 and 1903, but in the ensuing years, possibly because of the political developments during and after the CUP period outlined in Chapter 4, its educational role and importance appears to have gradually diminished.

Çoğrafya-yi Osmânî divides Ottoman lands into three separate entities: Ottoman lands in Europe (*Avrupa-yı Osmânî*); Ottoman lands in Asia (*Asya-yı Osmânî*); and Ottoman lands in Africa (*Afrika-yı Osmânî*). Kurdistan, along with the Anatolian Peninsula, Arabian Peninsula, Yemen, Hejaz and the islands of Crete and Cyprus, is a constituent territory of *Asya-yı Osmânî*, and it consists of the provinces (*eyalets*), sub-provinces (*sancaks*) and judicial districts (*kazas*) displayed in Table 1.1. (Kürdoloji Çalışmaları Grubu, Kürt Tarihi Araştırmaları-I, Osmanlı Kürdistanı, 2011).

Cemal's demarcation of the geographical extent of Ottoman Kurdistan is in accord with the detailed map of Kurdistan produced by Britain's military attaché at Constantinople[8], Major F. R. Maunsell[9] (1894: 81–2).

[8] Maunsell remained in this post until 1905, and was responsible for the War Office's maps of the Middle East during the period prior to the First World War.
[9] For other investigations of Maunsell on Kurdistan, see F. R. Maunsell (1901: 121–41).

Table 1.1 Eyalets, sancaks *and* kazas *in Ottoman Kurdistan, ca. 1890*

Eyalets	Sancaks	Kazas
Erzurum	Erzurum	Bayburt
		Ova
		Pasinler
		Hınıs
		Kiğı
		Tercan
		Tortum
		Kiskim
		İspir
	Erzincan	Kemah
		Kuruçay
		Refahiye
	Bayezid	Diyadin
		Kara Kilise
		Eleşkirt
		İntap
Mamuretülaziz		
	Mamuretülaziz	Harput
		Arapgir
		Keban Madeni
		Eğin (Kemaliye)
	Malatya	Hısnımansur-Adıyaman
		Besni
		Akçadağ
		Kahta
		Şiro
	Dersim	Ovacık
		Çemişgezek
		Çarsanacak
		Mazgirt
		Pah (Kocakoç)
		Pülümür
		Kızıl Kilisa
Diyarbekir		
	Diyarbekir	Silvan
		Lice
		Derik
	Mardin	Nusaybin
		Cizre
		Avniye
		Midyat
		Şırnak
	Ergani	Palo
		Çermik
		Siverek
Bitlis	Bitlis	Ahlat
		Hizan
		Mutki

Table 1.1 *(cont.)*

Eyalets	Sancaks	Kazas
	Muş	Malazgirt
		Bulanık
		Varto
		Sason
	Siird	Garzan
		Şirvan
		Eruh
		Pervari
	Genç	Çapakçur
		Kulp
Van		
	Van	Karcikan
		Şatak (Çatak)
		Gevaş
		Adilcevaz
		Erçiş
		Bargiri (Muradiye)
		Müks (Bahçesaray)
	Hakkari	Albak
		Gever (Yüksekova)
		Şemdinan (Şemdinli)
		Mahmudiye
		Nurdüz
		Hoşab
		Beytüşşebab
		İmadiye
		Oramar (Dağlıca)
Musul	Musul	Akra
		Zebar
		Duhok
		Zaho
		Sincar
		İmadiye
	Şehrizor	Revandiz
		Erbil
		Köy Sancak
		Salahiye
		Ranye
	Sülemaniye	Gülanber
		Bazyan
		Merge
		Şehripazar

Source: Çoğrafya-yi Osmânî, Ahmed Cemal, 1895: 105, 114, 130–51, 181–94, 231–8 in Kürdoloji Çalışmaları Grubu, Kürt Tarihi Araştırmaları-I, *Osmanlı Kürdistanı*, 2011: 181–232.

Ever since the First World War – by virtue of the political and military affairs that had surfaced in the Ottoman Empire and the neighbouring polities at the dawn, during and after the war (explored in Chapters 2–5) – there is much debate,[10] albeit with little consensus, on the issue of where the borders of Kurdistan lie.

Discussions pertaining to the territorial confines of Kurdistan are with regard to the political and social nature of the concept of Kurdistan, because in the wake of the First World War, Kurdistan was divvied between the various countries of the Middle East. Today, the bulk of the Kurds lives in Turkey, Iran, Iraq and Syria, and a tiny fraction within several republics of what used to be the Soviet Union (i.e. Azerbaijan, Armenia, Georgia, Kazakhstan, Kirghizstan and Turkmenistan), which had passed into these areas when territories were ceded by Persia in 1807–20, and by the Ottomans in 1878 (Meho, 2001: 4).

Population

The Kurds in Turkey constitute the majority of the population in ESA. These domains today consist of ethnically and religiously mixed provinces such as Malatya and Erzurum, with various combinations of Kurds, Turks, Sunnis and Alevis. As appropriately pointed out by H. Bozarslan, this diversity has geared nearly all scholars to use the geographical designation of 'predominantly Kurdish regions' rather than 'Kurdistan' (2008: 335), and this study will follow suit.

On account of forced displacements during the 1920s and 1930s and as part of the counteroffensive against the guerrilla insurgency by the PKK in the 1990s, as well as voluntary migration throughout the 1960s and 1970s, Kurds currently inhabit all cities in Turkey. Moreover, since the 1960s, particularly from the 1980s onwards, there has been a rapid increase in Kurdish immigrant communities in many Western European countries.

According to the Turkish census data, the inhabitants of the Turkish Republic whose mother tongue was Kurdish were 1.4 million in 1935, 1.4 million in 1945, 1.8 million in 1950, 1.8 million in 1960 and 2.3 million in 1965. That means Kurds constituted 9.2 per cent of the population in 1935, 7.9 per cent in 1945, 8.9 per cent in 1950, 6.7 per cent in 1960 and 7.7 per cent in 1965 (Heper, 2007: 36). It is apt to point out that such censuses do not equip one with the actual size of

[10] For a detailed exploration of the contentions surrounding the geography of Kurdistan from the onset of the First World War, see O'Shea (2004).

Table 1.2 *Kurdish population estimates, 2000*

Country	Total Population	Kurds	% of Population
Turkey	60,000,000	13,200,000	22%
Iraq	19,300,000	4,400,000	23%
Iran	61,000,000	6,100,000	10%
Ex-Soviet Union		500,000	
Elsewhere		700,000	
		Total 26,000,000	

the Kurdish population in Turkey during these years. This is for two main reasons. The first of these is – bearing in mind the suppressive political milieu in Turkey in the years 1935–65 – many Kurds were somewhat reluctant to stigmatise themselves by pronouncing their Kurdish identity. The other factor is that some of the enumerators may have 'corrected' their data in order to arrive at politically acceptable data (van Bruinessen, 2006: 22–3).

After 1965, the Turkish state abandoned and suppressed official censuses to establish ethnic distribution in Turkey. As a result, ever since 1965, there has been much speculation regarding the population of Kurds in Turkey. Commentators in the past two decades or so have given estimates ranging from 7 million to 30 million. This study will employ the breakdown of the Kurdish population prepared by McDowall, which falls in the middle of range approximations (2000: 3–4).[11]

1.2 Differing Theories on the Kurdish Question in Turkey

The socioeconomic disparities between the predominantly Kurdish ESA regions and the rest of the Turkish Republic, the lack of recognition of the collective rights of the Kurds in Turkey, their mass mobilisation around the demands of political pluralism and autonomy and the PKK-led Kurdish insurgency continue to be constitutive aspects of a thorny and multidimensional issue in Turkey: the Kurdish question. Although Turkey's Kurdish question is today generally examined as an amalgam of complex problems, for many decades after the proclamation of the Turkish Republic this question was conceptualised and

[11] For alternative studies regarding the size of the Kurds in Turkey, see Mutlu (1996: 517–41) and Sirkeci (2000: 149–75).

analysed in a rather static and unilinear fashion, largely dominated by the paradigms devised by the Turkish state.

Up until 1990, the Turkish state authorities denied the Kurdishness of the Kurds and the Kurdish question, or, put differently, they negated the existence of the Kurds as a separate people and the ethno-political component of the Kurdish issue, and generally controlled representations regarding this matter. This success in dominating characterisations of the Kurdish question was largely by virtue of three key factors: first, the Turkish state authorities' ability to quell pro-Kurdish movements and, concomitantly, to encumber all alternative formulations and projections of the Kurdish question; second, state-centric representations of the Kurdish question regularly attaining international acceptance and recognition, allowing the Turkish state to govern the Kurdish population in Turkey with very little international interference; third, the poverty of knowledge on Kurds in Turkey because of the state ceaselessly bowdlerising publications[12] and investigations on Kurds. As these features indicate, and as the exploration that follows will emphasise, the formulations and evolution of the Kurdish question are inextricably linked to political and socioeconomic events within and beyond the borders of the Turkish Republic and, as a result, ever since 1920 the Kurdish issue has been both an international and a transnational issue.

The Kurdish Question as a 'Question of Underdevelopment'

From the establishment of the Republic up until the 1950s, the Kurdish question was formulated as an issue of perseverance of the feudal or backward structures, to be resolved by relevant modernising social reforms. Relatedly, the founders of the Turkish Republic portrayed the question as a clash between a progressive modern state and archaic reactionary structures. The unsuccessful revolts of the Kurds in the initial years of the Republic – i.e. the Şeyh Said Revolt (1925), the Ararat Revolt

[12] One of the earliest texts on the socioeconomic and political structures of the Kurds, Şeref Han's 1597 manuscript *Şerefname* on the Ottoman Kurdish principalities, was translated into Turkish for the first time in 1971. Upon its publication, the public prosecutors in Turkey immediately filed a case against the book on the grounds of it 'making propaganda aimed at destroying or endangering [Turkey's] national feeling on the basis of race' (M. E. Bozarslan, 1990: unpagenated), and asking for its collection. Until 1980, the study by Basile Nikitine, *Les Kurdes: Etude Sociologique et Historique*, published in Paris in 1956, and Vladimir Minorsky's subject entries for 'Kurds', 'Kurdish' and 'Kurdistan' in the *Encyclopedia of Islam*, both of which were translated into Turkish, constituted the main sources on Kurds and Kurdish history unblemished by state-centric perspectives in Turkey.

(1927–30) and the Dersim Revolt (1937–8) (see Chapter 4) – were portrayed as the work of reactionary feudal leaders against a modern state structure that promised progress and prosperity.

As Yeğen rightly observed, this representation of the Kurdish question in Turkey is exhibited in the following speech of the chairperson of the Court of Independence in 1925, which condemned the leaders of the Şeyh Said Revolt to death:

> [S]ome of you used people for your personal interest, and some of you followed foreign incitement and political ambitions, but all of you marched to a certain point: the establishment of an independent Kurdistan. . . . Your political reaction and rebellion were destroyed immediately by the decisive acts of the government of the Republic and by the fatal strokes of the Republican army. . . . Everybody must know that as the young Republican government will definitely not condone any cursed action like the incitement and political re-action, it will prevent this sort of banditry by means of its precise precautions. The poor people of this region who have been exploited and oppressed under the domination of sheikhs and feudal landlords will be freed from your incitement and evil, and they will follow the efficient paths of our Republic which promises progress and prosperity. (2011: 69)

As the problem was conceived as a socioeconomic problem, rooted in the philistine and premodern structure of the region, it was thought it could be resolved by Kemalist *mission civilisatrice*. For example, Prime Minister İsmet İnönü portrayed the Dersim Rebellion as follows:

> The Government has been implementing a reform program for Tunceli [Dersim] for the past two years. It includes wide-ranging work . . . in order to civilise the region. Some of the tribal chiefs of the region . . . have not welcomed the [governments'] program. [Nevertheless], the program of reform as well as the civilising of Tunceli [Dersim] shall go on! (Beşikçi, 1990: 82–3)

By the 1950s, armed Kurdish resistances had ended, but socioeconomic disparities between the predominantly Kurdish ESA regions and the rest of Turkey had widened and reached an unquestionably inequitable level. In this context, the state represented the Kurdish question as a by-product of socioeconomic underdevelopment emanating from a lack of economic integration. Accordingly, as accentuated by Yeğen, the government programmes during the 1950s and 1960s promised to diminish the economic divergences between the principally Kurdish regions and the rest of Turkey (2009: 159–70). For instance, the 1969 government emphasised the issue of 'the development of the eastern region' and stressed the importance of 'special measures in the regions where backwardness is massive and acute' (ibid.: 164–5). Some of governments in the 1970s, 1980s and

1990s also portrayed the Kurdish question as a 'socio-economic problem of underdevelopment enhanced by the feudal structure' (Gençkaya, 1996: 94–101). Hence, after 1950, the question came to be titled the 'Doğu Sorunu' (the 'Eastern Question') and was perceived as a socioeconomic question by an increasing number of scholars and researchers in Turkey.

The representation of the Kurdish question as a problem of endurance of the traditional structure by nearly all of the governments in the years after the transition to multi-party democracy in 1946 was rendered paradoxical by the continual alliance between the Kurdish rural elite and political parties leading these governments. Most of the mainstream political parties that came to power after 1950 successfully obtained a Kurdish clientele group that consisted of the receptive elements within the Kurdish landed and/or religious elites, who were able to garner a large number of votes. For example, Mustafa Remzi Bucak and Ziya Şerefhanoğlu – members of venerated Kurdish tribes – were elected as candidates of the Democrat Party (Demokrat Parti, DP) in 1950.

In the succeeding years, with the exception of the far-right Nationalist Action Party (Milliyetçi Hareket Partisi, MHP), all of the mainstream parties co-opted a section of the Kurdish propertied class and had Kurdish representatives belonging to this segment in the National Assembly. As well as legitimising state rule in the predominantly Kurdish provinces in ESA, this integrative policy also revitalised the traditional structure in these regions and reinvigorated the power of the Kurdish rural elite – most of whom were deported during the single-party era and were granted the right to return only with the rise of the DP to power in 1950.

In the late 1950s and throughout the 1960s, Kurdish activists and intellectuals played a key role in the discussions of the 'Eastern Question' and saw them as a conduit to raise demands of social and economic equality for the Kurds. The leading members of the new Kurdish politically active intellectuals included Musa Anter, Yusuf Azizoğlu, Mehmet Emin Bozarslan, Faik Bucak and Sait Elçi, all of whom played a pivotal role in debates surrounding the Kurdish question in Turkey in the later years.[13] M. E. Bozarslan authored a very influential study titled *The Problems of the East* (*Doğu'nun Sorunları*) in 1966, wherein the socioeconomic problems in ESA were addressed and possible solutions were hypothesised.

[13] For more information on this period and the role of these leading members, see Anter (1990), Edip Karahan (2005) and Gunes (2012: chapters 3–4).

The Kurdish Question as a 'Natural and Instinctive Impetus for Liberation'

At a time when the Kurdish question was mainly perceived through the lens of the 'Eastern Question' in Turkey, in Europe, particularly in France, Kurdish nationalists were circulating publications outlining the nature and necessity of the 'national liberation movement' of Kurds with a view to influencing the European communities (Scalbert-Yücel and Le Ray, 2006: 4–8). As a result, Kurds living abroad and writing in French made the first explicit reference to the 'Kurdish question'. In 1930, a book authored by Dr. Bletch Chirguh, the penname of Celadet Bedirkhan, published by the Kurdish nationalist organisation Khoybûn,[14] described the Kurdish question as a political one, and more specifically as a question of 'national liberation'. Chirguh in *The Kurdish Question: Its Origins and Causes* (*La Question Kurde: ses Origines et ses Causes*) posits that the Kurdish question consists of 'the struggles that have lasted for more than three centuries and that have always aimed at national independence' (1930: 3 in Scalbert-Yücel and Le Ray, 2006: 4).

Three decades after the publication of *La Question Kurde: ses Origines et ses Causes*, Kamuran Bedirkhan, in another study in French, *The Kurdish Question* (*La question Kurde*), defined the Kurdish question as:

> [T]he fight of the Kurdish people since one century for its *liberation*. It is the *natural and instinctive impetus* of this people who wants to remain Kurd, to speak freely his language and preserve his national patrimony. … The Kurdish question consists in convincing the states that share Kurdistan to behave towards the Kurds in accordance with the judicial and moral principle universally acknowledged and inscribed in the United Nations Charter and in the Declaration of Human Rights. (1958: 8–9 in Scalbert-Yücel and Le Ray, 2006: 4–5, italics mine)

As can be deduced from the quotation, maiden formulations of the Kurdish question by Kurdish nationalists framed it as a question of 'national liberation' emanating from the perturbed relationship between the oppressive states and the oppressed Kurds. Moreover, these representations, akin to the aforementioned primordialist or essentialist studies on Kurds, considered the nation and national

[14] Khoybûn (Independence) was formed in Bhamdoun, Lebanon, in October 1927 by Kurdish intellectuals living in exile. Leading figures of Khoybûn included Kurds of aristocratic background such as the Bedirkhan brothers, Celadet Bedirkhan and Kamuran Bedirkhan, scions of the princely family that once ruled the Kurdish emirate of Bohtan. Khoybûn sought to establish a strong Kurdish national liberation movement. It instigated the unsuccessful Ararat uprising of the Kurds in Turkey in 1927–30, discussed in Chapter 4.

identity as 'natural and instinctive impetuses' or, put differently, conceived of identity as a fixed entity assuming it to be an essentially unchanging quality. Despite influencing the views of, in particular, French researchers studying the Kurdish question like Joyce Blau and Gerard Chaliand (see Scalbert-Yücel and Le Ray, 2006), the studies by the Bedirkhan brothers were not influential in Turkey at the time of their publication, largely because of the aforementioned expurgation of studies regarding Kurds.

The Kurdish Question as a 'Foreign Conspiracy'

The other prevailing conceptual framework intermittently used by the Turkish state to characterise the Kurdish question in Turkey, particularly at times of rising Kurdish discontent, was that it was a consequence of foreign provocation and thus the issue was reduced to a matter of the state subduing the disorder incited by the foreign elements. Underlying this sporadically used characterisation for the Kurdish question is the 'Sevres Syndrome', a long-enduring trauma shared by the post-Ottoman rulers and society in Turkey owing to the 'divisive' promises made by the triumphant Allies or Entente Powers of the First World War to the Armenians and Kurds in the Treaty of Sevres (1920). Despite this Treaty overriding the Treaty of Lausanne (1923), the spectre of the past haunted and recurrently informed the state's notion that foreign powers were provoking Kurdish rebellions in Turkey. This view is exemplified by the judgement of a case in 1963, wherein prominent members of the Kurdish opposition of the time were sentenced:

> During the Republican period . . . some foreign states intended to cause trouble in Eastern Anatolia. As a matter of fact, the Sheikh Said, Ağrı and Dersim rebellions were due to the counter revolutionary actions of some tribes which were incited by foreign powers. . . . The content of foreign incitement at present [however] is not the same as that of the past. While previous foreign incitements . . . were caused by the imperialists states which had interests in the Middle East, at present, these incitements are caused by communist activity. Today, . . . the Kurdish ideal is entirely the product of incitement by international communism. (Yeğen, 2011: 72)

Mahmut Rışvanoğlu's extensive study, *The Tribes of the East and Imperialism* (*Doğu Aşiretleri ve Emperyalizm*), published by Türk Kültür Yayınlar in 1975, offers an emblematic defence of the 'foreign incitement' hypothesis. Rışvanoğlu postulates that the Kurdish identity is a construct of Orientalist scholarship built to cater for the needs of international imperialism. According to him, initial studies on the Kurds by Russian scholars Vladimir Minorsky and Basile Nikitine, who settled in Britain and France after the October Revolution (1917), served the interests of the imperialist countries to where they had migrated by inciting Kurdish unrest.

The Turkish state and pro-state researchers or academics laid the blame for the existence of Kurdish uprisings and the Kurdish question on the foreign powers that they perceived as an external threat. The nature and the source of the peril to Turkey changed in accordance with who/what the Turkish state perceived as the enemy. Immediately after the War of Independence, the threat was the Western imperialist powers. During the Cold War, Turkey allied with the West and acted as an eastern embankment against the spread of communism, thus the source of the Kurdish unrest in the 1960s and 1970s was the Soviets. With the end of the Cold War, Kurds were portrayed as the agents of Greece, Israel and the European Union (EU).

The Kurdish Question as a 'National Liberation Struggle against Colonialism'

During the 1970s and 1980s, Kurdish left-wing movements in Turkey – i.e. the Ala Rizgarî, the Kawa, the PSK and the PKK – emphasised the political nature of the Kurdish question and articulated it as an issue of national self-determination. Such a conceptualisation by Kurdish organisations in Turkey altered the question from being discoursed and theorised as a socioeconomic problem to one of national oppressions. All of these Kurdish political currents, through appropriation of certain elements of Marxist and/or Leninist theory, espoused the notion that Kurdistan was a colony of Turkey, Iraq, Iran and Syria, and began to look towards the anticolonial liberation struggles in Asia and Africa.

In the 1978 manifesto of the PKK, the founder of the Party, Abdullah Öcalan, outlined the colony thesis[15] with the following words:

[15] Dr. Sait Kırmızıtoprak (Nom de guerre Dr. Şivan) (1935–71) initially formulated this thesis and the necessity of waging an anticolonial liberation struggle against the Turkish state in the late 1960s. Dr. Kırmızıtoprak was from Tunceli (Dersim). He studied medicine in university. During Adnan Menderes' government's crackdown on Kurdish intellectuals in 1959, he was arrested and tried – this episode came to be known as the '49'ers Incident' (see Section 4.5 for further details). Dr. Kırmızıtoprak was one of the leading figures of the pro-Kurdish movement in the 1960s. Kırmızıtoprak published articles in newspapers and magazines such as *Akis, Forum, Vatan, Yön, Dicle-Fırat, Sosyal Adalet* and *Milliyet*. His published books include *The Problem of Oppressing and Oppressed Nations* (*Ezen ve Ezilen Millletler Sorunu*); *Kurdish National Movements and the Kurdish Revolution in Iraq* (*Kürt Millet Hareketleri ve Irak'ta Kürdistan İhtilali*); *Kurdish Language* (*Zımanê Kurdî*), co-written with Kamuran Bedirkhan; and *Ferheng Kurdî û Tırkî* (Joyce Blau's Kurmanji-English-French dictionary translated to Turkish by Dr. Şivan with numerous additions).

In political terms, Kurdistan is under the rule of four colonialist states that collude with imperialism. Each of these states, in accord with its interests and the interests of the international monopolies, plays a central role in developing colonialism in the part it keeps under its rule. ([1978] 1992: 100)

Deriving from such an analysis, Öcalan emphasised the importance of a national liberation struggle in order to attain economic independence and political unity in Kurdistan:

Economic independence could only develop in an environment where there are no exogenous imperialist intrusions and internally there is political unison. In Kurdistan these conditions have not materialised, and, in the present conditions, can only develop subsequent to the victory of the national liberation struggle. (ibid.: 142)

PSK's founder, Kemal Burkay,[16] in a conference in London in 1984, postulated a similar description of Kurdistan, and hypothesised that one of the reasons for socioeconomic underdevelopment in Kurdistan was its colony status:

The states that have divvied Kurdistan have reduced each part of it to a colony. When compared to Western countries, Turkey, Iraq and Iran are backward countries. Yet, within the last 40–50 years, important developments have taken place [in each of these countries]. Despite [these developments] there exist major developmental divergences between Kurdistan and the remaining parts of these countries. ... The vast natural resource wealth of our country [Kurdistan] is an important factor in its division and the poverty endured by our people [Kurds]. The states that have apportioned Kurdistan and their imperialist chiefs have aggressively plundered and scrambled the natural and mineral resources, reducing our country to a colony. We are yet to see a development policy from Turkey. (1995: 5)

Despite the similarity in their theoretical analysis of the socioeconomic and political conditions and relations in ESA, the PKK, when compared to the aforementioned Kurdish left-wing organisations in Turkey, emphasised extensively and systematically the need for violent resistance in order to achieve the 'national liberation of Kurdistan' from the

[16] Burkay and a few other authors quoted in this section of the book, by virtue of being both organic intellectuals and instigators of pro-Kurdish political activism in Turkey, have authored scientific and militant/political works. Since up until very recently scientific and militant/political works on the Kurds were heavily bowdlerised, it was common for both forms of publications to be jointly published. Thus, on account of these two factors, in the writings of these influential Kurdish authors it is not always possible to distinguish clearly between scientific and militant/political publications. That said, this study has carefully surveyed articles penned by these individuals and has cautiously quoted their works; that is to say, this book has given special care to avoid employing militant/political publications by these figures.

'colonisers' and bring about a 'socialist revolution'.[17] Moreover, Öcalan considered violent struggle as not only a means and necessity of national liberation but also the very condition of individual manumission. The PKK launched its guerrilla campaign on 15 August 1984.

From the mid-1980s on, the trajectory and perceptions of the Kurdish question in Turkey were to be determined by the success of the projections and actions of a constellation of actors. That is, the Turkish state, the PKK, pro-Kurdish legal political parties in Turkey, Kurdish clientelist formations, the Kurdish nationalist movements in Iraq, Iran and Syria and global-imperial actors, most notably the United States and the Western European powers, played a fundamental role in the delineation of the political borders in the region throughout the twentieth century.

In the early 1990s, the increasing number of armed clashes between the PKK and state forces, the electoral success of the pro-Kurdish Peoples' Labour Party (Halkın Emek Partisi, HEP) alliance with the Social Democratic Populist Party (Sosyaldemokrat Halkçı Partisi, SHP) in the 1991 general elections, winning twenty-two seats in Parliament, and the Iraqi Kurds attaining *de facto* autonomy following the Gulf War in 1991, had made the negationist paradigms of the Turkish state regarding the Kurds and the ethno-political component of the Kurdish question unsustainable. As a result, in 1991, Prime Minister Süleyman Demirel made an unprecedented speech in Diyarbakir, wherein he declared that the state recognised 'the Kurdish reality' and, within the same year, the Turkish Assembly enacted a law annulling the 1983 ban on speaking Kurdish in public. The recognition of the presence of the Kurds, however, did not implicate or result in the recognition of their collective rights.

The Kurdish Question as a Question of 'Separatist Terror'

The Anti-Terror Law of 1991 (Act No: 3713), enacted within the same year as the speech by Demirel, defined terror in an across-the-board manner: it included nearly all of the activities tied to the advancement of Kurdish rights and culture, and it has since been invoked to detain and imprison Kurdish activists, intellectuals and politicians (Gunes and Zeydanlıoğlu, 2014: 13–14). The enactment of this draconian law was not only emblematic of the confines of the recognition policy of the Turkish state; it also was illustrative of the dominant

[17] For an extensive comparative study of the political manifestos and organs of the Ala Rizgarî, the Kawa, the PSK, and the PKK, see Gunes (2012: 65–100).

paradigm that would replace the negationist model of discourse and theorisation of Turkey's Kurdish question. That is to say, having acknowledged the ethnic constituent of the Kurdish question, the state throughout the 1990s would characterise the question as one of ethnic insurrection with a secessionist and divisive aim, which therefore necessitated military/security measures. Expectedly, as mentioned in the previous chapter, during the late 1980s and the 1990s the central focus of nearly all of the academic literature and discussions came to be the political history of Kurdish nationalism and conflict analyses. Whereas in the 1960s and 1970s the focus of the discussion about the Kurdish question was the socioeconomic features of the issue, from the latter part of the 1980s the political dimension of the question took precedence.

Because the political and cultural aspects of Turkey's Kurdish question constitute the main source of contention or conflict between the pro-Kurdish actors and the Turkish state, since 1990, scholarly research and debates regarding this issue have concentrated on these two components, resulting in the economic constituent of the question being under-researched. As van Bruinessen rightly observed, '[when compared to the political and cultural features of the Kurdish question] on the nature of the economic aspect of the question, there is broad range of agreement between Kurds and non-Kurds' (2004: 5), which has been a contributing factor to the economic feature of the question attaining relatively little attention.

1.3 Alternative Perspectives on Economic Development in ESA

The central focus and vantage point of virtually all of the literature analysing the linkages between economic development in ESA and the Kurdish question has been the hypothesis of regional underdevelopment. That said, two opposite poles of thought exist with regard to the causality of underdevelopment in these regions. Some of the literature attempts to account for the thesis of underdevelopment by prioritising the role and impact of economic, social and infrastructural factors such as the level of regional infrastructure, the logic of capitalist accumulation, regional industrialisation and the tribal structure in these regions (M. E. Bozarslan, [1966] 2002; Boran, 1974; Z. Aydın, 1986; Sönmez, [1990] 1992; Özer, 1994; Heper, 2007). Others instead have sought to understand and explain the postulate of underdevelopment via the binary and hierarchical state-versus-society model and thus have given pride of place to ethno-political issues as explanatory factors, i.e. the conflictual relationship between the state and the Kurdish population inhabiting these regions (Beşikçi, [1969] 1992, [1990] 2004; H. Yıldız, 1989; Aytar, 1991; Burkay, [1992] 2008, 1995; Bayrak, 1999).

The overview contained in this section seeks to map this theoretical field by providing an introductory presentation of the core assumptions of the main proponents of these differing perspectives. Drawing on that, this study will then account for the specific theoretical foundations and limitations of each perspective. This book has purposively selected literature from different periods and extremes of thought in order to exhibit the diversity, continuities and change regarding discussions on the correlation between the Kurdish question and economic development.

Contributions from the initial strand of studies commonly identify the dominance of the tribal social structure, the non-existence or inadequacy of modern infrastructure and the destruction of manufacturing after the nineteenth century as factors that have played a central role in shaping social, economic and political processes and structures in ESA. Relatedly, the roots of underdevelopment in these areas are sought in the interplay of these factors. The decision of the Ottoman state in the sixteenth century to recognise the political, legal and administrative autonomy of the tribal Kurdish lords in the provinces of Diyarbekir, Bitlis and Van, in exchange for military obligation and regular payment of tribute to the state, is regularly hypothesised to have constituted an incessant impediment to socioeconomic development in these areas, as well as a persistent factor influencing political events involving Kurds (Z. Aydın, 1986: 15–17; Pamuk, [1987] 2010: 98–9; Sönmez, [1990] 1992: 79–80; Heper: 2007: 5). This agreement is alleged to have entailed the dominance of tribal rule by dint of which not only had the Kurdish notables accumulated excessive landed and fiscal wealth, but there had also been 'minimal implementation of the governing *timar* system'. Consequently, the Ottoman state had 'never been able to become a powerful force in the Region'[18] (Sönmez, [1990] 1992: 79).

Moreover, these studies habitually hypothesise that the centuries-long autonomy of the Kurdish notables 'remained unbroken during the nineteenth century' (Pamuk, [1987] 2010: 98; Sönmez, [1990] 1992: 79; Heper, 2007: 5). Since the enactment of the Land Code of 1858, which *de facto* recognised the existing land distribution, it is argued that large tracts of land remained in the hands of the Kurdish rulers, who had

[18] In most of the publications on the Kurdish question and/or ESA, the term *the Region* is used to denote the predominantly Kurdish-populated provinces in ESA.

not 'been interested in increasing productivity in agriculture' (Heper, 2007: 16). Thus, the centralisation attempts by the state during and after the 1830s are often recognised as hardly affecting the political, social and economic powers of the tribal elite in these regions, to the detriment of social and economic development in ESA (Pamuk, [1987] 2010: 98–9; Sönmez, [1990] 1992: 86–8; Heper, 2007: 5).

The deeply inadequate and expensive means of transportation and the absence of railroads in ESA is also consistently posited to have largely 'secluded' these territories from the transformatory changes goaded by the capitalist world market in the Ottoman Empire throughout the nineteenth and early twentieth centuries (Pamuk, [1987] 2010: 97–9; Sönmez, [1990] 1992: 79–80). Owing to the absence of modern infrastructure up until the early twentieth century, the argument goes, the agricultural produce of these areas of Anatolia could not regularly be transported to long-distance markets (Pamuk, [1987] 2010: 97; Sönmez, [1990] 1992: 105). As a result, ESA, when compared to other areas of the predominantly agrarian Ottoman Empire, was least affected by the world market–induced commercialisation of agriculture during the nineteenth and twentieth centuries (Pamuk, [1987] 2010: 97; Sönmez, [1990] 1992: 79).

The unavailability of the indispensable modern infrastructure, it is commonly contended, cannot be imputed to the policies of the Ottoman state owing to two factors. First, the western quarters of present-day Turkey were provided with railroads by the industrialised capitalist countries, which were interested in importing raw materials from this region. And, second, the rail line projects of the dominant Western countries in these regions – namely, the United States' Chester Railway Project (1908–13) and Germany's Berlin–Baghdad Railway Project (1914–89) – had not materialised on account of exogenous events. The former was dropped by the U.S. state when the Mosul region remained in the hands of the British state, who also blocked the Berlin–Baghdad Railway Project, for it had its own eyes on the Middle East's resources (Sönmez, [1990] 1992: 104–6; Heper, 2007: 6–7). Unfavourable agronomic conditions, largely emanating from the enduring supremacy of the Kurdish landed or propertied elite, are usually construed as being influential in the success of manufacturing in ESA:

'[T]he relative scarcity and poor quality of agricultural land and the low level of commercialization of agriculture may also have been an important factor in the flourishing of manufactures in these areas [Eastern Anatolia and Northern Syria]' (Pamuk [1987] 2010: 112).

The most important concentration of Ottoman textile manufacturing activity existed in northern Syria, south eastern Anatolia and to some extent eastern Anatolia during both the earlier and later parts of the nineteenth century. However, in the period after the first quarter of the nineteenth century, manufacturing in ESA, especially cotton textile manufacturing, had, as elsewhere in the Ottoman Empire, met with immense competition from European imports, which on account of the Industrial Revolution in Europe had the advantage of rapid mechanised production. Such competition, plus the tariff policies in the 1838 Anglo-Turkish Convention, had initiated a 'period of destruction' of cotton textiles in the eastern Anatolian provinces in the 'latter part of [the] nineteenth … and early twentieth centuries' (Sönmez, [1990] 1992: 104–5).

Studies that have sought to elucidate regional underdevelopment by giving primacy to the obstructive role and impact of social, economic and infrastructural factors additionally have regularly argued that, in spite of the remarkable advancements witnessed after 1923, these regions maintained their relatively worse-off positions in present-day Turkey. It is claimed this is principally because, even after the establishment of the Turkish Republic, the feudal relations in these areas did not dissolve and ESA remained predominantly rural territories bereft of modern industry and infrastructure, which made it difficult to attract private-sector investment to these regions. Most of these studies emphasise the destruction wrought by the armed conflict between the Turkish state and the PKK after 1984 to the economy of these regions – i.e. the loss and/or removal of the local populace, stagnation of private investment, incomplete state-subsidised projects and destruction of the local infrastructure (Sönmez, [1990] 1992: 249–51; Heper, 2007: 6).

Nonetheless, there are differing assessments on the question of why, before 1984, the predominantly Kurdish-inhabited ESA regions lagged behind other parts of Turkey in social and economic development. Some of the literature correlates the paucity in development with the powers of the Kurdish tribal leaders and/or the absence of transformation in the social tribal structure (M. E. Bozarslan, [1966] 2002; Özer, 1994; Heper, 2007). Others alternatively attribute underdevelopment to the uneven development of capitalism in Turkey (Boran, 1974; Z. Aydın, 1986; Sönmez, [1990] 1992).

Studies of the frequently quoted sociologist Ahmet Özer are exemplary of the former approach. Özer, who regularly conducted research for the GAP and SPO in south eastern Anatolia, in his oft-cited *GAP and Social Change* (*GAP ve Sosyal Değişim*), published after two years of field research in the province of Urfa, has two inextricably linked conclusions: the first, the structure in these regions is traditional and has to be modernised; and, the second, the GAP regional development project is a socioeconomic initiative that could play an instrumental role in modernising the age-old social structure as well as fostering socioeconomic development in these regions (Özer, 1994: 88–9 and 150). Thus, the Kurds' discontent and the underdevelopment of the predominantly Kurdish regions were hypothesised to have been engendered by perseverance of the social tribal structure and relations.

Additional studies on the question of development in modern-day Turkey have proposed an alternate account of the hypothesis of underdevelopment by attributing underdevelopment in these regions to the logic of capital accumulation and the uneven development of (Turkish) capitalism, postulated by Karl Marx. According to Behice Boran,[19] the underdevelopment in ESA is an inevitable consequence of the capitalist Turkish economy, the aim of which is to grow continually through investment in the areas where the highest rate of profit is possible. Investments, according to the same argument, are unequally distributed within Turkey because the factors determining the rate of profit are unevenly distributed. Consequently, Boran argues, 'the people of the East [of Turkey] do not experience differential treatment because of speaking another language[;] [differential policies concerning the East of Turkey] stem from the uneven development of capitalism [in Turkey]' (1974: 189). Zülküf Aydın in *Underdevelopment and Rural Structures in Southeastern Turkey* (1986: 26–9) further develops the very general characterisation of regional underdevelopment posited by Boran by adopting Ernest Mandel's theory on underdevelopment and applying it to the specific conditions of Turkish capitalism.

Aydın claims 'that uneven development and underdevelopment are basic features of capitalism, and regional uneven development is the spatial juxtaposition of these two features of capitalism' (ibid.: 26). Bourgeois states, in creating the national market, ensure the flow of labour from the underdeveloped to the developed regions. Underdeveloped regions are not only a source of labour for the developed regions; they are also an important market. For instance, during the early years of the Turkish Republic – i.e. the ètatist period – the state

[19] Behice Boran (1910–87) was an immensely influential Turkish Marxist sociologist, author and politician. Boran, who was an associate professor at Ankara University, Faculty of Language and History-Geography, played a prominent role in shaping the views of many on the left on, among other things, the question of capitalist development in Turkey.

took advantage of the labour reserves in 'the Region' and by building railways connected the remote parts of 'the Region' with the developed western regions of Turkey (ibid.: 29). Deriving from such a causal theory of underdevelopment, Aydın argues that the 'Kemalist policy [in Eastern Anatolia] stemmed from the profit logic of capital, not from the fact that Eastern Anatolia was Kurdish' (ibid.), since 'capitalists are interested in accumulating capital; they are not concerned with the ethnicity of the people whose surplus product they appropriate' (ibid.: 25). Accordingly, 'the transfer of the surplus produced in the region is the prime reason of underdevelopment [in these regions]' (ibid.: 17). In a similar vein, Sönmez ([1990] 1992) argues that the role of ESA in the regional division of labour in Turkey is to provide energy and agricultural products, whilst being a market for the industrial west of Turkey. Consequently, the underdevelopment of these regions, above all, should be sought in the regional divisional of labour in Turkey (ibid.: 247–8).

On the other hand, studies that attempt to explain the economic, social and political features and processes in the predominantly Kurdish provinces in ESA by employing a binary model of state-versus-society have devised an alternative interpretative framework for the correlation between regional underdevelopment and the Kurdish question. The theoretical paradigm of underdevelopment formulated in these studies is based on a critique of the causality of underdevelopment embodied in all of the previously surveyed literature. Specifically, this body of literature classifies the causes of underdevelopment – i.e. the social, economic and infrastructural factors – as the *effects* of the conflictual relationship between the Kurdish people and the Turkish state. The source of the perturbed ties between the central state authority and the Kurdish populace, as well as the underdevelopment of ESA, is habitually purported to lie in the 'colonial' and 'assimilationist' policies implemented by the rulers of Turkey (Beşikçi, [1969] 1992, [1990] 2004; H. Yıldız, 1989; Aytar, 1991; Burkay, [1992] 2008, 1995; Bayrak, 1999).

Advocates of this dualistic model customarily posit that long-standing issues pertaining to tribalism and inequitable land tenure are results of the Ottoman and the Turkish state policy of maintaining and consolidating the traditional Kurdish ruling stratum and of burgeoning divisions and enmities amidst territorially segmented Kurdish tribes in ESA since the early sixteenth century. It is argued that the decision to incorporate the Kurdish principalities into the Ottoman Empire derived from the strategic objectives of: (i) making the predominantly Sunni Kurdish principalities Ottoman protectorates against the rival

Shi'i Safavid forces in Eastern Asia Minor; (ii) formalising and preserving the tribal kinship system; and (iii) apportioning the Kurdish principalities on the basis of territoriality and kinship ties (Beşikçi, [1969] 1992: 128–9; H. Yıldız, 1989: 38–9; Burkay, [1992] 2008: 279–82). The 'differential' and 'ambivalent' policies the Ottoman state executed in ESA in accord with these aims are hypothesised to have nurtured tribalism and inter-communal rivalries, and thereby laid the foundations for the underdevelopment in ESA (Beşikçi, [1969] 1992: 113–27; H. Yıldız, 1989: 37–41).

The advocates of this theoretical model commonly maintain that ever since the creation of the Turkish Republic, the Turkish ruling classes have pursued a policy akin to that of the Ottoman state and have thereby preserved the traditional structures and hindered the reforms necessary for social and economic development in ESA. The 'failed promise' of a land reform during the single-party period and the 'institutionalisation' of the 'feudal hegemonic forces' in the multi-party system post-1945 are regarded as quintessential examples of the enduring 'cooperation' between the Turkish state and the dominant 'feudal forces' in the predominantly Kurdish provinces of Turkey (Beşikçi, [1969] 1992; Burkay, 1995).

Authors that employ the binary model of state versus Kurdish society argue that the Turkish state inhibited socioeconomic development in these regions by infinitesimal public investment in infrastructure, and insistence on not recognising the Kurdish identity of the local populace:

> The East has been neglected for centuries and as a result it became a zone of deprivation (mahrumiyet bölgesi). This negligence continued during the republican era. Regardless of their party belonging, every politician, in order to assimilate the people and the intellectuals of the East, systematically and purposefully, represented the East, to the world and Turkey, as an area full of fanaticism, ignorance and the enemy of civilisation. (Edip Karahan, 1962: 4 in Gunes, 2012: 54)

In addition, it is hypothesised that the predominantly Kurdish areas are 'colonised' in order to cater for the needs of Turkey's industrialised regions: 'like most colonized regions, Kurdistan's stores of raw material, its vast natural wealth in petroleum, copper, coal and phosphate, soil, forests, and water are exploited and marketed for industry' (Beşikçi, [1990] 2004: 19). Relatedly, studies informed by this theoretical viewpoint agree on the proposition that the state-sanctioned GAP project constitutes an archetype of the Turkish Republic's 'colonial' policy in ESA.

The GAP project was implemented as a regional project in 1989 and, it is argued, under the 'façade' of 'regional economic development' this project enables the 'exploitation' and 'colonisation' of ESA (Aytar, 1991; Burkay, 1995). The GAP initiative is therefore conceptualised as being 'the new chain of exploitation and colonisation of natural and human resources in the Region' (Aytar, 1991: 7). This 'feature' of the GAP project is evinced, the argument goes, with the energy-oriented state investment in predominantly Kurdish-populated provinces in south east Turkey, which substitutes the exigent needs of the local dwellers for the requirements of industrialised western quarters of Turkey (Beşikçi, [1969] 1992, [1990] 2004; Aytar, 1991; Burkay, 1995).

The Limitations of Existing Theories

Despite shedding light on issues that impede social and economic progress, the existing literature on the question of development in ESA merely enables one to *understand* the obstacles to development in these territories, but does not *explain* them. This is due to two common omissions of the current studies. The first of these is that they do not systematically account for the historical antecedents of eastern Turkey's economic development. Put differently, political and economic changes that have fostered or hindered development in ESA during the Ottoman period are not thoroughly examined in the current investigations of the question of development in these domains. The second lacuna in the development literature on these regions is that it fails to analyse comprehensively the relationship between the Turkish state and the predominantly Kurdish-populated regions of Turkey. A closer and critical exploration of these studies will help to elucidate these explanatory limitations.

Modernisation Theory

Studies that correlate underdevelopment with the persistence of inhibitive premodern or feudal structures and relations have constituted the bulk of the development literature on ESA. Some of the proponents of this hypothesis, like Özer (1994) and Heper (2007), in the same vein as the aforementioned government programmes after 1950, ascribe the endurance of these unfavourable economic conditions primarily to the perseverance of inimical and obstreperous primordial values and practices in these regions. They advocate the view that the question of underdevelopment and the Kurdish question hinge, above all, on modernising the traditional tribal structure in ESA.

Scholars characterising the difficulties and deficiencies of economic and social transformation from the viewpoint summarised earlier borrow heavily from modernisation theory, in that the prevailing traditional tribal organisations and ties are professed to have persistently conserved underdevelopment in these regions. The modernisation school of thought initially developed in the Cold War era of the 1950s and comprises a range of perspectives inspired by the sociological theory of Max Weber that follow the same basic argument. That is, nations remain underdeveloped when traditional customs and culture hamper individual achievement and kin relations dominate, thus the development of societies is dependent on the adoption of modern capitalist values and practices. Modernisation theorists attempt to explain the diffusion of Western styles of living, technological innovations and individualist types of communication as the superiority of secular, materialist, Western, individualist culture and of individual motivation and achievement (Lerner, 1958; Schramm, 1964).

Scholars influenced by the modernisation approach frequently construe the tribal social structure in ESA as persistently impeding the Kurds from partaking in Turkey's modern social life and adjusting to latter-day lifestyles, as Heper alluded to in *The Kurds and the State*: 'In Turkey, as compared to those who live on the plains, the Kurds, who live in the mountains, have not intermingled with the Turks to any great extent. The tribal social structure of the area also rendered difficult the acculturation of the citizens' (2007: 7).

However, the hypothesis that the tribal structure is the perpetual obstacle to structural economic changes in the principally Kurdish areas of Turkey is founded on a deterministic and ahistorical conception of Kurdish tribes and tribalism. It depicts the Kurdish tribal identity and structure as an immutable and fixed feature of Kurdish society, devoid of wider processes of nation-building, capitalistic property relations, urbanisation and trans-border relations with other Kurds situated in neighbouring states. It is indubitable that tribes and tribalism have been features of Kurdish history, but that does not entail or validate an immutable and static conceptualisation of tribes, unaltered by economic and political transformations in or around the society in which it exists. In other words, tribes are not *explanans*, as they themselves need explaining.

As Eugene Kamenka rightly pointed out, tribalism – akin to national consciousness – is historically specific, reliant on 'specific social and historical content, deriving from specific social and historical conditions' (1973: 6). The Kurdish tribe *seems* to be permanent and unchanging due to its continued presence throughout different societies with different modes of production, but this is a *pretence*; the tribal entity of today is substantially different from its pre-capitalist antecedents.

Many examples exist of the changing nature of Kurdish tribal identity and structure throughout the history of the Ottoman Empire and the modern Middle East, as alterations are made in accordance with economic and/or political changes[20] (see Chapters 2–4). One of the many illuminating and relatively recent examples of the fluidity of the Kurdish tribal organisation and identity was witnessed after the transition to multi-party democracy, when the traditional Kurdish elite – in line with the Turkish state's policy of incorporating landed and/or religious Kurdish rulers into the state apparatus – was integrated into the Turkish political system. This policy resulted in the bulk of the old Kurdish elite, unlike its descendants, disavowing Kurdish origin in order to become more closely integrated members of the Turkish ruling class. Villages controlled by the traditional Kurdish rulers became political fiefdoms of various rival mainstream political parties previously loathed by the local populace.

Studies that ascribe the lack of economic advancement primarily to the absence of transformation in the archaic customs and practices in ESA fail to account properly for the corollaries of the cooperation between the traditional Kurdish elite and the Turkish state for the social, economic and political relations and structures in these domains. As a result, these studies avoid an exploration of the issue of how this collaboration might have maintained feudal relations in these regions by dint of the state not implementing the long-awaited land reform persistently opposed by the co-opted traditional Kurdish elite and thus leaving the land tenure bequeathed from the Ottoman era fundamentally untouched. Besides, the possible connection between the Turkish state–Kurdish traditional elite alliance and Turkey's Kurdish question is omitted. In other words, the likely links between the bourgeoning sociopolitical and economic demands of the Kurds during and after the transition to multi-party democracy in Turkey, starting with the 'Eastern Meetings' of the 1960s, and the desire of the Turkish state to block these demands by preserving the feudal structure in these regions are not examined.

[20] On the Kurdish tribes and their evolution, see H. Bozarslan (2006: 130–47).

In addition, researchers who have sought to explain underdevelopment by, above all, imputing it to the persistence of feudal social organisation in Kurdish society tend not to examine incidences and developments in the pre-Republican period. In so doing, 400 years of Ottoman Kurdish history are overlooked, and the seismic social, political and economic changes during and immediately after the First World War are eluded. Consequently, these explanations of underdevelopment fail to assess the links between the uprooting and seizure of the resources or properties of the indigenous people in ESA after 1913 and the lack of capital and the absence of innovation or 'entrepreneurial spirit' in these regions.

Other investigations that have associated underdevelopment in ESA with the perseverance of feudal relations have sought to explain this anomaly with the enduring excessive powers of the Kurdish tribal and religious leaders (M. E. Bozarslan, [1966] 2002). M. E. Bozarslan' epoch-making work in the late 1960s, *Doğu'nun Sorunları*, has identified the absence of land reform as well as the lack of industrial development and infrastructural modern facilities in ESA as the main reasons for Kurdish tribal and religious leaders' powers. The problem of underdevelopment in these regions or the 'Eastern Question' will be remedied, according to M. E. Bozarslan, with state-sponsored industrialisation, the reform of the age-old land tenure and adequate public investment, because these measures could play a catalytic role in dissolving the feudal structure and ties necessary for development.

Albeit illuminating pivotal issues overlooked in the works of the previously surveyed authors, most notably the negative ramifications of the collaboration between Kurdish *aghas* and the Turkish state for socioeconomic advancement, the influential study by M. E. Bozarslan ([1966] 2002) embodies nearly all of the inadvertences of the modernisation approach. More specifically, *Doğu'nun Sorunları* fails to analyse exhaustively the structures, processes and events before 1923, and thereby paints a rather unhistorical picture of 'the East' by treating the year 1923 as 'Year Zero'.

This influential study also does not systematically analyse the question of how the forced displacement and confiscation policies of the Ottoman and Turkish states have influenced social, political and economic developments, or the lack thereof, in ESA. In addition, underdevelopment in these domains is conceptualised solely as a socioeconomic and cultural problem devoid of political components or demands, as evinced in the following definition of development postulated by M. E. Bozarslan:

Development . . . is a multidimensional problem that does not have the possibility of being realised from one dimension [only]. The development of a country, or a region, is also tied to the industry and transportation as much as it is tied to culture. Because social, economic and cultural matters are tied to each other . . . development in the East [of Turkey] cannot solely be attained by economic incentives, nor can it be accomplished by cultural activities; it can only be attained by the combination of both [economic and cultural means]. ([1966] 2002: 203)

In 2002, *Doğu'nun Sorunları* was republished with a revised preface wherein M. E. Bozarslan in harmony with the aforementioned critique argued that what he described as being exclusively socioeconomic and cultural 'problems of the East' in the 1966 publication of this work were in fact germane to or spin-offs of the Kurdish question in Turkey. Consequently, M. E. Bozarslan further argues, if he were to write a separate book about development, he would title it *The Kurdish Question* and not *The Problems of the East* (ibid.: 9–14).

Dependency Theory

Studies that have accounted for underdevelopment in ESA by correlating it with the economic and structurally asymmetric relationship between the overwhelmingly Kurdish areas of Turkey and the Turkish state are largely informed by the theoretical paradigm that arose as an alternative to modernisation theory, namely, dependency theory. The authors of these studies regularly define the Kurds as a 'dependent nation' and draw heavily from the national movements in the Third World context. Moreover, they emphasise the role of 'national oppression' to which the Kurds were subjected, with Turkey engendering the socioeconomic 'backwardness' of the predominantly Kurdish regions, which these authors believe to be the root cause of regional underdevelopment.

Dependency theory is a theoretical current that came to the fore in 1960 as a heterodox response to the politics of modernisation and its in-built bias towards capitalist-induced development. Architects of the dependency theory include Andre Gunder Frank, Samir Amin, Fernando Henrique Cardoso, Walter Rodney and Immanuel Wallerstein. Dependency theorists commonly maintain that the inadequate development witnessed in 'peripheral' countries is the product of a process of impoverishment and distortion, or the 'development of underdevelopment' (Frank, 1966), which is an offshoot of subordinated participation in a polarised and hierarchical world system. The principal focus of the attention of the latterly mentioned theoreticians has therefore been trained on the mechanisms that generate dependent or peripheral underdevelopment.

Dependency theorists have posited two types of mechanisms to cause underdevelopment and the impoverishment of the 'periphery' to the advantage of the 'core'. The first consists in the systematic extraction of the surplus and resources from the periphery to the core through such means as plunder and unequal exchange. The other consists in the distortions introduced to the national political and economic structures of peripheral social formations as a consequence of their subordination – e.g. through the establishment of a 'comprador bourgeoisie' that earns its gains from collusion with the international extraction of the surplus rather than from 'autonomous' capitalist exploitation.

As often indicated by studies that characterise the Kurdish areas as a colony of the Turkish state, centre–periphery relations determine the relationship between the predominantly Kurdish ESA and the Turkish state, with the latter as the dominant 'centre' economy and the former as its 'subordinated' counterpart. The colonial policies of the Turkish state in the primarily Kurdish-populated ESA, the argument goes, is directed to meet the Turkish states' requirements for natural and human resources. This lopsided relationship between the former and the latter not only obstructs the Kurdish regions from freely integrating with the world capitalist system, it also shapes underdevelopment in these regions. Additionally, the distortion of local political and economic structures by virtue of the incorporation of traditional landed and/or religious Kurdish elite into the Turkish state apparatus, according to the advocates of the colony postulate, preserves and exacerbates underdevelopment in these regions.

Burkay argued that colonialism constituted a major impediment to development in Kurdistan and hypothesised the persistence of feudalism in ESA as a corollary of colonial rule in these regions:

> Capitalism [in Turkey], even if in an evolutionary form, has superseded feudalism to become hegemonic. In Kurdistan though, the feudal structure perseveres. This situation is undoubtedly fostered by the Turkish bourgeoisie's colonialist mechanism in Kurdistan. Kurdistan's raw materials (in particular oil, copper, iron, chrome, and coal) are being exploited; Kurdistan is the region that provides the cheap workforce for the west [of Turkey]; the capital accumulated in this region is flowing to the west; and Kurdistan became a very convenient market for the bourgeoisie to introduce its products. (1995: 5)

Similarly, Bayrak, in *The Kurdish Problem and the Democratic Solution* (*Kürt Sorunu ve Demokratik Çözüm*), through examining a range of state-sanctioned reports and policies after 1923 concerning ESA, describes how the Turkish state has 'colonised Kurdish lands', and thereby nurtured underdevelopment in these areas (1999: 188–98). In spite of there being no definitional or critical exploration of the notion of colonialism, it appears that Bayrak conceives ESA as a colony based on the 'continual seizure' and 'turkification' of Kurdish lands in these regions by the Turkish state after 1923.

One of the most influential explorations of the colony thesis was posited by Ismail Beşikçi in his seminal work *Inter-state Colony Kurdistan* (*Devletlerarası Sömürge Kürdistan*).[21] Beşikçi described the history of colonialism and 'colonial rule' in Kurdistan with the following words:

> The history of colonialism separates colonies into two main groups: full colonies and semi-colonies. Full colonies are societies which have not yet reached the stage of founding a state. ... Semi-colonies are societies which have a state founded on a traditional social order and possessing a long history. ... Kurdistan is neither a full nor a semi-colony. The political status of the Kurdish nation is far less than the status of a colony. The Kurds are a people the world wants to enslave, render devoid of identity, and wipe off the face of this earth ... until every trace of Kurdish identity has been eliminated. ... Turkey, Iran, Iraq, and Syria, in addition to being collaborators with outside powers, are also occupation forces which have portioned and annexed Kurdistan. ([1990] 2004: 18–19)

Recent scholarly publications on Kurds do also employ the colony thesis. For instance, Nader Entessar's relatively recent publication, *Kurdish Politics in the Middle East*, brands the predominantly Kurdish territories of Turkey as an 'internal colony' of the Turkish state (2010: 7). Likewise, in the introduction of another recent study, *The Kurdish Question in Turkey: New Perspectives on Violence, Representation, and Reconciliation*, Gunes and Zeydanlıoğlu characterise the Turkish state's rule in 'Kurdistan as an undeclared internal colony' (2014: 18).

Based on the different descriptions of the 'colony' postulate it can be argued that there are two separate claims, namely, colonialism and internal colonialism, which are distinct. Colonialism is the imposition of monopoly control by an alien state over the economic, political and social life of another land or polity. In the case of internal colonialism – which is a process of exploitation of one group or groups of people by another within a state through structural arrangements – the following conditions exist:

[21] For a contemporary defence of this thesis, see the following interview conducted with Beşikçi: 'The Turkish advocate of the Kurds – Dr. Ismail Beşikçi', in *Kurdish Globe* (2013).

(i) a high degree of administrative and legal integration, between what is considered an internal colony and the rest of the polity;
(ii) all of the subjects are citizens of the same state;
(iii) the relationship between the colonial core area and the territory deemed to be the internal colony has a long history (Hechter, 1975: 32–3).

Based on this distinction, it would stretch the definition of colonialism to apply it to the relationship between the Turkish state and the principally Kurdish ESA.

Unlike many of the Third World formations described by dependency theorists, these territories do not comprise a sovereign state. ESA is administratively and legally integrated with the Turkish Republic, and these territories are geographically contiguous with the rest of Turkey. Furthermore, the discriminatory policies of the Turkish state vis-à-vis the Kurdish people notwithstanding, the primarily Kurdish inhabitants of these regions are citizens of the Turkish Republic. Some aspects of the policies of the Turkish state in the years 1923–90 vis-à-vis its Kurdish citizens, as comprehensively analysed in Chapters 3–5, could however, be placed in the realm of the colonial. The policies implemented by successive governments in Turkey during the seven decades after the proclamation of the Turkish Republic were intolerant of local cultures, were determined to impose a single hegemonic culture (i.e. Turkish culture) and they were accompanied by a large-scale campaign against those who refused to be browbeaten. Relatedly, internal colonialism is the only viable theoretical toolkit that can be used by the advocates of the colony thesis.

The explanatory value of the internal colony postulate in elucidating the relationship between the Turkish state and the Kurdish people is dubitable, since all of the applications of this model are founded on a unidirectional and static conceptualisation of the relation between 'powerless and peripheral' Kurdish areas and the 'all-powerful and dominant' Turkish state. Albeit shedding some light on certain features of the relationship between the latter and the former, this characterisation obscures many aspects of the relationship between the central state authorities and the Kurdish populace or regions because it fails to account systematically for the influence of the periphery over the core. For instance, the impact of the altering interests of the propertied traditional elites in these regions, and their project to woo Turkish statesmen in order to establish new networks of support so as to enhance their authority, particularly during the post-Republican era, in shaping the Kurdish policy of the Turkish state is not properly analysed in these studies.

In addition, the mass migration of the Kurdish people to the industrialised metropolis of Turkey and its impact on the Turkish economy and society is not methodically investigated in publications that draw heavily from dependency theory.

The relationship between the Kurdish-majority regions and the rest of Turkey extends the dependency bonds to one that acknowledges relations of mutual dependence. In order to analyse aptly this reciprocal tie, it is essential to recognise that the social, the political and the economic in Turkey, as elsewhere, do not have one single centre, but many. Hence, it is necessary to analyse activities and deeds of a range of actors and dynamics, networks and interactions. As H. Bozarslan rightly highlighted, Kurds are not mere 'passive agents of a system imposed by Ankara. Various mechanisms of subordination, clientelism and participation link them to the center. … [These] links imply negotiation and a constant game of legitimization between them and the center as well as the political parties. The terms of these negotiations and legitimization game are determined, among other elements, by army pressure, Kurdish radicalism and ongoing guerrilla warfare since 1984, evolution of clientelist groups and the transborder nature of the Kurdish issue' (1996: 136).

It is also worth noting that the authors of the colony postulate do share some of the common deficiencies of the previously summarised alternative theoretical approaches on the question of development and underdevelopment in ESA. They do not thoroughly interrogate the ramifications of economic and political transformations in the Ottoman period for regional development, or lack thereof, in these territories. This is because they take for granted two interrelated postulations: (i) the dominance and manipulation of Ottoman Kurdistan via the divide and rule policy of imperial Istanbul; and (ii) the relatively worse-off position of ESA, when compared to other regions of the Empire, because of the fragmentation arising from the divisive policy of the Ottoman rulers with regard to Ottoman Kurds.

The protagonists of the colony hypothesis, moreover, do not systematically account for the population policies implemented in the years 1915–90. Despite regularly referring to policies of displacement and seizure of Kurdish lands, they habitually only refer to policies in the single-party period. Consequently, the mass deportations and confiscation of immovable and moveable properties belonging to the indigenous dwellers of these regions prior to the establishment of the Turkish Republic and/or after the single-party period is not adequately explicated.

Traditional Marxist Perspectives in Turkey

As displayed with the foregoing literature review, studies that have analysed the question of development in Turkey based on a Marxist perspective concur on the hypothesis of underdevelopment in ESA. Advocates of this standpoint argue that when compared with other regions of Turkey, the late interaction of these areas of Turkey with the transformatory changes induced by capitalism is a consequence of the uneven development of capitalism in Turkey. One of the merits of this approach is that it provides a valuable insight concerning certain aspects of the evolution of Turkish capitalism, which is often not detailed by the previously mentioned development literature swayed by non-Marxist interpretations of (under)development.

Nevertheless, their analysis of underdevelopment in ESA has commonly embodied a number of vulnerabilities. One of the central weaknesses of this interpretation is that it regularly presents a notion of development that is economistic – i.e. in analysing development and underdevelopment in Turkey, priority is given to economic relations, often without considerable regard to pivotal political, social and cultural relations. This is demonstrable with the overarching role ascribed to the logic of capital accumulation or surplus appropriation when analysing (under)development in Turkey by Boran (1974) and Aydın (1986).

This economistic conceptualisation of development is founded on a deterministic and univocal interpretation of the relationship between the economic base and the political superstructure, which implicates a 'vulgar materialist' analysis of development avidly criticised by leading Marxist scholars, amongst others. As the Marxist historian Eric Hobsbawm rightly highlighted, 'economic development is not a sort of a ventriloquist with the rest of history as its dummy' and neither are humans 'exclusively money-making machines ... immune to the political, emotional, ideological, patriotic or even racial appeals' ([1997] 2004: 62). Thus, noneconomic factors that underlie social progress or its absence need necessarily to be systematically considered by investigations that make socioeconomic development their thematic concern.

The second drawback of this approach pertains to the diminutive role imputed to the national conflicts and struggle of the indigenous populaces of ESA in shaping the social and economic history of these regions. Since precedence is given to economic relations or antagonisms as explanatory factors for (under)development, economic issues or conflicts are conceived of as the dominant force of history, frequently with little regard for other questions or struggles, like national and cultural conflicts, which influence how history unfolds. As a result, sociopolitical issues of the Kurdish population in these areas and the role of these problems in influencing the social and economic history of ESA have not been adequately analysed.

This deficiency in the historical accounts of the Marxists in Turkey cannot solely be understood by imputing it to their economistic approach; it is also a result of the influence of Kemalism on the political left in Turkey (Yeğen, 2007: 1208–36). Throughout the history of the Turkish Republic, virtually all of the left, including most Marxist currents, in Turkey have been heavily influenced by the dominant ideology of the Republican elite, Kemalism. For instance, the leaders of the Turkish Communist Party (Türkiye Komünist Partisi, TKP) welcomed the Republican government by agreeing that the basic problem was to wage a nationalist struggle against the imperialist powers and feudalist social forces (ibid.). The paradoxical modus operandi of Marxists under the influence of Kemalism has been to approve the ethnic dimension of the Kurdish question, while distancing themselves from the secessionist ideas or struggles acknowledging national unity and/or delaying the resolution of the question to a future post-revolutionary socialist Turkey.

The other shortcoming of this perspective consists of what the Marxist scholar Jairus Banaji refers to as substituting 'theory for history' – i.e. reducing the investigation of the concrete 'to a programme of verifying "laws" already implicit . . . in the materialist conception of history' (2010: 47). A corollary to this, in the context of the discussion of development and underdevelopment in Turkey, consists of using the process of uneven capitalist development Marx proposed as a necessary feature of capitalism in order to describe the underdevelopment of ESA as a by-product of this in-built predisposition of capitalism. This teleological form of analysing history inhibits a thorough examination of the role and impact of other intervening noneconomic factors or processes stated earlier that have played an influential role in prompting regional disparities in Turkey. In other words, it hinders an understanding of the concrete as the site of many determinations, requiring careful analysis as opposed to merely serving to validate *a priori* theoretical postulates. As Marx suggested in the following passage in *Grundrisse*: 'the concrete is concrete because it is the concentration of many determinations, hence unity of the diverse' (Marx, [1857] 1973: 101).

On account of deputising history for theory, authors like Boran and Aydın have failed to adequately address the relations between uneven capitalist development in Turkey and the policies of dispossession and destruction of productive resources systematically implemented by both the late Ottoman and Turkish polities in ESA. Another common shortcoming of these researchers is that they do not thoroughly investigate the repercussions of the rise and fall of Kurdish polities more than 300 years old on the social, economic and political developments, or lack thereof, in these regions.

The selective and problematic employment of certain features of Marxist theory in interpreting underdevelopment in ESA by the aforementioned authors, however, do not annul the important contribution that the historical materialist approach formulated by Marx and Friedrich Engels and other Marxist authors can provide to the study of historical development of societies. Once historical materialism is detached from deterministic and teleological interpretations or applications critically assessed earlier, it can offer useful tools for analysing development.

Scholarly analyses on the question of development in ESA surveyed previously do converge along a number of lines that are particularly relevant for this study. All of the theoretical models surveyed here are founded on a structuralist interpretation of development. Structuralist theories of development are those that regard development as a process of structural socioeconomic change whereby underdeveloped economies overcome specific structural barriers, by dint of which they are able to pursue a path of growth. Development is therefore understood as the qualitative growth-enabling process of overcoming those barriers. This thesis concurs with the structuralist interpretation of development.

All the theoretical explorations surveyed earlier, albeit on dissimilar and conflicting causal grounds, posit that two long-standing structural barriers engender underdevelopment in the predominantly Kurdish populated regions of ESA: (i) the dominance of the traditional elite in landownership and tenancy patterns; and (ii) the very low level of industrialisation in the years ensuing the destruction of manufacturing in these regions after the nineteenth century. There is also scholarly unanimity regarding the unilinear continuum of inadequate development characterising the economic history of these regions.

In the following chapters, by exploring the political and economic history of the ESA regions, these oft-postulated factors for underdevelopment and the paradigm of continual underdevelopment in ESA will be critically analysed in order to verify the veracity of these interrelated perspectives and to attest their relevance to the Kurdish question of Turkey.

A central tenet of this research is that the question of development in ESA and the Kurdish question of Turkey are inseparable and can be aptly comprehended only in relation to the political, social and economic history of the polities of which it has formed a part, namely, the Ottoman Empire and the Turkish Republic. Hence, this study will examine the economic, political and social features of these regions within the context of the larger geographical area and political entity it has comprised since the sixteenth century. In doing so, this book has relied heavily on a historical, structural and political-economic approach.

As universally agreed in the development literature on the ESA, there has been relatively late and little contact with capitalist development in these predominantly Kurdish regions, compared to other regions of Turkey. This book will argue that this is on account of the de-development process initiated by the dominant forces in these regions in order to prevent the formation of an economic base for the autonomous existence of the non-Turkish autochthonic societies in ESA that could jeopardise the political-national imperative of maintaining Turkey's national unity and territorial integrity.

De-development, as Sara Roy outlined in *The Gaza Strip: The Political Economy of De-development*, is an economic process generated and designed by a hegemonic power 'to ensure that there will be no economic base, even one that is malformed, to support an independent indigenous existence' (1995: 4). This process consists of policies that not only hinder but also 'deliberately block internal economic development and the structural reform upon which it is based' (ibid.: 6). It is qualitatively different from underdevelopment, which allows for some, albeit distorted, indigenous development, and thereby does not rescind the prospect of autonomous indigenous existence.

Relatedly, contra to the scholarly wisdom apparent in the development literature reviewed previously, this research hypothesises that continual inadequate development has not been a characteristic feature of ESA's economy. Ever since the early sixteenth century, these regions have witnessed economic prosperity, followed by underdevelopment and de-development. De-development in ESA commenced as a product of the state policies implemented in these regions after the Unionist seizure of power in the 1913 *coup d'état* that differed greatly from those of the previous regimes. The CUP rulers, and their political and ideological heirs, the Kemalists, pursued ideological, political and economic programmes – i.e. the construction and preservation of a Turkish national economy and state as well as the pursuit of population homogeneity based on Turkist ideals – that were qualitatively different from those of their predecessors. These objectives spurred policies of mass murder, deportations, expropriation and dispossession of economic resources, and the suppression of all forms of non-Turkish identities and cultures in the ethnically heterogeneous provinces in ESA. In addition to laying the foundations for the Kurdish question of Turkey, these unusual features of state policy have engendered de-development in these lands by not only distorting, but also forestalling economic development, which deprived the ESA economy of its capacity and potential for structural transformation.

Underlying ESA's de-development as well as the Kurdish question of Turkey is the incessant political-national objective of constructing a strong Turkish nation-state and maintaining Turkey's national unity and territorial integrity. Turkish governments throughout the history of the Turkish Republic have incessantly adopted these objectives. As a result, the identity and the collective rights of the Kurds have been negated. In order to foil the capacity of autonomous existence of the Kurds, de-development policies – albeit with varying methods – have been pursued by successive Turkish administrations in the years following the transition to multi-party politics in Turkey.

A Summary of the Theoretical Foundations

Thus far, this study has presented introductory synopses of the key theoretical debates on its central themes: Kurdish identity, the Kurdish question in Turkey and regional development in ESA. When outlining these debates, the presentation follows an analogous format: an overview of the main differing perspectives, followed by an elucidation of my views on those theoretical positions. The unifying approach linking the theoretical choices consists of the endorsement by this book of a structural, historical and materialist position. This study has argued that the most apposite form of investigating any social process is one that is constituent of these three approaches. First, it seeks to ascertain structural causes of any given social process, as opposed to treating it as a natural or perennial entity or impulse. Second, it draws on the premise that to a large extent, these structural causes consist of or stem from the dynamics of material reproduction of societies. Third, it employs a historical method when analysing social processes. In other words, it utilises historically and geographically concrete data when examining and making generalisations concerning social processes.

Moreover, this book has recurrently criticised essentialist and teleological interpretations of the concrete by abstract notions. The concrete, being multifaceted and largely indeterminate, should not be used selectively to reflect *a priori* theory, but as the locus for evaluating the relational and contingent nature of abstract categories and theoretical discernments, making it possible to revise and improve those categories and discernments. Last, this investigation asserts the primacy of political-economic factors in accounting for both the Kurdish question in Turkey and the regional de-development in ESA, and, at the same time, recognises the operation of a diverse array of other factors, including history, culture and violence, in bringing about these interrelated issues.

1.4 Research Design, Methods and Sources

This study makes use of interviews and archival investigation. Obtaining geographically concrete historical and contemporary empirical data constituted the prerequisite of investigating the role and impact of economic development in the predominantly Kurdish-populated regions of ESA on the rise and evolution of Turkey's Kurdish question. Relatedly, the empirical research of this thesis consists of three main phases explicated next. These stages take place consecutively, and the information attained in each stage is used to prepare the subsequent phases and triangulated with the information that had previously attained.

Preliminary Stage of the Research: Surveying Existing Literature

The initial phase involves the survey of the secondary literature available through two main types of repositories: first, physical libraries, in particular at the School of Oriental and African Studies (London), the British Library (London), the London School of Economics and Political Sciences (London) and the Institut Kurde (Paris); and, second, electronic sources. Accompanied by the information provided by international organisations – i.e. the EU, the United Nations (UN), the International Monetary Fund (IMF), the World Bank (WB) – and official Turkish sources, namely, the Turkish Statistical Institute (TÜİK), the data obtained hitherto were used to prepare a background chapter presenting a synopsis of the relevant research issues and setting the groundwork for the consecutive phase of the empirical work: fieldwork.

Exploratory Phase of the Research: Fieldwork

The subsequent phase, which is essentially the exploratory stage, took place over a four-month-long stay (March–June 2011) in the ESA provinces of Diyarbakir, Urfa, Mardin, Van and Gaziantep, besides Ankara and Istanbul, during the course of which fifteen semi-structured interviews (listed in Appendix I) were conducted, additional sources were consulted and supplementary statistical data were obtained. I employed the snowballing method[22] during my fieldwork. This method offers the opportunity to reach the most relevant information with the least cost and time. One interviewee or document leads to other interviewees, documents and so forth. The primary aims of this part of the research consist of collecting as much information as possible that would complement the previously acquired as well as make it feasible to identify relevant themes that had previously gone unnoticed.

The main systemic procedure consists of a series of semi-structured interviews with key informants: academics; senior members of public agencies dealing with development, economic or statistical matters; politicians; executives of chambers of commerce; non-governmental organisations' (NGOs) sources specialising in regional development in ESA; and the local agents of multilateral organisations. These interviews were conducted to attain detailed information regarding the historical and current trends in ESA of the following topics germane for this study: agricultural and industrial production; commerce and trade; credit and banking facilities; voluntary and involuntary migration; public and private investment; and agrarian and labour relations. The list of interviewees and the capacity under which they were interviewed is given in Appendix I.

The interviews were semi-structured: a list of eight to twelve questions was prepared prior to each interview in accordance with the interviewees' area of expertise. The interviews took between one and two hours, depending on the interviewees' availability and the relevance of the information they provided. All of the individuals were informed in advance of the identity of the researcher, the objectives of the research project, the purpose of the interview and the conditions under which the information obtained might be used. Some of the interviews were tape-recorded; others were documented in my notebook, depending on the consent of the interviewees. In all cases, the recording or notes were transferred onto my laptop within twenty-four hours. Content analysis methodology[23] was used to analyse interviews.

[22] Snowball sampling is set within the link-tracing sampling methodologies (Spreen, 1992) which benefit from ties of identified respondents or documents to provide the researcher with an ample set of potentially relevant information (Thomson, 1997).

[23] *Content analysis* denotes a research technique for the objective, systematic and quantitative description of the manifest content of communication (Rubin and Babbie, 2013). It is a technique from a local text to its social context in an objectified form (Bauer, 2000).

Overall, the interviews were more useful in obtaining or accessing sources related to the contemporary and/or historical trends of the aforementioned themes of research than in providing information about these trends. I was thus able to attain very beneficial and rich publications produced by or kept in the libraries of the following organisations that previously were not available to me:

Administration Regional Directorate (GAP) (Urfa);

The Union of Southeastern Anatolia Region Municipalities (Güneydoğu Anadolu Bölgesi Belediyeleri Birliği) (USARM) (Diyarbakır);

Delegation of the European Commission to Turkey (Ankara);

Republic of Turkey, Prime Ministry State Planning Organisation (T.C Başbakanlık Devlet Planlama Teşkilatı Müşteşarlığı) (Ankara);

Republic of Turkey, Ministry of Industry and Trade (T.C Sanayi ve Ticaret Bakanlığı) (Ankara);

Diyarbakir Chambers of Commerce and Industry (Diyarbakır Ticaret ve Sanayi Odası);

Gaziantep Chamber of Commerce (Gaziantep Sanayi Odasi).

Discourse analysis methodology[24] was used to examine the data provided in these publications. All of the information was used both directly – as one of the bases for writing Chapters 4 and 5 – and indirectly – in the context of the preparation of the subsequent phase of the research.

Moreover, these interviews and the collected secondary data led to the following realisation that on economic and social phenomena in ESA – particularly industrial and agricultural production, commerce and trade, labour and agrarian relations and voluntary and involuntary migration – there is a lack of longitudinal data and research. Nearly all of the existent data and analysis on economic and social activities and events in these territories covered the years after the proclamation of the Turkish Republic. There existed scant information on economic and social changes, structures and relations in Ottoman Kurdistan. Accordingly, I decided to collect data on social, economic and political structures, relations and changes in Ottoman Kurdistan, mainly by exploring the official British archival repositories. In addition, this book has also consulted the published Ottoman, Russian and German archival sources on Ottoman Kurdistan.

[24] This methodology denotes a deconstructive reading and interpretation of a problem or text (Powers, 2001). In this technique, analysts are interested in texts *per se*, rather than seeing them as capturing some reality that is supposed to lie behind the discourse (Gill, 2000). Thus, instead of conceiving the texts as a conduit to some other reality, discourse analysts are interested in the content and organisation of texts.

Final Phase of the Research: Archival Investigation

The final phase of the research took place over just under a year (October 2011–September 2012) and was conducted in London. The archives of the United Kingdom Foreign Office (FO) on Kurdistan, either stored in the Public Record Office (PRO) at Kew, or published online on the House of Commons Parliamentary Papers (HCPP) website, was the first port of call for data. These archival sources consist of reports prepared by British consuls reporting regularly on events in Kurdistan in the years 1850–1945. In the absence of systematic official Ottoman records in the nineteenth and early twentieth centuries (see Chapters 3 and 4), and the non-existence of any other long-drawn-out official foreign reports on events in Ottoman Kurdistan, this documentation, as McDowall rightly pointed out, constitutes 'possibly the single most important historical archive on Kurdistan' (2000: xii). The deficiencies and strengths of each of the archival resources employed in this research are discussed in the subsequent chapters.

Naturally, a growing number of scholars researching the Kurds and Kurdistan have referred to the UK Foreign Office archives on Kurdistan. Nevertheless, thus far, almost all of these researchers have utilised these reports to analyse the political history of the Kurds and Kurdistan (Olson, 1989; McDowall, 2000; Koohi-Kamali, 2003; O'Shea, 2004; Özoğlu, 2004). This study made particular but not sole use of the understudied information provided in these records concerning economic activities, relations and changes in the nineteenth and early twentieth centuries in Ottoman Kurdistan. I have consulted the quantitative and qualitative data presented in the reports prepared by the British consuls or diplomats in the years 1857–1914 on commerce, on manufacturing, on agrarian relations and production and on social structures in Ottoman Kurdistan and bordering regions. For purposes of triangulation, the data in these reports have been studied comparatively, where pertinent and available, with the data provided in the Ottoman official statistics (i.e. population and agricultural censuses) and/or the influential studies of important scholars, most notably, Ömer Lütfi Barkan, Vital Cuinet, Vedat Eldem, Suraiya Faroqhi, Halil İnalcık, Şevket Pamuk, Donald Quataert and Ahmet Tabakoğlu, who have contributed immensely to our understanding of Ottoman economic and social history. The information attained from the archival repositories was used directly in Chapters 3 and 4.

Unless specified, the translations of all of the materials in foreign language employed in this study belong to me.

2 The Formation of Ottoman Kurdistan: Social, Economic and Political Developments in Ottoman Kurdistan before the Nineteenth Century (1514–1800)

2.1 Overview

The pivotal events that materialised during and after the early sixteenth century played an immensely influential role in the foundation and progression of the social, economic and political structures in Ottoman Kurdistan and hastened the Kurds' self-awareness as a distinct group. Three occurrences in particular facilitated these interrelated processes: the battle of Çaldiran in 1514, which determined the general pattern of political relations between the Ottoman state and the Kurdish periphery for about the next 300 years; the maiden unified vision of Kurdish history presented in the *Şerefname* authored by Şeref Han (1543–1603), the famous *mir* of Bitlis, in 1595; and the utopia of Kurdish unison vociferously advocated by the poet Ehmed-ê Khanî (1650–1706) in 1695 in his epic poem *Mem û Zin*. Khanî espoused Kurdish unity against the perceived suppression of the Kurds after the first official division of Kurdistan resulting from the Treaty of Zuhab (also known as the Treaty of Qasr-i Shirin) in 1639 between the Ottoman Empire and the Safavids (McDowall, 2000: 25–36; Özoğlu, 2004: 21–40; H. Bozarslan, 2008: 333–7):

> I leave it to God's wisdom
> The Kurds in this world's state
> Why are they deprived of their rights?
> Why are they all doomed?
> See, from the Arabs to the Georgians
> Everything is Kurdish and, as with a citadel,
> The Turks and the Persians besiege them
> From four sides at once.
> And they both make the Kurdish people
> Into a target for Fate's arrow.

After the battle of Çaldıran, with the exclusion of Kelhor, Erdelan, Baban, Şehrizur and Mukri, which had either opted to stay independent of both the Safavid and the Ottoman Empires or continued to recognise the former' suzerainty (Özoğlu, 2004: 49), the rest of the existing Kurdish principalities incorporated into the Ottoman Empire. The newly conquered province of Diyarbekir[1] (1515) hosted all of the acquired Kurdish chiefdoms in return for their acknowledgement of Ottoman sovereignty. The formalisation of the Kurdish principalities occurred as a result of Sultan Selim I (1470–1520), the Ottoman sultan from 1512 to 1520, when in returning from the battle of Çaldıran, on the advice of İdris Bitlisi[2] (ca. 1455–1520), consented to gaining the support of the predominantly Sunni Kurdish chiefs and integrating the Kurdish principalities in eastern Asia Minor.

As per the formalisation of the Kurdish structures, autonomous Kurdish *hükümets* were formed, and the terms and conditions of their independence were negotiated *per se*. Alongside these self-governing entities, two other administrative structures were instituted: Kurdish *sancaks*, governed by hereditary Kurdish rulers, and classical *sancaks*, centrally controlled by Ottoman officials appointed by the Ottoman central authorities (van Bruinessen, 1988; Celil, 1992; Özoğlu, 2004). As will be elaborated later, the number and boundaries of these Kurdish administrative units were in a constant state of flux due to the changing balances of power between the Kurdish rulers, the central Ottoman government and local authorities in Ottoman Kurdistan. Ottoman rulers after the early sixteenth century also established nomadic peoples' or tribal confederations, *uluslar*,[3] that were not subject to the jurisdiction of the aforementioned Kurdish polities (İnalcık, 1994: 34–8; McDowall 2000: 28–9).

The battle of Çaldıran, moreover, revised the boundary between the Ottoman Empire and the Safavid Empire as the border relapsed to the line marked by Sultan Selim I after the battle of 1514 in Çaldıran, which is equidistant between Erzincan and Tabriz. This line attained official recognition with the signing of the Treaty of Zuhab (1693) and – despite disputes and invasions – it formally persisted until 1914. The battle of Çaldıran, the formalisation of the Kurdish principalities and the Treaty of Zuhab rendered Ottoman Kurdistan to a zonal or border area between

[1] In some of the Ottoman official documents, the province was also designated as Amid.

[2] İdris Bitlisi was the son of a respected Kurdish religious figure, Şeyh Hüssameddin Ali-ül Bitlisi. He was a political official in the region who had the confidence of both the Kurdish chiefs and Sultan Selim I.

[3] See Table 2.1.

the two empires, which had crucial political and economic implications for this region thereafter.

The events that materialised in Kurdistan post-1514 were largely initiated by the imperial objectives of the Ottoman Empire. By the early sixteenth century, the Ottoman state had established itself in western Anatolia and Thrace and from then on embarked on the project of conquering ESA. The predominantly Sunni Kurdish principalities were conceived as protectorates in the newly occupied territory against the disobedient Turcoman and Kurdish tribes and the Safavid rival. Furthermore, Ottoman ascendency in ESA enabled the Ottomans to assume control of the silk trade routes, since the silk caravans from Iran would arrive at Aleppo by way of Erzurum, following the Euphrates valley, or more often along the Tabriz-Van-Bitlis-Diyarbekir-Birecik route (İnalcık, 1970: 210–11). By 1517, the Ottoman state took control of these routes and of the Aleppo market too. Consequently, all outlets for Iranian silk open to Europeans were in Ottoman hands.

After conquering and formalising the Kurdish principalities, and attaining control of the aforementioned outlets, the Ottoman Empire had turned its attention further eastwards to territories such as Gilan and Shirvan, which were northern Iranian centres of silk production. Subsequently, the wars with the Safavid Empire began in 1578 and persisted alternatingly until 1639. The war with the Habsburg Empire was also ongoing between 1593 and 1606. These wars, particularly the wars for Azerbaijan, Shirvan and Gilan, were highly destructive, not only for the Turkish military structure but also for the Ottoman finances, as after 1590, the Ottoman treasury suffered huge deficits (İnalcık, 1994: 24).

Concomitantly, the penetration of the Ottoman Empire by the developed European countries by the use of trade that began after 1580 had devastating effects for the former. The financial impact on the Ottoman Empire of cheap and plentiful silver from the West was immediate and catastrophic (Lewis, 1968: 29). To deal with the sudden and devastating flow of European silver, the Ottoman currency, *akçe*, was devalued in 1584–6 (Barkan, 1975: 12). The judgement to debase the Ottoman *asper* occasioned a monetary and financial crisis. Owing to this calamity, the *sipahis*, or the mounted soldiers attached to the central government, in order to cover their loss of income, raised the rates of taxes and created novel forms of taxation. This decision of the *sipahis* deepened the deprivation of the *reaya* – i.e. the dominated groups, Muslim or non-Muslim, outside the tax-exempt *askeri* (military or religious) ruling elite, engaged in economic activities and thus subject to taxes – and formed the socioeconomic background to the Celali rebellions organised by the Muslim *reaya* in Anatolia (Faroqhi, 1994: 433–8).

The rural populace in the Empire attempted to flee both the exactions of the Celali' and those of the soldiers sent out to suppress them (Jennings, 1976: 39; Erder and Faroqhi, 1979: 323; Murphey, 1987: xix–xx). For instance, in the 1640s, compared to the 1560s and 1570s, Amasya, Bozok, Harput and Samsun had lost, respectively, 79 per cent, 89 per cent, 90 per cent and 83 per cent of their rural tax-paying populations (Özer, 1994: 191). However, it is apt to point out here that the effects of the Celali rebellions, despite being a pivotal factor in rural depopulation, cannot solely explain the large-scale abandonment of villages during the seventeenth century. The opportunities the cities offered to the villagers in difficulty, the urgent need of the Ottoman state for more soldiers using firearms and the employment of the dispossessed peasants to this end (İnalcık, 1980: 283–337; İslamoğlu-İnan, 1994: 185), the climatic changes as evinced with the increasing rainfall and occurrence of heavy snow (McGowan, 1981: 85–94; Griswold, 1993: 36–57) and the famine, typhus or plague epidemics (Faroqhi, 1994: 441–2) were all contributory factors for the devastation that befell the rural structure and populace in the Empire from 1600 onwards.

Since the rural economy, both agricultural and pastoral, was the principal source of wealth for the imperial treasury, the destabilisation of the rural economy and life created the condition for disaster in the seventeenth-century Ottoman Empire. In other words, compared with the general conditions of the sixteenth century that permitted, largely through military expansion, the growing population to integrate into an expanding system, the seventeenth century was a period of decreasing military and economic resources that generated the basis for general crisis and devastation. Overall, as lucidly highlighted and summarised by İnalcık, the Ottoman Empire of the seventeenth century was no longer the 'vital empire it had been in the sixteenth century . . . the Ottoman asper was replaced by the European currency; and the [Ottoman] economy entered the orbit of the European mercantilists' (1994: 25).

The diversion of world trade to the sea routes, the Capitulations[4] granted by the Ottoman sultan to the European countries, and the adverse consequences of the trade between the Ottoman Empire and the European states for the former had austere repercussions for the

[4] Capitulations were extraterritorial privileges granted by the Ottomans to subjects of foreign powers in commercial-economic and judicial areas. For detailed information, see İnalcık (1971: 1179–89).

Ottoman economy and increased Ottoman dependence on these powers during and after the seventeenth century. After 1650, owing to the foundation of British and Dutch trade establishments in certain parts of Asia, world trade was altered to river transportation. This shift had negative effects for Ottoman trade, because most of the trade hitherto was carried out using land routes due to the existence of a small number of navigable waterways in the Empire. Such a development, however, had put Ottoman Kurdistan in an advantageous strategic position for trade, as the only navigable waterway in all of Anatolia, Syria and Iraq on a regular basis was the Euphrates-Tigris system (Faroqhi, 1994: 483).

The 1744 Treaty of Capitulation between the Ottomans and France granted the citizens of the latter country the right to buy, travel and be exempt from all forms of taxation. Subsequently, Austria, England, the Netherlands and, later on, Russia signed like treaties with the Ottoman Empire. By virtue of these agreements, more foreign nationals became exempt from taxes that Ottoman citizens engaged in similar activities were obliged to pay (Fisher, 1959: 299–303). Concurrently, the value and content of trade between the European countries and the Ottoman Empire after the 1760s had unfavourable ramifications for the Ottoman economy. The latter provided the former raw materials – particularly cotton – while receiving finished products in return. The decline in trade of glass, soap, sugar, gunpowder and paper – which up until the mid-eighteenth century had been the engine of trade between the Ottoman Empire and the European countries – also played an influential role in the intensification of the adverse nature of the trade between these dominions (McGowan 1994: 639). Overall, the seventeenth and eighteenth centuries had engendered the gradual and persistent disintegration of the Ottoman Empire and increased its penetration by the developed countries.

2.2 Political Relations and Structures in Ottoman Kurdistan between the Sixteenth and Eighteenth Centuries

As outlined in Chapter 1, the atypical autonomous administrative entities founded in Ottoman Kurdistan after the incorporation of the Kurdish principalities into the Ottoman Empire are commonly hypothesised to have given rise to a peculiar landholding regime that constituted formidable impediments to socioeconomic development in ESA. In the ensuing part of this study, by analysing the nature and the evolution of the

Kurdish polities in the Ottoman Empire as well as the economic revenues and resources of these structures in the sixteenth, seventeenth and eighteenth centuries, this study will attest the veracity of this regularly proposed and readily accepted proposition.

Classical Ottoman Administration

The Ottoman administrative system consisted of two components: the central government and the provincial administration. *Dirlik*[5] is the Ottoman term for provincial administration, and it designated the state revenues in a given locality allocated to officials, who were mostly military men. In the course of collecting those revenues from the sultan's subjects, the military official supervised on matters of cultivation and other economic activities as well as maintaining public order. The primary duty of the *dirlik* holders was to partake in the military operations or campaigns of the sultan, paying for their expenses from the proceeds of their *dirlik*.

The provincial government traditionally consisted of two centrally appointed authorities to administer the *sancak*: the *sancakbeyi*, who was a member of the *askeri*, and the *kadı*, who was a member of the *ulema* and represented the legal authority of the sultan. Along with the *sancakbeyi* and the *kadı*, each *sancak* had also a *mufti* who interpreted Islamic law and via his *fetva*s stated his view on legal matters. The *kadı* had been adept in religious law, specifically Sharia law.

*Kanunname*s, that is, the statute books that laid the *kanun* (sultan's rules), were prepared separately for each *sancak*, and they legislated on matters of taxation, criminal law and tolls, as well as on the duties and privileges of officials. Numerous *sancaks* comprised an *eyalet*, which was administered by a centrally appointed *vali* or *beylerbeyi*. The *vali* or *beylerbeyi* was hierarchically superior to the *sancakbeyis* in the *sancaks*, except for military expeditions. The latter officials were responsible to the sultan and not to the *vali* or *beylerbeyi*.

The Ottoman lands were divided into three categories: *miri*, state-owned lands; *mülk*, freehold ownership of land as opposed to state-owned land; and *vakf*, land granted for pious or charitable purposes, which remained or was revised at the sultan's will. Income for the Ottoman state was attained solely from *miri* land, which had been apportioned or organised into three *dirliks* or administrative units: *timar, zeamet* and *has*. It is characteristic of studies on Ottoman history to classify *dirliks*

[5] Some of the scholarship on the Ottoman Empire employs the term *timar* – which is the smallest *dirlik* grant – interchangeably with *dirlik* and, as a result, in these scholarly works the Ottoman provincial organisation has been titled the *timar* system.

in accordance with their yields: a *dirlik* with revenues up to 20,000 *akçes* was termed a *timar*; a *zeamet* was the title given to a *dirlik* with revenues from 20,000 to 100,000 *akçes*; and a *dirlik* with revenues above 100,000 *akçes* was titled a *has*.

The *timar* was given to the hierarchically lowest-ranking military personnel, *sipahis*, in exchange for their services to the state. Higher-ranking military personnel, *subaşı*, were granted the *zeamet*. The *sancakbeyi* were granted with the largest *dirliks*, namely, the *has*. The *reaya* was dispensed to a *timar*, a *zeamet* or a *has*, and contingent on which of the three forms of *dirliks* the *reaya* were cultivating, they paid their taxes to the *sipahis*, the *subaşı* or the *sancakbeyi*. Nevertheless, the *cizye* (poll tax), paid by the non-Muslims, was directly transferred to the treasury of the central government.

The provincial proceeds held in the reserve for the sultan were termed *havass-ı humayun* (imperial reserve). Customs revenues of the most important ports and yields of all mining operations were reserved for the sultan's *has*. Furthermore, in exchange for the *dirlik* yields and based on their income, *sipahis* and *sancakbeyis* had to sustain a particular number of *cebelis* (cavalrymen) and upon appeal had to serve in the *sancakbeyi*' military campaigns. All of these details regarding the basic features of the *dirlik* system were specified in the *kanunnames*.

In the formalised Kurdish principalities, though, administrative variations and peculiarities existed, which were attributable to two predominant factors. The first of these is the geopolitical feature of Kurdistan. Due to Kurdistan being located in a frontier region behind which sat the rival Safavid regions and state, the Kurdish elites of this region, especially in the early years of the incorporation of the Kurdish principalities into the Empire, were granted more autonomy than the *sancakbeyis* closer to the Ottoman centre.

It is important to note here that such an administrative arrangement had not constituted a *sui generis* case: analogous provisions existed in other Ottoman borderlands. For instance, in the fifteenth and sixteenth centuries, the local families in Bosnia (*kapitanes*) had consolidated big *timars* and *zeamets* as hereditary prebends in their possession. Bosnia was the main defence region of the Empire against the Habsburgs and, thus, the Ottoman state often yielded to the pressure from these powerful families (İnalcık, 1994: 73–4). In addition, similar arrangements had existed in Turco-Mongol lands, such as north-central Anatolia, where Ottoman rule had not been firmly established. Therefore, it is not coincidental that in Amasya-Sivas-Tokat during the fifteenth and sixteenth centuries there existed the *divani-malikane* or 'dual ownership' land system as a compromise regime between ownership rights of the – mostly

Turcoman – local hereditary lords and Ottoman state ownership of land wherein the former and the latter shared the surplus of the peasants' production (İslamoğlu-İnan, 1994: 62–70).

The second factor for the existence of the unconventional administrative structures in Ottoman Kurdistan is the incessant struggle between the Ottoman central state and the Kurdish local elites, vying to establish and maintain political domination so as to extract larger shares of surpluses in the form of agricultural revenues. Accordingly, the magnitude and level of autonomy of the Kurdish principalities varied depending on the balances of power between the central state, provincial governor and the ruling families in a province (van Bruinessen, 1988: 13–28; Özoğlu, 2004: 52–63).

Ottoman Administration in Kurdistan

The Ottoman state, in contrast to the policies of the Aqquyunlu and the Safavid states prior to the sixteenth century, had initially aimed to govern Kurdistan by means of a dual policy. On the one hand, the Ottoman rulers, in order to govern the fragmented Kurdish groups, introduced a policy of organising them into larger and more controllable administrative units – i.e. the all-encompassing province of Diyarbekir – above the tribal level, and, on the other, they reinforced and consolidated the traditional tribal Kurdish ruling stratum in order to attain their support. The quintessential example of the Ottoman policy in Kurdistan is the *ferman* (imperial decree) issued by the son of Sultan Selim I after his death, Süleyman I (1495–1566), the Ottoman sultan from 1520 to 1566:

> [Sultan Süleyman] gives to the Kurdish beys who, in his father Yavuz Sultan Selim's times, opposed the Kızılbaş and who are currently serving the State (Devlet) with faith, and who joined specifically in the Serasker sultan Ibrahim Pasha's Iran expedition with courage – both as a reward for their loyalty and courage, and their application and requests being taken into consideration – the provinces and fortresses that have been controlled by each of them as their *yurtluk* and *ocaklık* since past times along with the places that were given to them with separate imperial licences (*berat*); and their provinces, fortresses, cities, villages, and arable fields (*mezraa*) with all their harvests, under the condition of inheritance from father to son, are also given to them as their estate (*temlik*). There should never be any external aggression and conflict among them. This glorious order (*emr-i celile*) shall be obeyed; under no condition shall it be changed. In case of bey's death, his province shall be given, as a whole, to his son, if there is only one. If there is more than one son, they (the sons) shall divide the province contingent upon mutual agreement among themselves. If they cannot reach any compromise, then whomever the Kurdistan beys decide to be the best choice shall succeed, and through private ownership (*mülkiyet*) he shall be the holder (*mutasarrıf*) of the land forever. If the bey has no heir or relative, then his province

shall not be given to anybody from outside. As a result of this consultation with the Kurdistan beys, the region shall be given to either the beys or beyzades [someone else from the bey's family] suggested by the Kurdistan beys. (Özoğlu, 2004: 53–4)

An often quoted *kanunname* of the *eyalet* of Diyarbekir alluded to by Evliya Çelebi[6] (ca. 1611–85), which is not dated but there is wide consensus in the relevant literature on it being from the mid-sixteenth century, is commonly hypothesised to concretise the administrative peculiarities of the Kurdish principalities. Çelebi postulates three different types of administrative units in Kurdistan. The first administrative category is the classical Ottoman *sancaks*. In these *sancaks* there existed *timar, zeamet* and *has*, and they were governed directly by a centrally appointed *sancakbeyi*. The second category is the Kurdish *sancaks*. These *sancaks* were granted to the Kurdish rulers as *yurtluk* and *ocaklık*, which implicated that succession to office will remain within the ruling family. The sultan or the provincial governor could not oust the ruler of the Kurdish *sancaks*. The Kurdish *sancaks*, like classical Ottoman *sancaks*, contained *timar, zeamet* and *has*, whose holders had the normal military obligations as those in the rest of the Ottoman Empire. The state did conduct fiscal surveys in these *sancaks*, which entails that a portion of their revenue was accrued to the central treasury. The third category is the Kurdish *hükümets*. In these administrative units, there were no *timar*s and *zeamet*s, and the taxes their Kurdish rulers levied were not passed on to the central treasury. According to the *kanunname* quoted earlier, the only obligation of these *hükümets* was to partake in military expeditions.

However, available official Ottoman documents suggest that there are incongruities between the administrative autonomy and privileges set out in the previously quoted *kanunname* and *ferman* and the veracities of the administrative structures in Kurdistan. Next, via describing and assessing the various documented official data[7] on the

[6] A diligent Ottoman traveller and author of *Seyahatname*, or *Book of Travels*, one of the most useful sources on the social, political, economic and cultural life of the Ottoman Empire in the seventeenth century. During 1655–6, Çelebi visited Ottoman Kurdistan and took extensive notes on almost everything he saw, all of which is outlined in the fourth volume of the ten-volume masterpiece, *Seyahatname*. His records on Ottoman Kurdistan are rich in detail on the military and administrative organisation of the provinces of Diyarbekir and Van, particularly on the relationship of the self-governing Kurdish polities with the central Ottoman state.

[7] This study does make use of the *Defters*, which are the official Ottoman administrative registers that are kept in the Topkapı Palace Archives, and the *Diyarbekir Şer'iyye Sicilleri*, which are detailed records of Ottoman courts containing information on imperial administrations, on affairs in towns and villages and on taxes and taxation regulations, price regulations, the *dirlik* system, agreement between guilds, theft, murder and other crimes.

Table 2.1 *Administrative division of the* eyalet *of Diyarbekir, 1527–1792*

	1527[8]	1540[9]	1578–88[10]	1626–37[11]	1733[12]	1747[13]	1785–92[14]
Major emirates[15]							
Ardalan	Not incorporated into the Ottoman Empire						
Hakkari	Not incorporated into the Ottoman Empire						
Imadiye	H	Transferred to Iran and then to *eyalet* Van					
Bitlis	H	Y	Transferred to *eyalet* Van				
Hisnkeyf	H	S	S	S	—	S	S
Cezire (Bohtan)	H	S	H	H	—	H?	H?
Minor emirates							
Sohran	H	—	—	—	—	—	—
Çemişgezek	H	—	—	S	—	—	S
*Mecengird (Mazgirt)	—	Y	Y	Y	—	—	S
*Pertek	—	Y	Y	Y	—	—	S
*Sağman	—	Y	Y	Y	—	—	S
Eğil	H	—	H	H	—	H	S
Palu	H	—	H	—	H	—	H?
Çermik	H	S	—	Y	S	S	S
Hazzo	H	—	—	H	—	—	—
Sasun	H	S	S	—	—	—	S
Zirqan	H	—	H	—	—	—	S
*Gürdükan	—	Y	H	—	—	—	—
*Ataq	H	Y	H	—	Y	Y	Y
*Tercil	—	Y	S	H	H	H	H
*Mihrani	—	Y	H	S	—	S	S
Hizan	H	S	S	Transferred to *eyalet* Van			
Suveydi							
*Hançük	—	—	—	—	—	—	—
*Genç	—	—	—	H	—	—	—
*Çapaqçur	H	Y	Y	Y	—	—	S
Süleymani							
*Qulp	—	Y	H	Y	—	S	S
*Mifariqın	—	—	—	Y	H	H	H
Sancaks that are not also Kurdish chiefdoms							
Amid	S	S	S	S	S	S	S

[8] Defter no. 5246, Topkapı Palace Archives in Kunt (1978: 130–1).
[9] Unnamed Defter in van Bruinessen (1988: 18–19).
[10] Defter Kamil Kepeci no. 262 in Kunt (1978: 162–4).
[11] Unnamed Defter from 1631 to 163 in Yılmazçelik (1995: 128).
[12] Diyarbekir Şer'iyye Sicilleri, No. 310: 62–3 in ibid.
[13] Diyarbekir Şer'iyye Sicilleri, No. 313: 174 in ibid.
[14] Diyarbekir Şer'iyye Sicilleri, No. 352: 25–7; No. 313: 30; No. 626: 1–32 in ibid.: 129–30.
[15] List of Kurdish and non-Kurdish chiefdoms as well as nomadic *sancaks* in this table was adopted from van Bruinessen (1988: 18–19).

Table 2.1 *(cont.)*

	1527	1540	1578–88	1626–37	1733	1747	1785–92
Mardin	S	S	—	—	—	S	S
Arabkir		Transferred to *eyalet* Sivas					
Kığı		Transferred to *eyalet* Erzurum					
Harput	S	S	S	S	—	—	S
Ergani	S	S	—	S	S	S	S
Siverek	S	S	S	S	S	S	S
Ruha (Urfa)	S	S	S	Transferred to *eyalet* Raqqa			
Bire	S	S	S	Transferred to *eyalet* Halep or Raqqa			
Raqqa	—	—	—	Made into *eyalet* Raqqa			
Suruc	—	S	S	Transferred to *eyalet* Raqqa			
Cammasa	—	—	S	Transferred to *eyalet* Raqqa			
Deyr ü Rahba	—	—	S	Transferred to *eyalet* Raqqa			
Beni Rabi'a	—	—	S	Transferred to *eyalet* Raqqa			
Mosul	S	—	S	Made into *eyalet* Mosul			
Ana ve Hit	S	—	S	Transferred to *eyalet* Raqqa			
Habur	—	—	S	Transferred to *eyalet* Raqqa			
Sincar	H	S	S	Transferred to *eyalet* Mosul			
Aqçaqal'e	—	—	S	Transferred to *eyalet* Mosul			
Nisibin	—	S	S	—	—	—	—
Si'ird	—	S	S	Y	—	S	S
Masyum u Tur	—	—	H	—	—	—	—
Hüsnru	—	—	H	—	—	—	—
Ahakis	—	—	—	Y	—	—	—
Zaho	—	—	—	—	—	—	—

Key: H = *Hükümets*, Y = *Yurtluk ve Ocaklık*, S = Classic *Sancaks*, H? = not mentioned in the document but based on other historical records discussed in this book, it is known to be a *Hükümet.*

administrative structures in Kurdistan between the early sixteenth and late eighteenth centuries, this study will trace the nature and evolution of the Kurdish polities.

As can be inferred from the summary of the administrative division of the *eyalet* of Diyarbekir, in the early years of the incorporation or formalisation of the Kurdish principalities into the Ottoman Empire, the Kurdish administrative structures in these principalities were in a constant state of flux. The bulk of the Kurdish administrative bodies had evolved from self-governing entities or *hükümets* in the sixteenth century to centrally governed classical Ottoman *sancaks* or semiautonomous administrative organisations, *yurtluks* and *ocaklık*s – wherein the governing *dirlik* or *timar* system was in operation – in the seventeenth and eighteenth centuries.

Table 2.2 *The* has' *of the* beylerbeyis, *late sixteenth or early seventeenth century*

Provinces	*Has'* of the *beylerbeyis* (in *akçes*)
Karaman	660,074
Zülkadriye	628,450
Rum	900,000
Diyarbekir	1,200,000
Van	1,132,000
Erzurum	1,214,000

Source: Cezar, 1986: 38.

An indication of this transformation is the increase in the official revenues of the *beylerbeyis*, or governors-general, of Diyarbekir in the seventeenth century when compared to their sixteenth-century counterparts. İ. Metin Kunt, in an extensive study of the appointment registers and financial registers of Diyarbekir, arrives at the following illuminating conclusion:

> [T]he political position of a seventeenth century governor-general is much stronger compared to his sixteenth century counterpart. The first and foremost obvious indication of this is supplied by the dimensions of Ömer Paşa's [*beylerbeyi* of Diyarbekir] official income. In the sixteenth century, the official income allocated to a governor-general was in the neighbourhood of one million *akçes*. In contrast, Ömer Paşa's income for the year 1670–71 in Diyarbekir exceeded sixteen million *akçes*. This increase in income cannot be explained solely as a result of inflation which emerged after the middle of the sixteenth century ... the increase in the governor's income was more than three time greater than the rate of inflation. (1981: 59)

Congruently, the figures corroborated by the chancery clerk Ayn-ı Ali Efendi (Table 2.2) suggest that in the late sixteenth or early seventeenth century the *has'* of the *beylerbeyis* of the provinces of Diyarbekir, Van and Erzurum, when juxtaposed with the bordering provinces of Karaman, Rum and Zülkadriye, were higher.

The detailed description of revenues and expenditures[16] of Ömer Paşa's annual accounts for 1670–1 illustrates that the provincial 'governor received a fee from all appointments within the province: all *sancakbeyis*, all *dirlik* holders, all central army troops stationed in Diyarbekir, and all guilds officials paid this fee, [which is] an excellent

[16] For a detailed and itemised version of this annual account, see Kunt (1981). An English version of these accounts is given in pp. 39–48.

indication of the supreme power of governor in his province' (Kunt, 1983: 92–3). The source of some of the incomes delineated in the annual accounts of the *beylerbeyi* of Diyarbekir in 1670–1 does shed light on the erosion of the autonomy Kurdish administrations enjoyed.

The incomes of Ömer Paşa were the appointment fees (*tahviller*) levied from *timar* and *zeamet* holders and fines (*cerimes*) that were imposed on the *hükümets* of Eğil, Palu and Hazzo (ibid.: 67). The provincial governor was acting within his jurisdiction with the collection of the former form of taxation, but the collection of the latter was an encroachment of the rights of the autonomous Kurdish rulers (van Bruinessen, 1988: 26). Such violations and interventions appear not to be atypical of the conduct of the centrally appointed governors or the Ottoman state in Kurdistan. In the early 1630s, Aziz Efendi in his *Nasihatname*, treatise of counsel or advice addressed to the sultan, outlined the incessant struggle between the Ottoman central state and the local elites, the corroding self-rule of the Kurdish administrations and the provincial governor ousting Kurdish leaders and appointing outsiders instead. Accordingly, Aziz Efendi suggested that the autonomous rights of the relevant Kurdish rulers should be reinstated (Özoğlu, 2004: 59).

Overall, the degree of autonomy the Kurdish principalities had in the early sixteenth century had gradually eroded and the majority of these Kurdish administrative structures had increasingly been dominated by and been very receptive to Ottoman demands. That said, despite the incessant struggle between the Kurdish local elites and the central state for political domination and control over the collection of the agricultural surplus, the Kurdish emirates reserved and conserved their infrastructure until the first half of the nineteenth century.

2.3 The Demography and Economy of Ottoman Kurdistan between the Sixteenth and Eighteenth Centuries

There is only a modicum of studies devoted to the socioeconomic and political structures and developments in Ottoman Kurdistan, and the existing works on this domain are commonly devoid of a comparative analysis of the demographic, social and economic features of this territory with the other regions of the Empire (Bois, 1966; Burkay, [1992] 2008; Celil, 1992). The latter lacuna constitutes a pivotal impediment for evaluating the relative social and economic importance of Kurdistan for the Ottoman Empire and for comprehensively analysing the evolution of the social and economic structures in ESA. This omission in the literature on Ottoman Kurdistan is largely due to two interrelated issues: first, the presence of trivial demographic[17] and economic primary data[18] for Ottoman ESA; second, the overreliance of the scholarship on Ottoman Kurdistan on travellers' estimates and observations for demographic and economic data for the period between the sixteenth and eighteenth centuries. It is not feasible to base a comparative study on annotations provided in these Traveller Books due to the existence of the descriptive information in these records and there being only one or two of these oft-quoted historical accounts[19] dealing with any one epoch.

Alternatively, by consulting studies on Ottoman imperial registers or *defter-i hakani*,[20] specifically *tahrir*[21] tax registers of the sixteenth century and the *avariz*[22] tax registers of the seventeenth and eighteenth centuries, this book will trace the main population trends as well as certain aspects of demographic change in the Empire.

[17] The existence of minimal demographic information is attributable to the absence of a population census up until 1831 in the Ottoman Empire.

[18] Owing to the existence of minimal economic data on ESA, these regions of the Ottoman Empire have generally been excluded from academic studies on the economic history of Ottoman Anatolia. A prime example of this is the laborious work of Suraiya Faroqhi on trade, crafts and food production in Ottoman Anatolia between 1520 and 1650, which, due to the less comprehensive and scant nature of the documentation on eastern Anatolia, opts to focus the study on western and central Anatolia (1984: 17–19).

[19] The often quoted and employed Traveller Books from the sixteenth to the eighteenth centuries are as follows: D'Aramon ([1555] 1864); Simeon ([1612] 2013); Tavernier ([1630] 1677); Çelebi, ([1655] 1988); and Niebuhr ([1766] 1968).

[20] These registers, until the beginning of the seventeenth century, were conducted every thirty or forty years, and they contained results of the surveys of the tax-paying population and taxable resources of the Empire. More specifically, they contained a listing of the Empire's adult male population; the entry for each person states his father's name, his legal status, the duties and privileges of his economic or social position, and the extent of his land (Barkan, 1970: 163).

[21] The *tahrir defters* are, in nature, and often referred to, as tax survey registers. The *tahrirs* were recorded and kept in the *defter-i hakani* (imperial registers) in Istanbul. Not all surveys have survived. In general, two sets of surveys are available for most of Anatolia (İslamoğlu-İnan, 1994: 25–6), and they form the basis of the demographic data that follows: one dating from the reign of Süleyman I (1520–60) and the other from the rule of Murat III (1574–95).

[22] The *avariz* was an emergency or irregular wartime tax paid in kind. It was converted into money in the course of the sixteenth century. During the first half of the seventeenth century, the *avariz* became an annual tax. In principle, though not always in practice, *avariz* taxpayers were taxed in accord with their ability to pay and therefore officially recorded as 'wealthy', 'middling' or 'poor'. In addition, taxpayers were grouped into units known as *avarizhane* (tax house), all of which were assessed the same amount of money. A 'tax house' consisted of two to fifteen households, and was kept small if the component households were considered wealthy, while in the case of the poor people, the number of the households were augmented (Faroqhi, 1994: 532).

Subsequently, based on the exploration of central treasury 'budgets'[23] and *icmal*[24] fiscal records, this study will analyse the provincial revenues and economic sources of these domains with the purpose of tracing the development and relative importance of the economic resources and local revenues of these territories for the general Ottoman economy.

Demographic Data in the Tahrir *and* Avariz *Registers*

The Ottoman state, prior to the late nineteenth century, enumerated its subjects' wealth, but not the people themselves. It counted only those liable for the payment of taxes (household heads, virtually always males), or likely to be conscripted (young males). As a result, population size for the Empire as a whole and/or for a given domain of the Empire can only be approximated until the 1880s, when the first actual censuses came into existence. That said, while the actual populace data for Ottoman lands cannot be identified, the basic patterns of demographic change can be based on tax surveys or registers,[25] which before the 1880s were conducted to quantify human and financial resources of the Empire.

Ömer Lütfi Barkan was the pioneering scholar to study and present Ottoman tax registers to the world of Ottomanists. In his seminal articles on these sources, Barkan posits, for the period 1520–35, a population of 12–12.5 million in the Ottoman Empire including the population not

[23] The 'budgets' in the sixteenth, seventeenth and eighteenth centuries differed from their twentieth-century counterparts. Ottoman 'budgets' pre-Tanzimat were used as balance sheets for the revenues and expenditures of the Ottoman state already undertaken, often encompassing a full solar or lunar year. On account of Ottoman 'budgets' from the sixteenth to the eighteenth centuries recording revenues already collected and expenditures undertaken, Ottoman historians conceive them as a reliable index for the general condition of the economy (İnalcık, 1994: 78; Barkan, 2000: 607).

[24] The *icmal* fiscal registers contained periodic summaries of the revenues and expenditures of the central imperial treasury and of the various provincial treasuries. They were used for verifying internal accounting as well as simplifying and summarising a mass of information for final reporting to the sultan in a synoptic form (Murphey, 1987: xvi).

[25] It is imperative to point out here that all of the demographic data shared in this section should be read with the following limitations in mind. The demographic information relayed in this section of this study are based on the records of the tax-paying population only, whose status was firmly defined by Ottoman law, and periodically, systematically recorded with meticulous care in the Ottoman tax survey registers, namely, *tahrir* and *avariz* registers. Tax-exempt groups, like the military, gypsies and certain sections of the peasantry owing to their services to the government, were not registered in the tax survey records. Despite these drawbacks, regularly and systematically recorded layers of Ottoman society in themselves do constitute an important and the only source for historical populace inquiry, permitting one to trail the main demographic trends and change in the Ottoman Empire.

entered in the tax registers in Asia Minor and the Balkans (see Table 2.3). For the end of the century, he surmises a larger population of 30–35 million; thus Barkan suggests a natural growth of 60 per cent and adds the population of the territories captured after 1535[26] (2000: 1421). The population growth in the all-encompassing Kurdish province of Diyarbekir seems to be in line with this suggestion. Between 1528 and 1548, the number of households in this province rose from 70,691 to 107,601, indicating a 64 per cent rise in the number of households (Barkan, 2000: 1420). Similarly, the number of households in the city

Table 2.3 *Distribution of the population of Turkey, 1520–1535*

	Household[27]			
Provinces	Muslim	Christian	Jewish	Total Population
Anatolia[28]	517,813	8,511	271	2,632,975
Karaman[29]	134,452	3,127	–	687,895
Zülkadiriye[30]	64,102	2,631	–	333,665
Diyarbekir[31]	70,858	11,938	288	415,420
Rum[32]	116,772	51,662	–	842,170
Arap[33]	113,358	914	–	571,360
Military classes	50,000	–	–	250,000
Total				**5,733,485**
İstanbul	46,635	25,295	–	400,000
Rumeli	194,958	862,707	–	5,308,995
Military classes	50,000	–	–	250,000
Total				**5,958,995**
Total				**11,692,480**
Total population (including the population not entered in the tax registers)				**12–12.5 million**

Source: Barkan, 1957: 20-3.

[26] Symria, Croatia, Hungary, Slovakia, northern Abyssinia, Hejaz, Yemen, Iraq, Al-Hasa and the North African coasts.

[27] Barkan, in his studies of the tax survey registers, employs the coefficient of five to measure households or *hanes*.

[28] Western Asia Minor.

[29] Konya, Beyşehri, Akşehir, Aksaray, Niğde, Kayseri and İçili.

[30] Maraş and Kaza: Bozok and Kırşehir.

[31] Amid, Mardin, Mosul, Sincar, Arapkir, Ergani, Çermik, Siverek, Kiği, Çemişkezek, Harput, Ruha (Urfa), Ana, Deyir and Rahbe and Kaza: Hisynkeyf.

[32] Amasya, Çorum, Tokat, Karahisar, Djanik, Trabzon, Malatya, Divriği, Dirende, Kemah and Bayburt.

[33] Damascus, Safed, Adjlin, Gaza, Jerusalem, Hama, Humus, Trablus, Ayintab, Birecik, Allepo, Adana, Uzeyir, Tarsus and Sis.

of Diyarbekir increased from 11,400 in 1518 to 31,450 in 1571–80 (van Bruinessen, 1988: 33).

As previously mentioned, while the sixteenth century was marked by swift population growth, research on various parts of the Empire, including Anatolia, Rumeli (the Balkans) and Syria, points to an opposite occurrence from the early seventeenth century onwards: a serious fall in population[34] (see Table 2.4). Owing to *tahrir* registers – which were utilised to attain an indication of the populace in the fifteenth and sixteenth centuries – seldom drawn up following the seventeenth century (McGowan, 1981: 113), the tax-paying population figures designated in the extant *avariz* registers, some of which are summarised next, constitute the only reliable means of understanding demographic patterns and changes after 1600.

Between 1600 and 1800, a relative decline in the global importance of the Ottoman Empire's population paralleled its fading international

Table 2.4 Avarizhanes *in four Ottoman zones, 1640–1786*

Date	Eastern Anatolia and Syria[35]	Rumeli[36]	Western Anatolia[37]	Total
1640	21,291 (220)[38]	110,901 (220)	–	132,192 (440)
1650	27,773 (224)	96,756 (159)	52,519 (275)	177,048 (658)
1662	33,280 (219)	103,100 (234)	50,384 (284)	186,764 (737)
1677	18,822 (219)	92,274 (221)	51,292 (281)	162,388 (721)
1688	30,759 (232)	53,122 (154)	41,689 (279)	125,570 (665)
1698	18,015 (213)	46,498 (180)	34,700 (288)	99,213 (618)
1718	18,490 (205)	44,426 (181)	30,373 (283)	93,289 (669)
1755	11,975 (185)	43,345 (228)	26,360 (289)	81,680 (702)
1786	12,967 (209)	43,455 (232)	22,561 (291)	78,983 (732)

Source: McGowan, 1981: 118–20.

[34] For a general evaluation of this phenomenon, see Faroqhi (1994: 438–47).

[35] Sivas, Amasya, Çorum, Bozok, Canik, Arabkir, Divriği, Konya, Niğde, Beğşehri, Akşehir, Kayseri, Aksaray, Kırşehri, Içil, Adana, Trablus-i Şam, Şam-i Şerif, Haleb, Bire'tül Firat, Maraş, Malatya, Ayntab, Diyarbekir, Erzurum, Karahisar-i Şarki, Trabzon, Gönye.

[36] Paşa, Vize, Çirmen, Köstendil, İsküb, Agriboz, Tirhala, Avlonya, Delvine, Selanik, Niğbolu, Silistre, Yanya, Ilbasan, Karli Eli, Inebahtı, Ohri, Pirzrin, Dukakin, Iskenderiye, Vidin, Mora, Kefe, Gelibolu, Ahur-i Edirne, Ahur-i Yanbolu, Ahur-i Zagora.

[37] Aydın, Saruhan, Menteşe, Suğla, Hamideli, Karasi, Biga, Teke, Alaiye, Kütahya, Hüdavengir, Karahisar-i Sahib, Anagara, Sultanönü, Kengri, Boli, Kastamonu.

[38] The figure between parentheses is the number of judicial districts or *kazas* in each *eyalet* or province.

political importance. The Ottoman population slipped from being one-sixth that of Western Europe to only one-tenth and from about one-eighth to one-twelfth that of China. In the early eighteenth century, the aggregate Ottoman population was less than it had been at the end of the sixteenth century. The total population is commonly posited to have equalled to some 25–32 million in 1800. According to one oft-quoted estimate, there were 11 million in the Asiatic provinces, 10–11 million in the European domains and an additional 3 million in the North African provinces. Moreover, by 1800, the populations of the Anatolian and Balkan provinces were about the same while, in the seventeenth century, that of the Balkan provinces had been greater. And last, in the eighteenth century, the populace of the Arab domains was declining, with very sharp drops after about 1775 (Quataert, 2000: 110–11).

As can be inferred from a comparative analysis of the figures in Tables 2.3–2.4, the paradigmatic Kurdish province of Diyarbekir and the other domains in and neighbouring eastern Anatolia were not immune to very severe population declines. As alluded to in the introductory pages of this chapter, epidemics and famine arising from natural disasters, as well as man-made factors, like wars, bad transportation and politics, witnessed during and after the seventeenth century in virtually all the great provinces of the Empire, played a crucial role in the sharp decrease of the Ottoman population (Faroqhi, 1994: 441–2; McGowan, 1994: 651–2). This was particularly pertinent for eastern Anatolia and Syria during the eighteenth century.

The most unfortunate territories of the Empire with respect to epidemic diseases were those that hosted ports and caravan terminals, especially Aleppo and Diyarbekir. Aleppo experienced eight major eruptions of the Black Death, lasting for about fifteen years, during the eighteenth century. Based on physicians' figures, deaths from plague equalled to 15–20 per cent of the population of Aleppo in the late 1700s (Quataert, 2000: 113). Diyarbekir endured a terrific famine in 1757 in the aftermath of a locust invasion, and Trablus was hard-hit by a famine in 1784 (McGowan, 1994: 651–2).

Provincial Revenues and Economic Resources of Ottoman Kurdistan

The first official balance sheet of state revenues or treasury 'budget' in 1527–8 takes account of the *timar, vakf* and *mülk* revenues and gives the total value of all revenues of the Ottoman Empire as 537.90 million *akçes*, which is equivalent to 9.7 million of gold ducat.[39] The state revenues

[39] In 1528, one gold ducat was equivalent to 55 *akçes* (İnalcık, 1994:78).

Table 2.5 *Total revenue of the Ottoman Empire, 1527–1528*

Sources of Revenue	Value (in millions *akçes*)
Imperial *Hass*	277
Other *Hass* and *Timar* distributed	200
Vakf and *Mülk* properties	60
Total	**537**

Source: İnalcık, 1994: 81.

Table 2.6 *Balance of provincial revenues, 1527–1528 (in million* akçes*)*

Province	Revenue	Expenditure	Balance
Anadolu, Karaman, Rum and Zülkadriye[40]	294.85	322.13	−27.28
Diyarbekir	21.46	20.10	+1.36

Source: İnalcık, 1994: 83; Barkan, 2000: 649–69.

consisted of 477 million, which constituted 89 per cent of the total revenue of the Empire (see Table 2.5).

The actual purpose of these 'budgets' was to determine whether surplus had been realised, thus for an efficient 'budget', Ottoman statesmen had anticipated a surplus after expenditures so that those in receipt of a salary from the sultan's treasury would not have concerns about their income (İnalcık, 1994: 77). When the revenues and expenditures of the province of Diyarbekir are compared with other Ottoman Anatolian regions (see Table 2.6), which today roughly constitute modern-day Turkey, it becomes evident that the latter areas were operating under a budget deficit whilst the former yielded surplus revenue. This is despite Diyarbekir having the third lowest population density out of the four compared provinces (see Table 2.3).

Such a development was not unique to the 'budget' of 1527–8, because more deficits were sustained from these regions – particularly Rumeli and Anadolu – in the later years of the sixteenth century, as evidenced by the

[40] In the published version of the 'budget' of 1527–8, the balance sheets of the provinces of Anadolu, Karaman, Rum and Zülkadriye are calculated together (Barkan, 2000: 649–69).

deficits incurred from the aforementioned provinces in the succeeding published 'budget' of 1547–8. The expenditure of the central budget reached 171,997,449 *akçes* in 1546 and 111,997,449 *akçes* in 1547. The revenue the central treasury received from the provinces of Anatolia and Rumeli in the same years was 135,402,022 *akçes* in 1546 and 94,543,349 *akçes* in 1547. Consequently, the deficits of 36,470,335 *akçes* and 17,454,694 *akçes* were incurred. The surplus revenues deriving from the newly conquered provinces of Egypt, Syria, Diyarbekir and Baghdad covered these deficits (Sahillioğlu, 1970: 239–40). The surplus revenue transferred from Diyarbekir to the central treasury had arisen from about 1.36 million *akçes* in the previous 'budget' to around 5 million *akçes* in the 'budget' of 1547–8 (Barkan, 2000: 891). In the only other published 'budget' for the sixteenth century, the 'budget' of 1567–8, the income revenues and expenditures for the province of Diyarbekir were not recorded in the form that it had been done with the latterly stated 'budgets' (Barkan, 2000: 962–73).

The periodic irregularities and altered content of the 'budgets' in the seventeenth and eighteenth centuries make it highly difficult to study systematically the spatial sources of state revenues and expenditures during this period. Summary accounts of incomes and expenditures were not calculated for a long time in the seventeenth century. Hence, the 'budget' of Tarhuncu (Grand Vizier 1652–3) possesses much importance and is generally looked on as the first Ottoman 'budget' of the seventeenth century (Sahillioğlu, 1970: 233). In addition, in the eighteenth century, summary financial or budgetary records were not collected regularly. With the exclusion of a few 'budgets' in the first decade of the eighteenth century, no accounts or 'budgets' existed in the subsequent thirty-six years (Tabakoğlu, 1985: 22).

More importantly for the purposes of this study, while sixteenth-century 'budgets' had registered revenues in accordance to their geographical origin, virtually none of the published 'budgets' in the seventeenth and eighteenth centuries provides the geographical distribution of all the revenue sources. Ottoman accountants in the seventeenth century had begun to register revenues in accordance with the treasury offices[41] in charge of their administration (Tabakoğlu, 1985: 21–5; Faroqhi, 1994: 539–40). The 'budgets' during the seventeenth and eighteenth centuries mostly contained the total amount of income and expenditures of these treasury offices – see the published 'budgets' for 1660–1, 1669–70 and 1690–1 (Barkan,

[41] For more information on the role, functions and evolution of the different treasury offices in the seventeenth and eighteenth centuries, see Tabakoğlu (1985: 33–69).

1955–6: 193–347, 2000: 727–881). Therefore, detailed information concerning provincial incomes and expenditures, which is necessary for a comparative study of the different regions of the Empire, was minimal compared to the sixteenth century. Another commonality of the Ottoman 'budgets' in the seventeenth and the eighteenth centuries was that, unlike their sixteenth-century counterparts, they contained information concerning the imperial *hass* revenues, which consisted to a great extent of *mukataa*[42] (tax-farm) and *cizye* revenues, thus information regarding the *dirlik* or *timar* revenues had not been accounted for (Tabakoğlu, 1985: 22–5).

These factors constitute insurmountable barriers to acquiring a complete analysis of all the provincial revenues and the fiscal or budgetary accounts of Ottoman domains in the seventeenth and the eighteenth centuries. Nevertheless, as Ahmet Tabakoğlu posits in a trailblazing study of the Ottoman 'budgets', *icmal* and *rüzname*[43] registers, provincial revenues in these two centuries – with the exclusion of Egypt – consisted of *mukataa* or tax-farm revenues administered by the Baş Muhasebe branch of the imperial treasury (1985: 168–9). Therefore, in order to attain an understanding of the evolution of the provincial revenues during the seventeenth and eighteenth centuries, this study will make use of the documented data on *mukataa* revenues of Ottoman provinces.

One of the existent official records from the seventeenth century is the *icmal* accounts in the tax-farm register for 1636–7, *Register Maliyeden Müdevver 7075.*[44] This documentation gives an insight into the amount and sources of *mukataa* revenues in the early seventeenth century from the following regions and provinces of the Empire: 'Western, Central, South-Central Anatolia (Anadolu, Zülkadriye, Karaman, Rum, Kastamonu and Bursa (Bolu)'; 'Southeastern Anatolian (Diyarbakir)'; 'Eastern Anatolia (Erzurum)'; and 'Northern Syria and parts of South-Central Anatolia (Aleppo)' (Murphey, 1987: 220).

[42] In Ottoman fiscal practice, a *mukataa* had meant a source of revenue projected and entered into the register of the finance department, which included a host of revenue sources. Collection of such revenues had been farmed out under a specific tax-farm system to independent agents called *mültezim* or *amils* or delegated to administrative officials such as the *emins* or *voyvodas*.

[43] *Rüzname* registers contained records of the day-by-day revenues and expenditures of the provincial treasuries and of various other government departments. For detailed information, see Shaw (1969: 1–12) and Tabakoğlu (1985: 40–3).

[44] This register was prepared in 1636 as a result of Sultan Murat IV (1612–40) ordering the preparation of a detailed report on the state of financial revenues of Anatolia (Murphy, 1987: xiii).

Table 2.7 *Provincial tax-farm revenues of Anatolia and the coastal and northern portions of Syria, early seventeenth century (in* akçes[45]*)*

Provinces	Amount
Aleppo	24,106,727
Zülkadriye	30,911,760
Karaman	2,390,000
Diyarbekir	25,019,750
Rum	3,063,000
Damascus	15,382,000
Erzurum	16,800,000
Kastamonu	2,656,113
Bursa (Bolu)	5,334,042
Anadolu	12,399,400

Source: Murphey, 1987: 220.

These tax-farm revenues suggest that the provincial sources of income in ESA in the early seventeenth century, when contrasted with the *mukataa* revenues of other Anatolian provinces, had attained a greater importance. *Mukataa* revenues in Diyarbekir alone had been almost equivalent to the *mukataa* revenues of the five bordering Anatolian regions, excluding Zülkadriye. The *mukataa* revenues in Erzurum had been triple the amount of the revenues in the bordering Rum and Karaman provinces.

When the available data on the principal provincial revenues of Diyarbekir and Erzurum (Table 2.8), the custom and production revenues/data (Maps 3–5), and the major export products from the Empire (Table 2.9) are juxtaposed, we can posit reasonably the following conclusion. The revenue base of the provincial revenues of Diyarbekir and Erzurum in the seventeenth century consisted of mine and mineral manufacturing and trade, sheep breeding and sheep trade, textile production and the custom revenues attained from long-distance trade passing from ESA.

Concomitantly, as described in the preceding section, the gradual integration of the autonomous Kurdish emirates into the Ottoman administrative system in the seventeenth century facilitated the rise in the number of Kurdish emirates becoming receptive to Ottoman

[45] There had been a four-fold increase in the exchange equivalent for one gold piece in circulating silver *akçe* coins in the period between 1526 (1 *altun* = 60 *akçes*) and 1636 (1 *altun* = 240 *akçes*) (Murphey, 1987: xxi).

Table 2.8 *Principal revenues for the provinces of Diyarbekir and Erzurum, early seventeenth century (in* akçes*)*

Diyarbekir	
Customs	6,021,950
Sales Tax on Cloths and Textile Production	551,800
Sheep Tax	555,000
Tax from Pastoral Peoples or Tribal Confederations	2,679,500
Erzurum	
Customs	8,000,000
Mines and Minerals	3,182,650
Revenues from Salt Flats	84,252

Source: Murphey, 1987: 226–33.

demands. This can also be identified as another factor in the growth of fiscal yields or revenues. As Hakan Özoğlu noted, 'although by the end of the seventeenth century there were autonomous Kurdish emirates, they were, for [the] most part, integrated into the Ottoman administrative system by increasing state authority. ... [B]ut the degree of autonomy they [Kurdish emirates] enjoyed was reduced to the point that a majority of the emirates became very responsive to Ottoman demands' (2004: 59).

The sources of income in the provinces of Diyarbekir and Erzurum maintained their relative importance in the eighteenth century. As exhibited in the summarised *mukataa* revenues in the 'budget' of 1706–7 in Table 2.10, the tax-farm or *mukataa* revenues of the provinces of Erzurum and Diyarbakir had been nearly equivalent to the total revenues of the three major Ottoman Anatolian provinces: Anadolu, Karaman and Sivas.

Tabakoğlu (1985), by collating *mukataa* revenues found in various Ottoman fiscal documents, traces the progress of the revenues of the ten prominent *mukataas* in the Empire between the late seventeenth and the mid-eighteenth centuries (Table 2.11). The findings of this study demonstrate that the provincial sources of revenue originating from ESA were vital sources of income for the Ottoman economy. *Mukataas* from Erzurum and Diyarbekir were among the most protuberant sources of income for Ottoman Empire.

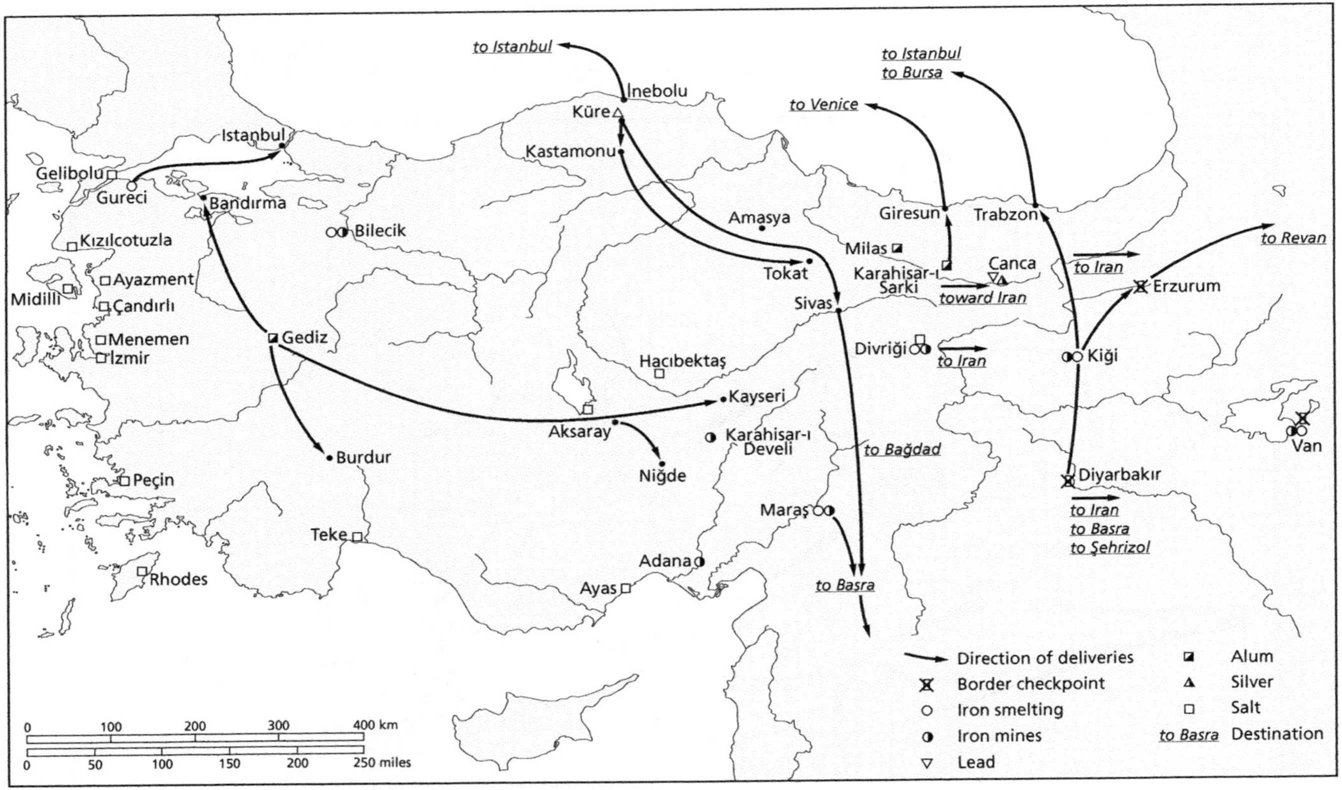

Map 3 Mine and metal manufactures and trade in Anatolia, sixteenth and seventeenth centuries
Source: Based on Faroqhi, 1984: 175.

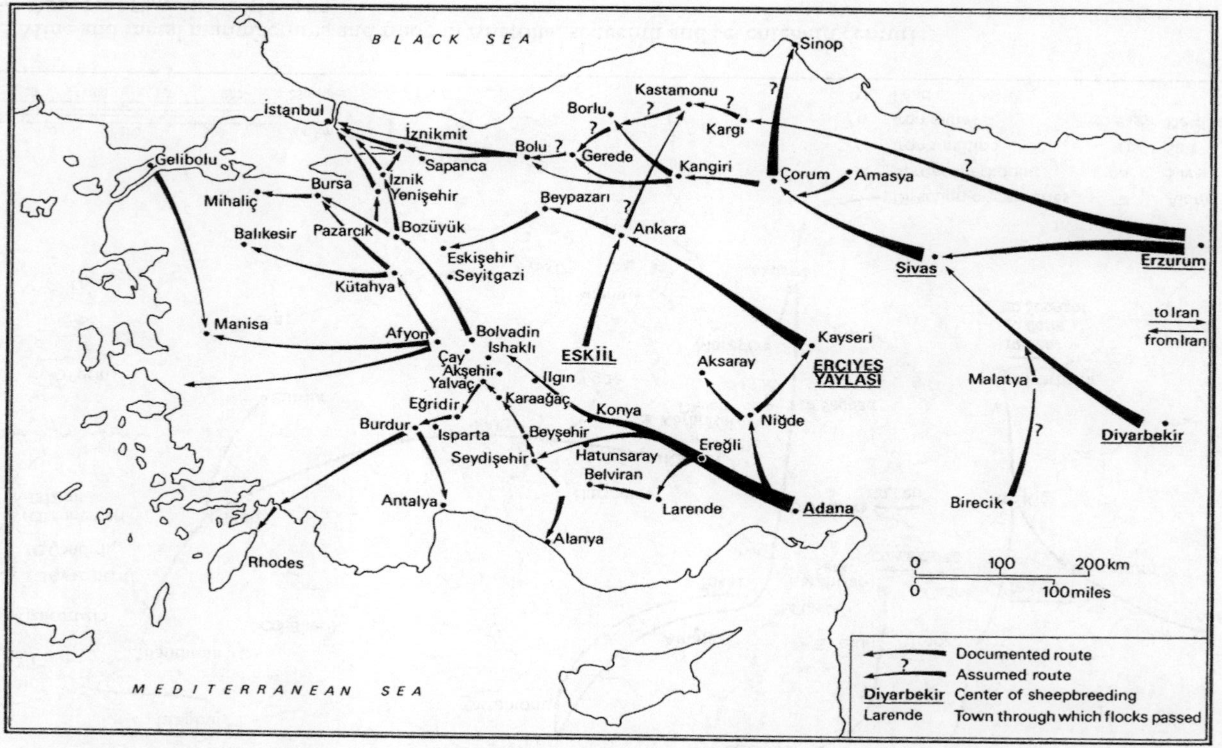

Map 4 Trade in Anatolian sheep, sixteenth and seventeenth centuries
Source: Faroqhi, 1994: 497.

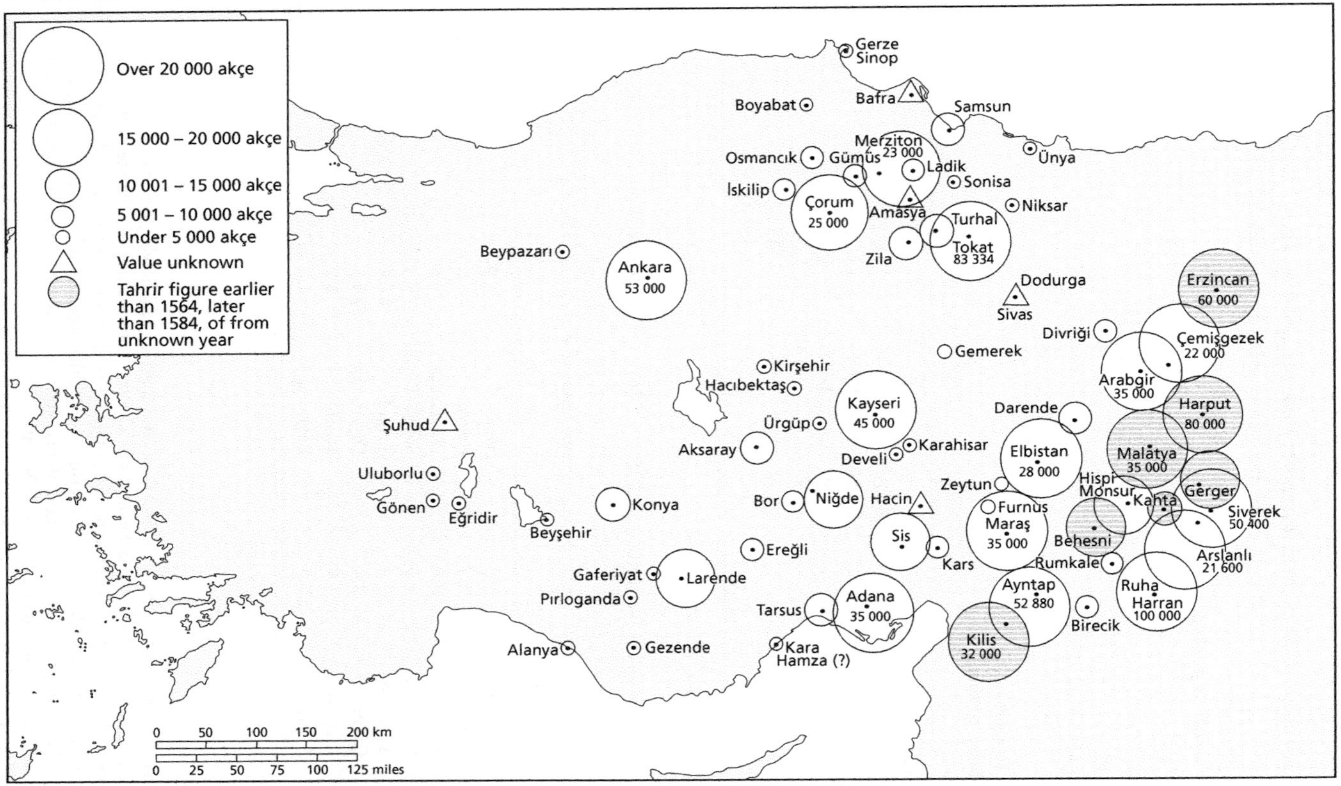

Map 5 Location and revenues of Ottoman dye houses or *boyahanes*, late sixteenth century
Source: Based on Faroqhi, 1984: 152.

Table 2.9 *English and French imports from the Levant, 1620–1789*

English Imports (*in thousands of pounds per year*)	**1621–34**	**1663–69**	**1699–1701**	**1722–4**
Raw Silk	73	172	219	274
Mohair Yarn	9	45	32	40
Cotton and Cotton Yarn	25	28	25	12
Galls	5	58	13	7
French Imports (*in millions of livres per year*)	**1700–2**	**1750–4**	**1785–9**	
Textile Materials				
Silk	2,416	2,095	1,683	
Cotton[46]	1,528	5,684	12,792	
Mohair Yarn	639	1,835	1,437	
Camel Hair	137	914	1,021	
Galls[47]	170	488	853	
Textile Manufacture	385	1,715	2,430	

Source: Davis, 1970: 202–4.

Table 2.10 Mukataa *revenues, 1706–1707 (in million* akçes*)*

Provinces			
Anadolu	4.6	Maraş	4.9
Karaman	2.3	Rakka	9.6
Sivas	8.0	Damascus	1.6
Erzurum	13.9	Sayda-Beirut	28.3
Trabzon	10.9	Tripoli	41.7
Çıldır	2.4	Diyarbekir	13.5
Aleppo	21.9	Mosul	3.2
Adana	13.8	Baghdad	4.4

Source: Tabakoğlu, 1985: 170.

46 Much cotton was locally processed into yarns and cloth in the following localities in Ottoman Kurdistan: Ergani, Mardin and Diyarbekir. The red cotton cloth of Diyarbekir was very famous and in much demand abroad during the seventeenth and eighteenth centuries. So much so that, according to the Tavernier, half of the population in the mid-seventeenth century had engaged in the production of this product and red Morocco leather. For more information, see van Bruinessen (1988: 36–40).

47 All galls exported originated in Diyarbekir, Van and Mosul (Davis, 1970: 200–1; van Bruinessen, 1988: 40).

Table 2.11 *Principal* mukataas*, 1698/99–1748 (in million* akçes*)*

	Years							
	1698–9	1700–1	1701–2	1706–7	1710–1	1716	1734–5	1748
Sources								
Erzurum Customs	11.4	11.5	11.6	13.9[48]	12.2	17.4	15.5	—
Aleppo Revenues	20.1	20.2	20.1	21.9	19.2	23.5	23.4	22.5
Rakka *Mukataas*	9.3	8.6	8.5	9.5	10.9	12.9	12.8	14.0
Sayda-Beirut *Mukataas*	26.5	26.7	26.7	28.3	27.4	26.9	27.4	27.6
Tripoli *Mukataas*	31.2	38.3	38.3	41.7	35.8	36.1	29.6	36.1
Diyarbekir *Voyvodalığı*	10.1	13.3	9.2	13.5[49]	9.5	9.3	10.3	10.5
Gümüşhane *Hass'*	10.0	10.1	—	—	9.5	9.6	—	—
Sakız and İzmir Customs	10.1	—	12.8	—	—	—	18.2	—
Eflak *Cizye*	17.0	—	17.0	—	—	—	22.2	—
İstanbul Customs	39.8	—	39.8	—	—	—	57.3	—

Source: Tabakoğlu, 1985: 173.

When the scale and sources of revenue of the most prominent *mukataa* of the province of Diyarbekir (Diyarbekir *Voyvodalığı*[50]) in 1797–8 (Table 2.12) are studied in tandem with the principal revenues of this province in the early seventeenth century (Table 2.8) and the total *mukataa* revenues in the early and mid-eighteenth century (Tables 2.10–2.11), we can arrive at two interrelated results. The first is that in the late eighteenth century, Diyarbekir increased its *mukataa* revenues. The other is that this province preserved the manufacturing and trade revenues base of the province, as is evident with the revenues yielded from

[48] This is the whole revenue of the *eyalet* of Erzurum.
[49] This is the whole revenue of the *eyalet* of Diyarbekir.
[50] The term *voyvodalık* originates from a Slavic term: *voyvoda*. A *voyvoda* refers to a sub-commander. During the sixteenth century, it was the title given to the civil governors of the Balkan states under the control of the Ottoman Empire. In the preceding centuries, the term had come to be used in northern Anatolia and Kurdistan for a class of officials who acted as intendants of tax farms. As a fiscal category *voyvodalık* denotes the stewardship of *hass* or sultan' properties assigned to the administration of a *voyvoda* or, in other words, extensive lands administered as imperial estates under the supervision of state officials titled *voyvoda*. The *voyvodalık* as an *eklâm* (provincial bureau) was a provincial fiscal bureau that had the stewardship of a bulk of the state-designated wealth in a given province. Moreover, one of the primary duties of the Diyarbekir *voyvoda* was to administer the *mukataa* of the Diyarbekir *Voyvodalığı*. The *mukataa* of the Diyarbekir *Voyvodalığı* yielded the highest revenues in the province of Diyarbekir. In return for this service, the *voyvoda*s attained an annual salary (Salzmann, 2003: 128–31).

Table 2.12 *Revenues of the Diyarbekir* Voyvodalığı, *1797–1798 (in* kuruş[51]*)*

Sources	Amount
Customs (*Gümrük*)	97,490
Dye House Dues (*Boyahane*)	35,000
Sales Tax (*Damga*)	33,550
Ground Rent (*Arsa*)	34,000
Craftsmen' Dues (*İhtisab*)	8,344
Total	208,384

Source: Başbakanlık Arşivi, Bab-ı Defteri Baş Muhasebesi, No: 6538 in Yılmazçelik, 1995: 285.

customs, dye houses and market dues. Thus, on the eve of the nineteenth century, the paradigmatic Kurdish province in the Ottoman Empire was as valuable, if not more, as a revenue source for the imperial treasury as it had been in the early sixteenth century, and its progression in the sphere of manufacturing and in international trade made it one of the promising hubs for production and commerce.

[51] In the years 1690–1844, 1 *kuru* equalled to 120 *akçes* or 40 *paras* (Pamuk, 1994: 967).

3 The Transformation of Ottoman Kurdistan: Underdevelopment in Ottoman Kurdistan in the Age of Centralisation, Westernisation and Crisis (1800–1914)

3.1 Overview

During the nineteenth and early twentieth centuries, the economic penetration of Europe into the Ottoman Empire deepened, and the Ottoman state had diminished its international position as well as its territorial possessions. Unavoidably, these and other significant changes, which will be deliberated in this chapter, in Ottoman social, economic and political life had major implications for the socioeconomic and political structures and processes in Ottoman Kurdistan. In this introductory section, as background to the ensuing analysis of the social and economic manifestations in Ottoman Kurdistan in the period 1800–1914, this study will provide a terse outline of the pivotal events that surfaced in this region in the years prior to the First World War.

The nineteenth century was a time of astounding change in Ottoman Kurdistan. In the first half of this century, the age-old Kurdish administrative structures established in the early sixteenth century foundered. The abolition of the Kurdish polities, which hitherto preserved their infrastructure despite intermittently being suppressed by the Ottoman state in the preceding three centuries, was a derivative of the centralisation and Westernisation policies unleashed by the reforms of Sultan Mahmut II and continued by subsequent Ottoman reformers: the Tanzimat statesmen; Sultan Abdülhamid II (1842–1918), the Ottoman sultan from 1876 to 1909; and the Young Turks.

The centralist restructuring policies, alongside a series of other political and military goals elucidated in this chapter, aimed to eradicate the increasing powers of the local notables, who accumulated fiscal or landed power because of the experiment in delegating tax collection and the levying of troops to local elites in the eighteenth-century Ottoman Empire. The concentration of fiscal and landed wealth in the hands of the locally powerful elements had forced the central government to recognise their power and to confirm formally their status. Relatedly, although the Ottoman state oversaw their functions, in the late eighteenth and early nineteenth centuries, the strong Kurdish emirates were in almost complete control of their own internal affairs. Such changes, as described by McDowall, were not only witnessed in the 'further flung areas of the empire; all over the Anatolia, let alone in Kurdistan, local derebeys (or "valley lords"), themselves theoretically holding military fiefs, turned their fiefdoms into hereditary holdings failing to submit the requisite taxes to the capital' (2000: 40).

This process enabled locally powerful groups, comparatively free from the supervision of the central authority, to respond to increasing opportunities of commodity production for long-distance markets by carving out large estates for themselves and by escalating the exploitation of the dependent peasantry. The issuing of the *Sened-i İttifak* in 1808 represented the zenith of the power of local notables or *ayan* as it implicated the devolution of state power to local potentates, among them the Kurdish notables, who derived their power from local sources.

The successor of Sultan Selim III (1761–1808), the Ottoman sultan from 1789 to 1807, Mahmut II, recognised that in order to rescue the ramshackle Empire from further demise or collapse, he would have to reform its institutions and oust the unreceptive elements of government. The centralist reforms implemented by Mahmut II and the succeeding Ottoman rulers entailed the suppression of the local notables all over the Empire and occasioned the destruction of the Kurdish emirates. Local Kurdish hereditary rulers were ejected and the Kurdish territories were brought under direct Ottoman control. In other words, the toppling of the Kurdish polities and the suppression of the fiscal and landed power of the Kurdish notables went hand in hand.

Reşid Muhammad Pasha,[1] and Hafiz Mehmed Pasha, who replaced Muhammad Pasha in 1836, played an active role in the eradication of Kurdish emirates (Jwaideh, 1961: 148–9; McDowall, 2000: 43–5). In 1834, Reşid Muhammad Pasha, formerly the grand vizier of Mahmud II and the governor of Sivas at the time, mobilised a substantial army with the particular task of suppressing the Kurdish emirates. His initial target was the Kurdish ruler, Mir Muhammad of Rawanduz (1783–ca. 1840), who by the early 1830s established control

[1] Reşid Muhammad Pasha, who was of Georgian origin, held the rank of Marshal of the East in the Ottoman Army (Jwaideh, 1961: 148).

and maintained a level of law and order that had been unknown for generations over a territory bounded by the Upper and Lower Zab Rivers, the Tigris and the Iranian border. As Reşid Muhammad Pasha entered Soran territory and approached the Rawanduz valley, forces from Mosul and Baghdad that were mobilised by the *vali* of Baghdad, Ali Riza Pasha, and the *vali* of Mosul, Muhammad Pasha Ince Bayrakdar, joined him. As a result, the powerful pasha of Rawanduz was captured and removed to Istanbul.

In addition to ousting Mir Muhammad in 1836, Reşid Pasha's campaign in Ottoman Kurdistan put an end to the revolt in Mardin which began in 1833, suppressed the rebellious Milli tribal confederation[2] in Upper Mesopotamia and subjugated the Sasun-Motkan region within the same year (Jwaideh, 1961: 149–50). Yet, from the perspective of the Ottoman rulers, the most momentous achievement of this two-year campaign in Ottoman Kurdistan had been the suppression of the 300-year-old *hükümets* of Hani, Hazro, Ilicak and Silvan (Aydin and Verheij, 2012: 31–2).

After the defeat of the *mir* of Rawanduz, the last supreme chief to present a stern challenge to the centralist Ottoman reformers was the ruler of the Botan emirate, Bedirkhan Bey (1802–68). Bedirkhan Bey had succeeded to his principality in 1820–1.[3] He was a member of the prominent Bedirkhani family who descended from the ancient Azizan family mentioned in the *Şerefname*. The Bedirkhani family enjoys a distinctive place in Kurdish history for producing numerous Kurdish nationalists after the dissolution of the Ottoman Empire, who will be analysed later.

The power Bedirkhan Bey accumulated during his rule had surpassed the authority of many of the authorities in the region. At the peak of his rule in the 1830s, an American traveller described his power:

[2] The Milli were a confederation of Kurdish *aşirets*, divided into two branches: the Timavizade branch living around Viranşehir and a second branch inhabiting between Resulayn and Mardin. Millis were largely semi-nomads. The Timavizade also practised agriculture. *Aşirets* in this study (i) are specified by their regional or, to be precise, the Middle Eastern context and their pastoral-nomadic character, determined by the necessity of transhumance; and (ii) are predominantly a construction on the basis of common political and economic goals and thus different to the 'tribe', which denotes kinship ties/groups of hunter-gatherers or agriculturalists in African American, Asian or Oceanic environments, to the extent that common descent is somewhat fictive.

[3] A controversy does exist about the exact year of Bedirkhan's coming to power; some of the sources suggest that the year 'was 1821' (Jwaideh, 1961: 176) or 'about 1820' (McDowall, 2000: 45), while others claim the period between 1835 and 1838 was the period during which he established himself as the emir of the emirate of Botan (Özoğlu, 2004: 70).

[Bedirkhan Bey's power] extend[ed] from the Persian line on the east to far into Mesopotamia on the west, and from the gates of Diarbekr to those of Mosul; and his fame was widespread. . . . Every chief in Northern Koordistan came to make their respects to him. . . . Even the Hakkary Bey, higher in rank, and once more powerful than he. (Jwaideh, 1961: 183)

By virtue of his cooperation with the Ottoman authorities and owing to the influence he wielded in Kurdistan, Bedirkhan Bey avoided the suppressive actions of Rashid Pasha in this region during 1834–6.

The relationship between Bedirkhan Bey and the Ottoman state remained relatively peaceful until 1842. The emir of Botan, however, was very disconcerted by the new centralist administrative arrangements of the Ottoman administration in the following five years and revolted against the Ottoman state in 1847. According to the new system, the Botan emirate would remain in Diyarbekir Province, but Cizre, a sub-district in the Botan emirate and the seat of the Bedirkhan administration, would be attached to Mosul. Although it was an arduous task, a heavily armed Ottoman military succeeded in defeating the revolt. Bedirkhan was captured and sent to Istanbul in 1847. Subsequently, the campaign was described in the official newspaper of the Ottoman state, *Takvîm-i Vakayi*, as 'reconquering of Kurdistan' (issue 345 in Kürdoloji Çalışmalar Grubu, 2011: 27), and a 'Medal of Kurdistan' was issued by the state to those who had fought against the Bedirkhan Revolt (Özoğlu, 2004: 71). The official designation of the campaign neatly epitomises the rationale for suppressing the Kurdish polity in Botan and other Kurdish emirates.

As part of the task of 'reconquering' Kurdistan, the Ottoman state established a new administrative unit and titled it Kurdistan Province (Kürdistan Eyaleti). As is evident in the imperial order (*irade*) cited later wherein the idea of creating the *Kürdistan Eyaleti* was explicated, this new administrative formation was formed with the aim of establishing direct control over Kurdistan, rather than recognising Kurdistan as a political entity. The imperial order of 1846 contains a letter from the office of the grand vizier on 6 May 1846 that reads:

The commander of the Anadolu army, illustrious Müşir Pasha, had some observations regarding the future of [the] Kurdistan region, which was saved – perhaps reconquered – from brigands (*eşkıya*). To present the requirement to, and to request permission from, the Sultan, two days ago his excellency Serasker Pasha, Fethi Pasha, the above-mentioned Müşir Pasha, Nazır Efendi, and the undersecretary met in the grand vizier's Residence (*Bab-ı Ali*). Müşir Pasha firstly stated that the village of Harput . . . although it is a suitable place to station the army, is peripheral to the headquarters of the army. On the other hand, Ahlat – which is located on the other shore of Lake Van, and has suitable weather and fertile soil, and is located at the centre of the Imperial Army (*Ordu-yu Hümayun*) – is, unlike Harput, close to the Iranian and Russian borders. **Ahlat provides better transportation and logistical support and is located in the heart of Kurdistan, where the Kurds can be better controlled with the iron fist (*pençe-i satvet*), which proves to be necessary**. Therefore, it is suggested to the exalted Sultan that Ahlat should become the headquarters of the Anadolu army. The appropriate action should be taken pending the Sultan's approval ... The second point of Müşir Pasha related to the administrative structure of Kurdistan. According to the pasha, the Kurdistan region was conquered to provide security and order to the region. Diyarbakir province (*eyalet*) and Van, Muş, and Hakkari districts (*sancak*) and Cizre, Botan and Mardin sub-districts (*kaza*) should be united under the name of Eyalet-i Kürdistan.[4]

The sultan approved the request in 1847, and for the first time in the history of the Ottoman Empire, the term *Kurdistan*, which until then was used as a geographical expression, was baptised to an administrative unit. *Eyalet-i Kürdistan* was short-lived, however. In the Devlet Salname of 1867, the name 'Kürdistan' was substituted by 'Diyarbakir' (Özoğlu, 2004: 61–2).

From the time of the defeat of Bedirkhan Bey in 1847 to the outbreak of the Turco-Russian war of 1877–8, there had not been a powerful Kurdish ruler in the region. This power vacuum within Kurdish society, originating from the eradication of the Kurdish emirates, led to the rise of the religious sheikhs belonging to Naqshbandi and Qadiriyya dervish orders, or *tariqas*, as they virtually were the only figures to mediate between tribal leaders. Capitalising on their religious prestige to act as intermediaries in inter-communal clashes, as well as presenting themselves as defenders of the Islamic order, resulted in the sheikhs accumulating extreme economic and political power.

After the Turco-Russian war, Sheikh Ubeydullah (1831–83) of the venerated Şemdinan[5] family had filled the political and military vacuity and assumed Kurdish leadership not only in Ottoman Kurdistan but also in Iran. His political rule extended over a vast region that was formerly controlled by the Botan, Bahdidan, Hakkari and Ardalan tribal confederacies, so much so that the sheikh was described by Henry Trotter (1841–1919), British consul-general at Erzurum, in 1880 as 'the most

[4] B. A., Mesail-i Mühimme, 1310, translated by and adopted from Özoğlu (2004: 60–1). The bold italics belong to me.

[5] The Şemdinan family was one of the greatest Naqshbandi families in Ottoman Kurdistan. Its prestige and popularity was due to the religious genealogy prior to the nineteenth century: the Şemdinans belonged to the Khallidiyya branch of the Naqshbandi *tariqa*, which, unlike some of the rival Sufi orders at the time, had a firm commitment to Sunni Islam, and the origins of the family had been traced back to Abd al Qadir Gilani, the twelfth-century mystic and saint who had founded the Qadiriyya order.

influential man in Eastern Kurdistan'.[6] The following critical and depictive verses of the late nineteenth-century Kurdish poet, Hacî Qadırê Koyî (1817–97), are also testimony to the dominance and the negative ramifications of sheikhs and Sufi dervish orders in Ottoman Kurdistan after the fall of the emirates:

> *Khanaqah* and Sheikh and *Tekke* all,[7]
> What is their benefit, tell me,
> What is the benefit of teaching laziness,
> And collecting treasure and lands,
> They do not test them once,
> Understand, its poison nay opium,
> If you rub them [the sheikhs] like gold,
> You will come to know whether they are highwaymen or guides,
> Don't beg sheikhs and alike,
> No one gives sustenance to another,
> This one [the sheikh] is busy with symbolism, coyness and wishing,
> While the science of Europe has reached the impossible.[8]

The influential revolt Sheikh Ubeydullah led in 1880[9] typified the rise of the sheikhs to supremacy in Ottoman Kurdish society. Assembling 220 tribal leaders and their supporters in Şemdinan, Ubeydullah formed the 'Kurdish Tribal League'. In 1880, the sheikh of Nehri invaded the north-western territories of Persia, allegedly in the name of the Kurdish nation. In the message he sent to William Abbot, the British consul-general in Tabriz, the sheikh outlines the purpose of this incursion with the following words:

> The Kurdish nation . . . is a people apart. Their religion is different, and their laws and customs are distinct . . . the Chiefs and Rulers of Kurdistan, whether Turkish or Persian subjects and inhabitants of Kurdistan, one and all are united and agreed that matters cannot be carried on in this way with the two Governments

[6] Great Britain: Parliamentary Papers, Accounts and Papers (hereafter, A&P) (1881), [Paper no. C.2851], [Vol. 361], p. 17. (Henceforth, all of the citations from A&P will be in the latterly stated format: session/paper number/volume number/page number).

[7] *Khanaqah* and *Tekke* denote venues used for gatherings of dervish orders.

[8] Hacî Qadırê Koyî's poem titled '*Udeba çak a*' written sometime between 1895 and 1897 in Bajalan (2013: 10).

[9] The rebellion was organised partially in protest of the suppressive policies the Ottoman state implemented as per its obligations under Article LXI of the Treaty of Berlin (1878): 'the Sublime Porte undertakes to carry out, without further delay, the improvements and reforms demanded by local requirements in the provinces inhabited by the Armenians, and to guarantee their security against the Circassians and Kurds' (in Jwaideh, 1961: 282). The rebellion was also in part a reaction to the perceived cavalier treatment of tribal chiefs in the villages located on the Ottoman–Safavid border by the local Persian authorities who had close links with Sheikh Ubeydullah (McDowall, 2000: 53).

[Ottoman and Persian], and that necessarily something must be done, so that European Governments having understood the matter shall inquire into our state. We also are a nation apart. We want our affairs to be in our own hands.[10]

As the phraseology of the epistle exhibits, it was not merely in terms of religious leadership, but also with regard to the explicit employment of nationalist discourse that this revolt diverged from preceding Kurdish upheavals. For this reason, some scholars, such as Wadie Jwaideh, conceive the Ubeydullah revolt as the origin of the Kurdish nationalist struggle. Özoğlu, however, disputes this viewpoint, because he conceives it as a 'trans-tribal revolt [rather] than a nationalist revolt' motivated by Ubeydullah's desire to be 'the ruler of Greater Kurdistan' (2004: 76). Regardless of whether Kurdish nationalism was the prime instigator of the sheikh and his supporters, the distinctive aspect of this rebellion was that it drew on the bourgeoning discourse of nationalism to appropriate and promote his actions, a sign of the permeation of capitalism and Western ideologies in Kurdistan.

Sheikh Ubeydullah' militias were defeated by the joint operation of Persian and Ottoman armies and upon his return to the Ottoman territories in 1881, the Ottoman authorities captured Ubeydullah. The Ottoman state exiled him to Istanbul and then to Hijaz. Thereafter, until the end of the Ottoman Empire, the Ottoman governors kept a close watch on Kurdistan and never allowed a strong Kurdish principality to emerge. Instead, particularly during the Hamidian period (1876–1909), the Sunni Kurdish *aşiret* or tribal forces were absorbed into the Ottoman military and the Kurdish nobility was largely resituated in Istanbul, where it could be controlled and manipulated.

Kurdish tribal sections were organised by the Ottoman state under the Hamidiya Cavalry (1891). The Hamidiya were an irregular mounted and proxy force in eastern Anatolia initially created by Sultan Abdülhamid II from selected Sunni Kurdish tribes to provide a bulwark against the Russian threat and to incorporate the Sunni Muslim Kurds – who had constituted the majority of the Hamidiya – into the Ottoman state system. Sultan Abdülhamid II also established tribal schools (*aşiret mektepleri*) in order to indoctrinate the children of Kurdish tribal leaders who remained in Kurdistan.

Inter-communal rifts and conflicts between the Kurds and the Armenians – which will be analysed in depth in subsequent sections of this study – and between the Sunni Kurds and the Alevi Kurds reached their peak with the establishment of the Hamidiya force. The most

[10] FO 371/953, Barclay to Gray, 3 January 1910.

notable example was the feud between the Alevi Khurmak and the Sunni Jibrans. The former were a leading Alevi landowning family, while the latter was one of the strongest tribes of Kurdistan. The Jibrans had assassinated the Khurmak chief Ibrahim Talu in 1894 and his son twelve years later (McDowall, 2000: 185). After the overthrow of the Abdülhamid regime by the CUP in 1908, the Hamidiya regiments were organised under the 'Tribal Light Cavalry Regiments'. Despite the change in appellation, the purpose imputed to Tribal Cavalry Regiments remained unchanged (Burkay, [1992] 2008: 399–411).

As can be inferred from these events, the suppression of the long-standing Kurdish polities wrought not only years of war to Ottoman Kurdistan but also prompted a power vacuum and, in turn, a reduction in law and order in most parts of ESA. Besides fostering the removal of the Kurdish administrative units, violent encounters between the Kurds and the Ottoman state all over Kurdistan stripped the Kurds of their indigenous political structures, empowered the traditionalist elements within Kurdish society and fuelled unprecedented inter-communal conflicts in this region.

With the elimination of the Kurdish rulers and dissolution of the emirates, their constituent parts, tribal confederations and *aşirets* became the most important political and social components in Kurdistan. Thus, rather paradoxically, in the wake of the modernisation reforms of the nineteenth century, a multitude of antagonistic Kurdish tribes were activated or empowered as political and social actors. Up to the second half of the nineteenth century, in spite of their existence, tribal structures had a subsidiary position in power relations. After the Ottoman state's policy of centralisation, however, according to the nineteenth-century French traveller Ubicini, some '1,000 independent [tribal] entities' (Celil, 1992: 121) replaced the few dozen former autonomous or semiautonomous Kurdish polities. In sum, the centralist restructuring of the Ottoman Empire gave birth to a period of immense insecurity in Ottoman Kurdistan and deepened the feudalisation of Kurdish society.

The centralist reforms of Mahmut II led also to the destruction of the Janissary corps in 1826, which in addition to being an act with a political purpose – i.e. the removal of military opposition to military reform – also had economic and social significance. As Quataert rightly noted, '[t]he sultan's actions in 1826 disarmed the urban guildsmen and eliminated the most powerful and best-organized advocates of protectionism. Thus, the 1826 event paved the way for the subsequent evolution of Ottoman economic liberalism' (1994: 764).

The Anglo-Turkish Convention of 1838 signed between the Ottoman government and Britain was the next step. In accordance with this Convention, British traders were permitted to import goods into the Ottoman Empire upon the payment of a 5 per cent *ad valorem* duty. As for exports from the Empire, traders were allowed to export Ottoman goods upon payment of a 12 per cent charge. The signing of this Convention had marked the beginning of a major increase in trade between the Ottoman Empire and Europe. British exports to the Empire, for example, increased from about 1 million pounds sterling in 1827 to more than 2.5 million pounds sterling in 1849; the British imports from the Empire consisted of agricultural produce and livestock products, such as mohair, wool, cotton, sheep, carpets, opium, raisins and figs (Jafar, 1976: 49).

The Convention of 1838 and the event of 1826 further integrated the Ottoman and European economies, and the 1839 and 1856 reform edicts more closely aligned Middle Eastern polities with Western political structures as a result of the following major political-administrative trends during the Tanzimat period:

1. the abolishment of the existing system of tax-farming and the creation of a monetised and rationalised system to levy taxes;
2. the secularisation and formalisation of education and of the administration of justice;
3. the functional differentiation of branches of government;
4. an increasing division of the powers of government leading to the establishment of an Ottoman parliament and constitution;
5. a differentiation of the means of physical force according to the separate realms of internal and external security;
6. the introduction of a new system of provincial administration.

During the re-centralisation and Westernisation period, the Ottoman Empire felt one of the greatest threats from its ambitious northern neighbour, Russia, which in 1828, after inflicting a series of military and political humiliations during the second half of the eighteenth century,[11] gained principalities as far as the Danube and penetrated eastern Anatolia as far as Erzurum in 1829. Kars, Erzurum and Bayazid were all returned to the Ottomans under the terms of the Treaty of Edirne

[11] In 1769, Russian forces pushed across the Danube, occupying Bucharest and destroying an Ottoman army at Kartal in 1770. The subsequent year, Russia destroyed the Ottoman fleet, leaving the entire eastern Mediterranean seaboard undefended. In 1774, it occupied Crimea, gaining access to the Black Sea. These mortifications were set out in the Treaty of Küçük Kaynarca, 1774. Although Russia withdrew from the Danube provinces and both parties recognised the independence of the Khanate of Crimea, it was clear that these two regions now fell within Russia's orbit. Crimea was directly annexed in 1779.

(1829), but the war had struck an entirely new note of danger as not only had the Ottoman Armenians assisted the Russian capture of Kars, but Muslim Kurdish tribes had also provided a regiment against the sultan (McDowall, 2000: 39). Such threats from Russia and the novel alliances between the Kurds and the Russians had also been influential in informing the policies of the Hamidian period.

At the beginning of the second half of the nineteenth century, the Crimean War (1853–6) broke out between the Ottomans and the Russians. The former, in order to meet its mounting military expenditures, contracted a number of loans with various Western European countries. The terms of these loans were very harmful to Ottoman finance and economy. In 1854, the first of these loans of 3 million pounds sterling was set at a 6 per cent annual interest rate. In 1855, 1858, 1860, 1862, 1863, 1865 (two loans), 1869, 1870, 1871, 1872, 1873 and 1874, new loans were contracted on similar terms to the one of 1854. By 1874, the total sum of these loans was 212 million pounds sterling, of which the Ottoman government actually received only 120,480,000 pounds, that is, 56.8 per cent of the nominal value of these loans (Lutsky, 1969: 319). Sixteen years after the first loan in 1854, the Ottoman state found itself completely dependent on foreign loans, while debt servicing consumed one-third of its treasury income (Zürcher, 1994: 67–8). Increasing integration in the capitalist world market, based on the disadvantageous terms of trade for the Ottoman economy and unsuccessful attempts to reform the financial administration of the Empire led to the fiscal crisis in the 1870s.

Following these turbulent events, the intra-Ottoman struggle between protectionists and pro-free trade forces continued while the basic commitment of the Ottoman polity to integration with the European economy remained intact until the 1908 Young Turk Revolution. The Ottoman state accepted the Public Debt Administration in 1881, which assured Western investors that the integration process would ensue without risking their investments. The Public Debt Administration was established as a result of the negotiations following the Ottoman fiscal crisis in the 1870s when the Ottoman state's ability to pay its international loans was in doubt. Hence, the Ottoman leadership had to agree to the rescheduling of these debts and to the formation of the Public Debt Administration, which represented the European creditors, for their collection.

Moreover, the 1908 Young Turk Revolution provided a different kind of reassurance to its European counterparts. The 1908 revolution entailed more than solely a reaction to the absolutism of Sultan Abdülhamid II and territorial losses. The emerging bureaucratic and military cadres launched their coup against a background of mounting social unrest: the rampant taxpayers' revolt and numerous labour strikes, among others, the 1908 strike at Ergani Copper Mine in Diyarbekir and violence during the half-decade prior to the revolution.[12] The Young Turks, as Quataert emphasised, 'seized power and prevented the spread of social revolution; thus, they circumscribed the kind of changes that would occur' (1994: 765). However, in the years between the 1908 Young Turk Revolution and the First World War, the proponents of a protected 'national economy' finally triumphed over the advocates of free trade, a theme explored in depth in the succeeding chapter.

3.2 Social Structures

Population

At the beginning of the nineteenth century, the European provinces held the majority of the population, but thereafter, as demonstrated by the Ottoman population figures tabulated in Table 3.1, the share of the European provinces gradually contracted. Owing to the rapid territorial losses in the last quarter of the century, the Balkans' share of the total Ottoman population fell drastically, which shifted the demographic centre of the Empire steadily towards Anatolia. For instance, during 1844–56, the Balkan lands contained 43 per cent of all Ottoman subjects (Table 3.1), whereas in the last census of the Empire in 1906, the

Table 3.1 *Ottoman population, 1844–1914 (in millions)*

Date	Balkan	Anatolia	Total
1844–56	15.5	10.7	35.4
1867	18.5	12.8	40.0 – with Egypt
1872–4	14.8	9.4	29.0 – without Egypt
			40.0 – with Egypt
1897	5.6	11.4	29.0 – without Egypt
1906			21.0 – without Egypt
1914	1.9	12.5	21.0 – without Egypt

Source: Derived from Karpat, 1985: 109–14 and Quataert, 1994: 779.

[12] For an exploration of the labour disputes in this period, see Yıldırım (2013) and Zürcher and Quataert (eds.) (1995).

Table 3.2 *Population of selected Ottoman towns, 1830–1912 (in thousands)*

Town/City	1830s–40s	1890	1912
Istanbul	375	900	1,125
Edirne	100	87	83
Izmir	110	200	300
Bursa	70	76	80
Sivas	40	43	60
Adana	12	30	42
Samsun	4	11	25
Trabzon	33	35	50
Erzurum	15	39	43
Diyarbekir	54	35	38
Urfa	50	55	50
Van	20	30	30
Bitlis	15	39	40
Antep	20	43	45
Muş	7	27	27

Source: Issawi, 1980: 34–5.

Ottoman government found that only 23 per cent of its citizens resided in Europe: 4.9 million of a total 20.9 million (Karpat, 1985: 35).

The majority of the Ottomans lived in the countryside and as a result, rural dwellers constituted around 80 per cent of the total population. During the nineteenth and early twentieth centuries, the urban-rural distribution changed. Between 1840 and 1913, the proportion of Ottoman urban dwellers had risen from 17 per cent to 22 per cent (Issawi, 1980: 33–5; Quataert, 1994: 780–1).

As the figures tabulated in Table 3.2 exhibit, during 1830–1912, Izmir and Istanbul increased in size. These port towns owed their demographic growth to the European trade. The expansion of the port communities, in turn, helps explain the expanding proportion of Ottomans living in the coasts. On the other hand, other cities, such as the predominantly Kurdish Diyarbekir in Anatolia and Edirne in Europe, as observed by Issawi (1980: 34–5) and Owen (1981: 24–5), respectively, fell some 20 per cent to 25 per cent over the same period owing to wars and/or secular shifts in trade route.

A demographic development that is often undetected in the scholarships on urbanisation in the Ottoman Empire during the nineteenth century is that, with the exclusion of Diyarbekir, other cities in ESA, such as Bitlis, Muş, Erzurum, Urfa and Van, had increased their

Table 3.3 *Population estimates of selected Ottoman towns, 1890 (in thousands)*

Provinces	Population
Adana	30
Konya	44
Diyarbekir	35
Van	30
Erzurum	39
Mamüretülaziz	101
Halep	127
Trabzon	35
Kastamonu	15

Source: Cuinet, 1890.

populations more than other eastern and south eastern domains of Trabzon, Samsun and Adana (see Table 3.2). Additionally, populace figures for towns prepared by Vital Cuinet (1833–96), based on *Salnames*[13] and additional population estimates[14] (Table 3.3), suggest that provinces in or on the borders of Ottoman Kurdistan, namely, Diyarbekir, Mamüratülaziz and Halep, when compared with other provinces in Anatolia, such as Adana, Trabzon, Kastamonu and Konya, had similar urban population densities during the late nineteenth century.

When compared with the minimal official demographic data in pre-nineteenth-century Ottoman Kurdistan, owing to the existence of the censuses from 1831 onwards, there is more information regarding the populace of this region of the Empire in the nineteenth century. The utility and veracity of the demographic details provided for Kurdistan in these official sources are highly questionable, however. The maiden 1831 'Census' did not include the principal provinces of Diyarbekir, Erzurum and Van (Behar, 1996: 23–5). Similarly, the contemporaries had received the data in the Ottoman Census of 1844 – which has been habitually employed by academic studies on Ottoman ESA to attain estimates of the populace of these regions in the early nineteenth century – with scepticism. For instance, in 1870, British Consul John George Taylor reporting from the Consular District of Kurdistan refers

[13] *Salnames* are state and provincial yearbooks published by the Ottoman state between the years 1847 and 1918.

[14] Cuinet does not specify the sources of his figures; however, it is postulated that he has made use of a 'wide variety of sources': various 'Ottoman Provincial *Salnames*' and 'population censuses' for the year 1300 (1881–93) (Behar, 1996: 45).

to the following deficiencies of the Census of 1844 and, alternatively, outlines the invaluable findings of his eight years of research in Kurdistan, which provide a comparatively more accurate and detailed demographic picture of this region (Table 3.4):

The data I give are merely the results of constant travel, careful inquiry, and research, noted day by day during an eight years' residence in the vialets of Erzeroom and Diabekr, composing the Consular district of Koordistan. ... The imperfect Turkish Census of 1844, as quoted by M. V. Heuschling, an official of the Belgian Ministry of the Interior, in his 'Empire de la Turquie', published in 1860, gives, as the population for the district of Erzeroom, Diabekr, Kharput, 1,700,000 souls. From all I have been able to collect, the actual amount in 1868 was 2,314,000, namely—

In the Erzeroom Vilayet ... 1,230,700
In the Diabekr Vilayet, including Kharput ... 1,083,000
Divided into the following races and creeds:

Table 3.4 *The ethnic and religious composition of Diyarbekir, Erzurum and Harput, 1868 (in thousands)*

Province/ District	Turks	Kurds	Christians	Jews	Yezidis	Qızılbaş Kurds	Arabs	Chechens	Terrek Iman (A Shiah Sect)
Erzurum	272	357	411	1	2	158	–	–	29
Diyarbekir	30	391	108	1	8	12	118	16	–
Harput	140	100	130	–	–	30	–	–	–
Total	**442**	**848**	**649**	**2**	**10**	**200**	**118**	**15**	**29**

Source: A&P, 1871, 'Report on the Condition of Industrial Classes' (in Kurdistan), C.414, LXVIII, p. 794.[15]

Official Ottoman statistics – as it is apparent with the data attained from the 1881/82–93 Census that is tabulated in Table 3.5 – had classed Kurdish-, Turkish- and Arabic-speaking Muslims together. Consequently, it is not always possible to extrapolate the proportional distribution of the different ethnic groups of the Muslim populace from the data provided in the official sources. Moreover, it is also not feasible to infer from the Ottoman censuses summarised later the figures of nomads and the individuals who are associates of the heterodox sects: Alevi (Qızılbaş) and Yezidi. In spite of these shortcomings, the data from the Ottoman Census of 1881/82–93 do

[15] The table is part of the text cited earlier and ends the quote.

Table 3.5 *The ethno-religious composition of various provinces of Ottoman Kurdistan, Ottoman census of 1881/82–1893*

Province	Muslim	Greek Orthodox	Armenian	Bulgarian	Catholic	Jewish	Protestant	Other	Foreign Nationals
Diyarbekir	289,591	1,166	46,823	73	9,793	1,051	4,021	16,552	–
Total Registered Population: 369,070									
Erzurum	445,548	3,356	101,138	–	6,630	6	1,940	15	292
Total Registered Population: 558,925									
Bitlis	167,054	–	101,358	–	4,948	–	46	–	–
Total Registered Population: 276,998									
Van	59,412	3	60,448	–	–	–	–	–	–
Total Registered Population: 119,860									
Elazığ	360,636	543	72,378	–	1,915	2	4,371	54	–
Total Registered Population: 381,346									

Source: Behar, 1996: 39–40.

provide us with an estimate of the populace in Ottoman Kurdistan on the eve of the twentieth century.

Employment

The aforementioned extensive research by Consul Taylor in Kurdistan also provides a unique compendium of the occupations and trades of the inhabitants in the three predominantly Kurdish eastern provinces of the Empire during the late nineteenth century. According to the findings of the British consul (Table 3.6), the agriculturalists constituted, like in other parts of the Empire, the bulk of the labouring classes in this region. At the time, their labour formed 'more than one-half the sum derived from every source of taxation or impost' in the provinces of Diyarbekir, Erzurum and Harput.[16] Agriculturalists, in order of density, were followed by the pastorals, small traders, handloom workers (i.e. silk and/or cotton weavers), artisans (i.e. carpenters,

Table 3.6 *Occupations and trades of the inhabitants of Diyarbekir, Erzurum and Harput, ca. 1869*

Occupation	Able-bodied Man exercising Trades	Working Adults helping the same	Remaining Members of Family, and Women and Children
Hand-loom Workers	11,700	6,000	52,500
Millers	4,300	500	21,000
Artisans	8,000	2,000	38,000
Jew[ish] Pedlars	2,000	–	–
People in Government Employ[ment]	7,000	–	–
Mollas, proprietors, Shop-keepers and Small traders	19,000	–	98,000
Agriculturists	200,000	200,000	800,000
Pastorals	109,800	109,800	439,200
Totals	**361,800**	**318,300**	**1,448,700**

Source: A&P, 1871, 'Report on the Condition of Industrial Classes' (in Kurdistan), C.414, LXVIII, p. 795.

[16] A&P, 1871, C.414, LXVIII, p. 809.

masons, smiths, tanners and dyers), government employees, millers and Jewish pedlars.

As Quataert rightly noted, owing to the non-existence of an empire-wide ethno-religious division of labour, 'neither agriculture nor industry were confined to areas of Christian, or for that matter Muslim, demographic predominance'. Christians, Jews and Muslims were present in all sectors and classes, and social stratification in Ottoman society was devoid of a coincidence of social class and ethno-religious origin. Thus, despite nineteenth-century contemporaries regularly 'reserving diligence to the Christians and aloof indifference to [the] Muslims, these stereotypes do not bear close scrutiny; instead, we find enterprising Muslim and Christian cultivators and manufacturers everywhere' (1994: 783). Or, to put it somewhat differently, the oft-cited truism – particularly with regard to the eastern provinces – that the Muslims were nomads or farmers whilst the Armenians were entrepreneurs or manufacturers is misleading as it does not posit an accurate observation of the diverse nature of the provincial and empire-wide economy and social classes.[17] Consequently, in the eastern quarters or elsewhere in the Empire, we search in vain, if we seek religion or ethnicity as the key to Ottoman economic activity.

Furthermore, as cogently expounded by Hilmar Kaiser (1998), the origin of the 'Ottoman ethnic division of labour' hypothesis lies in the essay of a German journalist/propagandist, Alphons Sussnitzki, titled 'On the Division of Labour According to Nationality in Turkey' ('*Zur Gliederung wirtschaftlicher Arbeit nach Nationalitäten in der Türkei*'), published in *Archiv für Wirtschaftsforschung im Orient* in 1917. In brief, this essay has two main contentions regarding the pre–First World War Ottoman Empire: (i) professions were each largely dominated by members of one racial group; and (ii) Armenian and Greeks, through usury and the exploitation of foreign imperialist protection, had abused Turkish tolerance and controlled nearly all trade and obstructed the development of other nationalities (Kaiser, 1997: 29–31). In other words, Sussnitzki's analysis, as accentuated by Kaiser, 'integrated a number of the familiar stereotypes: that Armenians were the political allies of Germany's enemies and that they played a negative role within the Ottoman economy. Accordingly, the author stressed the basic convergence of Ottoman Turkish and German interests' (ibid.: 32). In this study, following Quataert (1994, 1996) and Kaiser (1997), it will be argued that in the nineteenth- and early twentieth-century Ottoman Empire, there was no

[17] For a critical exploration of this thesis, see Kaiser (1997) and Quataert (1996).

ethno-religious division of labour, and the representatives of all nations and religions were present in all sectors of employment and trade.

3.3 Agriculture

From its birth to its demise following the First World War, the Ottoman Empire had been an agrarian empire. During the nineteenth and early twentieth centuries, 'four-fifths' of the Ottoman population lived on the land and drew some portion of their livelihoods from the soil (Eldem, 1970: 44). In an empire where agriculture was the dominant form of economic activity, the control of the land as an important means of production can naturally be conceived as one of the most important factors affecting the relations of production, class structure and the mechanisms of the articulation of the local structures with the larger structures. This explains why the role and influence of the Kurdish notables over agricultural land and surplus in the predominantly Kurdish provinces in ESA is commonly set as one of the central themes of enquiry by scholarships investigating socioeconomic and political developments in this region.

The prevailing view in these scholarly studies is that the centuries-long autonomy of the Kurdish rulers remained uninterrupted during the nineteenth century, despite the centralisation policies of the Ottoman state. As neatly summarised by Heper, common scholarly wisdom has held that 'since the enactment of the Land Code in 1858, large tracts of land were concentrated in the hands of a few local notables, particularly in the east and southeast of Turkey, [who] have not been interested in increasing productivity in agriculture' (2007: 5). Therefore, alongside transportation or communication barriers, which are discussed extensively in the subsequent section of this study, the unbroken autonomy of the 'disinterested' Kurdish notables, as well as the pervasiveness of the lord–peasant bond, during and after the nineteenth century is generally accepted to have hindered the (i) expansion of agricultural productivity and (ii) economic development of this region.

Owing to minimal industrial development during the Ottoman period, agricultural resources and productivity are the main source and measure of economic development. Below, by examining the evolution of patterns of landownership in Ottoman Kurdistan during 1800–1908, the correlation between patterns of landownership, agricultural productivity and economic development in this region of the Empire will be explored.

The Limitations of the Nineteenth-Century Ottoman Land Statistics

Prior to analysing the data pertaining to the land regime and agricultural activities in Ottoman Kurdistan, it is worth noting that during the nineteenth century, land statistics and quantitative information regarding agricultural production, unlike the previous centuries, were irregularly and poorly recorded and kept. We are made aware of this lacuna in a consular report drafted in 1869 by British Consul William Gifford Palgrave (1826–88), whose reports have often been utilised by the academic literature dealing with agriculture in Ottoman lands:

> Land statistics were formerly not ill-kept in the Ottoman Empire, and from what has been preserved of them in history and treatise, we are able to form a tolerably clear idea of the conditions of land tenure, cultivation, proprietorship, serfage, and the like ... in the anarchical condition of Constantinople during the troubled reigns of Seleen III and Mustapha IV (A.D. 1789–1808), the State records of the Empire were ill-kept, perished, or were dispensed beyond recovery, and the reforms of Mahmood II and Abd-el Mejeed did little to fill up the gap. Even at present, though personal statistics receive some degree of attention, land statistics are neglected; what little is accurately kept remains unpublished.[18]

Due to the aforementioned deficiencies and limitations of the Ottoman sources, the ensuing assessment of agriculture in nineteenth-century Ottoman Kurdistan will largely be based on the data presented in the consular reports prepared by British diplomats who had regularly reported on events from different parts of Kurdistan from the 1850s onwards. The data recorded in the British consular report make it very valuable and at times the only source of information for understanding manifestations in the agricultural sphere of nineteenth-century Ottoman Kurdistan. This said, the information in these reports rather than being treated as a definite reflection of the agricultural patterns or trends in this region will be taken as a rough indicator of the actualities in this sphere.

However, after the turn of the nineteenth century, Ottoman statistics regarding Ottoman agriculture became available. The Ottoman Agricultural Census of 1913 and 1914 for what comprises the present-day Turkey followed the maiden Ottoman Agricultural Census of 1907/09. For the purposes of this study, it is worth noting that the statistical information in these official documents, which usually constitute the

[18] A&P, 1870, C.75, LXVII, p. 285.

quantitative basis of most studies and research regarding Ottoman agricultural productivity and economic development, do not provide complete coverage of the predominantly Kurdish regions of the Empire. More precisely, the 1909 Census does not cover the Kars region. In addition to Kars, the census of 1913 did not cover the areas of Ağrı, Erzincan, Erzurum, Hakkari, Muş and Siirt. The census of 1914 omitted, along with the latterly mentioned areas, Bingöl, Bitlis, Urfa and Van (Güran, 1997: xxi). In consequence, when comparatively analysing the state of agricultural production and yields in Ottoman Kurdistan with those of the other regions of the Empire on the eve of the First World War, this study will not solely rely on the findings of the latterly mentioned censuses, but will also make use of alternate studies or research of Ottoman agriculture.

Agriculture in Ottoman Kurdistan, 1830–1876

As described earlier, the centralisation policies of the Ottoman state during and after the 1830s had not only occasioned the obliteration of the semiautonomous Kurdish administrative bodies, but had also resulted in the expropriation of large holdings of land that up until that point had been *de facto* properties of Kurdish notables. Contrary to what is customarily argued, the confiscation of large holdings of land from the Kurdish landed elites appears to have had unfavourable consequences for agricultural productivity in Kurdistan, and resulted in this region being less affected by the world-market-induced commercialisation of agriculture in the next four decades, predominantly because of two interrelated factors. The first of these factors is that after the 1830s, many of these confiscated lands were uncultivated owing to the neglect of these lands by the central state. The second factor is related to the inadequacies of the poverty-ridden peasants; with the absence of state support, peasants were not able to meet the demands of running the small estates/farms that they attained as a result of the very partial distribution of land to small peasants after 1830.

The initial consular reports prepared by British Consul William Richard Holmes (1822–82) in Ottoman Kurdistan during the 1850s track the latterly mentioned changes in the ownership of land and highlight the negative ramifications of the centralist policies of the central state on the agriculture of this Ottoman domain. The dates of these reports, 1857–8, are particularly important, coming nearly two decades after the confiscation of large landholdings and on the eve of the Land Code of 1858. In 1857, in a consular report on the conditions of Kurdistan,

Consul Holmes, who at the time was based in the province of Diyarbekir, notes the following informative changes:

The condition of the peasantry in general is extremely poor, and they seem on this account quite unable to cultivate the lands themselves. They therefore seek advances of money from the wealthier individuals of towns and villages. ... Land in this Pashalic [Kurdistan] can scarcely be said to have any value, as without artificial irrigation nothing can be produced, except wheat and barley, which are sown in the autumn or the very early spring. Formerly, the country was extensively irrigated, and covered with villages and cultivation, under the government of certain native Koordish families, who for years had ruled it. ...

Land in this Pashalic either belongs to the State... the Church, or to private individuals. That belonging to the State was acquired when the country was taken from Koordish Begs, by the confistication of their possessions.... Of these three categories of land freehold property is always the most flourishing... whereas the Crown and Church lands, particularly the latter, continually deteriorate.[19]

In addition, a survey on the land tenure in Kurdistan in 1858 on the eve of the Land Code of 1858 summarises the alterations that have taken place in this region of the Empire after the 1830s with the following words:

I. What are the different kinds of tenure of land and in what proportion are they, respectively, in use in your district?

About 20 years ago this part of Koordistan, which had previously been more nominally than really in the hands of the Turkish government, was wrested from the Koordish Beys, and the whole of the land, with the exception of some few parts the ownership of which was confirmed to its ancient proprietors, was confiscated to the Crown. Since then a portion has been sold and become private freehold property, a considerable portion is let as short leases of a year or two, a great deal has become Church property or 'Vakouf', but the greater part remains the property of the state and is waste and uncultivated ...

III. What is the condition of vakouf and other public lands as compared with that of freehold property?

Every individual takes care of his own private property to the best of his ability but the vakouf and crown lands are entirely neglected. ... Consequently freehold property is usually in a much better condition than any public lands. ...

XI. Are large estates or small holdings predominant, and what are the causes which most affect the distribution of land?

[19] A&P, 1857, 2285, XXXVIII, pp. 186–7.

Small holdings predominate.[20]

Erudite studies on the land tenure in the Ottoman Empire habitually hypothesise that the enactment of the Land Code of 1858 marked a watershed moment in agrarian relations and landownership in the Empire. As universally agreed, the intended purpose of this code had been twofold: (a) the recognition of private ownership of land; and (b) the demand by the central state that individuals possess a title deed to have legal use of *miri* land and thus to achieve complete registration; the state intended to survey all lands and give title deeds to those who controlled them. Scholars analysing the Land Code of 1858, nonetheless, have diverging views on its actual impacts. Some maintain the view that the code had been an instrument of the Ottoman government to reassert its fiscal domination over the peasantry (Baer, 1966; Jorgens, 2000). Others have insisted on its character as a facilitator that had transformed *miri* land into private property (Batatu, 1978). As outlined in Chapter 1, with regard to its implications for Ottoman Kurdistan, the latter view has been prevalent (Pamuk, [1987] 2010; Sönmez, [1990] 1992; Heper, 2007).

The code's role in facilitating the concentration of large tracts of land in the hands of the local notables in Ottoman Kurdistan and, as a result, not allowing the interruption of the autonomy of the Kurdish notables is dubitable. As can be deduced from the centralist policies of the Ottoman state, by the mid-nineteenth century, the central authorities had toppled all of the existing semiautonomous Kurdish emirates one after another, and thereafter kept a close eye on Kurdistan with the aim of preventing the creation of new autonomous Kurdish polities and elites. The Ottoman state was successful in achieving this aim through employing a trinity of complementary and sequential policies:

(i) Establishing a supersized administrative entity, *Eyalet-i Kürdistan*, through which it had asserted direct control of this region;
(ii) Suppressing any potential rivalry and demand for autonomy from the Kurdish notables, as evinced with the way it dealt with Sheikh Ubeydullah in the 1880s;
(iii) Promoting small peasant production, since peasant households were easier to tax than large landowners were, and the latter were more prone to posing political problems for the Ottoman state.

[20] FO 78/1419, 'Land Tenure in Kurdistan', 1858, Reply by Consul Holmes to Questionnaire in Issawi (1980: 220).

Table 3.7 *Landownership and distribution in the Asiatic provinces of the Ottoman Empire, ca. 1869*

	Acres
Total superficies in question:	**304,440,500**
Mubah or unreclaimed land:	152,200,250
Metrookah or common, forest and pasture:	101,480,167
Cultivated land:	50,740,083
Of the cultivated land:	
Vakıfs or endowment lands:	12,685,021
Miri or government property:	2,537,004
Mülk or private property:	35,518,058
Of *mülk* or private property:	
Larger estates, cultivated by tenancy or by hired labour:	5,074,008
Small estates, some cultivated by their peasant owners, some by *murabas* (sharecroppers):	30,444,050
Of *vakf, miri* and *mülk* property:	
Total of land divided into estates exceeding fifty acres, whether state property, endowment or private property, and cultivated partly by tenancy, partly by hired labour:	12,685,020
Total of land divided into estates from fifty acres and under, cultivated by the owners themselves, or by *murabas*:	38,055,062

Source: A&P, 1870, 'Report on Land Tenure in Turkey', C.75,LXVII, p. 285.C.75, LXVII, p. 286.

The information provided by Consul Palgrave regarding the land tenure in the Asiatic provinces[21] of the Ottoman Empire in 1870 offers quantitative data for doubting the role of the Land Code of 1858 in enabling the Kurdish notables and other landlords in these regions to retrieve large holdings of land. The date of this report, 1869, is vital: it is prepared three decades after the seizure of large landholdings, and just more than a decade after the Land Code of 1858. The extensive survey Palgrave conducted in Kurdistan, Anatolia, Syria and Iraq forms the basis of this survey.

According to the measurements Consul Palgrave gave, the Asiatic provinces had a total surface area of 1,219,762 square kilometres or 121,976,200 hectares – a hectare is equivalent to '2.5 English acres'.[22] Half of this land was considered un-reclaimed, and around two-thirds of it had comprised forests and pastures, leaving as cultivable land a total of 50,740,083 acres or 21,662,000 hectares.[23] As can be concluded from the figures prepared by Consul Palgrave that are tabulated in Table 3.7, of

[21] The report deals with land tenure in the provinces of Kurdistan, Anatolia, Syria and Iraq. Hereafter, the term *Asiatic provinces* denote these four regions.

[22] A&P, 1870, C.75, LXVII, p. 286. [23] Ibid.

all the cultivable land, 70 per cent had comprised *mülk* or private property, around 25 per cent belonged to *vakıfs* (endowments) and the remaining 5 per cent had been *miri* or state land. Yet around 85 per cent of the private or *mülk* land around was under small holdings whilst the remaining 15 per cent had been under large holdings. Around 75 per cent of all the cultivable land, that is, *mülk, miri* and *vakıf* lands, in these regions of the Ottoman Empire had been fifty acres or under, and only about 20 per cent of it had comprised estates exceeding fifty acres.

Consul Palgrave's assessment of the centralisation policies implemented during the Tanzimat era for the agriculture of the Asiatic provinces of the Empire is parallel to that of Consul Holmes delineated earlier. Palgrave contends that during this era as a result of four main factors – i.e. (i) subdivision of estates on land proprietorship; (ii) overweight of excessive taxation on land and its produce; (iii) official spoliation of land by the state for public works without any compensation for the landowners; and (iv) the 'forfeit of 10 per cent. *ad valorem* by the State from any proprietor' enacted by the Land Code of 1858[24] – the agriculture of this region had in general suffered gravely:

> The agricultural or land conditions of Eastern Turkey before and after the 'Tanzeemat' [Tanzimat] of the Sultans Mahmood II. and Abd-el-Mejeed [are] as follow:
>
> The tendency of the former period was to the security, permanence, and accumulation of land tenure; that of the latter to insecurity, change and disintegration. The tendency of the former period was to encourage agriculture, and to raise the value of land; that of the present, to discourage the former, and to depreciate the latter. The strength of the former period was in the permanence of large estates and numerous tenants; the weakness of the latter, in the multiplication of small estates and numerous landlords. ... That in such a state of things no advance, economic, social, moral, or intellectual, can be expected from the agricultural population, whether landlords or tenants, and that, none, in fact, exists; on the contrary, that cultivators and land are alike deteriorating.[25]

Agriculture in Ottoman Kurdistan during and after the Hamidian Era, 1876–1914

Towards the end of the nineteenth century, however, there appears to be a significant rise in the concentration of the land controlled by certain

[24] A&P, 1870, 'Report on Land Tenure in Eastern Turkey', C.75, LXVII, p. 283.
[25] Ibid.: 287.

Table 3.8 *Distribution of farm sizes ca. 1900 in the core regions of the Ottoman Empire*

	Distribution of farm sizes (% of farms)			
Regions	Under 10 *dönüms*	10–50 *dönüms*	Over 50 *dönüms*	Average Farm Size (*dönüms*)
Northern Greece and Thrace	40	42	18	21
Western Anatolia/Marmara	31	46	23	35
Eastern Black Sea	43	42	15	18
Adana	17	36	47	77
Central				
Anatolia	23	52	25	35
Eastern Anatolia				
Central Tier	41	41	18	21
Southern Tier	23	37	40	58

Source: Pamuk, [1987] 2010: 96

sections of the Kurdish notables. More specifically, as the findings of the Ottoman Agricultural Census of 1909 suggest, south eastern Anatolia – i.e. Diyarbekir, Bitlis and Van – had been second to the Adana region in terms of inequalities in the distribution of farm sizes within the following tabulated core regions[26] of the Empire (Pamuk, [1987] 2010: 98) (Table 3.8).

This change in land distribution and ownership in the southern tier of eastern Anatolia coincides with the policies implemented during the Hamidian period (1876–1909). As mentioned previously, in the course of this period, the Kurdish tribal forces in Ottoman Kurdistan were absorbed into the Ottoman military and political structure with the dual purpose of securing the eastern frontier districts from the real and perceived threats from Russia and Iran and integrating Kurds into the Ottoman state system. Thus, within Ottoman Kurdistan the Hamidiya became a channel for the power relationships between the sultan and the Kurdish rulers, operating as a tool for tribes to gain influence, and for the sultan to extend imperial rule

[26] Definitions of core regions as defined by Pamuk ([1987] 2010: 96)**: Northern Greece** (Salonica, Monastir), **Thrace** (Edirne), **Western Anatolia and Marmara** (Izmit, Biga, Hüdavendigar), **Aydın** (İzmir), **Eastern Black Sea Coast** (Trabzon), **Central Anatolia** (Kastamonu, Ankara, Konya, Sivas), **Eastern Anatolia, Central Tier** (Erzurum, Mamuretülaziz), **Eastern Anatolia, Southern Tier** (Diyarbakir, Bitlis, Van).

over this region of the Empire. The data from the late nineteenth century indicate that, particularly after the creation of the Hamidiya Cavalry (1891), the Kurdish religious and landed elite, with the active support of the Ottoman administration, attained vast amounts of land in ESA by the use of both economic and extra-economic means.

A case in point is the vast amount of power and land the tribal chiefs and urban notables in Diyarbekir accumulated during the Hamidian era. The data passed on by Mark Sykes[27] (1879–1919) in *Journeys in North Mesopotamia* (1907), and the present-day studies by Ali Arslan (1992) and Joost Jongerden (2012), shed much valuable light on the aggrandisement of the politically co-opted elite in this province throughout and after the Hamidian period.

In the initial years of his career as the regimental leader, Milli Ibrahim Pasha (?–ca. 1908), chief of the Milan confederation of tribes, had authority over a region extending from Viranşehir to Siverek and from Diyarbekir to Derik. At the peak of his power at the turn of the twentieth century, he had control over a much-extended region: the provinces of Diyarbekir, Mardin and Urfa. Relatedly, in 1902 following a visit by Milli Ibrahim to Sultan Abdülhamid II in Istanbul, he was awarded the rank of *pasha* (brigadier-general), and all four of his sons, Abdulhamid, Halil, Mahmut and Temur, attained the rank of *kaymakam* (lieutenant colonel). The power Milli Ibrahim Pasha accumulated enabled him to establish advantage over the land and villages as well as to control the trade routes in and out of the aforementioned regions (Sykes, 1907: 383–6; Jongerden, 2012: 63).

Similarly, Arif Pirinççizade (1853–1909), a prominent notable in Diyarbekir who was also the maternal uncle of Ziya Gökalp, had considerable wealth and power. After resigning from the *Diyarbekir Gazette* in 1877 as a journalist, Pirinççizade had concentrated on agriculture and trade. By the turn of the century, he became a large landowner, possessing around thirty villages near Diyarbekir, and was elected to Parliament in 1908 as an independent candidate for the district of Diyarbekir (A. Arslan, 1992: 52; Jongerden, 2012: 66).

The state encouraged the aggrandisement of the acquiescent Kurdish elites in order to strengthen their position in the provinces in the southern

[27] Mark Sykes was an English traveller, officer, honorary attaché and Conservative Party politician and diplomacy adviser known best as the co-author of the Sykes–Picot agreement (16 May 1916), a secret agreement between the governments of the UK and France, with the assent of Russia, to divide the provinces of the Ottoman Empire into spheres of British and French control. Sykes traversed Asia Minor both during and after his post as the honorary attaché to the British Embassy in Constantinople, in the years 1905–7, but also in the later years of 1908–9 and 1913.

and central tiers of eastern Anatolia vis-à-vis the Armenians who had occupied key positions in trade and business in certain quarters of these regions. For instance, in the province of Van during the late nineteenth century, Armenians held 80 per cent of the agriculture, 20 per cent of the livestock breeding and, out of the fifty moneylenders, thirty had also been Armenian (Issawi, 1980: 67). One of the common practices of the Ottoman authorities during this period was to settle in Armenian villages *hamidis*, i.e. tribal Kurdish forces serving in the sultan's irregular force, who, as pointed out by the Russian vice-consul in Bitlis in 1902, with time became the owners of these villages:

> These men [Hamidis] enjoying the protection of the administration dispensed justice and handed out punishment and, advancing to the every-needy Armenians funds secured by livestock, horses, and crops, gradually became the owners of the village or Aghas, and the Armenians, performing all their work for them . . . were unable to deliver themselves from the weight of their debts. (ibid.)

Concomitantly, the Kurdish notables with the backing of the Ottoman authorities employed economic means to increase their wealth and land as they bought the land of the Armenian inhabitants. Thereafter, in return for payment in kind to the landowner, the Armenian peasants worked on the majority of these lands. In addition, the landowning Kurdish notables provided cash and grain to the peasants in ESA on advantageous terms, which were repaid in kind at harvest time. These loans were at the time known as *selef*. The *selefdars* or the lenders soon became wealthy by taking the land of the defaulting debtors. The Russian vice-consul in Van, Consul Termen, described the exploitative consequences of the *selef* during the early years of the twentieth century with the following words:

> Thanks to this [selef] the whole village passes into the hands of the Kurds; the Armenians starting as miribe [*murabas*] – i.e. they receive from the Kurd seed and livestock for working the fields, giving in return half the crop – end up by losing their land and become simple laborers, i.e. the serfs of the Kurds. (ibid.: 64)

The *selef* was an important mechanism for the enrichment of the Kurdish elite. Based on the findings of the Archives of the Foreign Policy of Russia in 1908, Lazarev states the following telling cases:

> The Armenian village of Haskei, in [the] valley of Muş [Bitlis vilayet], lost through the selef 208 fields, 24 houses, and 6 mills, all of which had passed into the hands of the Kurdish selefdars. In the formerly prosperous village of Arench, in the kaza of Adilcevaz, out of the 115 houses only 70 remained in the hands of the local inhabitants; of these, however, only 55 were held in ownership, the other were being miribe [*murabas*]. In the village of Marmuss (vilayet of Van) the Kurdish

Bey seized all the land belonging to Armenian community and reduced the Armenian peasants to sharecroppers. (ibid.)

Agricultural Productivity Data

The Ottoman agricultural censuses prepared in the early twentieth century enable us to obtain information regarding agricultural output during these years. Owing to the minimal amount of recorded production figures, however, agricultural taxes, namely, tithes (*aşar*) and animal taxes (*ağnam*), and the revenues attained from these taxes continued to form the main means of measuring agricultural output. As outlined in the introductory section of the 1909 Census, unlike the agricultural censuses of most other countries in the modern era, the Ottoman agricultural production levels were estimated first on the basis of the tithe revenues and the cultivated areas were estimated afterwards (Güran, 1997: xxi). After the Tanzimat Decree of 1838, tithes were fixed at one-tenth of the gross agricultural output. This was paid partly in kind in the earlier period with a larger proportion repaid in crude money later on in the century. During the years of lower agricultural prices, the tax collectors routinely pressed for and received tax payments in cash. In addition, the 10 per cent rate was likely to escalate to 15 per cent, as it did in 1868, whenever the budgetary deficit of the state deepened. The practice of the tithe along with other forms of agrarian taxation, like the *ağnam*, meant that as much as a quarter of agricultural output was taxed (Pamuk, [1987] 2010: 89). However, it is worth noting that agricultural tax revenues only provide rough and indirect indications of the agricultural output, as they are dependent on the state's ability to tax and collect the taxes. Hence, the agricultural tax revenues cited later should be treated as rough indicators of output patterns.

The volume of annual gross agricultural production in the Empire is estimated to have doubled between the early 1860s and the First World War (ibid.: 83). In 1914, according to an educated guess, agriculture comprised 56 per cent of the Ottoman 'national' income (Quataert, 1994: 845). Agricultural taxes had thus remained the most important source of imperial revenues. By the end of the first decade of the twentieth century, moreover, Anatolia had overtaken the European provinces by becoming the leading contributor of the agricultural taxes.

In 1910, the Anatolian provinces had contributed 57 per cent of all the Ottoman tithes and animal taxes. The European provinces, which during the nineteenth century had contributed the bulk of the Ottoman agricultural taxes, provided 25 per cent of the total in 1910. Syria contributed 11 per cent, while Iraq yielded 6 per cent and Hejaz provided 3 per cent of

Table 3.9 *Population and agricultural output measured by tax revenues of Anatolia, 1910*

Province/Region	Population (thousands)	Revenue (million *kuruş*)
İstanbul, Çatalca	1,134	60
Hudavedigar, Karasi		
Izmit, Biga	2,128	1,068
Aydın (İzmir)	1,703	806
Ankara	1,160	448
Konya	1,254	521
Sivas	1,197	361
Adana	489	291
Maraş, Antep	417	169
Kastamonu, Bolu	1,109	252
Trabzon, Canik	1,265	374
Dıyarbekir, Mamuretulaziz,		
Urfa	1,036	413
Van, Bitlis	693	184
Erzurum	759	194

Source: Eldem, 1970: 86–7.

all the agricultural tithes in the Empire. The available data regarding actual production are very similar to those suggested by the tithe data. Agricultural output statistics for 1913 suggest that the Anatolian provinces contained 55 per cent and the European provinces held 24 per cent of the total estimated value of Ottoman agricultural production (ibid.: 845–7).

The contribution of the eastern Anatolia region to the Ottoman agricultural tax revenues in 1910/11,[28] just before the Balkan War, had been around 8.5 per cent, and the population of this domain at the time had constituted just under 9 per cent of the Ottoman population (Eldem, 1970: 86–7). When the agricultural tax revenues of the eastern Anatolia region are compared with the other Anatolian areas, the relative importance of the tax revenue contributions of this region witnesses a decline. In the face of forming the second most populated area of Anatolia, eastern Anatolia had only been the fourth biggest contributor of the agricultural tax revenues in 1910 (see Table 3.9).

[28] The value of agricultural tax revenues for 1910/11 is based on the figures attained from the statistics of the Ottoman Treasury Department or *Maliye Nezareti Ihsaiyat Mecmualari* for the years 1909–10, 1910–11 and 1911–12, which are derived directly from Eldem (1970).

Table 3.10 *Population and agricultural production measured by tax revenues of the different regions of Anatolia, 1910/11 and 1913/14*

	Population (thousands)		Revenue (million *kuruş*)	
Areas/Regions[29]	1910/11	1913/14	1910/11	1913/14
Istanbul	1,134	1,238	60	66
Marmara	2,128	2,204	1,068	1,188
Aegean Coast	1,703	1,761	806	942
Central Anatolia	3,611	3,636	1,330	1,749
Mediterranean Region	906	937	460	487
The Eastern Black Sea Coast	2,374	2,410	626	688
Eastern Anatolia	2,488	2,574	791	878

Source: Eldem, 1970: 81.

Similar results also arise when the agricultural revenues of the year 1913/14 are comparatively analysed, as is demonstrated with the figures tabulated in Table 3.10.

Overall, the details outlined previously elucidate the limitations and drawbacks of imputing agricultural productivity levels and land tenure in Ottoman Kurdistan to the 'unbroken autonomy' of the Kurdish notables. This prevailing and linear explanation does not fully account for the implications of the following pivotal political events on the agricultural output and the forms of landownership in Ottoman Kurdistan during the nineteenth and early twentieth centuries: (i) the suppression of the Ottoman Kurdish polities; (ii) the confiscation of land from the Kurdish notables; and (iii) the policies of the central state during the Hamidian era. Contrary to the commonly advocated correlation between the dominance of the Kurdish notables over land and agricultural unproductivity in Ottoman Kurdistan, the available data from the nineteenth century suggest that agricultural productivity in Kurdistan had begun to decline with the demise of the Kurdish emirates and expropriation by the Ottoman state of land owned by the Kurdish notables.

[29] The areas/regions are defined according to the geographical distinctions employed by Eldem (1970): **Central Anatolia** (Ankara, Konya, Sivas), **Eastern Anatolia** (Erzurum, Mamuretülaziz, Diyarbakir, Urfa, Van, Bitlis), **Istanbul** (Istanbul and Çatalca), **Aegean Coast** (Aydın (İzmir), **Mediterranean Region** (Adana, Hatay, Maraş, Antep), **Marmara** (Izmit, Biga, Hüdavendigar), **Eastern Black Sea Coast** (Trabzon, Kastamonu, Bolu).

Despite this deterioration, the recorded data from the early twentieth century on agricultural output levels of certain parts of Ottoman Kurdistan – i.e. Diyarbekir, Mamuretülaziz and Urfa – indicate that the agricultural output levels had been akin to provinces in the central Anatolian and the eastern Black Sea coast regions: Sivas, Kastamonu, Bolu, Trabzon and Ankara (see Table 3.9). A reasonable explanatory factor for this development in the early twentieth century is that the aggrandisement of the politically receptive Kurdish notables during the Hamidian era enhanced agricultural productivity in these domains by dint of ownership of large estates and acceleration of the exploitation of the dependant peasantry.

3.4 Transportation

As outlined in Chapter 1, the academic literature on the economic and social history of ESA, alongside the 'unbroken autonomy' of the Kurdish notables, frequently identifies the absence of railroads and the expensive forms of transportation in these regions as playing a determinate role in the underdevelopment in these areas. In other words, the transportation barriers are hypothesised to have 'secluded' ESA regions from the rest of the Ottoman Empire and the European markets throughout the nineteenth century and thereby delayed the destruction of the self-sufficient nature of the rural economies, the commercialisation of agriculture and the rise of demand for imported manufacture.

Nearly all of the scholarships on this region share the following interconnected claims made by Pamuk regarding transportation in eastern Anatolia:

> Because of the absence of railroads until the early 1910s, agricultural produce of this region [Eastern Anatolia] could not be directed towards long-distance markets. ... In general, barriers posed by transportation costs isolated Eastern Anatolia from the rest of the Empire and the European markets throughout the [nineteenth] century. ... A limited amount of mohair constituted the major export commodity of the region during this period. ([1987] 2010: 97)[30]

The list of prices and profits pertaining to the wheat trade at Diyarbekir, Urfa and Aleppo, summarised by the British consul in Kurdistan in 1866, is illustrative of the high prices of transportation Pamuk referred to:

[30] Also cited in Sönmez ([1990] 1992: 79, 105).

Diyarbekir:	
One Quarter of Wheat at Erzurum	13s.6d.
Expenses to Diyarbekir, 150 miles off	£1.4s.
Selling Price at Diyarbekir	£2
Profit	2s.6d.
Urfa:	
One Quarter of Wheat at Erzurum	13s.6d.
Expenses to Urfa, 258 miles off	£1.16s.
Selling Price at Urfa	£3.12s.8d.
Profit	£1.3s.2d.
Aleppo:	
One Quarter of Wheat at Erzurum	13s.6d.
Expenses to Aleppo, 120 miles off	£2.14s.
Selling Price at Aleppo	£4.1s.9⅔d.
Profit 14s.	3⅔d.

Source: A&P, 1867, 'Commercial Report for Kurdistan', 3938, LXVIII, p. 590.

However, expensive transportation costs were burdensome in almost all regions of the Empire throughout the nineteenth and early twentieth centuries, to the extent that high carriage fees had made it unprofitable to carry bulk goods like grain over anywhere but the shortest distances by land within the Empire. The effects of high transport costs in the nineteenth century were so severe that the British consul general in Istanbul, Consul Alison, thought it 'unbalance[d] Turkey's trade, since most of its imports were light and valuable while its exports were bulky and cheap, and were also severely restricting the zone in which its profitable to grow exports crops' (Issawi, 1980: 179). Strikingly, 'the cost of transporting one tonne of wheat from central Anatolia to Istanbul in 1924 was $8.8 whereas it was only $5 from New York to Istanbul; and, hence, it seemed more rational to feed the population of Istanbul from Iowa rather than Ankara and Konya and let the peasant vegetate in subsistence farming' (Boratav, 1981: 165). These data explain to a certain extent why '75 per cent of all crops grown' in Ottoman lands throughout the period 1800–1914 are estimated to have remained within the Empire (Quataert, 1994: 834).

Railroads

The issue of high transportation costs in the Ottoman Empire in the nineteenth century is attributable to the Empire arriving comparatively late to the railroad age. Up until 1859, not a single track was laid in any soil or area of the Empire. The first railway in the Ottoman Empire was built in 1859–60, between Chernavoda and Constanza, and was followed in 1863–8 by the Varna–Rustchuk line. The Oriental Railway Company, found by Baron Hirsch in 1878, built the main European lines. This company built 1,312 kilometres (km) of railway lines, and by 1888 Istanbul was connected to Vienna. Other major railroad lines were the Salonica–Constantinople Junction Railway and the Salonica–Monastir Railway, both of which were completed at the turn of the twentieth century.

As can be inferred from these railway projects, the European provinces took the lead and by contrast, the Anatolian provinces in 1890 contained only 900 km of railroads whilst the Arab provinces contained none at all. In the second half of the nineteenth century, mainly after 1890, Ottoman territories acquired 7,500 km of track (Quataert, 1994: 804). The increase in Ottoman rail-laying activities in a sense coincided with that in many other countries, but was significantly more modest in scale. For instance, railway lines in the Habsburg Empire extended 'to nearly 23,000 km by 1913, over three times the Ottoman level', and former Ottoman territories in the Balkans, namely, the independent states of Rumania, Bulgaria, Serbia and Greece, 'together built about 8,000 km of track, or slightly more than in the empire itself' (ibid.: 805). Some scholars have construed the relatively slow pace of rail-laying activities in the Empire during 1800–1914 as 'a measure of [the] low degree of development of the Ottoman Empire; in 1914, its 1,900, 000 square kilometers had only 5,991 kilometers of railways' (Issawi, 1980: 147).

The exact share of all the goods the Ottoman railways transported during the nineteenth and early twentieth centuries cannot be accurately deliberated since animal-back traffic cannot be calculated with any certainty because of the scant research and records left behind by the transporters (Quataert, 1994: 812, 821). Nevertheless, what follows are estimate figures for goods and passengers transported on various Ottoman railways during 1891–1910, which have been prepared by Quataert (1994) based on the information Hecker provided in 1914. As Tables 3.11–3.12 indicate, only after the turn of the century did transportation of goods and people via Ottoman railways gain prominence, which is instructive of the limitations of explaining the 'seclusion' of the predominantly Kurdish provinces in ESA regions throughout the nineteenth century on the absence of the railroads.

Table 3.11 *Goods transported on various Ottoman railways, 1891–1910 (thousand tons)*

Line	1891	1895	1900	1910
Ankara–Konya	–	118	357	585
Izmir–Konya	–	–	245	327
Aydın	–	–	–	342
Mersin–Adana	–	–	–	130
Damascus–Hama	–	–	–	309
Hejaz	–	–	–	66
Baghdad	–	–	–	28

Source: Quataert, 1994: 813.

Table 3.12 *Passengers transported on various Ottoman railways, 1891–1910 (millions)*

Line	1891	1895	1900	1910
Ankara–Konya	0.7	1.0	1.2	2.7
Izmir–Konya	–	1.5	1.7	2.4
Aydın	–	–	–	1.9
Mersin–Adana	–	–	–	0.3
Damascus–Hama	–	–	0.2	0.7
Hejaz	–	–	–	0.2
Baghdad	–	–	–	0.01

Source: Quataert, 1994: 813.

Overland Transport System

During 1800–1910, the overland transport system – the roads, highways, wagons and caravans – was used for 'one-half of all goods shipped overland in Anatolia and Syria' (Quataert, 1994: 818). This was despite the shortcomings of the overland transport system owing to the poor quality and maintenance of the roads, which was largely due to the Ottoman central state allocating transportation too few resources throughout the nineteenth century (Issawi, 1980: 150; Owen, 1981: 246). In 1858, Consul Holmes described the poor maintenance of the Ottoman roads and its repercussions on daily life and commerce within the Empire: 'One of the greatest drawbacks to the advancement of civilisation and commerce in Turkey, is the want of properly constructed roads; and the

Pashalic of Diabekir [Diyarbekir] is in no better condition in this respect, than the rest of the empire.'[31]

In the second half of the nineteenth century, the Ottoman state took extreme action with the hope of improving the poor quality of the roads in the Empire. In 1865, a law was enacted to oblige all males aged sixteen to sixty-five to work four days a year on local roads or pay a substitute tax; however, even such compulsory measures had minimal effect on improving the roads in the Empire and, as a result, in 1910, it was replaced by mandatory cash payments (Eldem, 1970: 150; Issawi, 1980: 150). A British consular report in 1878 summarises the severe conditions of the highways in the Empire, even after the enactment of this piece of legislation, by stating that the Beirut–Damascus road was the 'only road in the whole of the Turkish Empire which is kept in good order' (Issawi, 1980: 150). Furthermore, the overland transport system in Ottoman lands in the early years of the twentieth century does not appear to have improved. In 1904, the entire Ottoman Empire had only 24,000 km of roads: 'three-quarters of these were within the borders of modern Turkey, poor in quality and badly maintained' (Quataert, 1994: 818).

Animal-back transport was more common than wheeled transport in most areas because Ottoman roads were suitable only for animal-back transport; shipment by wagon often damaged the transported goods. Hence, caravans provided most of the overland and non-mechanised links within and between the different regions of the Empire (Issawi, 1980: 146; Quataert, 1994: 819). Alongside the shorter and more frequent routes of Alexandretta–Diyarbekir and Diyarbekir–Erzurum (Quataert, 1994: 818) there also existed long caravan routes, with *hans*[32] built at suitable intervals. The mains ones were (Issawi, 1980: 146):

1. the Trabzon-Erzurum-Beyazıt route leading to Tabrız (Iran);
2. the Samsum-Amasya-Zile-Tokat route to Sivas, at this point it bifurcated, one route passing via Kayseri and Cilician gates to Tarsus and the other to Deliklitaş, Harput and Diyarbekir, and thereafter to either Mosul, via Mardin, or Aleppo, through Urfa;
3. the Izmir-Bolu-Tosya route, touching the second route at Amasya;
4. the Bursa-Akşehir-Konya-Tarsus route leading to Syria.

The actual volume of goods handled by caravans, which is difficult to measure, appears to be very substantial. As described by Quataert

[31] A&P, 1857, 2285, XXXVIII, pp. 184–5.
[32] *Han*: housing for merchant entrepôts and craftsmen's shops, usually grounded around a courtyard and accessible by a single gate (Faroqhi, 1984: 343).

(1994: 817–19), in 1812, horses carried most of the goods from Salonica north towards the German lands and some 20,000 animals were used. In the mid-nineteenth century, caravans from Baghdad to Damascus were carrying Iraqi, Persian and Indian goods and in the reverse direction, Damascus sent local textiles as well as cloths from England and Germany. During the 1860s, the Tabriz-Erzurum-Trabzon caravans annually transported as much as 12,000 tons, requiring 48,000 pack animals. Moreover, in answer to a questionnaire of 1863, the British consul in Salonica stated that horses and mules transported most produce and that the ox-drawn carts had been used in the plains. Similarly, the consuls in Izmir and Trabzon reported that camels carried the majority of transit trade, while horses and mules were used only for transporting lightweight produce to the cities (Issawi, 1980: 177).

Sea Transport

Whilst the overland transport system maintained its importance throughout the nineteenth and early twentieth centuries, sea transport, sailing vessels and steamships had been increasing well into the late nineteenth century. In the early years of the nineteenth century, sea transport in the Empire had been very insignificant. For example, around 1800, it is reported that France – which at the time was the most important foreign trading partner of the Ottoman Empire – had annually sent 150 ships, and in many areas of the Empire sea traffic is reported to have been light (Quataert, 1994: 799). However, after the entrance of steamships into Ottoman waters in the 1820s, the volume of shipping had experienced a considerable rise (Table 3.13).

The introduction of steam implicated a dramatic increase in the size of vessels. Ships calling at Trabzon averaged an eightfold rise in size

Table 3.13 *Shipping tonnage entering main Ottoman ports, 1830–1913 (thousand tons)*

Port	1830	1860	1890	1913
Basra	10	–	100	400
Beirut	40	400	600	1,700
Istanbul	–	–	800	4,000
Izmir	100	600	1,600	2,200
Trabzon	15	120	500	–

Source: Quataert, 1994: 801.

between 1830 and 1888, and steamships calling at Istanbul in the 1830s ranged between 130 and 530 tons, but in the late nineteenth century averaged more than 1,250 tons (ibid.: 800). Steamship travel on the Euphrates and Tigris, which was navigable from Diyarbekir down to Mosul, Baghdad and the Persian Gulf, had begun in the late 1830s. The 215-mile journey from Diyarbekir to Mosul and Baghdad cost half as much as the cheapest land transport. Thus, steam power impacted travel and commerce in the interior regions of the Tigris–Euphrates basin (Quataert, 2000: 118).

Transportation in Ottoman Kurdistan

The available official data regarding custom duties remittances collected by the Diyarbekir *gümrük*[33] (customs house) indicate that up until the early 1830s the trade routes located in Ottoman Kurdistan were frequently used for the movement of goods (Table 3.14). Information regarding customs revenues of Diyarbekir has seen daylight as a result

Table 3.14 *Customs revenues collected by the Diyarbekir* Voyvodalığı, *1797–1834*

Years	Value (*kuruş*)
1797–8[34]	97,490
1804–5[35]	86,505
1805–6[36]	72,248.5
1822–3[37]	86,388
1824–5[38]	93,847
1833–4[39]	36,199

[33] After 1760–1, the central authorities handed over the management of the *gümrük* (customs house) of Diyarbekir to the Diyarbekir *Voyvodalığı*. The revenues of the Diyarbekir *gümrük* during the 1820s accounted for 43.76 per cent of all the incomes of the Diyarbekir *Voyvodalığı*, and up until the 1830s, it was by far the richest source of income of the *Voyvodalı*k of this province (Yılmazçelik, 1995: 285, 314–15).

[34] Başbakanlık Arşivi, Bab-ı Defteri Baş Muhasebesi, No: 6538 in Yılmazçelik (1995: 286).

[35] Başbakanlık Arşivi, Bab-ı Defter-i Baş Muhasebesi Diyarbakır Hazinesi, No: 16802 (1804–5/1805–6) pp. 1–10 in Yılmazçelik (1995: 286).

[36] Ibid.

[37] Diyarbakir Müzesi, Diyarbakır Şer'iyye Sicilleri, No: 351, pp. 7–8 (1822–3) in Yılmazçelik (1995: 286).

[38] Başbakanlık Arşivi, Kamil Kepeci No: 5132, pp. 1–150 (1824–5) in Yılmazçelik (1995: 286).

[39] Diyarbakir Müzesi, Diyarbakır Şer'iyye Sicilleri, No: 603, p. 15 (1833–4) in Yılmazçelik (1995: 286).

of the extensive archival work on the tax-farm records of the provincial fiscal bureau, or Diyarbekir *Voyvodalığı*, by Yılmazçelik (1995).

It is worth noting here that the jurisdictional range of the province of Diyarbekir during 1780–1845 had been such that it encompassed the vast majority of the Kurdish lands incorporated into the Ottoman Empire after 1514 (see Map 6). In the early decades of the nineteenth century, the province of Diyarbekir had in its jurisdictional boundaries vast areas of land, extending from Malatya to Mosul. During 1847–67, as mentioned earlier, Diyarbekir was renamed *Kürdistan Eyaleti* and it comprised parts of the provinces of Bitlis and Van. At the end of the nineteenth century, the province remained impressive in size, as it embodied the following provinces in present-day Turkey: Batman, Elazığ, Mardin, Siirt, Şanlıurfa and Şırnak. Thus, up until the twentieth century, the bulk of the aforementioned overland trade routes situated in Ottoman Kurdistan was located in Diyarbekir's provincial boundaries, which explains the importance of the customs revenue records kept by the *voyvodas* of this province for attaining an understanding of the trade to and from Ottoman Kurdistan.

The data consulted by this thesis also accentuate the following features of Diyarbekir, which is crucial to highlight in any investigation on transportation in this province:

(i) It was a meeting point for caravans from Samsun, Aleppo, Baghdad and Erzurum.[40]

(ii) It was a gateway for merchants entering the Empire from Iran and Dagestan heading towards Istanbul, Aleppo and Baghdad (Yılmazçelik, 1995: 314).

By virtue of these attributes, the British consul in Kurdistan described Diyarbekir as 'nearly equidistant west and east between the capital and Busreh, north and south between Erzeroom and Aleppo – [Diyarbekir] is admirably calculated for a great commercial central depôt.'[41] Throughout the nineteenth century, merchants from a wide range of other locations – Van, Manastır, Gümüşhane, Rakka – very frequently visited and stayed in the different *hans* of Diyarbekir (Yılmazçelik, 1995: 314–15). The Ottoman *hans*[42] provide a valuable source of information for transportation of goods and commerce – in particular for Anatolian cities that were linked by overland trade routes – because starting with the sixteenth century in the big *hans* of any of the urban business centres,

[40] FO 195/799, *Trade and Agriculture of Kurdistan for 1863*, enclosed in Taylor at Diarbekir, 13 July 1864.

[41] A&P, 1873, 'Commercial Report for Diyarbekir', C.824, LXVII, p. 682.

[42] For a detailed analysis regarding *hans*, see Faroqhi, 1984: 1–104, and for a detailed description of the *hans* in the province of Diyarbekir, see Yılmazçelik (1995: 23–74).

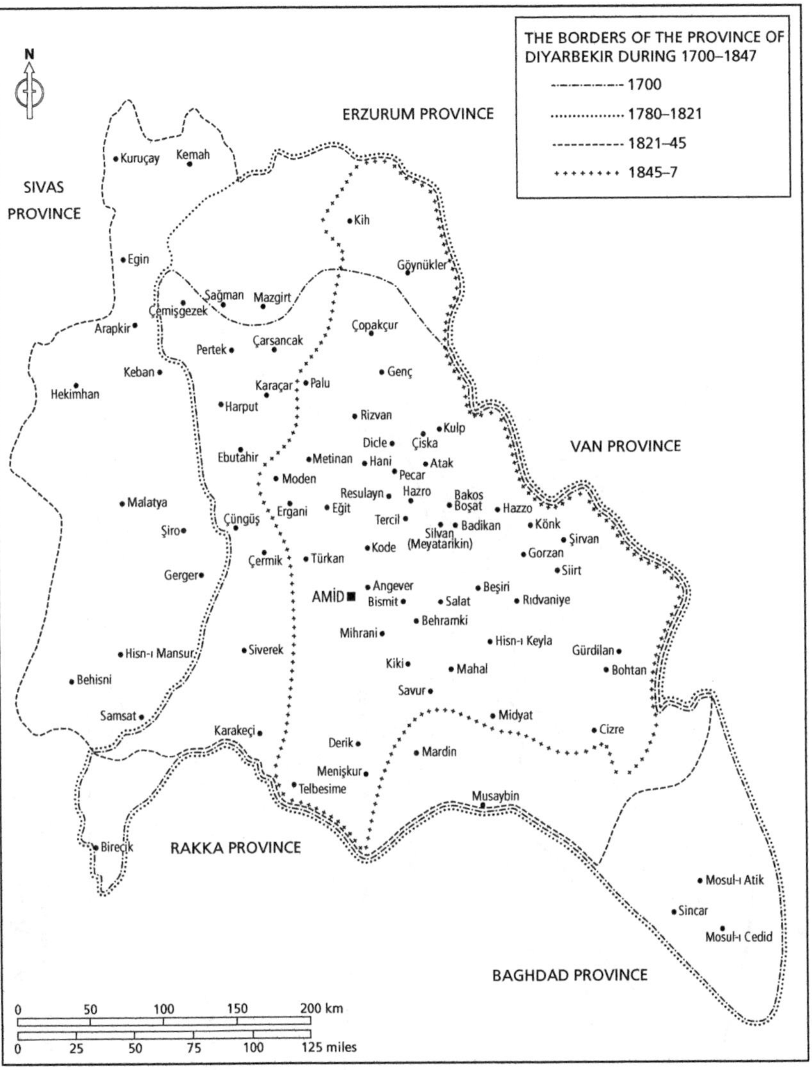

Map 6 The jurisdictional boundaries of the province of Diyarbekir, 1700–1847
Source: Based on Yılmazçelik, 1995: Appendix II.

merchants conducted negotiations that led to the formation of caravans (Faroqhi, 1984: 51–3).

Because of being located on an important crossing point for international and domestic trade, Diyarbekir – alongside, Aleppo, Bursa,

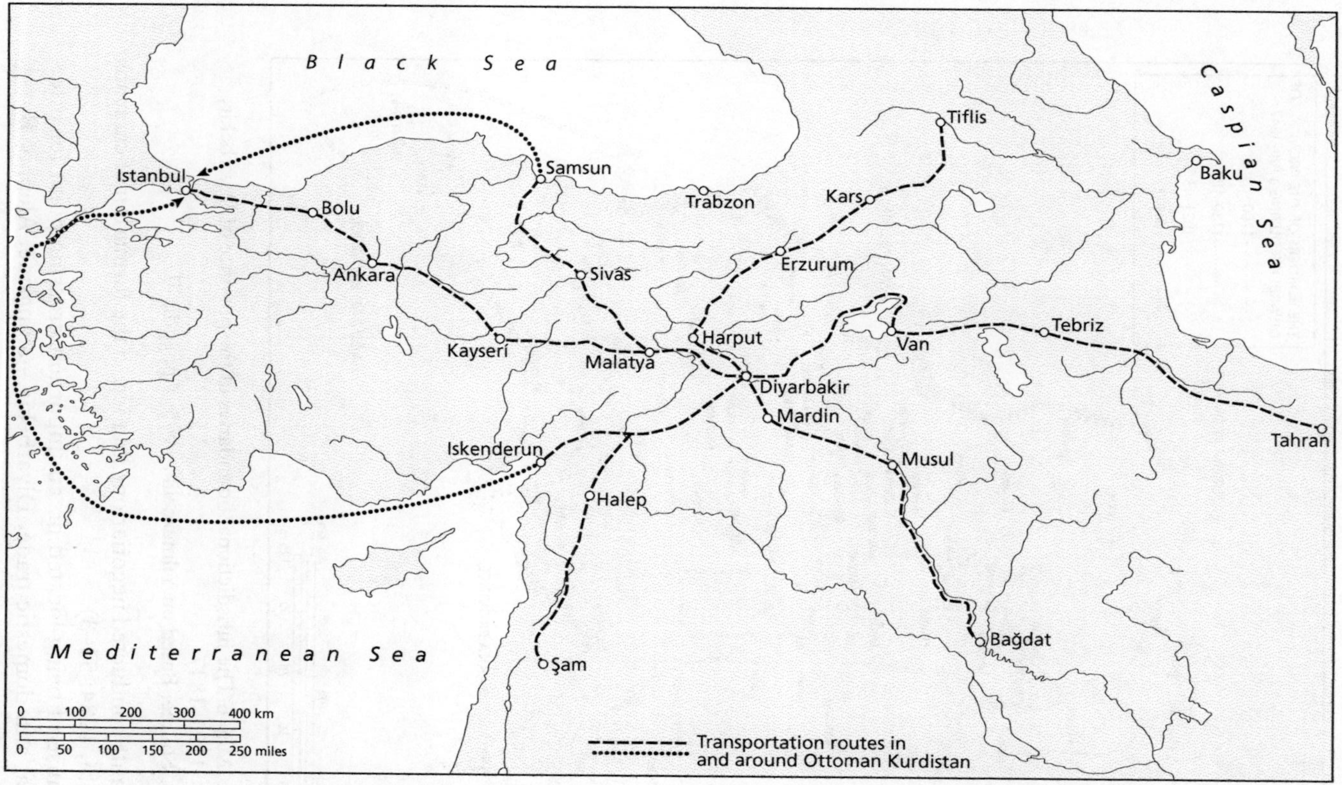

Map 7 Transportation routes in Ottoman Kurdistan
Source: Based on Yılmazçelik, 1995: Appendix I/A.

Erzurum and Tokat – was one of the few provinces that had tax farms incorporating customs and other transportation-related duties. Customs duties or *resm-i gümrük* were levied on all goods transported to and from Diyarbekir in accordance with the varying tariffs laid in the *Customs Tariff Book* (*Gümrük Tarife Defterleri*) (Yılmazçelik, 1995: 288).

When the customs revenues in 1833–4 are studied in conjunction with those of the preceding three decades (see Table 3.13), it becomes apparent that there had been a remarkable fall in the early years of the 1830s. The extensive historical details provided regarding Ottoman Kurdistan in the report from the British Consular District of Kurdistan in 1863, which hitherto has been overlooked by the existing scholarships on Ottoman Kurdistan, indicate that the sizeable reduction in the customs revenues in 1833–4 was a corollary of the military campaigns of Rashid Pasha against the Kurdish emirates:

> Though repeatedly taken and plundered; by Persians, Arabs, Saljooks [Seljuks], Tatars, Soofees [Sufis], and Turks it [Diyarbekir] always seems to have soon regained its riches and prosperity as history hardly records one of its many sieges and captures, without at the same time detailing the rich booty that fell a prey to the enemy. **In more modern times its commercial activity does not seem to have sensibly diminished; and I cannot trace its real decline any further back than thirty years ago, immediately subsequent to Rasheed Pasha's successful campaign against the Kurds in these regions. But from that time, as the merchants inform me, marked falling off took place and each succeeding year has been more unprofitable than the last.**[43]

Other foreign officials based in Ottoman Kurdistan during the nineteenth century have made similar observations in relation to the negative repercussions of the military activities of the Ottoman state in this region. In 1835, a few years after Rasheed Pasha's campaign commenced, British Consul James Brant reports two destructive results of the military assaults in Diyarbekir. The first of these relate to the demographic demolition: the number of houses found in Diyarbekir had reduced from '40,000' to '8,000', and the second devastation pertains to the 'severe damage' to the trade of Diyarbekir (Brant, 1836: 209–10). Correspondingly, German Field Marshall Helmuth Carl Bernhard von Moltke (1800–91), who participated in the Ottoman army in Ottoman Kurdistan under Hafiz Pasha, makes parallel observations vis-à-vis the ramifications of the military

[43] FO 195/799, *Trade and Agriculture of Kurdistan for 1863*, enclosed in Taylor at Diarbekir, 13 July 1864. Emphasis mine.

campaigns to social and economic life in Hasankeyf and Cizre (Moltke, 1968: 251). The information relayed earlier not only oppugns the validity of the postulate that the predominantly Kurdish regions of ESA was secluded from the local and foreign trade throughout the nineteenth century, but it also indicates that the military operations of the Ottoman state after the early 1830s in Ottoman Kurdistan created long-term constraints for the commerce of this Ottoman borderland.

3.5 Commerce

The commerce of Ottoman Kurdistan in the nineteenth and early twentieth centuries is an area awaiting systematic examination. The nominal documented data presently available on the commerce of this region, and the readily accepted truism that ESA regions had throughout the nineteenth and early twentieth centuries been 'secluded' from the rest of the Empire and the European markets, are two long-standing impediments to the actuation of this intricate task. While the currently existing quantitative evidence on the commerce of Ottoman Kurdistan in no way enables a complete understanding or analysis of the nature and scale of the commercial activities in this domain, it nevertheless does equip us with valid grounds to doubt the prevailing static assessments regarding the trade of this region.

The data surveyed by this investigation suggest that the trade of Ottoman Kurdistan during the nineteenth and early twentieth centuries had undergone decline, recovery and growth. These different trends in the trade of this frontier region appear to be very closely tied to political factors that surfaced in the years 1800–1914. Prior to analysing the commercial activities in Ottoman Kurdistan, it is apt to offer a terse description of the nature and limitations of the Ottoman trade statistics.

Limitations and Deficiencies of Ottoman Trade Statistics

As the consular reports penned by British diplomats frequently remind us, accurate and regular Ottoman statistics regarding the trade of Ottoman Kurdistan during the nineteenth century were extremely uncommon. In 1857, Consul Holmes, in one of the initial consular reports sent from the British consulate in Kurdistan, summarised the non-existence of clear-cut official trade data in the first half of the century:

I found it utterly impossible to obtain any satisfactory details of imports and exports [of Diyarbekir], for the simple reason that no correct account of them exists. The Custom House is the only place where any sort of account is pretended to be kept, but as regards to exports, a considerable amount of the produce is sent from the province, without passing through the town, direct to Aleppo, where it pays duty, and as with regard to imports, no note is taken of that which arrives having already paid duty at Aleppo, little or nothing is known, event at the Custom House, as to the real amount of the trade of this place.[44]

Correspondingly, the consul in Erzurum, Sir Robert Alexander Osborn Dalyell (1821–86), just before leaving his post in the mid-1860s, made the following informative remarks regarding commercial bookkeeping:

Up to the period at which I left Erzeroom [Erzurum] it was impossible to get definite commercial information, no regular books being kept at the custom-house; but in consequence of late alterations of [the] system in the administration of the custom-houses of the Empire, it is now to a certain degree possible.[45]

All of these lacunae regarding Ottoman trade records validate the following observation conveyed in 1870 by Consul Taylor, in a consular report titled the *Conditions of the Industrial Classes in the Consular District of Kurdistan*: 'In this country, statistics … and official returns are so negligently and loosely compiled as to render them perfectly useless for the purpose of judging of, or guiding the wealth of the nation.'[46]

Deriving from the previous assessment of Consul Taylor, one can conclude that the aforementioned limitations were not unique to trade statistics of Ottoman Kurdistan. As the findings of a range of scholarly studies (Eldem, 1970; Pamuk, [1987] 2010; Quataert, 1994) that examined the existing Ottoman official statistics illustrate, Ottoman trade statistics for the nineteenth century had been minimal and deficient. For the purposes of this study, it is apposite to summarise the findings of these pivotal studies, since they elucidate the deficient nature of the official Ottoman trade statistics.

No information is presently available from Ottoman sources regarding Ottoman foreign trade before 1878, with the exception of estimated customs revenues for each year, which are available from the budgets that were first prepared in the 1860s. The efficacy and veracity of the official Ottoman trade statistics for the years after 1878 are questionable,

[44] A&P, 1857, 2285, XXXVIII, pp. 184–5. [45] A&P, 1866, 3582, LXIX, p. 433.
[46] A&P, 1871, C.414, LXVIII, p. 793.

though, due to the following deficiencies identified by Pamuk ([1987] 2010: 153–4). Official Ottoman trade statistics until 1907 provided figures only for general trade; therefore, transit trade was not distinctively covered. The distinction between general and special trade is vital, argues Pamuk, since the transit trade through the Empire, which mostly consisted of European–Persian trade, was far from insignificant, particularly in the late 1870s and 1880s. The lack of distinction between special and general trade between 1978 and 1907 engendered an upward bias of the order of 3 per cent to 5 per cent for imports and exports of the Ottoman Empire.

The other deficiency of the Ottoman trade statistics after 1878 stems from the incomplete coverage of traded goods. Imports of arms and ammunition, agricultural and industrial machinery and all materials for railways and factory construction were not recorded in the official Ottoman statistics. Thus, Pamuk ascertains that the exclusion of these items introduces a significant amount of downward bias to the Ottoman imports for some years. Last, the existent official Ottoman trade data for the years after 1878 present grave problems for establishing the country of distribution of Ottoman trade. Until 1910, the destination/country of origin definition employed in the Ottoman statistics specified the country with which trade was conducted as that from which goods were directly received to or to which goods were directly sent. Therefore, whenever Ottoman trade with a country was carried out through ports of the third countries, it was not possible to determine the magnitude of Ottoman trade with that country on the basis of Ottoman statistics.

In addition, Eldem rightly points out that the varying political and administrative statuses or structures of the different provinces in the Empire, along with the inexperience of the state officials responsible for collating the statistical data, made it very difficult to generate uniform sets of statistical data for the whole of the Ottoman Empire (1970: 13). These two issues do also render a comparative study of the trade of Ottoman Kurdistan with other Ottoman regions for the most part of the nineteenth century a near-impossible task. Furthermore, as exemplified with the constantly changing borders of Diyarbekir delineated in Map 6, the administrative boundaries of ESA Ottoman provinces – i.e. Diyarbekir, Erzurum, Harput and Van – had been in a state of flux throughout the nineteenth century, making it highly difficult to track and undertake a longitudinal study of the trade of localities situated in Ottoman Kurdistan.

Owing to the aforementioned drawbacks of the official Ottoman trade statistics, the ensuing assessment of the trade of Ottoman Kurdistan will mainly be based on the trade data accumulated from the British consular reports for this region penned in the second half of the nineteenth and the early twentieth centuries. These reports contain invaluable information regarding the local trade of the two predominantly Kurdish provinces in ESA, Diyarbekir and Erzurum. Where available, this book will transmit data concerning other provinces in these regions – i.e. Van, Bitlis and Hakkari. Up until the 1880s, the trade figures for these three areas were either recorded under the trade data of the provinces of Erzurum and Diyarbekir or not recorded at all.

In this section, a particular emphasis will be given to the trade reports drafted by Consul Taylor who, unlike his predecessor and successors, had the unique opportunity to study comparatively the customs house archives of the provinces in ESA with those of the bordering provinces, such as Aleppo and Baghdad. As a result, he was able to attain a clearer picture of the state of the trade of Kurdistan: 'During my residence I had, under Vizirial orders, ample opportunities for examining the Custom-house archives, that establishment being then not formed but under the control of a paid officer under the Aleppo Nazir or Chief now, which enabled me to obtain a clearer view of local trade, whether native or British, than my predecessors had.'[47]

The General Trends in Ottoman Trade

Prior to analysing the trade of Ottoman Kurdistan, as background to the analysis of the commerce of this region in the nineteenth and early twentieth centuries, based on the formulations or findings of Quataert (1994: 827–30), a brief description of the general trends in Ottoman trade during 1800–1914 will be presented. Until 1820, trade within the Ottoman Empire and with Russia was more important than that with Western and Central Europe.

By the end of the century, Britain, France, Germany, Austria and Italy accounted for more than three-quarters of total Ottoman international trade. Between 1780 and 1830, a period of recovery and then growth had been experienced in international trade; Ottoman–European trade augmented at an annual rate below 1.5 per cent. After this period of recovery, foreign trade grew very swiftly between the early 1840s and the 1870s. Imports and exports each annually increased at compound growth rates of 5.5 per cent, nearly doubling in each successive decade. For example, during the mid-1870s, exports were about 6 per cent to 8 per cent of

[47] A&P, 1873, C.824, LXVII, p. 683.

Table 3.15 *Ottoman foreign trade, 1830–1913 (annual average, in millions of pounds sterling)*

Period	f.o.b. exports	c.i.f. imports
1830s	4.2	5.1
1840s	6.0	6.9
1850s	9.8	12.3
1860s	15.4	18.3
1870s	18.6	20.8
1880s	15.5	16.0
1890s	17.7	18.6
1900s	23.0	26.0
1910–13	27.3	38.6

Source: Pamuk, 2010 [1987]: 149.

estimated Ottoman gross national product (GNP), about double the proportion of the 1840s.

Stagnation followed boom in the 1870s as fiscal crisis and government bankruptcy coupled with the famine and the Russo–Turkish War had hampered international trade. Between the late 1870s and 1890s, imports and exports had increased at annual rates of 2.6 per cent or, in other words, half the rate of the three previous decades.

However, within a decade after the international depression had ended (1906–7), Ottoman exports are reported to have risen by 3.4 per cent as imports rose by 4.8 per cent. Subsequently, even in the face of major territorial losses suffered in the Balkans Wars, exports in 1913 equalled and imports surpassed, by 2.5 per cent, the level of 1907. In 1914, perhaps one-quarter of total agricultural production was exported; exports overall formed nearly 14 per cent of the gross national product and the ratio of imports to GNP was around 18 per cent. Thus, despite the relatively important and substantial changes in international trade in the nineteenth century domestic commerce continued to majorly surpass foreign trade and foreign trade remained a comparatively minor factor in Ottoman economic life.

Until c.1870s, textiles, in particular cotton, constituted the main form of imports to the Empire, but after the 1870s the relative share of the foodstuff imports gradually increased. By the end of the nineteenth century, wheat, flour, rice, sugar, coffee and tea formed 'about one-third' of all imports (ibid.: 832). Yet, Ottoman agricultural products, such as cereals and animal products, constituted the bulk of the exported articles, usually around '90 per cent' (ibid.). After the 1860s, however, the nature of the exported items had diversified in virtue of variations of foreign demands from Ottoman lands. In the second half of the nineteenth century, significant quantities of opium, raw silk, raisins, wool, cotton, tobacco, hides and manufactured carpets, as well as raw silk were exported.

Commerce of Ottoman Kurdistan

The only currently available regularly recorded data of the commercial activities in Ottoman Kurdistan for the first half of the nineteenth century is the tax-farm accounts of the provincial fiscal bureau, or *voyvodalık*, of Diyarbekir. For reasons outlined in the section on transportation in Ottoman Kurdistan, the records of Diyarbekir *Voyvodalık* is an important lens though which we are able to detect the commercial trends in Ottoman Kurdistan.

As alluded to by Faroqhi, in the absence of regular and accurate data 'for figures concerning the volume of urban economic activities and particularly of trade, our best and usually only guide consists of tax-farming accounts' (1984: 16). However, as it can be concluded from the information provided in the introductory pages of this Chapter, after 1839, due to the centralist reforms in the Tanzimat era, the tax-farm system had been transformed. Therefore, the availability and utility of the tax-farms accounts after the third decade of the nineteenth century is moot, which is why the study will only make use of tax-farm records up until the mid-1830s.

As outlined in the preceding section, the year in which Rashid Pasha's military venture in Ottoman Kurdistan (1833–34) commenced was identified by the contemporaries as the point at which the decades-long decline – which contemporary observers believed lasted until the 1860s[48] – in the commercial activities in this region began. This observation is supported by the data attained from the records of the fiscal bureau of the paradigmatic Kurdish province of Diyarbekir summarised earlier. One of the first things we realise when we look at the figures tabulated in Table 3.16 is the vast decrease during the 1830s in the second most important source of revenue of the Diyarbekir dye house (*voyvodalık: boyahane*) dues remittances. This drop is redolent of the fact that production of and trade in textiles was sorely affected by the military operations in this province. The other glaring fact is that there is no record of the ground rent (*arsa*) levied from external goods kept in the warehouses of Diyarbekir. According to archival research by Yılmazçelik, this void was

[48] FO 195/799 *Trade and Agriculture of Kurdistan for 1863*, Taylor in Diarbekir, 13 July 1864.

Table 3.16 *Revenues of the Diyarbekir* Voyvodalığı, *1797–1834 (in* kuruş*)*

Years	*Gümrük* (Customs)	*Boyahane* (Dye House Dues)	*Arsa* (Ground Rent)	*İhtisab* (Craftsmen' Dues)	*Damga* (Sales Tax)	Others	Total
1797–1798[49]	97,490	35,000	34,000	8,344	33,550	–	208,384
1804–1805[50]	8,6505	19,726	23,153	10,742	30,078	23,121	193,325
1805–1806[51]	72,248.5	21,946	29,868	12,000	32,519.5	12,067.5	180,798
1822–1823[52]	86,388	31,515	37,697	4,090	8,671	30,000	198,361
1824–1825[53]	93,847	39,872	51,198	9,613	11,854	8,956	214,440
1833–1834[54]	36,199	8,483	–	–	10,297	74,063	129,042

[49] Başbakanlık Arşivi, Bab-ı Defteri Baş Muhasebesi, No: 6538 in Yılmazçelik (1995: 285).
[50] Başbakanlık Arşivi, Bab-ı Defter-i Baş Muhasebesi Diyarbakır Hazinesi, No: 16802 (1804–5/1805–6) pp. 1–10 in Yılmazçelik (1995: 286).
[51] Ibid.
[52] Diyarbakir Müzesi, Diyarbakır Şer'iyye Sicilleri, No: 351, pp. 7–8 (1822–3) in Yılmazçelik (1995: 286).
[53] Başbakanlık Arşivi, Kamil Kepeci No: 5132, pp. 1–150 (1824–5) in Yılmazçelik (1995: 286).
[54] Diyarbakir Müzesi, Diyarbakır Şer'iyye Sicilleri, No: 603, p. 15 (1833–4) in Yılmazçelik (1995: 286).

because after the early 1830s, this form of taxation was conjoined or 'noted under the *Gümrük* [customs revenues]' (1995: 288) by the *voyvoda* personnel. This change in the records reinforces the drastic fall in Diyarbekir's custom and trade revenues immediately after the military activities of the Ottoman state in Kurdistan in the early 1830s. Furthermore, sales taxes (*damga*) intakes, when compared with the figures during 1797–1806, witnessed a severe reduction. The concurrence of these negative fluctuations led the total revenue of the *voyvodalık* to decrease, when compared to the revenues of the selected years in the preceding three decades, by around half in 1833–4. After sixteen years of sporadic war in the different parts of ESA, the Ottoman state had been successful in suppressing the Kurdish emirates and the rebellions in Ottoman Kurdistan, but with tremendous negative repercussions for the economic activities in this region.

The data pertaining to the commercial activities in Ottoman Kurdistan during the second half of the nineteenth century suggest that between the 1860s and the early 1870s, with the arrival of relative security to this domain, the commerce in this region witnessed a gradual revival. In 1871, the British consul in Kurdistan, based on his own previous trade reports and the archival research conducted in the relevant custom houses of the Empire, conveys the following information regarding the principal items of production and trade in the constituent *sancaks* of the consular district of Kurdistan during the late 1850s and early 1870s:

The important [foreign] trade that does actually exist ... is in the hands of the residents native agents at Erzeroom [Erzurum], Diarbeker [Diyarbekir], and Kharput [Harput], whose principals have their head-quarters at Constantinople, Trebizond, or Aleppo ...

Local industries consist:

At Erzeroom [Erzurum sancak], brass, iron, tin ware and swords for home exports

At Van, thick woollen stuffs used by the natives for trousers, cloaks, jackets and leggings

At Bitlis, cotton cloths in lengths and pieces, died red, with madders and plain

At Erzingan [Erzincan], fine bath cloths and Turkish towels of cotton, and stripped nankeens

At Diabeker [Diyarbekir], silk in lengths, silk, and mixed silk and cotton ... cotton piece goods of patters, woollen cloaks and dyed moroccos of colours

At Mardin, dyed moroccos of colours, woollen cloaks, shallees of mohair ... and silver and gold jewellery

At Deh and Eyruh, fine shallees, in different coloured stripes and colours, made of mohair …

All of the above goods are largely exported to the interior provinces of Russia and Constantinople

Local productions are, in the northern districts, rye barley, wheat and some mohair. In all the others the usual kind of grain, beside millet, Indian corn, sesame, castor oil seed, tobacco, hemp, flax and cotton.

At and about Erzeroom: sheep and cattle exported to Syria, Egypt and Constantinople; raw skins and entrails to Europe; jerked meat, soap, tallow and bone ash.

At Van: salt fish from the Lake, alkali, mohair, silk-worm seed from about that town and Hakkaree [Hakkari]. Sheep are largely exported to Syria and Egypt. Pack horses.

At Bitlis: madders, wax, honey (most superior) and walnut oil.

At Saert [Siirt] and Jezireh [Cizre]: mohair, wool, gall-nuts, wax, tallow, madders, scammony (oil made from the 'pistachio terenbinthus'), goat hair, different from the fine mohair, coarse and rough for sackings.

At Deyrsim [Dersim]: galls, valonea, acorn cups, all used in tanning.

At Mardin and Diabeker: wool, silk, gall-nuts, raw skins, cotton, sheep, clarified butter and camels exported to Syria and Kaiserieh [Kayseri]; horses …

At Hini: first quality flour, equal to the best English, though at the half price.

Minerals: silver, copper, lead, tin, iron and orpiment, fine yellow in flakes.[55]

In 1857, Consul Holmes estimates in tons the annual production and exports in the province of Diyarbekir as tabulated in Table 3.17. Although due to the meagre customs house records in Diyarbekir during the 1850s the information given by Consul Holmes is limited, it nonetheless gives us an idea regarding the profile and scale of the exported and produced articles in the province of Diyarbekir in the mid-1850s.

In 1864, in a separate British consular report prepared by Consul Taylor, a distinctively in-depth examination of the trade of the province of Diyarbekir for 1863 – which at the time was the central administrative unit of *Eyalet-i Kürdistan* – is given. According to the seventy-two-page elaborate trade and agriculture dossier, Diyarbekir's general trade in this year – including the transit trade which was worth around £200,000[56] – stood at £532,949. As it can be inferred from the trade figures tabulated in Appendix II, in 1863, the total value of the goods exported to foreign lands and interior (Ottoman) regions – after deducting the items that have been imported and re-exported – was £325,174.

[55] A&P, 1872, C.530, LX, pp. 125–6.
[56] FO 195/799, Taylor at Diarbekir, 13 July 1864.

Table 3.17 *Annual amount of the produce of Diyarbekir Province, 1857 (in tons)*

Articles	Amount	Remarks
Galls	441	Chiefly exported
Wool	441	"
Cotton	404.5	Consumed in local manufactures
Rice	735	Consumed and exported in equal quantities
Madder Roots	184	"
Gum	88	"
Antoof[57]	22	Consumed in the local tanneries
Sesame	250	Consumed and exported in equal quantities
Wax	7	Chiefly exported
Goats-hair	51.5	"
Silk	7	Consumed in local manufactures
Olive Oil	147	Chiefly consumed
Butter	294	Consumed and exported in equal quantities
Tallow	110	"
Tobacco	367.5	Consumed
Leather (pieces or skin)	112	

Source: A&P, 1857, 'Commercial Report for Diarbekir', 2285, XXXVIII, p. 196.

The aggregate value of goods imported from foreign countries and domestic regions totalled £187,224.

Unlike most consular reports for Kurdistan in the nineteenth century, Consul Taylor's gives a comprehensive list of all the imported and exported articles with their sums (see Appendix II). In view of the details transmitted in this report, as well as the trade data provided in separate British consular reports for Diyarbekir referred to later, it appears that the major export product of this province throughout the nineteenth century was not restricted to 'a limited amount of mohair' (Pamuk, [1987] 2010: 97). Alongside mohair, wool, cotton and galls, which from the 1860s onwards had been in demand by the foreign trading partners of the Ottoman Empire, constituted the greater part of Diyarbekir's export trade in the 1860s and the early 1870s.

In 1863, the amount of raw cotton, galls and wool exported had been higher than mohair. Additionally, when the values of wool and galls exported in 1863, tabulated in Appendix II, are analysed in conjunction

[57] A fungus of the gall oak used in tanning.

with those exported in 1860, which are outlined in a separate consular report,[58] it becomes evident that there had been a considerable rise in the export of these two commodities.

The amount of wool exported in Diyarbekir increased from £23,300 in 1860 to £74,999 in 1863. Similarly, the total value of galls exported in Diyarbekir augmented from £8,000 in 1860 to £34,893 in 1863. Exports of mohair, gall and wool from Diyarbekir continued thereafter. Just the amount of these native staple products transported to England had been £50,000 in 1871.[59] In a British consular report on Kurdistan's trade in 1872, the consul in Kurdistan had reported that 'the competitive demand for mohair, raw hides, and galls in Jezireh, Saert, Mardin, and Diarbekir, raised the price of all those articles, and increased the annual aggregate amount hitherto exported to Europe.'[60]

The export destinations of these products implicate the antithesis of the generally held postulation that ESA had been 'isolated' from the rest of the Empire and European markets throughout the nineteenth century. Goods produced in the Diyarbekir province were exported to a wide range of localities, from foreign countries to afar provinces in northern and central Anatolia, as well as all of the bordering provinces. For instance, the foreign exports of cotton, wool, galls and mohair in 1863, which amounted to more than £185,000, constituted nearly half of all the trade of Diyarbekir. In the same year, the manufactures of Diyarbekir sent to northern Turkey and Baghdad comprised the bulk of the interregional or interior exports.

In addition, according to the export data Consul Taylor provided in a subsequent report, a further £32,816 worth of manufactures from Diyarbekir had been exported in 1865–6.[61] All of these figures are illustrative of the industrial capacity and importance of this province for particularly the Ottoman market.

Based on the findings of Quataert in the seminal work *Ottoman Manufacturing in the Age of the Industrial Revolution*, we learn that the use of British yarn in the textile manufacturing industry at the Diyarbekir province had overall 'quadrupled or quintupled between the 1860s and late 1880s and, by [the] mid-1890s, had doubled again' (1993: 69). Contrary to the suggestions of the destruction of

[58] A&P, 1886, Appendix, Part II, 4715, Vol. XXI, p. 364.
[59] A&P, 1873, 824, LXVII, p. 684. [60] A&P, 1873, C.828, LXV, p. 1124.
[61] A&P, 1867, 3938–9, LXVIII, p. 587.

the manufacturing sector in the second half of the nineteenth century (Jafar, 1976; Pamuk, [1987] 2010; Sönmez, [1990] 1992; Burkay, [1992] 2008), Quataert establishes that 'aggregate textile production around Diyarbakir was stable, at c. 200,000 pieces, between the 1860s and 1903' (1993: 70). Accordingly, Quataert argues, 'despite the loss of Diyarbekir's international markets during the eighteenth century ... the Diyarbekir region continued as one of the most important Ottoman textile production centers' in the nineteenth century (ibid.: 66).[62]

The gradual revival witnessed in the trade of Diyarbekir during the 1860s was replicated in the province of Erzurum. The consul in Erzurum, Consul Dalyell, estimates the aggregate value of Erzurum's trade in the years 1862–5 as £615,071.[63] In 1871, according to Consul Taylor's figures, Erzurum province's total value of imports and exports was £515,000.[64] Due to the dominance of subsistence agriculture and animal husbandry in Erzurum, cattle, sheep and goats, alongside native galls, mohair, wax and hides, had constituted the best part of the export trade of this province. Manufactured goods, cotton and silk from Europe and other regions of the Empire dominated the imports to Erzurum.

The available documented data on the trade between Erzurum and England tabulated next, as well as bearing witness to the expansion of trade in Erzurum in the 1860s and early 1870s, do also ascertain one of the important sources of this increase. During this period, the main articles of exports from Erzurum to England had consisted of native produce, such as skins, galls, mohair and dried entrails, whereas imports from England to Erzurum consisted of woollen and cotton yarns, silk threads, grey cloths, sheet iron and tin in sheets, copper and tea.

The gradual revival and progression of commerce in Diyarbekir and Erzurum throughout the 1860s and early 1870s was followed by stagnation and regression in the second half of the 1870s. Alongside the fiscal crisis and government bankruptcy in 1875 and the famine in the 1880s, the Russo-Turkish War (1877–8) and the Sheikh Ubeydullah Revolt (1880), both of which took place in the borders of or in close proximity to Erzurum and Diyarbekir, severely

[62] For an exploration of manufacturing and manufacturers in ESA between ca. 1800 and 1914, see Quataert (1993).
[63] A&P, 1866, 3582, LXIX, pp. 457–9.
[64] A&P, 1872, 637, LVIII, p. 1347.

Table 3.18 *Trade between the province of Erzurum and England, 1863–1871 (in pounds sterling)*

Year	Exports	Imports
1863	8,000	135,000
1865	100,000	176,000
1866	47,500	100,500
1867	40,000	95,000
1868	60,000	120,000
1871	96,000	215,000

Source: A&P 1872 & 1873.[65]

hampered production and trade in these provinces between ca. 1875 and 1890.

In 1886, the acting consul of Kurdistan, George Pollard Devey, described the negative ramifications of the political instabilities in this region for manufacturing and commerce in Kurdistan:

> Some industries have altogether died out, as that of swords and dagger making. The manufactures of cotton, woollen, and silken stuff is much less than in former years. ... There can be no doubt that the death blow to Erzeroum['s] trade and industry was the war of 1877–78, followed by three years of famine, since this period trade has remained at the lowest point.[66]

The British consul at Diyarbekir, Thomas Boyajian, in the same report, transmits the following bleak manifestations:

> During the period from 1880–85, as compared with the preceding 15 years, export trade has, with the exception of opium, diminished. Imports have increased in volume but decreased 30 per cent. in value. ... This town in former years could reckon 1,500 silk and cotton looms, and carried trade with the remotest parts of the empire. ... The value of silk alone manufactured in 1865 was £35,000, that of 1884 £7,500. ... In the absence of trade returns of former years, I am not in a position to state precisely the difference of exports of the period 1880–85 as compared with the 15 previous years, but the following table of one or two of the chief items of export will suffice to prove the statement:

[65] For the years 1863–8: A&P, 1872,110, XLVII, p. 7. For the year 1871: A&P, 1873, C.824, LXVII, p. 684.

[66] A&P, 1886, C. 4715, XXI, p. 795.

	Value 1860	Value 1884
	£	£
Mohair	65,450	14,500
Wool	23,300	14,200
Galls	8,000	1,900
Total	**96,750**	**30,600**

Source: A&P, 1886, C.4715, XXI, p. 796.[67]

Table 3.19 *Imports and exports of Erzurum, 1871–1884 (in pounds sterling)*

Year	Import	Export	Total
1871[68]	300,000	215,000[69]	515,000
1883[70]	356,160	83,560	439,720
1884[71]	268,570	99,070	367,640

Source: A&P 1872, 1884 and 1884–5.

Although the non-existence of trade records for Diyarbekir and Erzurum makes it impossible to estimate the exact nature of the decrease in the export trade, we nevertheless are able to attain an idea of the nature of the deterioration by juxtaposing the trade data from the early 1880s with that of the previous two decades. The trade figures tabulated in Tables 3.19–3.20 are in harmony with the dismal state of the eastern Anatolian economy relayed by the British consuls cited earlier.

The relatively abundant quantitative data[72] after 1890 on Ottoman Kurdistan's trade regularly transmitted in the commercial reports

[67] The table is part of the text cited earlier and ends the quote.

[68] A&P, 1872, C.637, LVIII, p. 1347.

[69] Export figures of only items exported to Europe and the interior regions, not including Persia and Russia.

[70] A&P, 1884, C.4106, LXXXI, p. 1411. [71] A&P, 1884–5, C.4526, LXXIX, p. 1929.

[72] Tables 3.21–3.22 express the trade balance in ESA during 1891–1913 in nominal terms. This limitation is due to the existent and prevalent Consumer Price Index (CPI) – which used to calculate inflation and thus enumerate real (inflation-adjusted) growth – employed to understand and analyse price trends in the Ottoman Empire based on price indices in Istanbul (see Pamuk, 2004). Owing to the fact that throughout the lifetime of the Empire prices, as well as wages, in the imperial capital differed substantially with that of the other regions of the Empire, the utility and the veracity of using the CPI to work out the real growth in Ottoman ESA are highly dubitable. That said, when we bear in mind the following two actualities, it becomes apparent that the trade expansion in ESA posited by this study cannot be oppugned: (i) exchange rate of the British pound sterling against the Ottoman lira remained constant during the years

Table 3.20 *Imports and exports of Diyarbekir, 1863–1884 (in pounds sterling)*

Year	Import	Export	Total
1863[73]	187,224	325,174	512,398
1883[74]	129,850	118,150	248,000
1884[75]	132,980	108,838	241,818

Source: FO 195/799 &A&P 1884 and 1884–5

Table 3.21 *Imports and exports of Diyarbekir, 1891–1913 (in pounds sterling)*

Year	Import	Export	Total
1891[76]	151,184	145,282	296,466
1893[77]	169,885	193,338	363,167
1895[78]	216,636	179,181	395,817
1897[79]	287,000	275,000	562,000
1908[80]	436,560	445,049	881,609
1909[81]	478,500	510,000	988,500
1912[82]	648,000	455,400	1,103,400
1913[83]	693,960	503,300	1,197,260

Source: A&P.

prepared by the British consuls based in Diyarbekir and Erzurum – some of which have been tabulated here – specifies that commercial activities in these provinces had recorded an impressive recovery during 1890–1914. In more concrete terms, the paradigmatic Kurdish province of Diyarbekir and the province of Erzurum in 1913, when compared with that of 1891, had witnessed a near-fourfold increase in nominal terms (see Table 3.21).

1850–1914 (i.e. 1 British pound sterling = 1.10 Ottoman lira); and (ii) change in the CPI in Istanbul in the years 1891–1913 was not of a very substantial nature (i.e. CPI in 1891 = 282.91 and CPI in 1913 = 317.10.) (Pamuk, 2004).

73 FO 195/799, Taylor at Diarbekir, 13 July 1864, pp. 63, 77, 74, 79.
74 A&P, 1884, C.4106, LXXXI, p. 1411. 75 A&P, 1884–5, C.4526, LXXIX, p. 1940.
76 A&P, 1893–4, C.6855–129, XCII, p. 8.
77 A&P, 1895, C.7581 C.7828, XCVI, p. 3927.
78 A&P, 1897, C.8277, LXXXIX, pp. 4200–1. 79 A&P, 1898, C.8648, XCIV, p. 3974.
80 A&P, 1911, Cd.5465, XCVII, p. 1877 81 Ibid.
82 A&P 1914, Cd.7048–187, XCV, pp. 6–12. 83 Ibid.

Table 3.22 *Imports and exports of Erzurum, 1891–1913 (in pounds sterling)*

Year	Import	Export	Total
1891[84]	294,400	202,950	497,350
1892[85]	230,015	209,300	439,315
1893[86]	231,690	164,700	396,390
1895[87]	194,110	157,300	351,410
1897[88]	214,030	167,660	381,690
1912[89]	639,200	303,750	942,950
1913[90]	650,250	360,700	1,010,950

Source: A&P.

Based on the details provided in the commerce reports cited earlier, it becomes apparent that around 40 per cent of all the items exported from Diyarbekir during 1890–1913 had consisted of wool, silk, mohair, valonia oak and hides that had been sent to foreign countries. The remainder had consisted of industrial products and agricultural produce, such as butter, rice, sheep and camels, which had been exported to various regions of the Empire. The trade data for the province of Erzurum in the same period indicate that the bulk of all the trade had been with interior domains and had consisted of commodities and agricultural produce similar to that in Diyarbekir.

Although the level of interregional trade in native goods had varied in these provinces, it nonetheless had been a very important component of the trade of provinces in and around Ottoman Kurdistan during 1890–1913. Quataert deriving from the trade data attained for Diyarbekir, Harput and Mosul – all of which had been constituent parts of the central province of Diyarbekir in the early nineteenth century – during the 1890s arrives at the following revealing conclusion:

> In some cases, the value of a district's inter-regional trade in goods of Ottoman origins vastly exceeded the value of its exports to foreign countries. At Mosul, in some years, the ratios were nearly three and four to one. During a typical year in the 1890s, Diyarbekir, Harput and Mosul together inter-regionally sent goods worth more than one million pound sterling. . . . (Total Ottoman exports abroad during the 1890s averaged 18 million pound sterling). (1994: 837)

84 A&P, 1893–4, C.6855–129, XCII, pp. 3–4. 85 Ibid.
86 A&P, 1895, C.7581–C.7828, XCVI, p. 3918.
87 A&P, 1897, C.8277, LXXXIX, p. 4199. 88 A&P, 1898, C.8648, XCIV, p. 3971.
89 A&P 1914, Cd.7048–187, XCV, pp. 6–12. 90 Ibid.

All of the data presented here are indicative of the vibrant atmosphere and positive fluctuations in the spheres of commerce and production in Ottoman Kurdistan and bordering regions after 1890. Moreover, contrary to the prevalent static conceptions of the commerce in predominantly Kurdish provinces in ESA, the information, despite the lack of longitudinal data, draws a picture of constant flux in manufacturing and commerce in Ottoman Kurdistan in the nineteenth and early twentieth centuries.

3.6 Population Income Levels

In regard to the general income levels in Ottoman Kurdistan, we are able to attain an idea from the comparative study of the income levels in the different parts of the Empire undertaken by Eldem based on the income data available in the official Ottoman sources from the first decade of the twentieth century (1970: 302–8). According to the results of this study, in 1907, there were discernible regional disparities in the per capita levels of income, particularly between the Anatolian and European provinces. The per capita levels of income in the bulk of the latter provinces, i.e. 900–1100+ *kuruş*, were nearly double those of the former provinces, i.e. 600–800 *kuruş*, which constitute the bulk of present-day Turkey (ibid: 304–6).

When we comparatively analyse the income levels given for the Anatolian provinces, it becomes apparent that with the exclusion of the Adana region, the overall majority of the Anatolian region, i.e. provinces in north, central and the predominantly Kurdish eastern Anatolia, were not too dissimilar. As the income levels per head in the great majority of the latterly mentioned Anatolian regions were estimated at 600–700 *kuruş* and a minority of the Anatolian provinces, namely Konya and Trabzon, the income levels had been approximated at 700–800 *kuruş* (ibid: 306).

4 The Deformation of Ottoman Kurdistan and Bordering Regions: De-development in ESA from the First World War until the 1980 Coup (1914–1980)

4.1 Overview

The mass violence that accompanied the formation of nation-states in Europe during the nineteenth century erupted in the Ottoman Empire during the first two decades of the twentieth century. The succession of wars and revolutions, ferociously crushed rebellions and forced population exchanges and deportations, as well as ethnocide, massacres and genocide, only partially concluded in 1923 with the signing of the Treaty of Lausanne. It was not enough to have redrawn territorial boundaries, since the sustenance of the nation-state necessitated the consolidation of the social, economic and political foundations of modern Turkey that was born out of the ruins of the Ottoman Empire. This chapter assesses the economic, political and social ramifications of the profound changes that have taken place on the eve of and during the eight decades following the establishment of the Republic in the predominantly Kurdish-populated regions of ESA.

The signing of the Turco-German Treaty of Alliance[1] on 2 August 1914 opened a new chapter in Ottoman history. By virtue of this secret pact, the Ottoman Empire joined the Central Powers to form the Triple Alliance, namely, Austria-Hungary, Germany and the Ottoman Empire. As part of the Empire's unavoidable commitment to prepare for war, on 29 October 1914, the Ottoman navy, without a formal declaration of war, shelled the Russian Black Sea ports of Odessa, Sebastopol, Novorossisk and Feodosia. Within a week of this pre-emptive bombardment, the Entente Powers comprising Britain, France and Russia declared war on the Ottoman Empire and from 5 November on, the Empire was officially at war with the Triple Entente powers (Keegan, 1998: 217).

[1] For the terms of this Treaty, see *Primary Documents-Turco-German Alliance-2 August 1914*, www.firstworldwar.com/source/turcogermanalliance.htm.

During the First World War, the eastern borderlands of the Ottoman Empire were a major theatre of operations between the Ottoman Empire and Russia, as well as being the epicentre of Turkish-nationalist demographic engineering programmes implemented by the Young Turk regime on account of short-term war exigencies and long-term ideological objectives explored later in this volume. As a consequence, the war plunged Ottoman Kurdistan into greater chaos than at any time since perhaps the Battle of Çaldıran (1514) with austere and long-lasting social, economic and political implications. The Great War not only changed the social and economic fabric of the ethnically diverse eastern and south eastern Ottoman provinces, but it also had a deleterious impact on the economic developments witnessed in Ottoman Kurdistan between 1890 and 1913. The events that had taken place in the build-up to and during the war, moreover, had crucial implications for the pre-history of Turkey's Kurdish question, and the radicalisation of the then nascent Kurdish national movement – exemplified by the occurrence of the influential Bitlis, Barzan and Baban revolts, which were organised in 1914 with the demand of regional autonomy for Ottoman Kurdistan.

The escalation in the political activities of the Ottoman Kurds was inextricably linked to the suppressive policies the CUP government implemented after the 1908 Young Turk Revolution. Once the CUP leadership was directly confronted with secessionism, European intervention (e.g. annexation of Bosnia and Herzegovina by the Habsburg Empire in October 1908) and the counterrevolutionary activities of a diverse group of anti-CUP forces (i.e. the short-lived counterrevolution of April 1909), it steered away from political pluralism and consequently reneged on one of its main promises with which it had come to power in 1908: re-establishing a constitutional order in an 'ideal' fashion by giving freedom of expression to all the ethnic groups in the Empire.

In other words, the Turkist proclivities of the CUP,[2] which had been in existence since 1902 (Hanioğlu, 2001: 295–302), had gained momentum because of the Young Turks regime experiencing exogenous and endogenous threats to its rule. A quintessential example of this is the following incisive and unequivocal conceptualisation of an ideal society outlined by one of the influential members of the Central Committee of the CUP, Dr. Mehmed Nazım (1872–1926), in a letter to Zionist leaders in November 1908:

> The Committee of Progress and Union wants centralization and a Turkish monopoly of power. It wants no nationalities in Turkey. It does not want Turkey to

[2] For in-depth and differing interpretations of the evolution of Turkish nationalism, see Ahmad (1969), Hanioğlu (1995, 2001) and Karpat (2001).

become a new Austria[-Hungary]. It wants a unified Turkish nation-state with Turkish schools, a Turkish administration, [and] a Turkish legal system. (ibid.: 260)

Despite pan-Turkism not becoming a defining feature of the Ottoman state identity until after the *coup d'état* of January 1913, in the wake of the counterrevolution of April 1909, the CUP began to implement in a piecemeal fashion nationalistic and centralist policies,[3] which instigated the indiscriminate suppression of a range of non-Turkish Ottoman citizens, including the Ottoman Kurds. A case in point is the Law of Association (1909) that forbade the formation of associations that had an ethnic basis or national name (Ahmad, 1969: 61–2). With the enactment of this legislation, the leadership of the Kurdish organisations, which hitherto was in alliance with the Young Turks in opposition to the Hamidian regime during the preparatory years of the 1908 Revolution, was forced to swallow the bitter pill of betrayal.

Ironically, one of the first organisations to be proscribed in 1909 was the maiden Kurdish political society, The Society for the Rise and Progress of Kurdistan (Kurdistan Taali ve Terakki Cemiyeti) (1908), which had up until then supported the 1908 Revolution (Elphinston, 1946: 94). The two founding leaders of this society, Amin Ali Bedirkhan and Şerif Paşa, were condemned to death and had to flee the country. Amin Ali's eldest son, Sürreya Bedirkhan, who had resumed the publication of the initial and influential Kurdish nationalist journal *Kurdistan* (1898–1909) after returning to Istanbul in 1908, had also shared the same destiny as his father and had it to seek refuge in 1909. Similarly, the newly established Kurdish cultural and educational organisations, like Kurd Nashri Ma'arif Cemiyeti (Society for the Propagation of Kurdish Education), had also been forced to suspend their activities (Jwaideh, 1961: 297–9).

The implementation of the unanticipated authoritarian policies by the Young Turks, as well as the ideas of nationalism that had gained prominence throughout the Empire percolating into Ottoman Kurdish minds, severely deteriorated the relationship between the CUP government and its Kurdish subjects. In May 1912, numerous Kurdish organisations joined forces and convened the first Kurdish General Assembly, which unanimously agreed to create a Kurdish political party to defend the rights of the Ottoman Kurds (Celil, 1992: 202).

[3] In 1909, legislations circumventing the power of the sultan were approved. Consequently, the sultan's role in the appointment of ministers was reduced to the choice of the grand vizier. Moreover, the Young Turks tried to centralise and empower the government with legislative powers such as the Law on the Press and Printing Establishments and Law on the Public Meeting, which prohibited protest (Barlas, 1998: 76–7).

The conflictual ties between the Young Turk regime and the Kurds reached its lowest ebb immediately after the Balkan Wars of 1912–13. This was primarily because in the wake of the calamitous defeats – which resulted in the loss of the richest and most advanced core areas of the Empire (Macedonia, Albania and Thrace) – the CUP government had endorsed three highly controversial policies: (a) the implementation of the agonising 20 per cent rise in the profits tax (*temettü vergisi*) paid by the merchants and artisans; (b) the doubling of the customs dues; and (c) the rise in the *ağnam* tax. These much-reviled policies had been the last straw in the worsening relationship between the Ottoman state and its Kurdish subjects as they set in motion Kurdish uprisings all over Ottoman Kurdistan. Sixteen consecutive Kurdish revolts had taken place all over Kurdistan between 1913 and 1914. These rebellions culminated in the major rebellions led by the leaders of the Kurdish principalities in Bitlis, Barzan and Baban on the eve of the First World War with clear nationalist demands, including the rights to regional autonomy (Celil, 1992: 201–16; Burkay, 2008 [1992]: 457–69).

The outbreak of the war, however, interjected the contestations of the Kurdish nationalist movement. This was due to two successive events orchestrated by the ruling CUP, which after the January 1913 *coup d'état* regained complete control of internal political affairs. The first is the genocide of the Armenians (1915–16), which marked a new shift, pushing many Kurdish tribes and a considerable number of urban notables and religious sheikhs into an alliance with the Ottoman authorities. The other is the forced deportation of a substantial number of Kurds from their ancestral homes subsequent to the massacre and expulsion of the Armenians in 1916.

In sum, the pro-Muslim and Turkist sentiments of the Ottoman rulers intensified during the Balkan Wars and reached its peak with the eruption of the First World War. This was largely a consequence of the humiliating defeats endured during the former war and the heightened existential fears, as well as the corresponding imperative to save the Ottoman state from the CUP leadership at the onset of the latter war.

The successive defeats in the Balkan Wars resulted not only in the mortifying loss of almost all the remaining European provinces, but also in the humiliating forced expulsion of the Balkan Muslims. By 1914, the Ottoman rulers, having seen the Empire shrink from approximately 3,000,000 square kilometres in 1800 to 1,300,000 square kilometres, dreaded the imminent loss of the Empire's entire territory with the fear-provoking possibility that the reform agreement of February 1914 signed by the Russians would be implemented. According to this agreement, Armenians were to partake on an equal basis in the local administration of the six eastern provinces (i.e. Erzurum, Van, Bitlis, Mamuretülaziz, Diyarbakir and Sivas) where they were living in dense concentration. The parties involved in the negotiation of this reform agreement conceived this as a building block for the creation of an independent Armenian state (Akçam, 2012: xvii–xviii).

4.2 The Collapse of the Empire, the Rise of the 'National Economy' and the Implementation of Nationalist Population Policies

These summarised events and eventualities constituted the basis of the ideological shifts among the late Ottoman political elite from pan-Ottomanism to pan-Islamism and, later, to pan-Turkism. The swing to pan-Turkism or Turkish nationalism at around the same time as the outbreak of the First World War had entailed a dialectical process; involving not only destructive social engineering and economic policies targeting the non-Turkish citizens of the Empire, but the nationalist reorganisation of the Ottoman lands.[4] In other words, during and immediately after the war, the CUP's nationalist demographic policies aimed at homogenising the multiethnic landscape of the Empire, which mainly targeted the Armenians and the Kurds in the ethnically heterogeneous eastern provinces,[5] concurred with the radical reforms that laid the groundwork for Turkish capitalism and the unitary Turkish nation-state that ascended from the ashes of the Ottoman Empire.

This helps to explain the jubilation of the nationalist cadres of the CUP at the outbreak of the war, as exhibited with the following words from an article penned by a leading Young Turk journalist, Hüseyin Cahit Yalçın (1875–1957), published in the party organ of the CUP, *Tanin*, under the headline of 'The Awaited Day': '[The war] had come like a stroke of good fortune upon the Turkish people, who had been certain of their own debility. The day had finally come . . . the Turks would make an historical reckoning with those [with] whom they had hitherto unable to do so.'[6]

With the anticipation that a Europe at war would not be able to enforce its will on the Ottoman rulers, the CUP implemented far-reaching administrative reforms once the war began. The Ottoman Porte between

[4] For detailed analyses of the nature and implications of the nationalist spatial policies in the late Ottoman era and the Republican era of the Turkish Republic in eastern Anatolia, see Öktem (2004), Ülker (2005) and Jongerden (2007).

[5] The CUP also targeted other communities like the Christian Syriacs during this period. For a detailed study of the policies towards other Christian communities in eastern Anatolia, see Gaunt (2006).

[6] *Tanin*, 'The Awaited Day', 14 November 1914.

1908 and 1914 had already designed some of these restructurings, but the restructurings could not pass as law because of the vetoes of the European embassies. The European diplomats perceived these measures as an infringement of the 'treaty rights of the foreigners', since these blocked reforms had aimed to annul the regime of Capitulations (Ahmad, 1993: 40–1). In 1914, the much-loathed Capitulations were unilaterally abrogated, which facilitated the Porte to raise tariffs on imported goods, and the tasks of both the Public Debt Administration and the Ottoman Bank were overturned, enabling the Porte for the first time to undertake a monetary policy in printing paper money.

After 1913, more importantly, the CUP abandoned the English liberal model of economic development modelled on laissez-faire liberalism and began to embrace the economic model of 'national economy' centred on the ideas of the German economist Friedrich List. This shift in policy enabled the Unionists to combine the principle of state control over the economy with preferential treatment towards the Turkish/Muslim bourgeoisie.

List, in brief, contended that the liberal theories of the British economists Adam Smith and David Ricardo suited the national interest of England because of its industrialised economy and imperialist policies, but the model of development these economists advocated could not be universalised. According to List, if laissez-faire liberal ideas are adopted by countries that do not have the large-scale industries akin to those of England, they would end up reliant on England (List, 1856).

One of the prominent theoreticians of the CUP, Ziya Gökalp, paraphrased these concerns in the early 1920s. Gökalp maintained that the 'Manchester economics is not at all a cosmopolitan doctrine, it is nothing but the national economics of England which stands for big industry and, thus, derives only benefit from the freedom of exchange abroad and suffers no loss from it' (1959: 307). Deriving from this premise, Gökalp argued that if countries that do not have the industrial base and scale of England implement the ideas of the Manchester school, they would inevitably become 'economic slaves to industrialized nations like England' (1968: 123).

For List, states' ability to engender productive power enables them to participate in world trade on a 'value-adding' basis: through producing goods that represent relatively high levels of skills and command relatively high prices on international markets. The lack of productive power in an economy dooms a country to importing goods of higher value than those it exports, leading to debt and underdevelopment:

The causes of wealth are quite a different thing from wealth itself. An individual may possess wealth, that is to say, exchangeable values; but if he is not able to produce more values than he consumes, he will be impoverished. An individual may be poor, but if he can produce more than he consumes, he may grow rich. (List, 1856: 208)

Relatedly, the CUP with the purpose of nurturing the indigenous industry undertook fundamental economic measures (Toprak, 1982: 25–33). One of the core aims of these policies was the creation of the Turkish/Muslim bourgeoisie to supplant the existing non-Muslim/Turkish commercial class, which was content to play the role of commercial intermediary in an empire that served as a market for Europe's industry. The historian Yusuf Akçura (1876–1935), who alongside Gökalp had laid the theoretical foundations of the ideological shift to Turkish nationalism (Karpat, 2001: 374–407), believed that the fostering of the Turkish national bourgeoisie was an existential prerequisite for the 'national economy' (*milli iktisad*) that would sustain a Turkish nation-state, as manifested in the following postulation by Akçura:

The foundation of the contemporary states is the bourgeoisie; the modern prosperous states came into existence on the shoulders of the artisan, merchants and banker bourgeoisie. The Turkish national awakening can be a platform for a Turkish bourgeoisie in the Ottoman state and if natural growth of the Turkish bourgeoisie continues without damage of interruption, we can guarantee the solid ascendancy of the Ottoman state.[7]

In 1914, with the intention of developing national production, the CUP government enacted the Law for the Encouragement of Industry (Teşvik-i Sanayi Kanunu). The following year, under the tutelage of the CUP, Muslim businessmen founded the Tradesman's Association in order to take the domestic market under their control. In 1916, the Lower House of the Ottoman Empire, namely, the House of Deputies of the Ottoman Empire (Meclis-i Mebusan), approved a customs law and ruled that all trade-related business should be conducted in Turkish (Ahmad, 1993: 39–46; Barlas, 1998: 78–9).

However, the repercussions of the First World War and the project of building a 'national economy', which concealed a Turkist agenda that was entirely a novel feature in Ottoman history, were double-edged. Ethnocide, forced migration and the demolition of moveable and immovable property had become the destructive components of the policies implemented in the Ottoman Empire during the War. The examples of the recorded atrocities committed in the initial stages of the First World

[7] Akçuraoğlu Yusuf, '1329 senesinde Türk Dünyası', *Türk Yurdu* 6.3 (3 April 1914) in Toprak (1982: 410).

War shed much light on the devastations it had wrought to Ottoman Kurdistan and neighbouring Ottoman regions. For instance, when the Russian armies infiltrated beyond the Doğubeyazıt-Alaşkirt region in northern Kurdistan in December 1914, reportedly only 'one-tenth' of the predominantly Kurdish population of the area survived the vehemence of the Armenian units, some of whom were ex-Ottoman citizens attached to the Russian Army (Jwaideh, 1961: 363). In January 1915, when the Ottoman Army moved to capture Urumiya and Tabriz, most Armenians and Assyrians had fled in panic as the Russian armies stationed in Iranian Azerbaijan had at the time retired northwards. The Christian population who remained in these and surrounding areas was subjected to acts of savagery at the hands of the Turkish troops and Kurdish auxiliary forces (McDowall, 2000: 103).

The Armenian Genocide of 1915 and the Forced Deportation of Ottoman Kurds in 1916: A Social and Economic Catastrophe

Based on an archival study of the deportation orders issued by the CUP government, Fuat Dündar discerns that the deportation of the Ottoman Armenians had commenced in February 1915. The 'fifth and final stage of the deportations' is said to have begun after the leader of the CUP, Talaat Pasha, on 21 June 1915, ordered the deportation of 'all Armenians without exception' who lived in ten provinces of the eastern and south eastern regions of the Empire, including Diyarbakır, Sivas and Mamuretülaziz (Dündar, 2012: 281–3). Within a year or so after the initiation of forced deportation of the Armenians from their ancestral homelands, according to a report of a United Nations human rights subcommission, 'at least one million' Armenians perished (Hovannisian, 1999: 15).

The removal and the subsequent destruction of the Ottoman Armenians had severe social and economic consequences.[8] Prior to 1916, The CUP's 'national economy' targeted mainly the Armenian and the Greek communities in the Empire, and after 1916, it targeted the Kurds. The Ottoman Interior Ministry, in a circular on 2 November 1915, confessed to the occurrence of 'an economic vacuum arising from the transportation of Armenian craftsmen'.[9] Owing to the fact that the bulk of the Armenians, like the Ottoman Kurds, lived in the eastern provinces, the largest

[8] For a detailed examination of the social and economic repercussions of the Armenian Genocide of 1915, see Üngör and Polatel (2011).

[9] Başbakanlık Odası Arşivi (BOA), Dahiliye Nezareti Şifre Kalemi (DH.ŞFR) 57/261, Interior Ministry to all provinces, 2 November 1915 in Üngör and Polatel (2011: 93).

destruction was meted out to this region. A French report from Diyarbekir observed that 'the mass exodus of Christians, most of whom were artisans and merchants, had created a major economic crisis in this region' (Tachjian, 2004: 206).

After the forced expulsion and massacre of the Armenians, the CUP had designed and implemented a range of forced deportation policies targeting the Kurds. The settlement policies of the CUP entailed, on one hand, the deportation of Kurds from their homelands for resettlement in central and western Anatolia in accordance with the '5 per cent rule': ensuring that the Kurds constituted no more than 5 per cent of the total population in their new places of settlement. On the other hand, Muslim immigrants, or *muhacir*, from lost territories, such as Albanian Muslims, Bosnian Muslims and Bulgarian Turks, settled in eastern Anatolia, where they were not allowed to constitute more than 10 per cent of the local population (Jongerden, 2007: 178–9; Akçam, 2012: 43–50).

The mass forced deportation of the Ottoman Kurds[10] began with the following order issued, subsequent to the deportation of the Armenians, on 2 May 1916 by Minister of the Interior Mehmed Talat to the governor of Diyarbekir:

> It is absolutely not allowable to send the Kurdish refugees to southern regions such as Urfa or Zor [Deir ez-Zor]. Because they would either Arabize or preserve their nationality there and remain a useless and harmful element, the envisioned would not be accomplished and therefore the deportation and settlement of these refugees needs to carried out as follows.
> - Turkish refugees and the turkified city dwellers need to be deported to the Urfa, Maraş, and Anteb regions and settled there.
> - To prevent the Kurdish refugees from continuing their tribal life and their nationality wherever they have been deported, the chieftains need to be separated from the common people by all means, and all influential personalities and leaders need to be sent separately to the provinces of Konya and Kastamonu, and to the districts of Niğde and Kayseri.
> - The sick, the elderly, lonely and deprived women and children who are unable to travel will be settled and supported in Maden town and Ergani and Behremaz counties, to be dispersed in Turkish villages and among Turks.[11]

Orders with similar contents were also sent to the provinces of Sivas, Mamuretülaziz and Erzurum and to the provincial districts of Urfa, Maraş and Antep on 4 May 1916 (Akçam, 2012: 45–6). Another

[10] The deportation of the Ottoman Kurds was supervised by the Directorate for the Settlement of Tribes and Immigrants (İskân-ı Aşâir Muhacirîn Müdüriyeti) (İAMM), renamed the General Directorate for Tribes and Immigrants (Aşair ve Muhacirin Müdüriyet-i Umûmiyesi) (AMMU) in 1916.

[11] BOA, DH.ŞFR no. 63/172–3, coded telegram from Minister Talat to Diyarbekir, 2 May 1916 in Üngör (2012: 285).

telegram sent to the province of Mosul on 6 May even listed each step of the policy of forced deportation of the Kurds:

> (1) In order to reform the Kurdish element and transform it into a constructive entity it is obligatory to immediately displace and send [the Kurds] to the assigned places in Anatolia mentioned below; (2) The areas of resettlement are: the provinces of Konya, Ankara, and Kastamonu, and the provincial districts of Niğde, Kayseri, Kütahya, Eskişehir, Amasya, and Tokat; (3) In the place of resettlements the sheikhs, leaders and mullahs will be separated from the rest of the tribe and sent to different districts, either before or after the [other] member [of the tribe], in other words, to places from which they will be unable to maintain relations with the other members.[12]

The statistical data prepared by the Ministry of the Economy indicate that there were 'well over a million' Kurdish refugees and deportees during this period (Üngör, 2011: 117). Figures pertaining to the actual number of Kurdish deportations are non-existent, however. The common consensus in the scholarly studies on this issue is that approximately 700,000 Kurds were forced to flee their homelands, around half of whom are reported to have perished before reaching their various destinations (Safrastian, 1948: 76; Jwaideh, 1961: 369).

As briefly mentioned earlier, the deportation policy was a dual-track policy; along with the forced deportation of the Ottoman Kurds from their native lands, the CUP had ordered the settlement of non-Kurdish Muslims who had fled from the lost Ottoman territories in Kurdish lands. See, for instance, the following instructions sent by the İAMM on 21 May 1916 to the province of Mamuretülaziz: 'The Turkish refugees who surpass the province's absorptive capacity will be sent to the areas of Urfa, Zor [Deir ez-Zor], Maraş and Ayıntab via the Ergani-Diyarbekır, Siverek route, while the Kurdish refugees will be sent to Kayseri, Yozgat, Ankara and Canik via Malatya-Sivas-Tokat, and then via the route Malatya-Darende-Şarız-Aziziye.'[13]

The existent official records regarding the non-Kurdish Muslim settlers reveal that they resided in and worked on the 'abandoned properties' (*emvâl-ı metrûke*[14]) the Armenians and the Kurds had left behind. The precise number of the confiscated properties is not known, though,

[12] BOA, DH.ŞFR no. 63/215, coded telegram from the Interior Ministry's IAMM to the Province of Mosul, 6 May 1916 in Akçam (2012: 47).

[13] BOA, DH.ŞFR no. 64/93, coded telegram from the Interior Ministry's Office of Tribal and Immigrant Resettlement to the Province of Mamuretülaziz, 21 May 1916 in ibid. (43–4).

[14] The term *abandoned properties* had been designated by the CUP as a euphemism employed to veil and legitimatise the confiscated possessions of both the Armenians and the Kurds. Thus, in this study, this term will be interchangeably used with *confiscation* and *dispossession*.

since Turkish state officials allege that the registers of the 33 Abandoned Properties Commission (Emvâl-ı Metruke Komisyonu) are 'lost' (Üngör and Polatel, 2011: 72).

In 1924, an important report written by a research commission chaired by a leading CUP member, Cavid Bey, concluded that the new proprietors of the 'abandoned properties', who had possession of these properties as a result of 'extraordinary permissions', lacked 'economic education', and, as a result, wasted the wealth through 'squander and dissipation'.[15] This crucial documentation not only validates that Turkish and/or Turkophone migrants possessed the confiscated properties of the Armenians and the Kurds in the eastern and south eastern provinces, but it also indicates that the new occupiers failed to put these appropriated properties to efficient use. Thus, dispossession of land and properties, as well as resulting in the pauperisation of the Armenians and the Kurds, had burdensome negative repercussions for regional productivity and prosperity.

Overall, by the end of the war, the Ottoman economy shrank by around 50 per cent and its GDP fell by 40 per cent. The destruction the war caused in the different sectors of the Ottoman economy are succinctly summarised by the following figures pertaining to the declines experienced during the war. Mineral production fell by 80 per cent, coal production by 75 per cent, cotton textiles by 50 per cent, wheat production by 40 per cent, and sheep and goat raising by 40 per cent (Üngör and Polatel, 2011: 94). Life for the population in Ottoman Kurdistan who had survived the war had been reduced to abject misery and destitution as famine and bacterial diseases like typhus and typhoid took their toll. Due to the destruction of the eastern economy during the course of the First World War, the famine that began at the end of 1917 struck the eastern and south eastern provinces more acutely than elsewhere in the Empire (McDowall, 2000: 108–9).

4.3 From the Mudros Armistice of 1918 to the Lausanne Treaty of 1923

Istanbul signed the Mudros Armistice on 30 October 1918. Owing to the defeat of the Ottoman forces in Mesopotamia and Syria in the period leading up to the Mudros Armistice, it was unavoidable that the map of the Middle East would be redrawn, with inevitable spill-over effects for Ottoman Kurdish lands. The details of the Anglo-French plan for the Middle East, the Sykes-Picot Agreement (May 1916), which the

[15] 'İktisadi Kısım', *Şehremaneti Mecmuası* 7, March 1924, in Toprak (1982: 422).

Bolsheviks had exposed a month after the October Revolution (1917), revealed how the Allied victors proposed to redraw the map of the Middle East. This agreement projected that most of Anatolia be taken from Ottoman control and the Russian Empire be rewarded with the eastern provinces and the straits, Greece with the region around Izmir and Italy with south-west Anatolia. After the October Revolution, however, the Soviets had stated their opposition to this imperialist plan, and the British proposed that the void their withdrawal created be filled by endowing to Britain as 'zones of influence' the 'Cossack territories, the territory of the Caucasus, Armenia, Georgia, and Kurdistan' (McDowall, 2000: 115).

This decision triggered the Ottoman and British scramble for Kurdistan. For the former, the key objective was to preserve what remained of the Empire, and the loss of the strategic and naturally rich eastern provinces would have been a major setback. For Britain, the issue of Kurdistan had been secondary to the main territories Britain had been interested in, namely, Mesopotamia (Iraq) and Syria, but it unavoidably partook in the decision-making process regarding the future of Kurdistan because of its strategic position in Mesopotamia. The following words of Arnold Wilson, acting civil commissioner in Baghdad, in 1919, deftly summarises the objectives of Britain: 'The whole basis of our action as regards [the] Kurds should be in my opinion the assurance of a satisfactory boundary to Mesopotamia. Such a boundary cannot possibly be secured, I imagine, in the plains, but must be found in the Kurdish mountains ... [and that] entails a tribal policy.'[16]

With the latterly mentioned apprehension concerning the eastern provinces in Ottoman minds, the recognition of the Kurdish claims appeared prudent to the Ottoman statesmen in order to dissuade the Kurds from making common cause with the Armenians. Accordingly, both components of the (dual) state power that emerged in the years between the end of the First World War and the establishment of the Turkish Republic (i.e. the palace-backed government in Istanbul and the new government led by Mustafa Kemal in Ankara) acknowledged the previously suppressed demands of the Kurds. The *Amasya Protocol*, a document signed in 1919 at a time of accord between the Istanbul government and the founders of the Ankara Assembly and later the Turkish Republic, testifies that both of these constituents had recognised that the Kurds would be granted ethnic and cultural rights in order to warrant their free development (Yeğen, 2011: 68).

[16] FO 371/4192, Memorandum by Wilson, 12 September 1919.

In a public interview held immediately before the proclamation of the Turkish Republic, Mustafa Kemal stated: 'In accordance with our constitution, a kind of local autonomy is to be granted. Hence, provinces inhabited by the Kurds will rule themselves autonomously. . . . The Grand National Assembly of Turkey is composed of the deputies of both Kurds and Turks and these two peoples have unified their interests and fates' (ibid.).

Besides these assurances, Mustafa Kemal making Islam the lynch-pin of the Kemalist struggle against the 'Christian invaders', promising to conserve the caliphate and pledging to liberate the province of Mosul from British occupation, played a determinate role in persuading the mainstream Kurdish leaders to coalesce with Ankara during the War of Independence (1919–22) (McDowall, 2000: 187; H. Bozarslan, 2008: 338).

This collaboration, however, had been threatened by the Kurdish uprisings that began in Dersim and spread to other parts of Ottoman Kurdistan between 1921 and 1922 by Kurdish notables who were discontent and fearful of Ankara's headship. Colonel Alfred Rawlinson (1867–1934), a British liaison officer in Anatolia, conveying the general perception and attitude of the Kurds vis-à-vis the Ankara government in one of the Foreign Office Memorandums in 1922, notes the following observation that sheds much light on the growing disgruntlement of the Kurds towards the end of the War of Independence: 'the Kurds are left enormously in the majority in the eastern districts of Anatolia and all Turkish posts there being very weakly held at the mercy of the local Kurds . . . the principal Kurdish chiefs are entirely dissatisfied . . . and extremely antagonistic towards Turks.'[17]

Despite these conflicts, the Kurds were unable to create a unified and effective opposition because of their inability to develop a cohesive idea of Kurdish identity owing to being fragmented by tribal and religious allegiances as well as by language and socioeconomic activity. This disunity amongst Kurds had been evident with the differing approaches to the question of Kurdish autonomy on the eve of and during the War of Independence.

At the onset of the War of Independence, the Kurdish national movement that had organised around Kurdish societies re-emerged. The official representative, Şerif Paşa, of the most influential Kurdish society, the Society for Kurdish Advancement (Kürd Teali Cemiyeti) (1918), started

[17] FO 371/7858, Memorandum by Rawlinson, 4 March 1922.

negotiations with the Armenian delegate, Bughos Nubar, for the Paris Peace Conference (1919–20) to assure the independence of the two countries. The negotiations concluded with a Kurdo-Armenian accord. In a joint declaration on 20 November 1919, both parties affirmed that they agreed on an independent Kurdistan and Armenia, only to be rejected by a sizeable section of Kurdish leaders because of their bitter memories of the Armenian troops and their willingness to ally with Ankara due to the promises made by Mustafa Kemal. The majority in Armenia who were in favour of the Armenian case for six eastern provinces also opposed this accord (Jwaideh, 1961: 376–8).

The only major Kurdish revolt against the Kemalists during the War of Independence had been the Koçgiri revolt, which took place in 1921 in the predominantly Alevi Dersim area. This revolt had endangered the Kemalist–Kurdish alliance as the rebel leaders had the following demands:

(i) Acceptance by Ankara of Kurdish autonomy as agreed by Istanbul as per the Sevres Treaty;
(ii) The release of Kurdish prisoners in Elaziz (Elazığ), Erzincan, Malatya and Sivas;
(iii) The withdrawal of all Turkish officials from areas with a Kurdish majority;
(iv) The withdrawal of all Turkish forces from the Koçgiri region in west Dersim, which because of lying west of the Euphrates had been excluded from the area formally designated at Sevres as part of an autonomous Kurdistan.

Aside from being badly organised, the revolt had not been able to mobilise sufficient support from the Sunni Kurds since they perceived it as an Alevi uprising. Predictably, the Turkish forces defeated it by April 1921 (Olson, 1989: 26–33).

On account of the successful War of Independence, the Sevres Treaty (10 August 1920) was superseded by the Treaty of Lausanne (24 July 1923). This new treaty carved up Kurdistan and annulled the possibility of its independence and autonomy. The only protection offered to the Kurds was the safeguarding of their linguistic rights under Article 39:

> No restrictions shall be imposed on the free use by any Turkish national of any language in private intercourse, in commerce, religion, in the press, or in publications of any kind or at public meetings. Notwithstanding the existence of the official language, adequate facilities shall be given to Turkish nationals of non-Turkish speech for the oral use of their own language before the courts. (McDowall, 2000: 142)

4.4 Society, Economics and Politics in the Republican People's Party Era (1923–1950)

Consolidation of the 'National Economy' and the 'Reform' of the East (1923–1929)

With the proclamation of the Turkish Republic (29 October 1923), the aforementioned Kemalist–Kurdish alliance collapsed, and many Kurdish notables followed the path of the Alevi Kurdish rebels in Dersim. This rupture stemmed largely from three principal factors. First, after the armistice in October 1923, Turkish nationalism had become Turkey's official and hegemonic ideology. This new ideology conceived national and linguistic differences as existential threats to the Turkish Republic and for that reason ruthlessly repressed them. Second, the promises Mustafa Kemal made to the Kurds before 1923 were reneged on with the foundation of the Republic. After the proclamation of the Turkish Republic, the existence of Kurdish identity was negated, the caliphate was abolished (3 March 1924) and the *vilayet* of Mosul in southern Kurdistan was not liberated from British occupation as promised under the National Pact (*Misak-ı Milli*) in 1920.

Third, the Lausanne Conference produced a major problem: the future of the *vilayet* of Mosul. Kemalists were alarmed by the apparent willingness of Britain to offer the Kurds in Mosul a certain degree of local autonomy during the Lausanne negotiations, because of the possible spill-over effects of such a Kurdish polity for the Kurds in the north of the border.[18] In other words, the Turkish officials were fretful that an autonomous Kurdish political entity would foster autonomist tendencies amongst the Kurds living in Turkey; in the same way that the successful revolt led by Ismail Ağa Simko in 1920 established a short-lived independent Kurdish state in eastern Kurdistan (Arfa, 1966: 48–64; McDowall, 2000: 141–2; Koohi-Kamali, 2003: 66–83).

The predominantly Kurdish ESA comprised the only domains in Turkey not to be turkified at the inception of the Turkish Republic; therefore, in the eyes of the Kemalist rulers, these territories were areas wherein potential secessionist threats could originate. The perceived risk of Kurdish self-rule by the Republican rulers informed the discriminatory Kurdish policies during the single-party period, which led to neglect and further peripheralisation of these primarily Kurdish regions of the new Turkish nation-state, a theme explored later. This perhaps explains why

[18] See Mustafa Kemal's (Atatürk) Speeches in Eskişehir and İzmit in 1923 in Perinçek (1993: 94–6).

the alteration in the Kemalist attitude towards the Kurds had overlapped with the Lausanne Conference, which was held in two sessions, from 20 November 1922 to 4 February 1923 and then from 23 April until 24 July 1923.

The Izmir Economic Congress

The major change of policy vis-à-vis the Kurds took place at the Izmir Economic Congress (17 February–4 March 1923). This Congress convened during the interval in the deliberations of the Lausanne Conference, with the attendance of 1,135 delegates (İnan, 1972: 12) mostly from the dominant classes i.e. big landowners and the merchant bourgeoisie, as well as from the labouring classes (Boratav, 1982: 14–18). When Mustafa Kemal's speech[19] to this Congress was published, all references to the Kurds had been excised (McDowall, 2000: 191), which implied a fundamental shift in the policies of Ankara towards the Kurds in Turkey.

Such an alteration was not adversative to the purpose and principles of the 1923 Congress of Economics, as this Congress espoused to consolidate the foundations of the Turkish 'national economy' envisioned and set out by the CUP during the First World War as the basic strategy of the new Turkish nation-state. The principles adopted in the Izmir Economic Congress pertained to the preparation of: a property regime, an institutional structure required for the operation of a modern market economy and special incentives designed for the enrichment and development of the indigenous bourgeoisie. Specifically, the Congress decided to encourage domestic production, prohibit the import of luxury goods and permit foreign direct investment if the investors refrained from seeking political concessions. Other important decisions included the abolishment of the tithe and its replacement with a tax on soil produce, the establishment of an industrial bank, which would provide credit to the industrialists, and the adoption of the Law for the Encouragement of Industry (Boratav, 1982; Toprak, 1982 Yalman, 2009).

After this Congress, and throughout the Republican era, one of the central objectives of the Kemalists was, in the words of an official report of the ruling Republican People's Party's General Secretariat in 1939–40, to 'dismantle the territorial unity of Kurds' and to 'Turkify the Eastern population' (Bulut, 1998: 185–9). The rulers of Republican Turkey did not hold back from openly propagating their plans for the Kurds in

[19] For the speech by Mustafa Kemal Atatürk to the İzmir Economic Congress, see İnan (1972: 57–69).

Turkey. Quintessential examples of this are the exchanges the foreign minister of the Turkish Republic, Tevfik Rüştü Aras (1883–1972), had with the foreign diplomats in 1926–7.

Aras, in 1926, stated to the British administrator of Iraq, Sir Henry Dobbs (1871–1934), that the central governors of Turkey were 'determined to clear out the Kurds of their valleys, the richest part of Turkey to-day, and settle Turkish peasants there', and averred that 'the Kurds would for many generations [be] incapable of self-government'.[20] Consequently, the forthright foreign minister made plain to the representatives of the international community that the Kemalist governors of the Turkish Republic were adamant to forcibly displace the Kurds from their ancestral lands, and encumber any form of Kurdish self-determination or polity. In 1927, the Turkish foreign minister had in the presence of Sir George Clerk (1874–1951), the British ambassador to Turkey, reiterated similar policy objectives based on social Darwinian premises: 'They [Kurds] will die out, economically unfitted for the struggle for life in competition with the more advanced and cultured Turk[s], who will be settled in the Kurdish districts. After all there are [fewer] than 500,000 Kurds in Turkey to-day, of whom as many as can will emigrate into Persia and Iraq, while the rest will simply undergo the elimination of the unfit.'[21]

In order to ensure the 'elimination' of the so-called economically unfit Kurds, moreover, Fevzi Çakmak (1876–1950), the first chief of the General Staff of the Republic of Turkey and an architect of the Kurdish policy of the Turkish state during the Republican era, had around the same time argued that the predominantly Kurdish provinces of Turkey should deliberately be kept underdeveloped. Marshal Çakmak suspected that 'economic development and wealth would accelerate the level of consciousness and thus lead to the development of nationalism among the Kurds' (A. H. Kılıç, 1998: 97). Put differently, the influential marshal maintained that in order to nullify the probability of the existence of a Kurdish polity, it is necessary to forestall social and economic development in areas predominantly populated by Kurds, namely, ESA. Thus, the denial of economic opportunity for Kurds, which could provide the economic base of an indigenous Kurdish state, was construed as the best possible shield against the ostensible separatist threat, as well as increasing the strength and viability of the Turkish state.

The avowals by the two senior figures of the CHP government indicate that since the foundation of the Turkish Republic, the Kemalists sought to procure the densification and power of the dominant ethnic group, the

[20] FO 424/265, Memorandum by Henry Dobbs, 22 November 1926.
[21] FO 424/266, Clerk to Chamberlain, 4 January 1927.

Turks, at the expense of the Kurds in ESA with the anticipation that the latter would gradually be extinguished or become a powerless ethnic entity. The cornerstones of this strategy were threefold: (a) the forced deportation of the Kurds from their native lands; (b) the assimilation of the Kurds into the Turkish identity; and (c) the underdevelopment of the areas predominantly inhabited by the Kurds.

The Republican rulers' aim of 'turkifying' the heterogeneous eastern provinces and, in turn, extinguishing the Kurdish identity or rendering the Kurds a feeble entity had played a determinate role in the creation of a chaotic atmosphere in the predominantly Kurdish southeast of Turkey in the early years of the Turkish Republic. During the first two decades of the Republic, there were twenty-seven Kurdish revolts, and only one out of the eighteen Turkish military expeditions during the years 1924–38 transpired outside of Kurdistan. Three of these revolts, namely, the Şeyh Said Revolt (1925), the Ararat Revolt (1930) and the Dersim Revolt (1936–8), had a distinctive influence on the evolution of the CHP regime and its Kurdish policy.

The Şeyh Said Revolt and the 1925 Reform Plan

The Şeyh Said Revolt had taken place against the backdrop of increasing hostility between the Kurds and the Kemalist state largely due to the contested decisions the latter implemented between 1923 and 1924. During the election of the new Grand National Assembly in the summer of 1923, Kurdish deputies were denied the right to return to their constituencies and candidates selected by the government replaced them. In the same year, the Kemalists had also abolished the caliphate, which the Sunni Kurds interpreted as an attack on their collective and religious identity. Furthermore, in March 1924, despite Article 39 of the Treaty of Lausanne, the Turkish state had officially prohibited the use of Kurdish in schools and law courts and insisted on the use of Turkish in official domains – traditional Kurdish clothing and music were also banned.

The 1925 revolt, led by a Kurdish religious dignitary, Şeyh Mehmed Said of Piran[22](1865–1925), was initially organised with the aim of establishing an independent Kurdistan by the leadership of the Azadi (Freedom) Committee composed of Kurdish intellectuals and officers who had been arrested in September 1924 after the failed mutiny attempt. The Şeyh Said uprising truly threatened the Kemalist state to the extent that Ankara mobilised 52,000 soldiers, spent around a third of its annual budget, proclaimed martial law in almost all of the predominantly

[22] For a biography of Şeyh Mehmed Said of Piran, see Aras (1992).

Kurdish provinces and negotiated with the French authorities to gain use of the southern railways in order to supress it. These measures by the Turkish were not to no avail as the revolt was crushed in spring 1925 at the gates of Diyarbekir (renamed Diyarbakır) (Olson, 1989: 91–127; McDowall, 2000: 192–6; H. Bozarslan, 2008: 339–41).

Subsequent to the Şeyh Said Revolt, Atatürk, on 8 September 1925, authorised the creation of the Reform Council for the East (Şark İslahat Encümanı)[23] in order to devise concrete policy prescriptions to deal once and for all with any potential separatist threat from Kurdish society. Pursuant to this, on 24 September 1925, a special report titled the *Report for Reform in the East* (*Şark İslahat Raporu*) was prepared and presented to the Turkish Assembly. This secret report, which saw daylight as a result of a series of official reports published by Mehmet Bayrak (1993, 1994) in the 1990s, made the following critical recommendations:

(i) Preventing the Kurdish political and social elite from reviving as a ruling class;
(ii) Clearing persons, families and their relatives whose residence 'in the east the government deems inappropriate';
(iii) Reuniting and governing all of the provinces located on the east bank of the Euphrates River via the military administrative unit of 'Inspectorates-General'[24] by martial law for an unspecified period of time;
(iv) Emphatically prohibiting the use 'of all non-Turkish languages' and the 'employment of the Kurds in even secondary offices';
(v) Allocation of 7 million Turkish Lira (TL) in order to finance the settlement and the livelihoods of the Turkish refugees and transportation of the Kurds (Bayrak, 1993: 481–9).

Consequently, a series of deportation laws was implemented between 1925 and 1927 actuating the recommendations in this report. On

[23] Prime Minister İsmet İnönü (1884–1973) chaired the Reform Council for the East. Major positions in this body were held by the following senior military officers and government bureaucrats who had attained experience in the field of policy-making as CUP officials: Chief of Staff Marshal Mustafa Fevzi Çakmak, Interior Minister Lieutenant-Colonel Mehmet Cemil Uybadın (1880–1957), Lieutenant-General Kazım Fikri Özalp (1882–1968), Şükrü Kaya (1883–1959), Mahmud Celal Bayar (1883–1986) and Mustafa Abdülhalik Renda (1881–1957) (Bayrak, 1993: 481).

[24] The Inspectorates-General (Umûmî Müfettişlikler) were regional governorships whose authority prevailed over all civilian, military and judicial institutions under their domain in large areas of the Turkish Republic. During the 1920s and the 1930s, four of them were established in ESA provinces. On 1 January 1928, the CHP government established the First Inspectorate-General (covering the provinces of Bitlis, Diyarbakır, Van, Hakkari, Muş, Mardin, Urfa and Siirt), and appointed Dr. İbrahim Tali Öngören (1875–1952) as its first Inspector-General. For a detailed study of the Inspectorates-General, see Koçak (2003).

10 December 1925, the ruling CHP government led by Prime Minister İsmet İnönü had passed law number 675, titled 'Law on Migrants, Refugees, and Tribes Who Leave Their Local Settlements Without Permission'. On 31 May 1926, the government enacted the 'Settlement Law'. This piece of legislation permitted the Interior Ministry to identify:

(i) 'Individuals who do not fall under Turkish culture, those infected with syphilis, persons suffering from leprosy and their families, and those convicted of murder except for political and military crimes, anarchists, spies, gypsies, and those who have been expelled from the country' (the appendix to this law considered the 'Pomaks, Bosniaks, and Tatars' in the Turkish culture);

(ii) 'Migratory tribes in the country and all the nomads', with the aim of 'transporting [them] to suitable and available places' (Üngör, 2011: 138).

This was not the last of the deportation orders. The CHP government on 10 June 1927 passed the 'Law Regarding the Transportation of Certain Persons from Eastern Regions to the Western Regions'. This new deportation law was akin to the expulsion orders of 1915–16. In the words of British Ambassador Sir George Clerk, it empowered the government to 'transport from the Eastern Vilayets an indefinite number of Kurds or other elements ... the Government has already begun to apply to the Kurdish elements ... the policy which so successfully disposed of the Armenian Minority in 1915'.[25] Despite the lack of factual data, according to the figures cited by contemporary Kurdish authors, from 1925 to 1928 more than 500,000 people were deported of whom some 200,000 were estimated to have perished in the aforementioned provinces (Bedirkhan, 1958: 52–3).

The Law on the Maintenance of Order 1925–1929

The 1925 revolt was a catalyst for more than the suppression of the Kurdish national movement as it led to the implementation on 4 March 1925 of an extraordinary law titled 'The Law on the Maintenance of Order' (Takrir-i Sükün Kanunu), which remained in force until March 1929. The Law on the Maintenance of Order marked the end of political pluralism and free press in Turkey. This piece of legislation was used within the first few months of its enactment by the Republican government to outlaw the opposition party, the Progressive Republican Party (Terakkiperver Cumhuriyet Fırkası), and the only publications not banned were the government publication, *National*

[25] FO 371/12255, Clerk to Chamberlain, Istanbul, 22 June 1927.

Sovereignty (*Hakimiyet-i Milliye*), and the pro-establishment national paper, *Republic* (*Cumhuriyet*).

The Law on the Maintenance of Order empowered the government to enact a wide range of legislations in order to attain a top-down transformation of society according to the Western model, which the Kemalist perceived as the universal model of civilisation and progress as well as a precondition for economic progress (Ahmad, 1993: 79–93; Zürcher, 1994: 179–84; McDowall, 2000: 198–202). The direct and indirect effects of these new acts, which will be elucidated later, are commonly posited in the literature on the initial years of the Turkish Republic to have stimulated modernisation and capitalist development in Turkey (Herschlag, 1968; Issawi, 1980; Z. Aydın, 1986; Ahmad, 1993). Put differently, despite the economic restrictions agreed to as per the economic concessions appended to the Lausanne Treaty,[26] the new acts implemented during the lifetime of the Law on the Maintenance of Order are commonly thought to have instigated important socioeconomic changes. These pivotal developments were the fostering of the indigenous capitalist class, the nurturing of a legal and institutional structure that provided the conditions for capital accumulation and the transformation of society in accordance with norms of the idealised Western civilisation.

During the period between the enactment and repeal of the Law on the Maintenance of Order, the Gregorian calendar was adopted (1 January 1926). Within the same year, the Islamic code of law, *sharia*, was annulled. Subsequently, the government introduced a civil code patterned on the Swiss civil code, followed by a penal code based on the penal code of Mussolini's Italy, and a commercial code centred largely on the German and Italian codes (Issawi, 1980: 367; Ahmad, 1993: 79–80).

According to the 1927 Census, Turkey had 65,245 industrial enterprises, the overwhelming majority of which had been small workshops. The enterprises with more than five workers constituted only 8.94 per cent of these registered industrial firms (Herschlag, 1968: 54; Zürcher, 1994: 204). Relatedly, in 1927, the state implemented the 'Law for the Encouragement of Industry'. This new piece of legislation made state lands available to entrepreneurs, exempted many essential materials from import duties and reduced freight charges and taxes. One of the indicators of the impact of this law during the 1920s is the fact that out of the 1,473 industrial enterprises which reaped the benefits of the law

[26] These concessions compelled Turkey to free its customs tariffs at the 1916 rates, with prohibitions on differential rates for imported and locally produced goods, and to remove the quantitative restrictions on foreign trade until 1929.

in 1932, only 342 had been established before 1923 (Thornburg, 1949: 24–5; Herschlag, 1968: 54–5).

In 1928, the Kemalist state replaced the Arabic script with the Latin script in the writing of Turkish (Ahmad, 1993: 80–2). In addition, after the mid-1920s, for purposes of accelerating economic development and maintaining political control, the Turkish state had set as one of its central aims the task of modernising transportation. In accordance with this objective, the state nationalised the foreign concessions in this sector and embarked on the development of an extensive transport network in order to cover the country with a dense network of railways and roads, stretching to the distant regions of Anatolia. Railway projects in particular absorbed high state investments during the first decade of the Republic. Eight hundred kilometres of track were laid between 1923 and 1929, and in 1929, another 800 kilometres were under construction (Rivkin, 1965: 63–4; Herschlag, 1968: 231–6; Barlas, 1998: 89–92).

In order to overcome one of the main drawbacks of the nascent national industrial enterprises, that is, adequate initial capital, great importance was imputed to banking facilities, in particular to the Business Bank (İş Bankası) established in August 1924 (Herschlag, 1968: 56–7; Ahmad, 1993: 96). Its nominal capital was raised in 1927 to 4 million TL. The short- and long-term deposits held in this bank increased from 8,061,377 TL in 1925 to 43,839,567 TL in 1929 (Herschlag, 1968: 56).

The role of the Agricultural Bank (Ziraat Bankası), established in 1889, underwent magnification by the Kemalist state after 1924 to granting of loans, purchase and sale of agricultural produce, purchase of land, participation in companies dealing with agriculture and dealing with the materials needed by the peasants. The augmentation in the role and capabilities of this bank in the early years of the Republic was uneven and not attuned to the actual needs of the peasantry, since it did not overcome the overreliance of the peasantry on usurers and big landowners (Herschlag, 1968: 48–9; Z. Aydın, 1986: 31–7).

In line with the newly defined roles, there had been an increase in the outstanding credit limit of this bank: from 53 per cent of the paid-up capital during the War of Independence to more than 100 per cent after 1924. As a result, a drastic rise took place in the level of loans handled by this bank: from 928,000 TL in 1922 to 25,880,000 TL in 1929 (Herschlag, 1968: 48–9). Such expansions are believed to have played an influential role in the recovery and development of agriculture in Turkey after the mid-1920s (Issawi, 1980: 367). The main beneficiaries of the thrust of agricultural policies between 1923 and 1929 were, however, the large commercial producers of exportable cash crops, concentrated in the Aegean and Mediterranean regions (Margulies and Yıldızoğlu, 1987: 273).

Uneven Post-war Recovery

Between 1923 and 1929, the Turkish economy recovered, and by 1929, it appeared to have regained its pre-war level. For instance, per capita GDP in 1923 was 40 per cent below its 1914 level, but by the end of the 1920s, it had attained the levels prevailing prior to the First World War (Pamuk, 2008: 276–7). Besides, as illustrated in Table 4.1, when compared to the pre-war Ottoman levels, considerable developments had taken place in the sphere of education and in transport.

However, the predominantly Kurdish provinces[27] in ESA (Beyazıt, Bitlis, Diyarbekir, Elaziz (Elazığ), Erzincan, Hakkari, Kars, Malatya, Mardin, Siirt, Urfa and Van), which in 1927 were home to around a quarter (14.6%) of the general population of Turkey (13,660,275[28]), did not develop in parallel with the rest of the country. These regions had been the least affected quarters by the post-war recovery witnessed in the Turkish Republic between the years of 1923 and 1929. Despite the aforementioned transport infrastructure projects, by 1930 no railroads were constructed in these provinces.[29] In 1927, only 900 of the 14,000 schools in Turkey were located in these domains.[30] In the whole of ESA, furthermore, by 1930 there was only one bank, namely, the Elaziz İktisat Bankası, established in 1929, which had a nominal capital of 50,000 TL.[31] Thus, obtaining loans was virtually impossible.

According to the official data from 1927, when compared with the nine designated agricultural districts in Turkey, each of which was composed of five to nine provinces, the districts comprising the predominantly Kurdish provinces in ESA, i.e. districts five and six, contained the least amount of agricultural tools and machinery. Only 119,665 out of 1,413,509 of the necessary agricultural tools and machinery were to be found in the provinces located in these regions.[32]

[27] Mustafa Abdülhalik Renda, one of the co-authors of the aforementioned *Report for the Reform of the East,* in September 1925 traversed the eastern provinces/districts of Gaziantep, Urfa, Siverek, Diyarbekir, Siirt, Bitlis, Van, Muş, Genç, Elaziz, Dersim, Ergani, Mardin, Malatya and Maraş in order to identify 'where the Kurds live and how many they are'. As a result of this field research, Renda discerned that out of the 1,360,000 registered population east of the Euphrates in 1925, 993,000 were Kurds, 251,000 were Turkish and 117,600 were Arabs. Moreover, Renda, subsequent to an elaborate socioeconomic analysis of the eastern provinces, concluded that the Kurds had been in a 'dominant economic position' in this region of Turkey (Bayrak, 1993: 452–67).

[28] TCBIUM, *Annuaire Statistique,* 1928: 24–5. [29] Ibid.: 1932: 359.

[30] Ibid.: 1928: 28–9. [31] Ibid.: 1934: 305. [32] Ibid.: 1933: 188–9.

Table 4.1 *Indicators of development, 1913–1928*

Year	1913	1923	1928
Population (millions)	15.7	12	13.8
Foreign Trade (million dollars)	179	137	202
GDP per capita (1948 prices Turkish lira)	—	254	330
Agricultural Production (millions of liras 1940 prices)	—	1,522	2,254
Industrial Production (millions of liras 1948 prices)	—	421	662
Wheat (million tons)	3.4	1.0	1.9
Tobacco (thousand tons)	49	45	50
Cotton (thousand tons)	30	44	51
Coal (million tons)	0.8	0.6	1.3
Refined Sugar (thousand tons)	—	—	4.3
Cement (thousand tons)	—	—	59
Electricity (million kWh)	20	40	90
Railways (thousand kilometres)	3.6	4.1	4.8
Students in Schools (thousands)	—	359	517

Source: Issawi, 1980: 368.

In the late 1920s, as evinced by the following figures demonstrative of the calamitous imbalance between the unproductive and productive sectors in the predominantly Kurdish towns in 1927, the productive sector in these provinces had been in a dismal state:

> 45,863 soldiers (this figure is solely of the soldiers stationed in this region and therefore it is not inclusive of the armies mobilised to deal with specific military tasks in the region) and 1,841 magistrates as against 25,327 merchants, 32,496 artisans and workers and 21,095 in various other unclassified professions. This was at a time when 1,400,209 active people were unemployed in this region, which accounted for over 16 per cent of the total number of unemployed people in Turkey.[33]

Although there are no official regional trade statistics to cite, the following report from the British consul in Trabzon in June 1926 indicates that the trade in the mid-1920s in the Kurdish provinces was a shadow of what it had been during the First World War: 'Travellers report having seen great numbers of Kurds with their families and cattle being driven along [the] Erzurum–Erzinjan [Erzincan] road presumably bound for Angora [Ankara] and Western Anatolia. Whole villages are deserted, and trade is at a standstill over a large area.'[34]

[33] Ibid.: 64–5. [34] FO 371/11528, Knight to Lindsay, Trebizon, 16 June 1926.

The policy of deporting the Kurdish political and economic elites, moreover, adversely affected trade and wealth creation in this region of Turkey, as revealed by the following observation of a British traveller in the summer of 1929: 'One of the main weapons employed was the deportation of the rich and powerful Kurdish families ... in the process they have lost all their belongings, and there is not, so I was told, a single wealthy or powerful Kurd in Turkish Kurdistan to-day.'[35]

The Great Depression, Ètatism and the Resettlement of Kurds (1929–1939)

The year 1929 was a critical one for the Turkish Republic. On one hand, the economic restrictions agreed to in the Lausanne Treaty ended. On the other, the negative impacts of the world economic crisis began to be felt by Turkey, and the Kemalist regime were, yet again, facing a rapidly growing Kurdish resistance led by the pro-self-rule Khoybun (Independence) Committee. By the autumn of 1929, Khoybun dominated an area from Ararat as far south as Khushab, south of Van, and pressed for Kurdish autonomy. Within a year or so, by means of massive military expeditions, in close alliance with Iran, the Ararat rising was supressed by the Kemalist forces (van Bruinessen, 1992: 376–93; Alakom, 1998) whereas the negative ramifications of the 1929 Great Depression had kept aggravating.

The initial effects of the economic crisis were to be seen in the fall in the prices of agricultural produce: the principal source of income of the population of Turkey and the lion's share of Turkish exports. Agriculture was by far the largest sector; it accounted for approximately half of the GDP and employed three-fourths of the labour force (Pamuk, 2008: 279). For example, compared to 1925, agricultural prices in 1932 and 1933 fell by one-third, and, in turn, the value of exports declined vastly. Turkey had received more than 1 million TL for around 14,000 tons of wheat exported in 1926. In 1931, it was in receipt of the same amount for almost 26,000 tons (Barlas, 1998: 81).

The year 1929 saw the greatest deficit, amounting to 101 million TL, with imports at 256 million TL and exports at 155 million TL (Herschlag, 1968: 66). The economic situation in Turkey worsened with a corresponding depreciation of the Turkish lira against the sterling pound. Consequently, the cost of paying public debt rose very sharply to the extent that the state was forced to suspend payments to foreign creditors in 1930.

[35] FO 371/13828, Clerk (Istanbul) to Henderson (London), 15 July 1929.

Turkey's reaction to the Great Depression was similar to that of America and Western European countries. It implemented a protectionist trade policy and increased government activity in the sphere of the economy. This was done with the aim of stabilising the economy and strengthening the national industry, a target set in the 1920s but the implementation of which proved slow due to the economic restrictions appended to the Lausanne Treaty. Accordingly, between 1929 and 1931, the state ratified a wide range of measures in order to attain stability and to promote the indigenous industry. A new tariff policy, Tariff Regulation of 1929, came into effect at the beginning of the Depression in order to protect the local industry. This policy was followed by the introduction of foreign exchange controls in December 1929, after a very high demand for foreign currency for large imports in that year. It was this excess in demand that initiated the aforementioned depreciation of the Turkish lira. In addition, a system of import quotas and restrictions on the import of certain commodities was implemented by the Turkish state as of November 1931 (Herschlag, 1968: 66–7).

Ètatist Turkey

Despite the steps towards implementing ètatist policies when the Great Depression took its toll on the Turkish economy, it was not until the third congress of the CHP (10–18 May 1931) that the ruling party formally adopted ètatism[36] (*devletçilik*) as a new economic policy and made it one of the pillars of Kemalist ideology. *Ètatism* in this study will denote the direct intervention by the state in the economic life of a capitalist society, by way of nationalisation, by the administration of prices and by control of wages, as well as by social welfare legislation. After its official adoption at the CHP Congress, ètatism, along with the other five principles or 'arrows' (i.e. Republicanism, Nationalism, Populism, Secularism and Revolutionarism) adopted at the same Congress, was officially inscribed as Article 2 of the Turkish Constitution in 1937.

In the party programme of the RRP, moreover, ètatism was described with the following words: 'Although considering private work and activity a basic idea, it is one of our main principles to interest the State activity in matters where the general and vital interests of the nation are in question, especially in the economic field, in order to lead the nation and the country to prosperity in as short time as possible.'[37]

[36] For detailed and differing interpretations of ètatism in Turkey, see Herschlag (1968: 61–122), Hale (1981: 53–85) and Boratav (1982).

[37] The quoted passage is an excerpt from the official translation of the aforementioned party programme, reproduced in Barlas (1998: 103).

The central feature of this new economic policy was to protect and strengthen the national private sector by assisting and carrying out economic ventures that the private sector was unable and/or unwilling to carry out. With this aim in mind, a five-year economic plan was drawn up in 1933. The anonymous authors of this plan stated that the top priority for Turkey had to be nationalistic industrialisation:

> Despite the political and economic disagreements between them, the powerful industrial countries are essentially in agreement in reducing agricultural countries to a status of primary producers and in dominating their internal markets. To this end, they will eventually use their political influence to prevent the present movement in the agricultural countries. Some agricultural countries may accept this situation in return for minimal concessions. This reality, in particular, drives us to establish the industry we need without any delay. (Boratav, 1981: 186–7)

Consequently, the Five-Year Plan, which the government approved on 9 January 1934, aimed at establishing twenty industrial plants, with a special focus on setting up import substituting industries in textiles, sugar, cement, paper and mining (İnan, 1972: 15; Tezel, 1982: 141). As outlined in Table 4.2, almost all of these plants were to be located in central and western Anatolia. Only two factories had been situated in ESA (i.e. the textile factories in Iğdır and Malatya), which is considered one of the main drawbacks of the Five-Year Plan (Küçük, 1978: 248–9).

With Soviet technical assistance and loans of $8 million, the first quinquennial plan had been launched in May 1934, and between 1934 and 1938, it was put into operation. The loan attained from the Soviet Union covered a small portion of the total investments, which stood at around 100 million TL by 1938 (Herschlag, 1968: 81; Hale, 1981: 56). In order to finance and control the operation of the projects in the Five-Year Plan, important agencies were established during the 1930s.

The state bank, Sümerbank, which replaced the Bank for Industry (Türkiye Sanayi Kredi Bankası) and the State Industry Office (Devlet Sanayi Ofisi) in June 1933, became a pivotal institution in the field of industrialisation throughout the Five-Year Plan. It took on the role of planning and establishing new enterprises, operating state-owned factories and carrying out banking functions (Hale, 1981: 57; Boratav, 1982: 197–8; Barlas, 1998: 96). A second state agency, Etibank, was established in 1935, with the development of mining as its main function. The law that had established Etibank, moreover, attributed a wide range of roles to this bank, from the purchase and sale of mines of minerals to establishing or participating in the foundation of trade organisations in the mining sector and dealing with all kinds of banking transactions

Table 4.2 *Industrial plants established under the First Five-Year Plan*

Industry	Type/Location
Chemical	Artificial silk (Gemlik)
	Semicoke (Zonguldak)
	Attar of roses (Isparta)
	Sulphuric acid (Izmit)
	Superphosphates (Izmit)
	Chlorine and caustic soda (Izmit)
Cotton Textiles	Yarn and cotton fabric
	(Bakırköy, Kayseri, Ereğli, Nazilli and Malatya)
	Yarn
	(Iğdır)
Earthenware	Ceramics (Kütahya)
	Glass and bottles (Paşabahçe-Istanbul)
Hemp	Kastamonu
Iron	Karabük
Paper and Cellulose	İzmit
Sponge	Bodrum
Sulphur	Keçiborlu
Worsted	Bursa

(Herschlag, 1968: 92–3; Hale, 1981: 57). Hence, both organisations, which acted as state-owned holding companies with banking functions, unified investment and financing activities.

The number of large private firms benefitting from the Law for Encouragement of Industry reached 1,397 in 1935. The investment in these establishments rose from 63 million TL in 1935 to around 266 million TL in 1939. At the same time, the value of net output in these enterprises rose from 104 million TL in 1935 to 266 million TL in 1939 (Herschlag, 1968: 106).

The state had also intervened in the agricultural sector during the 1930s. A case in point is the action the state took in 1932 to rescue farmers from plummeting world prices[38] by authorising the Agricultural Bank to regulate prices via building up and selling off stocks of wheat – a duty transferred in 1938 to the newly established Office for Soil Products (Toprak Mahsulleri Ofisi, TMO) (Ahmad, 1993: 98; Zürcher, 1994: 207). Moreover, during the ètatist period, the state had also taken

[38] The price index for wheat, one of Turkey's principal exports, fell from 100 in 1929 to 32 in 1931.

the following noteworthy measures to support and encourage agriculture: increasing and promoting agricultural credit, setting up research and training schemes, forming small irrigation programmes, reducing rail transport rates by 50–75 per cent and importing machinery and modern implements (Thornburg, 1949: 43–75; Tezel, 1982: 284–315; Margulies and Yıldızoğlu, 1987: 274–5).

As it can be inferred from the overview of the ètatist decade, significant developments had taken place in this brief period. It is estimated that GDP and GDP per capita grew at average annual rates of 5.4 and 3.1 per cent, respectively, during the 1930s (Pamuk, 2008: 278). Besides, during the ètatist period the process of industrialisation was accelerated and resultantly the share of industry in the GNP grew from 10 per cent in 1927 to 16 per cent in 1938 (Yerasimos, 1987: 90). This is despite the stagnation or decline in wages, and the severely deteriorating working conditions on account of the implementation of a labour law in 1934 which forbade forming unions and partaking in strikes as well as lockouts (Boratav, 1981: 169; Yerasimos, 1987: 100; Ahmad, 1998: 99).

In the course of the ètatist period, a massive expansion of cultivated land was also witnessed as the total amount of cropped area, which amounted to 4.86 per cent of the total area in 1927, reached 12.25 per cent in 1940 (Margulies and Yıldızoğlu, 1987: 274). Relatedly, agricultural output is estimated to have increased by 50–70 per cent during the 1930s (Pamuk, 2008: 279). Relatively significant developments were also recorded in the sphere of education and transportation (see Table 4.3). During the same period, foreign trade recovered, too, in spite of the fact that more than 80 per cent of Turkey's trade was conducted under bilateral agreements, around 50 per cent of which in the years before the Second World War was with Germany and its allies (Tezel, 1982: 124–34; Herschlag, 1986: 115–17).

1934 Settlement Act: Third Wave of Kurdish Deportations

The influence of Nazi Germany in the 1930s had not been limited to trade; the CHP government had embarked on social engineering policies that at the time had currency in Germany. Put differently, during the 1930s, the CHP government implemented ètatist policies in conjunction with nationalist population policies, which is a dark feature of the 1930s that is often glossed over, if not ignored, by influential economic historians analysing this period (Thornburg, 1949; Rivkin, 1965; Herschlag, 1986). The operation of the practical expression of ètatism, the Five-Year Plan, had coincided with the implementation of the

Table 4.3 *Indicators of development, 1933–1938*

Year	1933	1938
Population (millions)	15.5	17.2
Foreign Trade (million dollars)	83	234
GDP per capita (1948 prices Turkish lira)	370	474
Agricultural Production (millions of liras 1940 prices)	2,490	3,791
Industrial Production (millions of liras 1948 prices)	1,019	1,423
Wheat (million tons)	2.3	3.6
Tobacco (thousand tons)	36	68
Cotton (thousand tons)	40	64
Coal (million tons)	1.9	2.6
Refined Sugar (thousand tons)	65.1	42.5
Cement (thousand tons)	143	287
Electricity (million kWh)	152	312
Railways (thousand kilometres)	6.1	7.2
Students in Schools (thousands)	657	944

Source: Issawi, 1980: 368.

draconian 1934 Settlement Act[39] (Law No. 2510), which facilitated the third wave of deportation of Kurds from ESA and was a contributory factor in the upsurge of socioeconomic problems and political turbulence in this region, as exhibited with the Dersim Uprising (1936–8). The execution of this new Settlement Act hindered the overwhelmingly Kurdish provinces in ESA from reaping the aforementioned benefits of ètatism in Turkey.

For the purposes of tracing the evolution of the population policies targeting the Kurds and making sense of the causality of the 1934 Settlement Act, it is worth remarking that this piece of legislation was ratified a few years after the Turkish foreign minister, Aras, had informed the British representatives to the League of Nations in Geneva in November 1930 of the 'possibility of a future intense Turkish colonization in order to smother the Kurds in a considerable mass of Turkish population'.[40] On the day when this new Settlement Act came into force, 14 June 1934, the points raised by Interior Minister Şükrü Kaya in the deliberations of this law in the Turkish Assembly made crystal clear that what Aras had alluded to as a possibility was now set as a project of demographic engineering by the Kemalist state.

[39] Iskan Kanunu, Nr. 2510, 13 June 1934 in *Resmi Gazete*, 21 June 1934, Issue No. 2733.
[40] FO 371/14578, Drummond (Geneva) to Cadogan (London), 18 November 1930.

During this parliamentary debate, the interior minister not only espoused the task of the CHP government to be to 'render the Turk the master of the soil' in the East but also stated that 'there are around two million pure Turks abroad in our near environs. It is somewhat mandatory for them to come to the homeland in a piecemeal fashion. … It is then our obligation to settle them in accordance with the social and economic principles necessitated by the science of settlement' (Üngör, 2011: 149). Kaya, during these discussions, did also express the ethno-territorialist nationalist nature of the new Settlement Act in the plainest way possible: 'This law will create a country speaking with one language, thinking in the same way and sharing the same sentiment' (Ülker, 2005 5).

Notwithstanding the relatively meticulous nature of the 1934 Settlement Act,[41] the new Settlement Act was directly modelled after the aforementioned deportation orders and laws. In other words, this new Settlement Act akin to the deportation decrees and laws put into effect over the previous two decades had intended to assist: (a) the deportation and assimilation of the Kurds; and (b) the resettlement of the non-Kurdish Muslim settlers. The latter included migrants from the lost Ottoman territories and Turkish peasants who had been relocated from most densely populated areas of the country, like the eastern Black Sea littoral.[42]

In order to determine the criteria for the identification and the selection of the deportees and the settlers, the first article of the new Settlement Act stated that 'the Ministry of Interior is assigned the power to correct … the distribution and location of the populace in Turkey in accord with affiliation to Turkish culture.'[43] In the 1920s and 1930s, the Kurds in Turkey, as exemplified by the 1926 deportation law, were commonly described by the Kemalist statesmen as 'people who do not share the Turkish culture' or as a 'tribal populace that do not speak Turkish' and so were one of the main targets of this law.

Pursuant to the criteria outlined in Article 1, in Article 2 of the 1934 Settlement Act, under the rubric of 'Settlement Regions', Turkey was divided into three zones (Articles 12, 13 and 14[44]):

[41] For differing and detailed accounts and discussions of the 1934 Settlement Act, see Kökdemir (1952), Beşikçi (1991), Jongerden (2007) and Üngör (2011).

[42] The *Report on Reform in the East* of September 1925 had authorised the resettlement of the inhabitants of Rize and Trabzon provinces in the Murat river valley as well as in the Lake Van basin (Bayrak, 1993: 483). Accordingly, on 5 November 1933, the CHP government decided to resettle '9,836 landless peasants from Trabzon and Çoruh' provinces around lake Van (Çağaptay, 2006: 71), which under the provisions of the 1934 Settlement Act had been located in the Zone 2 area wherein Kurdish settlement was prohibited.

[43] Iskan Kanunu, Nr. 2510, *Resmi Gazete*, 21 June 1934, Issue No. 2733, p. 4003.

[44] Ibid.: 4004–5.

Zone 1: Localities in which it was deemed desirable to increase the density of the culturally Turkish population or set aside land for 'populations who share the Turkish culture'.

Zone 2: Regions for the 'relocation and resettlement of populations which are to be assimilated into the Turkish culture'.

Zone 3: Areas, which for 'spatial, sanitary, economic, cultural, political, military and security' needed to be evacuated and settlement prohibited.[45]

Under the provisions of this law, the Turkish state was vested with full powers to:

(a) settle immigrants of Turkish origin or culture in Zone 1, which as outlined in Article 12 was synonymous with the eastern provinces;
(b) forcibly deport Kurds to Zone 2, which for the most part was Turkish areas in the western regions of Turkey, where they were never to form more than 10 per cent of the local population and had to stay a minimum of ten years in their new homes;
(c) prohibit the resettlement of non-Turkish speakers in Zone 3, that is, localities where there was previously active Kurdish opposition to the Turkish state and vicinities where there were railways, highways, transit roads and natural resources in southeast Turkey.[46]

In order to attain the aim of resettling Kurds in Zone 2 areas, Article 9 of the new act authorised the resettlement of 'nomads, who do not share the Turkish culture, by dispersing them to Turkish towns and villages'.[47] The subsequent article specified that the Ministry of Interior was to 'disperse tribal members, who were Turkish subjects and who were not affiliated to the Turkish culture, to Zone 2', and, furthermore, laid down that all the properties belonging to the tribesmen be surrendered to the state, which would redistribute it to various settlers.[48] The measures outlined in these two articles were analogous to the procedures delineated in the previous deportation laws that aimed to diminish the size and influence of the Kurds in ESA by breaking up Kurdish society, by deporting Kurdish leaders and by dragooning the members of Kurdish society into the Turkish culture. To this end, during the 1930s, Kemalist social engineers prepared confidential reports about the Kurdish tribes in the eastern provinces in which they scrutinised the relationships of these tribes with the Turkish state (i.e. whether they were 'loyal' or 'disloyal'), as well as their relationships with each other. These reports were augmented in the 1970s, and published in book form in 2000 (Aşiret Raporları, 2000).

Judging from the appraisals outlined in a report presented to the ruling CHP's General Secretariat in 1939–40, the 1934 Settlement Act, aside

[45] Ibid.: 4003. [46] Ibid.: 4003–6. [47] Ibid.: 4003. [48] Ibid.

from the administrative glitches, was commended and seen as an effective instrument of 'assimilation and internal colonisation' and 'dismantling the territorial unity of the Kurds' by the Republican rulers of Turkey. The report is, moreover, a testament to the Kemalist zeal for nationalist homogenisation during the 1930s. The anonymous author of this document not only called for the continuation of 'widespread' deportation of the Kurds, but also vociferously argued for the furtherance of settling Turks 'in their [the minorities'] richest and most fertile villages at a rate of at least 50 per cent [of the local population]'. In order to 'Turkify' successfully the eastern provinces, it was deemed necessary to complement 'deportation measure' with 'incorporeal measures' or, in other words, assimilative cultural policies. The expansion of formal education and the construction of a modern transportation system in this region were seen as the 'backbones' of assimilation or 'Turkification' (Bulut, 1998: 185–99).

The demographic repercussions of the new Settlement Act were significant. Based on the recorded deportation figures in the official sources, throughout the 1930s the total number of Kurdish deported to the western provinces was 25,381 people in 5,074 households. Despite the lack of detailed and firm factual information regarding the total number of settlers in ESA, based on existent official counts for the provinces of Diyarbekir and Elazığ, it is known that from 1928 to 1938 at least 1,988 households were sent to the Diyarbekir province, and another 2,143 households were expected to settle there in 1938. In addition, from 1932 on, 1,571 households were settled in the neighbouring province of Elazığ. Almost all of the non-Kurdish Muslim settlers from Bulgaria, Greece, Yugoslavia and Syria were peasants, and they settled rural areas (Üngör, 2011: 162).

The dual-track policy of settling non-Kurdish migrants and deporting Kurds in the 1930s, however, further deepened the socioeconomic and political problems from which the eastern provinces had been suffering since the First World War. In the 1930s, owing to poor planning by the state and inefficient use of land by its new occupiers, the settlement of the migrants in the rural areas of ESA had negative implications for the agricultural productivity in these regions, which, in turn, had inauspicious consequences for the well-being of the settlers toiling on the land allocated to them. In an internal report in 1935, Prime Minister İsmet İnönü confessed to the existence of these issues with the succeeding informative remarks: 'There have been efforts to settle immigrants from everywhere. A population of about fifteen hundred work[s] on every fertile and water-rich terrain. There are three groups of immigrants with a gap between them of three to five years. . . . Almost all of them complain to government officials about their conditions. . . . The people are needy, destitute, the fields have not yet been productive. The pastureland has been distributed poorly.'[49]

A year later, under the instructions of Atatürk, Economic Minister Celal Bayar embarked on an expedition to survey the state of the economy in the eastern provinces. At the end of this mission, Bayar prepared a secret report wherein the seasoned state official bewailed the collapse of the economy in ESA and described the underdeveloped nature of the eastern economy in the most unequivocal form possible: 'this is an entirely primitive economy without markets and production beyond what is necessary for personal use' (Bayar, 2006: 69). At this point, in order to understand the level of regression that befell these regions, it is worth going back about forty years and comparing the bleak picture painted by Bayar with that of the vibrant ESA between 1890 and 1910. These regions had gone from inter-regionally sending goods worth more than 1 million pounds sterling in a typical year in the 1890s to self-sufficient domains in the late 1930s.

Moreover, since the Kurdish tribe was, in the last analysis, a site of reproduction of Kurdish identity, the Republican rulers, as part of their policy of rendering the Kurds a feeble ethnic entity, aimed to liquidate tribal structures by means of relocating the Kurdish kinfolks. The policy of resettling the Kurdish tribes in the 1930s, which, in the words of the contemporary British consular Thomas Henry Matthews (1869–1941), had been conducted by the CHP government 'in a manner which resembled the operation against Armenians in 1915',[50] wrought more disorder and destruction to ESA. A prime example of this is the events that had been staged in the latter part of the 1930s in the defiant Dersim region, which since the 1921 rebellion had remained tranquil.

The 1936–8 Dersim Uprising started after the Tunceli Law of 1935 (Law No. 2884). This legislation aimed at the removal of this 'abscess' by forcibly deporting the Kurdish Alevi population and replacing it with a Turkish population. As early as 1926, in a report prepared by the Ministry of Interior for the Turkish Assembly, Dersim had been described 'as an abscess on the Turkish Republic which must be removed, for the sake of the country's well-being' (Beşikçi, 1991: 29).

The Dersim rebellion was led by Kurdish intellectuals such as Dr. Nurî Dersimî (1893–1973)[51] and the Alevi dignitary, Seyid Rıza (1863–1937), who, after the commencement of the military operation in the spring of

[49] Saygı Öztürk, 'İsmet Paşa'nın Kürt Raporu', *Hürriyet*, 8 September 1992, p. 7.
[50] FO 371/14580, Matthews to Clerk, Trebizond, 15 November 1930.
[51] For Dersimî's memoirs, see Dersimî (1992).

1937, alongside other chieftains in the region pleaded with the secretary-general of the League of Nations in a letter sent on 20 November 1937 with the following words:

> The tyrannies of the Turkish government against human rights and the Kurdish nation, of which the ethnic and national existence has been recognised by diplomatic conferences and by international conventions, are incompatible with the essence and entirety of the inspiring and liberating principles of your organisation. ... In order for the League of Nations to be able to take various apposite measures to prevent the continuation of these tyrannies and the total extermination of the Kurdish nation, it needs ... to infiltrate the thoroughness of these tragedies. To that we will reply: it suffices to send onto our soil an international commission of inquiry.[52]

However, the people of Dersim – which as a result of the Tunceli Law of 1935 was re-designated as a province, to be known by the Turkish name Tunceli – were never to receive any external assistance against the resolute Kemalist military offensive, which continued until Dersim was occupied in 1938. The contemporaries estimated that by the end of 1938, some 40,000 Kurds perished in this province (Rambout, 1947: 39). The Tunceli Law, which was initially to last up until 1 January 1940, remained in force until 1 January 1947. The ramifications of this law are deftly summarised by a report sent by Osman Mete, special correspondent for the Turkish Daily *Son Posta*, who visited Dersim in 1948:

> I went to Tunc Eli, the old Dersim. The place was desolate. Tax collectors and policemen are still the only state officials the people have ever seen. I tried to meet the people, to get to know their way of life, their spirit. But unfortunately very little remains from the period before the revolt. There are no more artisans, no more culture, no more trade. I met unoccupied people whose life now seem[s] to revolve around a flock of hundred goats. ... There are no schools, no doctors. The people don't know what 'medicine' means. If you speak to them of the government, they translate it immediately as tax collector and policemen. We give the people of Dersim nothing; we only take. We have no right to carry on treating them like this. (Kendal, 1982: 72)

The Second World War and the End of the Republican Era

During the Second World War, all of Turkey's neighbours either were at war or occupied by one or other of the belligerents. Turkey succeeded in not participating actively in the war though it was faced with the constant risk of invasion. Thus, full-scale mobilisation was maintained throughout

[52] Letter of Dersim tribal leaders to the League of Nations dated 20 November 1937. Translated from Dersimî (1997: 299–303).

the war. The maintenance of an army of more than 1 million placed massive strains on the economy. Under these circumstances, ètatism was gradually pushed aside.

In the course of the Second World War, Turkey's GDP declined by 35 per cent, and the wheat output dropped by more than 50 per cent (Pamuk, 2008: 280). Concomitantly, per capita income fell by around a quarter. On account of financing defence expenditure via monetary expansion, the CHP government encouraged inflation, which, in turn, triggered hardship for large segments of society: the cost-of-living index rose from 100 in 1939 to 350 in 1945 (Issawi, 1980: 369). The implementation of the 1940 National Defence Law (Milli Koruma Kanunu), through which the government could confiscate 'idle economic resources', and the 1942 Wealth Levy (Varlık Vergisi), which was applied in a disproportionate and confiscatory manner on non-Muslims and ethnic minorities (Robinson, 1963: 122), only rubbed more salt into the wounds of an impoverished nation.

The defeat of Germany and the non-renewal of the Friendship Treaty with the Soviet Union after the war[53] pushed Turkey towards the United States. In accordance with its long-term objectives, the United States wanted Turkey to be a part of the US-dominated world order that was in the making, and to act as a bulwark against Soviet expansion in the Cold War era, as outlined by the following US National Security Council statement in 1949: 'Turkey's independence and the maintenance of her status as a buffer against expansion of the Soviet Union into the Mediterranean and the Middle East is of critical importance to the Security of the US' (Yalman, 2009: 183).

In light of the strategic importance imputed to Turkey, she was permitted to benefit from the military assistance provided as part of the Truman Doctrine, which stipulated that the United States would help defend 'free nations' whose existence was threatened by foreign forces or by radical minorities inside their borders. Additionally, Turkey was allowed to take advantage of the economic aid granted by the Economic Recovery Plan (ERP), better known as the Marshall Plan, even though Turkey had not been actively involved in the Second World War.

[53] In 1945, the Friendship Treaty with Turkey had come to an end, and the Soviet Union had formulated a number of important conditions which Turkey would have to meet before a new friendship treaty could be signed: (a) retrocession to the Soviet Union the provinces in north-eastern Anatolia, which had been under the control of the Russians between 1878 and 1918 (i.e. the provinces of Kars and Artvin); (b) the establishment of joint Turco-Soviet defence installations in the straits; and (c) the revision of the 1936 Montreux Convention, governing access through the straits, in favour of the Soviet Union. Despite the Soviet Union dropping these demands in 1946, as a result of the firm refusal of Turkey, a new Friendship Treaty was not signed.

However, if the strategic significance of Turkey was a determinate factor in shaping US–Turkish relations in the post-war era, another was the imposition of a specific role to the Turkish economy by the United States within the context of the Marshall Plan:

> Turkey's primary role in the recovery program will be to augment its production of essential commodities in conformity with European and world requirements. ... Since Turkey is predominantly an agricultural country in its economy and in its exports, the anticipated gains in agricultural output will be of greater importance to the recovery program as whole than increases in industrial output. (ibid.: 182)

Relatedly, after the Second World War, the quandary facing ruling politicians in Turkey was how to reconcile post-war adjustment (i.e. reintegrating the Turkish economy into the world economy in agreement with the liberalisation of international trade relations as espoused by the architects of the new world order) with industrialisation (i.e. maintaining the objective of nationalistic industrialisation which was the *sine qua non* of the 'national economy' and national development). Hence, in the post-war years, the restructuring of the political, economic and legal architecture of Turkey necessitated by the intensified incorporation of Turkey into the world capitalist system created thorny predicaments for the governors of the Turkish Republic in all realms of government.

Despite the two world wars and the Great Depression, per capita levels of production and income in Turkey were 30–40 per cent higher at the end of the Republican era in 1950 than on the eve of the First World War (Pamuk, 2008: 280). Per capita income in Turkey in 1950 was at US$ 1,620 constant or inflation adjusted, which was equal to 24 per cent of the per capita income capita of the high-income countries and 188 per cent of developing countries of Asia, Africa and Latin America (ibid.: 270). In addition, Turkey's GDP growth rate between 1929 and 1950 was 83 per cent – high when compared, for example, with other developing countries such as India, Egypt, Yugoslavia and Greece for the same period: 21, 59, 30 and −12 per cent, respectively (Tezel, 1982: 450).

However, when the focus of development economics is shifted from GDP per capita to a more comprehensive measure in the form of human development index (HDI),[54] a less remarkable picture emerges. That is to say, when the HDI of Turkey in 1913 and 1950 is compared with those of other developing countries with similar levels of GDP in Eastern Europe,

[54] Human Development Index, first used by the United Nations in 1990, is a broader measure of development based on three components: education as measured by a weighted average of adult literacy and schooling; health as measured by life expectancy at birth; and income as measured by GDP per capita.

Table 4.4 *Changes in the Human Development Index, 1913–1950*[55]

Country	1913	1950
Western Europe	0.580	0.707
North America	0.643	0.774
Japan	0.466	0.676
China	n.a.	0.225
India	0.143	0.247
Africa	n.a.	0.271
Greece		0.625
Russia	0.345	0.694
Bulgaria	0.403	0.607
Argentina	0.511	0.526
Mexico	0.270	0.484
Brazil	0.249	0.448
South Korea	n.a.	0.459
Malaysia	n.a.	0.407
Thailand	0.388	0.603
Indonesia	n.a.	0.337
Tunisia	n.a.	0.303
Iran	n.a.	0.331
Egypt	n.a.	0.291
Nigeria	n.a.	0.194
Turkey	**0.190**	**0.382**

Source: Pamuk, 2008: 272.

Latin America and East Asia, it becomes apparent that Turkey's human development measures had been lagging behind developing countries with similar levels of income (see Table 4.4).

The feeble performance of Turkey in the HDI is considered a by-product of two central issues that have haunted its development since 1923. The first is the large regional disparities between the predominantly Kurdish ESA and the rest of the country. The second is the gender inequalities – i.e. Turkey falling behind developing countries with analogous levels of income in indices aiming to measure gender equality and the socioeconomic development of women (Pamuk, 2008: 272–3).

The available data[56] on living standards demonstrate that from the promulgation of the Republic up to the end of CHP rule, the

[55] Regional or continental averages are measured by the population of the individual countries. The maximum possible improvement in HDI is 1(HDI in 1950).

[56] It is apposite to state here that prior to 1968, statistical information on the geographical distribution of income and wealth in Turkey had been non-existent. The maiden statistical study on the spatial distribution of income and wealth based on direct observation in the form of income surveys was undertaken in 1968. For a comprehensive analysis of the

improvements in living conditions in the ESA provinces had been considerably inferior to that of the other parts of Turkey, as exhibited by the figures tabulated in Table 4.5.

The policies implemented during these twenty-seven years did not narrow, but deepened the gulf between ESA and the rest of Turkey. In concrete terms, the difference in the literacy rates between the western provinces (excluding Istanbul, Ankara, Izmir, Bursa and Adana) and the eastern provinces (to the east of Hatay, Zonguldak, Bolu, Eskişehir and Konya) went up from 4 per cent in 1927 to 15 per cent in by 1950 (Tezel, 1982: 460–1). Similarly, regional disparities in industrial development had further widened in the Republican period. It is worth remembering here that changes in the regional distribution of industry reflect both the character and the results of the development programmes conducted under the Republicans. Industrialisation, throughout the Republican era, was not only considered the dominant technological economic force with the potential of reshaping the socioeconomic and political structures in the country, but also was conceived as the precondition for regional and national development.

As outlined in Table 4.6,in 1927, 17.8 per cent of the industrial enterprises in Turkey were located in ESA. In 1939, this figure dropped sharply to 8 per cent. By 1955, only 7.7 per cent of the industrial enterprises in the country were based in these regions. In contrast, the percentage of the industrial enterprises situated in the western Aegean region augmented from 17.9 per cent in 1939 to 19.8 per cent in 1995. Likewise, the proportion of industrial firms sited in the north-western Marmara region increased from 29.6 per cent in 1939 to 47.8 per cent in 1955. The low level of industrialisation witnessed in ESA provinces made agriculture virtually the sole source of income.

The findings of a study in 1949 by the director general of the Central Statistical Office, Şefik Bilkur, indicate that disparities between the ESA regions and the rest of Turkey also widened in the agricultural sector. Irrespective of the estimated 30 per cent increase in national per capita agricultural income between 1935 and 1943, the agricultural income of the rural populace in ESA was found to be less than half of the national average agricultural income in 1943. More specifically, 34 TL per hectare was verified by the aforementioned research as Turkey's average agricultural income per capita in 1943, the agricultural income per head was at its lowest level in ESA where the income per hectare was 16 TL and reached its highest point in the western Aegean region where

nature and historicity of studies on the spatial distribution of income and wealth in Turkey, see Karaman (1986) and Hansen (1991: 275–87).

Table 4.5 *Indicators of regional differences in living standards, 1923–1950*

Regions/ Provinces	Population	7+ Literacy Rate			The number of doctors per 100,000 population 1950 (1)	The number of land vehicles per 10,000 population 1950 (2)	The number of radios per 10,000 population 1950
	1950 (1,000)	1927 %	1950 %	Changes in 1927–50 as %			
Istanbul Ankara Izmir	1,180	45	73	+28	316	64	981
Adana Bursa	2,637	12	47	+35	56	26	272
Western Provinces (3)	7,322	10	38	+28	24	9	115
Eastern Provinces (4)	9,341	6	23	+17	15	6	53

Key:
(1) The number of doctors is inclusive of dentists, and the figures are attained from the statistics for the year 1953.
(2) Land vehicles comprise automobiles, lorries, buses and jeeps.
(3) Zonguldak, Bolu, Eskişehir, Konya, Hatay and the provinces to the west of these, excluding Istanbul, Ankara, Adana, Izmir and Bursa.
(4) Provinces to the east of Hatay, Zonguldak, Bolu, Eskişehir and Konya.

Source: Tezel, 1982: 461.

Table 4.6 *The regional distribution of industrial enterprises, 1927–1955*

	1927(1)		1939(2)		1955	
Region	No.	%	No.	%	No.	%
Marmara	19,170	29.6	581	51.0	1,961	47.8
Aegean	11,550	17.9	232	20.0	812	19.8
Central Anatolia	10,220	15.8	83	8.0	488	10.9
Eastern Black Sea	7,947	12.3	73	6.0	280	6.8
Eastern and Southeastern Anatolia	11,448	17.8	96	8.0	316	7.7

Notes:
(1) Figures include the small industrial enterprises.
(2) Only includes industrial enterprises benefitting from the 1927 Law for Encouragement of Industry.
Source: Serin, 1963: 147.

it rose to 51 TL. The 'remaining regions [of Turkey] were situated between these two limits' (Bilkur, 1949: 11).

4.5 Transition to a Turbulent Democracy and 'Incorporation' of ESA (1950–1980)

Economic Integration of the Kurdish Region and the Revival of the Kurdish ağas *and* sheikhs *during the Democrat Party Decade (1950–1960)*

On 14 May 1950, the first democratic elections in the history of the Turkish Republic took place. The electorate inflicted a humiliating defeat to the CHP, giving it only 39.5 per cent of the overall votes whilst its rival, the Democrat Party (Demokrat Parti, DP) – which was officially established on 7 January 1946 – received 52.7 per cent of the votes. In the new Assembly, the DP had 408 seats against the CHP's 69. The 1950 elections had taken place five years after 'National Chief' President İsmet İnönü's famous speech of 19 May 1945 in which he indicated that the time was ripe to move in the direction of democracy.

The judgement to do away with the single-party regime had been taken in light of significant domestic and international factors. On the home front, the different social classes became highly disillusioned with the single-party regime. Owing to the wartime inflation, taxes and confiscations, as well as the controversial decisions taken since the proclamation of the Turkish Republic, disfranchisement amongst the peasants and other sections of the labouring masses reached a critical level. Therefore, in order to prevent a social explosion, the multi-party electoral regime was seen as a viable option to channel public discontent.

Moreover, the Turkish bourgeoisie became increasingly apprehensive of authoritarian rule and lobbied for political pluralism. Despite the substantial benefits of the policies implemented during the Republican era, the multi-party system was regarded by the bourgeoisie as a safety net against dependency on a single party. The root causes of this anxiety were the Wealth Levy of 1942 and the Land Distribution Law of 1945, which the CHP wanted to implement in order to regain its waning public support. International factors were also influential in shaping the political architecture in Turkey after the Second World War. The post-war adjustment policies designed by the United States as the dominant world power entailed adhering to a liberal economic model and political system, which necessitated a shift from the one-party dictatorship.[57]

The transition to multi-party rule, however, did not lead to a qualitative shift in the Kurdish policies of the Turkish state, principally because the Democrat Party government (1950–60) did not sufficiently detach itself from the hegemonic Kemalist ideology and failed to deal with the legacy of CHP rule in the ESA provinces. During the decade in which the DP was in power, not a single implementation and/or crime from the Republican era was debated, let alone punished. This is unsurprising considering that the four defecting CHP deputies who launched the DP when the government pushed for the Land Distribution Law in 1945, in spite of their steadfast opposition, were long-standing Kemalists.[58]

Their loyalty to Kemalism was reaffirmed when establishing the DP with the adoption of the 'six arrows' of Kemalism, albeit declaring that they would not intransigently practise them but would interpret them according to the needs of the Republic. Indeed, they did not dogmatically pursue the 'six arrows'. In harmony with the advice of ERP, from its inception, the DP government, headed by Menderes, replaced ètatism with liberal free-market economics and substituted the industry-oriented model of development for the agriculture-led model at a time when agriculture continued to be the dominant sector. In 1950, agriculture accounted for 54 per cent of the GDP, and its share of total employment

[57] For a detailed account of the transitional years 1945–50, see Karpat (1959) and Lewis (1968).

[58] The four seasoned ex-Republican politicians who founded the DP were Celal Bayar (1883–1986), the banker and confidant of Mustafa Kemal; Adnan Menderes (1899–1961), a prominent landowner from the Aegean region; Fuad Köprülü (1890–1966), a historian and a professor of Turcology; and Refik Koraltan (1889–1974), a veteran bureaucrat.

was 80 per cent (Pamuk, 2008: 268–9). The DP also brought an end to the dichotomy of state versus the traditional institutions, which had been a major source of the frustration amongst those who opposed the top-down Western-centric modernisation policies implemented during the Republican era. In other words, the DP pragmatically accommodated traditional institutions, structures and ways of life.

Incorporation of the Kurdish Elite

The Democrat Party government allowed the bulk of the Kurdish deportees, including the tribal chieftains and religious figures, to return, and, in turn, akin to the policies of Sultan Abdülhamid II, it incorporated the traditional Kurdish elite into the Turkish political system. Despite the suppressive measures during the single-party period, the old landowning elite (be it *ağas*, large landed families or *sheiks*) still held title to the lands in their ancestral provinces, as the new civil code in 1926 confirmed private land from the Ottoman period. The most notable example of the DP co-opting the traditional elite was the promotion of Abdülmelik Fırat[59] (1934–2009), the grandson of Şeyh Said, to the prestigious position of deputy of the National Assembly. Thus, the agriculture-led development strategy during the Democrat decade marked the beginning of two interrelated processes: the economic incorporation of the Kurdish region into the Turkish economy, and the co-opting of the old Kurdish elite into Turkish political life. As an offshoot of these changes, a new breed of Kurdish propertied elites developed. Unlike their predecessors, the new elites repudiated their Kurdish origin and exploited their relationship with the peasants not as a means to semi-independence from the centre as in Ottoman times, but in order to become more closely integrated members of the Turkish ruling class.

Agriculture-Led Growth

The strong emphasis placed on agriculture enabled the agricultural output to more than double from 1947, at the time when pre-war levels of production were already attained, through 1953 (Pamuk, 2008: 281). This increase was largely due to the drastic enlargement of the acreage under cultivation – from 14.5 million hectares in 1948 to 22.5 million in 1956, far exceeding the population growth (Zürcher, 1994: 235) – and

[59] For a biography of Abdülmelik Fırat, see Kaya (2005).

the rapid commercialisation of agriculture.[60] These developments in agriculture were engendered by the following three complementary government policies: (a) the provision of cheap credit to large landowners; (b) distribution of state-owned lands and open communal pastures to peasants with scarce or no land; and (c) the maintenance of high prices for agricultural products through TMO, the government-buying agency.

The DP government used Marshall Plan aid[61] to subsidise the importation of agricultural machinery, particularly tractors, whose number soared from 1,756 to 43,727 in the years 1948–56 (Margulies and Yıldızoğlu, 1987: 281). The Menderes-led administration began to distribute about 1.8 million hectares of land to around 360,000 families between 1947 and 1962, but as few as 8,600 were taken from private landlords; nearly all lands distributed belonged to the state and were already in use for grazing (Aktan, 1966: 325). Agricultural producers also immensely benefitted from the high world market demand for wheat and other export commodities, by virtue of American stockpiling programmes during the Korean War (25 June 1950–25 June 1953) (Hansen, 1991: 338–44).

Pauperisation of the Kurdish Peasants, Aggrandisement of the Landlords

The distribution of land and the extensive use of agricultural machinery, however, did not lead to improvements in the living condition of the peasants, because, as the Kurdish novelist Yaşar Kemal recounted, '*the peasant was again share-cropping on the lands distributed by the government; he provided the land, the ağa provided the tractor.*'[62] A significant number of peasants who acquired land were forced to sell off their lands to the tractor-owning *ağas* or large landowners because of not being able to fund the hiring costs. This process increased the number of landless peasants and triggered migration to local towns and/or large metropolises in western Turkey. The proportion of landless peasant families in Turkey increased from 5.9 per cent to 30.7 per cent between 1950 and 1960, and the annual rate of urban population growth during 1950–5 stood at

60 For a detailed analysis of the commercialisation of agriculture during this period, see Margulies and Yıldızoğlu (1987: 269–92).

61 Between 1950 and 1962, $831.8 million in total grants was tendered by US economic assistance, and when we include loans and sales under PL 480 programmes involving soft currency payments by the United States during this period, the total US economic assistance amounts to $1,615.9 million (Rivkin, 1965: 97).

62 *Cumhuriyet*, 23 June 1955 (Yaşar Kemal's italics).

Table 4.7 *Landless peasant families in ESA, 1950–1968*

	1950 (%)	1962–8 (%)
Turkey	5.9	30.7
Urfa	36.7	55.0
Diyarbakir	37.1	47.0
Bingöl	20.0	40.0
Mardin	11.8	40.9
Siirt	12.0	42.0
Van	20.0	37.5
Tunceli	22.7	37.0
Elazığ	12.0	32.0
Ağrı	10.7	36.1
Erzincan	10.7	38.0
Erzurum	6.0	32.0
Kars	8.0	23.0
Adıyaman	–	34.0

Source: Sönmez, [1990] 1992: 144.

55.6 per cent in Turkey (Sönmez, [1990] 1992: 144–5). As a result, the gradual mechanisation of agriculture that commenced in the 1950s further intensified social differentiation in the countryside and accelerated rural migration into towns (Karpat, 1973: 58).

The rise in the number of landless peasant families between 1950 and 1960 in the predominantly Kurdish provinces far exceeded the national average (see Table 4.7). This was largely predicated on the more extensive use of agricultural machinery in ESA, to the extent that small and tenant farmers with plots that could not afford tractors would hire them from the large landowners in return for a proportion of their crop (Beşikçi, [1969] 1992: 195–8; McDowall, 2000: 398–9).

The increase in seizures and purchases of land by the landowning class concurred with the raising of the upper limit of landownership from 500 *dönüms*, as specified by the 1945 Land Distribution Act, to 5,000 *dönüms* by the National Assembly in 1950. These developments resulted in the Kurdish *ağas* or prominent landowning families accumulating more land as well as reducing the lands available for distribution. Consequently, the overwhelmingly Kurdish provinces in ESA constituted one of the important exclusions to the owner-cultivated smallholdings, which had been the predominant unit of agrarian production in Turkey during the Democrat period, as Herschlag observed in the 1960s:

> The present land tenure system can be roughly classified into four major categories: 1) old feudal land ownership devoid of modernisation – in the south-east; 2) the modern management type of large absentee ownership, under wage-relations – in the west and north-east; 3) small and medium ownership, with a growing tendency towards large ownership – in central Anatolia and in the Adana region; and, 4) small, fractioned and poor villages, the chief reservoir of rural wage-earners. The total number of families was estimated in the early 1960s at 3 million. Of these, 2 million were full land-owners, mainly of mushroom units, while another 1 million were partial owners, share-croppers, tenants and landless. (1968: 209)

According to the first modern agricultural census in Turkey in 1950, 1.5 per cent of families owned 25 per cent of the total cultivable land; the remaining 98.5 per cent owned 75 per cent of the cultivable land. Additionally, 72.6 per cent was owner-cultivated, and a further 21.5 per cent was partly owned. The findings of the Agricultural Census of 1963 suggest that owner-cultivated smallholdings remained the main form of land tenure since 68.7 per cent was 5 hectares or under and 85.3 per cent was under owner cultivation.[63]

However, data pertaining to nine of the fourteen predominantly Kurdish provinces in ESA collated in the Autumn Survey of 1952, which uniquely gives a detailed statistical data concerning land distribution amongst families, demonstrated the dominance of family-owned large holdings in this area. Two per cent of families in these provinces owned 30.5 per cent of the total cultivable land, while 59.5 per cent of the families owned only 18.6 per cent of the cultivable land. The findings of the 1960 The Village Inventory Studies of the Ministry of Village Affairs, which cover fifty-six of the then total sixty-seven provinces of Turkey, certify that concentration of land in the hands of large Kurdish landowners continued throughout the Democrat decade, as increasingly more villages became the private property of *ağas* or prominent landowning families. For example, in Urfa, out of the total 664 villages, 51 were owned by *ağas*, 72 by wealthy landowning families. In Diyarbakir out of the 663 villages, 70 were owned by rich landowning families, and in the province of Siirt, 11 *ağas* and 21 families owned in total 32 villages (Sönmez, [1990] 1992: 142).

These villages operated as political fiefdoms of one of the rival mainstream parties, depending on the partisan affiliations of the landowning class. The incorporation and aggrandisement of the landed elite during the 1950s fostered an axis of mutual reliance between the political parties in Ankara and the Kurdish landed elites that yielded a bloc of votes.

[63] Derived from Istanbul İktisadi ve Ticari İlimler Akademisi (1973: 47–8).

The much-sought-after communal votes were exchanged for top positions in the regional parties. When the DP came to power in 1950, a significant share of its votes in the ESA provinces were from the wealthy landowning families or large tribes, as a result of which the following leading members of these tribes and families attained seats in the National Assembly: Edip Altınakar (Sürgücüzâde tribe – Diyarbakır), Mustafa Ekinci (Seydan tribe –Lice) and Mehmet Tevfik Bucak (Bucak tribe – Siverek).

The '49'ers Incident' and the End of the 'Period of Silence'

In contrast, a section of the well-educated children of this traditional rural class along with other Kurdish students from less affluent backgrounds constituted the nucleus of the new generation of Kurdish organic intellectuals[64] who played a focal role in public debate of the Eastern Question: the socioeconomic underdevelopment in ESA. In the late 1950s, Kurdish university students from prominent landowning families, like Yusuf Azizoğlu (1917–70), alongside their peers from less well-off backgrounds, such as Musa Anter (1920–92), who were handpicked by state officials and sent to university in order to be made into 'good Turkish citizens', spearheaded an alternative and progressive movement.

This movement centred on raising awareness and promoting the socioeconomic development of the neglected Kurdish provinces. Despite avoiding an explicit campaign demanding national rights for the Kurds and concentrating on socioeconomic issues, for instance, tackling drought and encouraging government investment, they could not evade the suppressive measures of the DP government. Soon after the movement's birth in 1959, its activities were halted.

The Kurdish rebellion that had surfaced across the border in northern Iraq with the return from exile of the influential Kurdish leader Mullah Mustafa Barzani (1903–79) after the Iraqi Revolution in July 1958 played a significant role in the government clampdown on this movement. Turkish state officials were fretful that it might incite Kurds in Turkey to take similar forms of action (Tan, 2010: 323–34). On 17 June 1959, forty-nine leading Kurdish intellectuals, including the two mentioned

[64] The notion of organic intellectuals is based on Antonio Gramsci's distinction between 'organic' and 'traditional' intellectuals, with the former wedded to a particular social class (bourgeoisie or proletariat) and the latter connected to the older socioeconomic order and 'hegemonic project' (1971: 131–3). The role of the organic intellectuals is not simply to associate themselves with a social group but, much more importantly in terms of the struggles of hegemony, they are responsible for enabling the social group to attain some kind of political, social and cultural self-awareness. Thus, the organic intellectuals are both the producers and the products of sociopolitical interests.

earlier, were arrested. President Bayar and Prime Minister Menderes wanted the forty-nine hanged, but the prospect of hostile international reaction made them renege on their decision. The '49'ers episode' let the Kurdish genie out of the bottle, and the two decades of silence that had followed the 1936–8 Dersim rebellion came to an end.

In Ankara and Istanbul, alongside the small but highly active Kurdish intellectuals, there was a growing number of migrant Kurdish workers, who became members of the new expanding urban proletariat of Turkey. As briefly alluded to earlier, a sizeable segment of the landless Kurdish peasants in ESA sought employment in one of the local towns, and if not successful at their first port of call, they moved to industrial cities mainly in western Turkey. In six of the fourteen predominantly Kurdish provinces, the annual rate of urban population growth during 1955–60 surpassed the national average of 49.2 per cent: Elazığ (62.4%), Siirt (76.4%), Van (49.6%), Erzincan (87.7%), Hakkari (64.4%) and Tunceli (50.9) (Sönmez, [1990] 1992: 145). And of those migrants who moved beyond local towns, around 41 per cent went to Istanbul, 18 per cent to Ankara, 15 per cent to Adana and 4 per cent to Izmir (McDowall, 2000: 401). Eventually, the migratory process made the Kurdish question a perceptible reality for people living in Ankara and Istanbul, hundreds of miles away from the predominantly Kurdish provinces.

The movement from the countryside to towns and cities was not *sui generis* to the Kurdish provinces, as the 1950s witnessed mass migration from the rural to urban areas all over Turkey. More than a million people had left the countryside and by the end of the decade, the major cities were growing by 10 per cent a year (Zürcher, 1994: 237). Surplus labour began to flock to the cities, where employment was more readily found (Karpat, 1973: 191). The economic boom years of the DP government ended in 1953; the ensuing deteriorating economic conditions were a major push factor for rural-to-urban migration.

Crisis of Agriculture-Led Growth

With the end of the Korean War, international demand decreased, and prices of export commodities began to decline. Economic growth fell from the average rate of 13 per cent per annum in the 'golden years' (1950–3) of the Democrat decade to 9.5 per cent in 1954, and as a result the trade deficit in 1955 was eight times that of 1950 (Ahmad, 1977: 135). These years were followed by years of spiralling inflation (1956–9). During these years, prices rose around 18 per cent a year (Ahmad, 1993: 116), because regardless of slackening international demand and decline in prices of export commodities, the DP government continued with investment programmes and initiated a large price support programme for wheat, financed by increases in the money supply (Herschlag, 1968: 146; Pamuk, 2008: 282). In 1958, Western foreign allies announced that they would 'rescue' the Turkish economy and Menderes government by agreeing to provide Ankara with a loan of $359 million and the consolidation of the $400 million debt (Herschlag, 1968: 147). The Organisation for Economic Co-operation and Development (OECD) and IMF-backed economic programme introduced in August 1958 imposed certain 'stabilising measures', the most significant of which was the *de facto* devaluation of the lira from TL 2.80 to TL 9,025 to the dollar (ibid.).

The deteriorating economic situation combined with Menderes' increasingly authoritarian style of government, to the extent that in his 21 September 1958 Izmir speech, he openly threatened 'an end to democracy' and brought the country to the brink of chaos. The trend towards totalitarianism by the government representatives was based on the fear of being toppled, which was instilled by the January 1958 rumours of a military conspiracy and aggravated because of the July 1958 revolution in neighbouring Iraq as well as the rising popular unrest at home. The robust anti-government demonstrations – some of which the CHP encouraged – towards the end of the 1950s severely undermined government authority. The most resilient popular movements were the student rallies and large street demonstration on 28 April 1960 – first in Istanbul and then in Ankara – which continued virtually uninterrupted until the military takeover by the thirty-eight officers of the self-proclaimed National Unity Committee (Milli Birlik Komitesi, MBK), on 27 May 1960.[65]

The 1960 Coup

The coup involved more than a change of government. On the very day of the military takeover, the MBK, headed by the former commander-in-chief of the land forces, Cemal Gürses, set up a commission under the leadership of the rector of Istanbul University, Professor Sıddık Sami Onar, to rewrite the constitution and provide recommendations for the restructuring of Turkey's institutions. The junta's decision to engage five distinguished law professors from Istanbul University, who on 28 May 1960 through their initial report justified the coup on the basis that the DP had governed unconstitutionally, enabled it to portray the 27 May movement as more than a mere coup: as 'a revolution of the intellectuals'.

[65] For a detailed analysis of the Democrat Party era, see Eroğlu (1998) and Ahmad (1977).

On 12 June 1960, the MBK set up an interim government legalised by the professors with a provisional constitution enabling the MBK to rule until a new parliament had been elected. Undoubtedly the most important enactment of the interim government, which had governed the country until the first CHP and Justice Party (Adalet Partisi, AP) coalition government (10 November 1961–30 May 1962), was the 1961 constitution. The new constitution signalled the MBK's readiness to return to a civilian rule, albeit under the guardianship of the military, and demonstrated its proclivity to incorporate large segments of the population into the political system and the domestic market through liberal constitutional readjustments and institutional reorientations.

The 1961 Constitution

The 1961 constitution further developed the existing quasi-parliamentary system by introducing a bicameral parliament, with a lower house (National Assembly) elected by proportional representation, and an upper house (Republican Senate), consisting of 150 members, some elected and others appointed by the president. Both chambers constituted the Grand National Assembly of Turkey (GNAT). The new constitution as well as separating the executive from the judiciary, did also create the Constitutional Court, which vetted the legislations of the parliament.

Furthermore, the novel constitution established two central state institutions, namely, the National Security Council (Milli Güvenlik Kurulu, MGK) and the SPO. For the first time in the history of the Republic, Article 3 of the 1961 constitution gave the military a constitutional role by setting up the MGK, which was composed of the chief of the general staff, representatives of the armed forces and a government minister. The MGK's function was to assist the cabinet on matters vaguely defined as 'national security', which encompassed virtually all issues pertinent to running the state, and in March 1962 an additional bill increased the powers of this body by permitting it to interfere in the deliberations of the cabinet. Thus, the military was made the custodian and partner of the new regime.

Having recognised that the Democrats' aversion for drawing up and applying long-term plans of economic development had played a pivotal role in the economic downturn in the late 1950s (Hale, 1981: 117, Pamuk, 2008: 283), Article 129 of the new constitution stipulated the establishment of the SPO[66] so as to initiate the development of the

[66] The SPO was in charge of proposing and implementing plans for economic, social and cultural development under the High Planning Council.

country on a planned basis. In other words, the coup denoted a shift from a free-market economics approach to a planned economy. Accordingly, four consecutive five-year economic development plans were designed by the SPO (1963–7, 1968–72, 1973–7 and 1979–1983[67]).

Long Period of Import Substituted Industrialisation (1963–1979)

The economic policies of the military rule and the civilian rule that followed in the 1960s and 1970s aimed, primarily, at the protection of the domestic market and industrialisation through import substitution (ISI). In order to achieve the ISI objectives, governments made abundant use of a restrictive trade regime, investments by state economic enterprises (SEEs) and subsidised credit.

Akin to the ètatist period during the long period of import substitution, not only were SEEs imputed a central role in attaining set economic goals, but the public and the private sectors were also conceived as complementary and not mutually exclusive or antagonistic components of the Turkish economy. The private sector, moreover, was provided with a wide range of state incentives in order to enhance capabilities. For instance, private manufacturing and distribution companies, in addition to being provided with cheap inputs produced by the SEEs, were also permitted to borrow from the Treasury at much lower rates than inflation (Aydın, 2005: 37). As a result, by the 1980s, large corporations, big family holdings and banks were in far stronger positions than at the beginning of the 1960s (Pamuk, 2008: 283).

In order to safeguard the enlargement of the domestic market for the sustainability of the ISI, large segments of the society were incorporated into the internal market by means of the fundamental rights and freedoms granted under the 1961 constitution. The new liberal constitution vowed freedoms of thought, expression, association and publication, and promised social and economic rights and the freedom to work. Trade unions were granted the right to strike and partake in collective bargaining, and the dominated classes even established a political party, the Workers' Party of Turkey (Türkiye İşçi Partisi, TİP).

Systematic Denial of the Kurds

The interim government led by the MBK, in juxtaposition to the liberal dispensations granted by the 1961 constitution, gave an end to the

[67] The fourth five-year plan was delayed by the foreign exchange crisis of 1977–9 (Hansen, 1991: 352).

political overtures of the 1950s and adopted the suppressive Kurdish policies reminiscent of the Republican era. Turkey's Kurdish policy of the 1960 coup was philistinely expressed in the following words of the new national chief, General Gürsel, which he uttered standing on an American tank in the overwhelmingly Kurdish city of Diyarbakir: 'There are no Kurds in this country. Whoever says he is a Kurd, I will spit in his face' (Muller, 1996 177).

The disclosure in 2008 of a special report, titled *The Principles of the State Development Programmes in Eastern and Southeastern Anatolia*, prepared in 1961 by the SPO under the instructions of the MBK, revealed details of the policy prescriptions authorised by the new guardians of the Republic for the predominantly Kurdish provinces. A working group within the SPO, namely the 'East Group', which had toured the region on 8, 10 and 16 February 1961, drew up this report in early 1961. The junta-sanctioned 'East Report' comprised three core policy recommendations in order to 'fill the power vacuum [left by the state and] occupied by separatists, ağas and sheiks' and to give an end to the previously witnessed 'separatist activities' threatening the 'unitary structure' of the country.

First was 'transforming the existing social structure' in ESA by 'assimilating those who feel they are Kurdish'. Pursuant to this aim, the 'East Group' advised a set of complementing tools of assimilation: (a) wide circulation of existing and/or novel 'sociological and anthropological research' which posit that Kurds are of Turkish stock; (b) 'cultural propaganda' on radio; and (c) building more schools in the region in order to train 'missionaries' to spread the Turkish language and culture.

Second was 'changing the population structure' in this region by procuring the 'densification of Turks' so that they could gradually 'outweigh those who feel they are Kurds'. The numerical dominance of the hegemonic nation in this region could be achieved, the report argued, by means of transferring the 'excess Turkish population in the Black Sea littoral', by settling Turks migrating from overseas and by giving 'economic incentives to those who feel they are Kurds to move' where 'the sons of the Turks' are predominant. Last was 'increasing the income of the region and appropriately redistributing it' in order to overcome the 'neglect of the region by previous governments' and end the 'endurance of the backward social structures'.[68] This shift in

[68] This secret report was kept in the personal archives of the veteran statesman Bülent Ecevit (1925–2006) who received it when serving as the minister of work in the first CHP and Justice Party (Adalet Partisi, AP) government. The report came to light in the process of preparing Ecevit's biographical documentary by two influential journalists in Turkey,

policy with regard to augmenting public investment in the predominantly Kurdish regions of Turkey was advised by the 'East Group' with the objective of earning the loyalty of the Kurds who thus far were neglected by the state.

The interim government led by the MBK and the successive civilian governments actuated the assimilationist recommendations put forward in this report. In the early 1960s, as sanctioned by Law No. 1587 (1960), Kurdish place names were systematically changed into Turkish ones, and Turkish radio stations were set up in order to propagate the ideas set out in the East Report as well as discouraging listening to broadcasts in Kurdish from neighbouring countries (Nezan, 1993: 65). Additional measures taken by the state involved granting the registrars the right to refuse to record Kurdish names on birth certificates as well as establishing more regional boarding schools in the overwhelmingly Kurdish ESA with the specific aim of assimilating Kurds (McDowall, 2000: 405). By the end of the 1960s, of seventy boarding schools in Turkey, sixty were located in ESA (Beşikçi, [1969] 1992: 551–3).

On the other hand, the other two policies the 'East Group' advocated were either not adopted or not thoroughly implemented by governments that came to power after 1961 in light of the changing circumstances and/or priorities of the Turkish state. The ambitious task of gradually 'turkifying' ESA did not materialise, as the envisioned dual-track policy of resettling Turks in these regions and deporting Kurds from these regions through economic incentives had not been put into effect. The Forced Settlement Law No. 105 appended to the Settlement Law No. 2510 on 19 October 1960[69] by the interim government in order to deport 55 of the 485 most prominent Kurds detained immediately after the coup was annulled on 18 October 1962[70] by the second coalition government which comprised the CHP, New Turkey Party (Yeni Türkiye Partisi, YTP) and Republican Peasants' Nation Party (Cumhuriyetçi Köylü Millet Partisi, CKMP). With the implementation of the First Five-Year Plan in 1963, the Turkish state prioritised the policy of 'absorbing' the region over that of 'dismembering' it, espoused by the former Republican rulers, and thus the assimilationist programmes summarised earlier were preferred to the previously implemented social engineering policies advocated by the 'East Group' in a relatively mild form.

Can Dündar, and Rıdvan Akar. For an extensive version of this report, see Dündar and Akar (2008).

[69] *Resmi Gazete*, Issue No. 10638, 25 November 1960.

[70] *Resmi Gazete*, Issue No. 11239, 23 November 1962.

Restoration of the Status Quo Ante *and the Failed Promise of Land Reform*

The annulment of the Forced Settlement Law of No. 105, moreover, permitted the deported *ağas* to return to their old places of residence and reinstated all their land and property (Ahmad, 1977: 216–17). Accordingly, the state restored the order existing before the coup in the eastern and south eastern provinces. Despite the recurrent theme in the official rhetoric of the successive governments in the 1960s and 1970s of the need to 'break up the backward structure' in ESA (Yeğen, 2011: 71), the 'feudal land ownership devoid of modernisation in the south-east' – alluded to by Herschlag – existent at the beginning of the 1960s remained intact in the ensuing two decades. The failure to implement the much-needed root-and-branch land reform implicated the endurance of the traditional land tenure patterns and agrarian relations.

The junta's promise of land reform in 1960, like the promises of the various elected governments of 1961–9 succeeding it, failed to materialise (Ahmad, 1977: 276–8). It was not until June 1973, during the period of semi-military rule, that a new land reform was passed, which in May 1977 the Constitutional Court nullified. In the lifetime of this law, as little as 23,000 hectares of land was distributed to 1,200 peasant families (Hale, 1981: 185–6). Thus, the landed property of the large landowning families remained virtually untouched. In 1980, 8 per cent of the families in ESA owned more than 50 per cent of the cultivable land, while 80 per cent of the families were evenly matched between those holding up to five hectares and those who were landless (McDowall, 2000: 243).

The continuity in the concentration of land in the hands of wealthy landlords during the 1960s and 1970s was, furthermore, an indication of the preservation of the alliance built in the 1950s between the co-opted traditional (tribal/religious) landed Kurdish elites and the Turkish state. The collaboration between these two parties had openly manifested itself with the harsh measures the state authorised to suppress the occasional peasant revolts that took place in the 1970s. When the peasants occupied the land belonging to the *ağa* and demanded that it be redistributed, they were on each occasion confronted by the military who would not shy away from using heavy-handed tactics to remove them and give the land back to the owners (Nezan, 1993: 91).

The Kurdish peasant actions in the 1970s came about against the backdrop of a period of political mobilisation spearheaded by the previously mentioned mass demonstrations in 1967: 'Eastern Meetings' (Beşikçi, 1992). By 1969, one of most important left-wing Kurdish groups, the Revolutionary Eastern Cultural Hearths (Devrimci Doğu

Kültür Ocakları, DDKO), was formed. The DDKO provided the kernel for a large number of other revolutionary Kurdish groups, including the PKK.[71] Alongside economic concerns, political factors, like the aforementioned regeneration of the Kurdish revolt in Iraq after the 1958 coup, and the development of a robust left-wing movement in Turkey, which by advocating social justice and equality became a point of attraction for the Kurds, had a tremendous effect on the revival of Kurdish activism in 1960s and 1970s Turkey. Consequently, from the 1960s on, the conservation of the state-landed Kurdish elite's alliance was grounded on the shared objective of maintaining the prevailing economic and political order increasingly opposed by large segments of the Kurdish society in Turkey.

Intensification of Regional Inequalities and Massive Underdevelopment of the Kurdish Region

One of the factors fuelling the disillusionment and dissent of the Kurds in this period was the immense underdevelopment of the largely Kurdish ESA. Relatedly, the programmes of the 1965, the 1969 and the 1970 administrations contained pledges to undertake 'special measures' in an attempt to overcome the socioeconomic disparities between regions and encourage the development of the 'Eastern regions' (Yeğen, 1999: 163–7). Yet, as outlined in the programme of the 1969 administration, the aim of the 'special measures' was not to 'initiate the formation of privileged regions, but to *forge integration*' (Yeğen, 1999: 164). Put differently, the overarching aim of the 'special measures' was to incorporate the ESA provinces in accord with the requirements and necessities of the domestic market, and not to privilege or prioritise the exigent needs of these lagging and long-neglected provinces. Hence, in the 1960s and the 1970s, despite the main economic development strategy centred on ISI successfully bringing about significant economic growth, the underdevelopment of the predominantly Kurdish eastern and south eastern provinces deepened.

When the period of planned import substitution of 1961–3 to 1977–9 is compared to that of the Democrat decade of 1951–3 to 1961–3, the GDP growth rate increased from 4.9 per cent to 6.4 per cent, with an equally robust increase in the gross national income (GNI) growth rate from 4.4 per cent to 6.3 per cent. In addition, GDP growth per capita increased from 2.1 per cent to 3.9 per cent, with GNI growth per capita income

[71] For an expanded study of the influence of the DDKO on the establishment of the PKK, see Marcus (2007: 21–30).

increasing from 1.6 per cent to 3.8 per cent. Thus, the growth of per capita income more than doubled, which compared well with that of the industrialised and developing countries. The average growth of GNP per capita for the period 1960–77, as set by the World Bank, for middle-income countries was 3.6 per cent, for industrialised countries 3.4 per cent and for low-income countries 1.4 per cent (Hansen, 1991: 354).

Even with this impressive economic performance, the socioeconomic disparities between different geographic zones inherited from previous decades intensified during 1960–80, to the detriment of ESA, as the SPO conceded in 1979:

> Ever since the 1st Plan [First Five-Year Plan] the issue of regional imbalances have been addressed and within all three of the [Five-Year] Plans a range of policies have been designated to overcome this issue. Despite all efforts and policies, regional imbalances have exacerbated. … With the exclusion of the Eastern and Southeastern Anatolia regions in all of the other regions the share of national income has been similar to the share of total population. (SPO, 1979: 75)

Throughout the long period of planned import substitution, the national income share of the seventeen eastern and south eastern provinces continually decreased: in 1965, it was 10.39 per cent, in 1975, it reduced to 9.56 per cent and by 1979, it further dropped to 8.17 per cent (USARM, 2009: 18). This persistent decline in the national income share of these provinces was in spite of the constant increase in their proportion of the total population during the 1960s and 1970s, as demonstrated by the census figures tabulated in Table 4.8.

Thus, income disparities between the ESA provinces and the rest of the country did not reduce in the heyday of the period of planned import substitution, that is, the years before the first oil shock of 1973–4,[72] and persisted until the end of this period because of the incessant decrease in the national income share of the former provinces.

Derisory Public and Private Investment

A significant causal factor for the perseverance of the regional income disparities between the ESA and the rest of the country was the low and inadequate level of public and private investment in the latter domains during the long period of planned import substitution, which was

[72] The first oil shock quadrupled the price of oil in the international market and further deteriorated the balance of trade and balance of payments deficit of an oil-dependent Turkish economy, a natural predicament for a rapidly industrialising economy that was not export-orientated (Hale, 1981: 203–6; Zürcher, 1994: 280–1).

Table 4.8 *Population of ESA, 1950–1970*

Population	1950	1960	1970
General	20,947,188	27,754,820	35,605,176
Eastern and Southeastern Anatolia	3,528,932	4,713,101	6,178,964
Eastern and Southeastern Anatolia' Share in Turkey (%)	16.8	17.0	17.3

Source: Sönmez, [1990]1992: 259.

nowhere near enough to counterbalance the past years of neglect and massive underdevelopment. It is worth noting that state investment during 1960–80 is estimated to have constituted more than 50 per cent of the overall investment in Turkey (Aydın, 2005: 35). Despite the SPO designating the whole ESA as 'Priority Development Regions' (PDRs) as of 1968, between the First Five-Year Plan and the Fourth Five-Year Plan, public investment in the provinces situated in this part of country decreased by 40 per cent. In total, forty provinces were classified as PDRs, that is, provinces in need of extra investment and incentives: all eighteen of the provinces in ESA, plus twenty-two other provinces located in the Black Sea littoral and central Anatolia. The share of public investment for ESA provinces in the four consecutive Five-Year Plans was as follows, respectively: 11.85, 11.90, 7.11 and 7.20 (Sönmez, [1990] 1992: 158). The share of public investment in the western Marmara region, on the other hand, increased from 11.70 per cent in the First Five-Year Plan to 15.70 per cent in the Fourth Five-Year Plan (ibid.).

From 1962–3 to 1974–8, private investment in Turkey increased from 8.8 per cent to 11.2 per cent (Hansen, 1991: 369), but private-sector investment in ESA provinces remained nominal, owing in part to the little effort the state put in to encourage private investment in this area. From 1968, in order to encourage private investment in the PDRs, the SPO introduced state-sanctioned incentive schemes, which involved exemption from financial tax and stamp duties. Albeit the provinces in ESA accounting for almost half of all the PDRs in Turkey, only 5.8 per cent of the total 5,918 incentives the state approved during 1968–80 were for these provinces (Sönmez, [1990] 1992: 188).

Unbalanced Sectoral Distribution of Public Investment

The other factors fuelling the disparities between ESA and the rest of Turkey during the long period of planned import substitution emanated from the following two perennial features of public investment in these regions: (a) unbalanced sectoral distribution; and (b) prioritisation of the needs of the industrialised western economic centres over that of the primary and immediate requirements of ESA. The heavy investments in the energy and mining sectors, which, with the exclusion of the Third Five-Year Plan, constituted the main part of the public investment in the four quinquennial plans in east and south east Turkey, exemplify both of these aspects (see Table 4.9). As it will be explicated, very little, if any at all, of the production in the energy and mining sectors, was locally used. These minerals were exported overseas and to other areas in Turkey. The earnings from these were retained mainly by the Turkish state as well as the private sector based outside of ESA. In consequence, the region has had very little benefit from the flow of its resources, as these potential investments were not available for its further development.

During 1965–75, one of the major investment projects in ESA was the 900-Megawatt (MW) Keban Dam scheme on the Upper Euphrates, which opened in 1975 (Hale, 1981: 205). Within the first five years, the Keban hydroelectric power plant was generating 504 MW of electricity (i.e. 56 per cent of its total generation capacity), 400 MW of which was transmitted to western Turkey. When the Keban hydroelectric power plant operated at its full capacity, it had the potential of generating a quarter of the total electricity produced in Turkey in 1980 (Sönmez, [1990] 1992: 157–60). Six other hydroelectric power schemes in ESA provinces that received large amounts of government investment during and after the Second Five-Year Plan were Elazığ-Hazar II, Van-Engil, Van-Erçiş, Elazığ-Hazar, Mardin-Cağ-Cağ and Kars-Kiği.

Between 1960 and 1980, the other main area of public investment in ESA was Turkey's largest and one of the world's richest chrome mines situated in the eastern province of Elazığ: Güleman chromite (chromium ore) deposits operated by the state-owned Etibank (Sönmez, [1990] 1992: 160). Chrome ore production statistics indicate that Turkey's chrome output was 22,183,406 tons between 1942 and 1979 (Engin et al., 1981: 34), 30 per cent of which was produced in the Güleman area and the remainder came from a number of smaller mines in various different parts of Turkey: Bursa, Eskişehir, Fethiye and Antalya (ibid.). Since the 1960s, chrome exports from the Güleman mines accounted for the greatest foreign exchange earnings among Turkey's mining exports (Europa, 2003: 1142). For instance, in 1967, chrome exports from the Güleman area were worth $7.2 million and in 1972, they increased to $17.5 million (Jafar, 1976: 68). Yet little chrome was processed locally; almost the entire chrome output was exported (Europa, 2003: 1142).

Table 4.9 *Sectoral distribution of the public investment in ESA, 1963–1983*

Sectors	I. F. Y. P.[73] %	II. F. Y. P. %	III. F. Y. P. %	IV. F. Y. P. %
Energy	24.1	40.0	16.0	19.8
Mining	9.6	6.0	4.0	11.8
Agriculture	13.2	14.6	9.4	8.4
Manufacturing Industry	8.0	11.0	27.4	23.2
Transport	11.2	7.3	13.6	8.0
Education	17.0	11.8	15.0	11.3
Health	5.0	3.0	2.9	2.5
Other	11.9	6.3	11.7	15.0

Source: Sönmez, [1990] 1992: 158.

Moreover, the Second Five-Year Plan (1968–72) included projects to enhance the production of copper, zinc and lead mined in Elazığ by Etibank. The set output targets were as follows: (a) augmenting the output of Elazığ's Ergani copper mines to 1,200,000 tons/year; (b) increasing lead production to 8,000 tons/year; and (c) expanding zinc production to 6,000 tons/year (Jafar, 1976: 68–9). Systematic or longitudinal statistical data on the actual amount and value of production and/or exports for zinc, lead and copper production in Elazığ in the 1960s and 1970s are hard to come by. Nevertheless, the available data from 1969 indicate that production of blister copper (or raw copper) by Etibank in the country's oldest copper mines, the Ergani copper mines, amounted to around 24,000 tons, 16,000 tons of which were exported to the United States, the United Kingdom and West Germany. These exports were worth $17 million in foreign currencies (Europa, 2002: 1130).

The petroleum sector had been the other main beneficiary of public investment during the period of planned import substitution (Aytar, 1991: 62–8). Petroleum in Turkey was discovered in 1950 in ESA, and all successive discoveries have been in these domains (Europa, 2002: 1130). Thus, provinces located in ESA were the sole producers of petroleum during the 1960s and the 1970s. From the mid-1950s to the early 1970s, owing in part to state investment, there was a noticeable increase in petroleum production: from 178,000 tons in 1955 to 3,500,000 tons in 1973 (ibid.). Between 1955 and 1972, production of petroleum is

[73] Five-Year Plan (F.Y.P.).

estimated to be worth $27 million (Jafar, 1976: 68). Up until 1980, it maintained the same level of production as 1973 (Europa, 2002: 1130). The great majority of the petroleum production was exported, since only 6 per cent of the total petrol refining capacity was located in ESA in the 1970s, and the proceeds attained from the petroleum exports were 'seldom re-cycled into the Region's [ESA] economy' (Jafar, 1976: 68).

In juxtaposition to the sizable state investment in the energy and mining sectors in ESA, there was little and insufficient investment in the manufacturing industry, especially in the first two Five-Year Plans, considering the exceptionally low level of industrial development witnessed in this area during the Republican and the Democrat era. As a result, the stunted industrialisation of ESA deepened in the Planned Period.

Stunted Industrial and Agricultural Development

Even in the face of the value added by the manufacturing industry precipitously increasing from 6,636 million TL in 1963 to 148,014 million TL in 1977 (Hale, 1981: 197), eastern and south eastern provinces' share of the value added in manufacturing decreased from 7.8 per cent in 1968 to 4.0 per cent in 1974 (SPO, 1979: 75). It is worth noting that the SPO's calculations of the share of value added in manufacturing for these provinces take into account the crude oil output in the Batman Refinery.[74] In 1968, 34.3 per cent and in 1974, 42.3 per cent of the total share of valued added in manufacturing in ESA was generated by the Batman Refinery (ibid.). The Batman Refinery accounting for the bulk of the valued added in manufacturing generated by these provinces is indicative of the dismal state of the manufacturing industry in ESA.

According to the 1978 data tabulated in Table 4.10, the share of the manufacturing industry in the GDP of ESA regions was 10.5 per cent, while agriculture accounted for nearly half of the regions' GDP. In the western Marmara region, manufacturing industry accounted for 33.7 per cent of this region's GDP, and agriculture's contribution to the region's GDP was a mere 7.9 per cent. Therefore, ESA continued to be a predominantly agrarian region in the 1960s and 1970s.

During the period of planned import substitution, agricultural productivity rates in ESA witnessed a downward slide. In 1960–2, the ESA

[74] The Batman Refinery was the first refinery built in Turkey in 1955 with a capacity of 330.000 tons/year. Due to increasing demand, the capacity of the refinery was increased by the Debottlenecking Project to 580.000 tons/year in 1960. The crude oil–processing capacity of the Batman Refinery, which was continuously being upgraded with the modernisation studies, reached 1.1 million tons/year with commissioning of a new crude unit in 1972.

Table 4.10 *Sectoral breakdown of GDP in ESA and the Marmara region, 1978*

Sectors	ESA (%)	Marmara Region (%)
Agriculture	46.2	7.9
Manufacturing Industry	10.5	33.7
Construction	6.4	4.5
Trade	7.0	20.0
Transport	6.6	9.4
State Services	12.6	7.7
Others	10.7	16.8

Source: Sönmez, 2012: 351.

Table 4.11 *The GDP share and rankings of the ESA provinces, 1965 and 1979*

	1965		1979	
Provinces	Share (%)	Ranking	Share (%)	Ranking
Kars	1.20	18	0.70	40
Urfa	1.14	21	0.58	47
Erzurum	1.10	22	0.98	24
Elazığ	0.95	30	0.87	31
Malatya	0.88	36	0.68	41
Diyarbakır	0.78	43	0.83	34
Siirt	0.75	45	0.44	51
Mardin	0.72	47	0.58	46
Erzincan	0.56	49	0.40	54
Van	0.51	52	0.40	55
Adıyaman	0.42	57	0.41	53
Ağrı	0.35	61	0.33	61
Muş	0.33	63	0.32	62
Bitlis	0.23	47	0.20	64
Tunceli	0.18	65	0.16	66
Bingöl	0.16	66	0.18	65
Hakkari	0.13	67	0.11	67

Source: Sönmez, [1990] 1992: 190.

provinces accounted for 17.01 per cent of the total cultivated area and 17.10 per cent of the total crops produced in Turkey. In 1978–80, despite the share of these provinces in the total cultivated land rising to 19.89 per cent, the share of these provinces in the total crops produced

Table 4.12 *Literacy and educational attainment data for ESA for individuals aged six and older, 1985*

Provinces	Population Aged 6+	Illiteracy Rate	Non-schooling Rate
Adıyaman	341,248	38.2	60.5
Ağrı	326,893	43.7	64.5
Bingöl	190,508	42.2	63.2
Bitlis	231,520	45.5	70.2
Diyarbakır	739,419	47.7	65.8
Elazığ	408,607	31.0	50.0
Erzincan	257,212	23.7	41.6
Erzurum	703,872	30.4	49.9
Hakkari	138,266	54.3	69.5
Kars	592,916	28.9	51.5
Malatya	559,586	27.7	47.2
Mardin	502,747	52.0	70.3
Muş	260,757	44.6	65.4
Siirt	398,505	48.3	68.3
Tunceli	126,248	30.2	50.8
Şanlıurfa	627,269	52.0	68.7
Van	416,891	49.2	68.6
Turkey	43,112,337	22.5	40.9

Source: Sönmez, [1990] 1992: 263.

decreased to 14.61 per cent (Sönmez, [1990] 1992: 164). The decrease in output is believed to be inextricably linked to two region-wide issues: (i) the inefficient irrigation system deprived of modernisation; and (ii) the limited availability and use of chemical fertilisers (ibid.: 162–3).

During 1965–79, because of the stunted growth of agriculture and industry, with the exception of Diyarbakir and Bingöl, the GDP share of all the ESA provinces descended. Out of the overall sixty-seven provinces, the seventeen eastern and south eastern provinces, with a few exemptions, were the lowest-ranked provinces in the national GDP rankings.

In each of the successive four Five-Year Plans, the investment in education decreased (see Table 4.9). Therefore, the low level of literacy and schooling inherited from the Republican era could not be overcome in the Planned Period. Illiteracy and non-schooling rates of individuals aged six and older remained far above the national average in almost all of the provinces in ESA in 1985 (see Table 4.12). Inadequate state investment in education, coupled with formal education being in a language foreign to the majority of the inhabitants in this region, played a pivotal role in the persistence of low levels of literacy in the predominantly Kurdish ESA in the two decades after the single-party era. In other words, unlike other regions of Turkey, large sections of the populace of these regions were taught to read and write in a language other than their native language, Kurdish, which unsurprisingly constituted additional linguistic or literacy barriers.

In summary, the preconditions for socioeconomic development in ESA, that is, adequate public investment oriented towards the exigent needs of these long-neglected regions, land reform and the resultant removal of the *ağa* class, as well as the introduction of Kurdish-medium formal education, could not be implemented because all of these measures were antithetical to the Turkish state's policy of controlling the overwhelmingly Kurdish regions. Thus, the transition from a one-party autocracy to a multi-party political system, which was temporarily suspended by military intervention in 1960–1 and 1971–3, did not lead to a qualitative alteration in the Turkish state's perception of and preoccupation with the Kurdish question, largely because none of the regimes post-1950 sufficiently de-Kemalised or dealt with the legacy of the Young Turk rule. As a result, by the end of the 1970s, Turkey remained locked in contradictions created by the Kemalist shibboleths on the Kurdish issue and the predominantly Kurdish provinces in massive underdevelopment born of state negligence and paranoia.

5 Turkey's Kurdish Question in the Era of Neoliberalism: From the 1980 Coup to the AKP's Kurdish Overture (1980–2010s)

5.1 Overview

In the late 1970s, Turkey found itself in one of the gravest political and economic crises since the establishment of the Republic, prompting a military coup and the authoritarian implementation of a structural adjustment programme as well as a shift to export-led growth from 1980 on. In other words, in the wake of the economic crisis and political turmoil of the late 1970s, Turkey abandoned the ISI policies and instead adopted a neoliberal strategy focussed on the long-term objectives of export-oriented trade, a development strategy based on the neoclassical principle of comparative advantages and a more market-directed system of resource allocation. After a brief overview of the pivotal events in the late 1970s, this chapter will evaluate the implications of the political economy of post-1980 Turkey on the Kurdish policy of the Turkish state and the socioeconomic issues in the predominantly Kurdish ESA.

Turkey had a persistent balance of payment and balance of trade deficit throughout the 1960s and the 1970s as a result of Turkey's ISI giving birth to new labour-intensive industries which were not only heavily dependent on foreign subsidies,[1] manufacturing inputs and technology, but also not export-oriented.[2] Put differently, increasing import bills

[1] Foreign subsidies in the form of aids and loans, particularly from the United States. After the Second World War, the Turkish state was able to persuade the United States, supranational organisations and the funding agencies that the development of capitalism in Turkey should be subsidised externally largely because of the geostrategic importance of Turkey, as discussed in the previous chapter. Relatedly, between 1960 and 1974, American loans and aid constituted the principal mode of covering the trade deficit as they covered 'about one-third' of the deficit up until 1974 (Keyder, 1987: 180). From 1970 on, however, workers' remittances from Europe gained prominence: remittances 'peaked in 1974 with a total of $1.426 million' (Zürcher, 1994: 280).

[2] The export sector's share in 'GDP averaged less than 4 per cent during the 1970s, and about two-thirds of these revenues came from the traditional export crops' (Pamuk, 2008: 284).

coupled with meagre exports led to rapidly increasing trade deficits that had to be financed by foreign funds. The decline in the profits of the SEEs during the 1970s, resulting from the mismanagement of these state-owned enterprises by fragile and short-lived political coalitions with short-term horizons (Richards and Waterbury, 2008: 218–19) and the oil crises (1973–4 and 1979–80), only exacerbated the difficulties. As a result, the strategy of ensuring satisfactory profits for industrialists while also creating and sustaining an internal market resulted in a dismal failure.

In less than a decade, Turkey's debt grew almost five-fold: increasing from $3.3 billion in 1973 to $15.3 billion by 1980. Since rising budgetary deficits were met with monetary expansion, inflation jumped to 90 per cent in 1979 (Pamuk, 2008: 285). The second oil price shock in 1979–80, which depleted one-third of foreign reserves of the Central Bank, compounded the problems in the country. Oil for industry and electricity generating became increasingly limited, so much so that by 1979 power cuts of up to five hours a day were the rule, even in winter (Zürcher, 1994: 281). Unemployment rose officially from 600,000 in 1967 to 1.5 million in 1977, though the unofficial figures were much higher as each year only 40 per cent of new entrants to the labour market could find employment (McDowall, 2000: 411). Moreover, the number of days lost to strikes rose from 323,220 in 1970 to 2,217,347 in 1979 (Işıklı, 1987: 325). The economic crisis fuelled political instability as more people, especially the youth, were being disenfranchised by the existing system. Economic crisis, combined with political instability and violence, brought Turkey to the verge of civil war.

Radical left-wing groups, which were driven underground when the political left was proscribed after the 1971 military coup,[3] clashed with extremist right-wing groups, most notably Idealist Hearths or Grey Wolves: the youth organisation of MHP, a constituent member of the National Front coalition governments.[4] The latter was given

[3] After the coup, one of the top priorities of the generals was the 'restoration of law and order', and that meant the elimination of the political left, which was seen as a threat to the status quo, such as the TİP, the Federation of the Revolutionary Youth of Turkey (Dev-Genç) and the Confederation of Revolutionary Trade Unions of Turkey (DİSK).

[4] There were two successive National Front coalition governments. The First National Front governed the country from 31 March 1975 until 5 June 1977 and was composed of four parties: the AP, the National Salvation Party, the Reliance Party and the Nationalist Action Party (Milliyetçi Hareket Partisi, MHP). The MHP had two of its three deputies in the cabinet, thereby legitimising its far-right ideology. After the elections on 5 June 1977, Ecevit's CHP formed a minority government, but he failed to win a vote of confidence on 3 July. As a result, the Second National Front government was formed, and it was in power between 21 July 1977 and 31 December 1977.

unhampered freedom and protection to act as vigilantes against its ideological rivals[5] (Ahmad, 2008: 250–4). The number of victims of these clashes arose rapidly from around 230 in 1977 to between 1,200 and 1,500 in 1979 (Zürcher, 1994: 276). Thus, in the second half of the 1970s, political violence plagued Turkey.

In addition to university campuses and the shanties of Ankara and Istanbul, ESA provinces that were overwhelmingly Kurdish and/or ethnically mixed, like Maraş and Malatya, became the focus for these conflicts. By the end of 1978, twenty to thirty were being killed daily in these provinces. The Grey Wolves organised pogroms against Kurdish and Turkish Alevis, who generally supported the political left. There was a major outbreak of violence in Malatya in April 1978. In December of the same year, the Maraş massacre occurred wherein, according to official reports, the Grey Wolves left 109 people dead and seriously wounded 176 individuals, as well as destroying 500 shops and houses. The victims were largely Alevi Kurdish slum-dwellers (McDowall, 2000: 412–13). The political turmoil in these regions was in part due to the Turkish nationalist shibboleths on the Kurdish question advocated by the National Front coalition governments, which openly articulated 'the need to Turkicize these [Kurdish] inalienable regions of the Turkish nation' (Nezan, 1993: 86), and to some extent due to politically co-opted *ağas* who feared the social and economic challenge of the leftists.

The draconian measures of particularly the Second National Front coalition government in ESA were brutal and indefensible. On 31 December 1977, Demirel, the leader of the coalition government, failed to win the vote of confidence when twelve AP deputies who had resigned voted against the government on account of the ongoing violence and oppression against the Kurds in these provinces (Ahmad, 2008: 253). The Second National Front coalition government was succeeded by a CHP government led by Ecevit from January 1978, which immediately responded to the disorder in ESA by putting the whole of these regions under martial law. It is in this political climate that the Ankara University student Abdullah Öcalan founded the PKK in November 1978, with the aim of establishing a socialist Kurdistan.

5 As Zürcher noted: '[t]he struggle between right and left was an unequal one. During the "Nationalist Front" governments of 1974–7, the police and the security forces had become the exclusive preserves of [Alparslan] Türkeş's NAP [MHP], and even under Ecevit's government of 1978–79, they remained infiltrated by right-wing extremists who shielded and protected the Grey Wolves' (1994: 276).

After taking office, the other important step Ecevit's government took was to begin negotiations for new credits with the IMF, the World Bank and the OECD. Owing to the radical austerity measures demanded by the creditors, the talks dragged on. Turkey finally bowed to the impositions of the creditors and in July 1979, an agreement was reached which would release $1.8 billion in new credits, dependent on the Turkish government executing reform packages, including cutting government expenditure, cutting subsidies, abolishing import and export controls and freeing interest rates. This agreement put the CHP government in a perturbed position, as it neither gave an end to the downhill slide of the economy nor curbed the mounting political unrest.

After suffering a humiliating defeat at the by-election of 19 October 1979, Ecevit resigned. Following his resignation, an AP minority government took office on 12 November.

On 24 January 1980, the new government announced a new stabilisation programme akin to the reform packages announced by the preceding government. The architects and advocates of neoliberalism, however, alleged the 24 January programme to be a turning point in the history of Turkey, since they conceived it to be more than a standard stabilisation programme on account of it seeking to attain structural adjustment by changing the development strategy that Turkey hitherto followed (World Bank, 1980). In other words, the IMF-inspired 24 January measures were emblematic of Turkey's full embracement of the neoliberal development strategy.

The new programme involved, among others, the following critical measures: greater liberalisation of the trade and payments regime; a devaluation of the lira against the dollar by 33 per cent and the limitation of multiple exchange rate practices; increased competition for SEEs and abolition of most government subsidies; promotion of foreign investment; additional promotional measures for exports; and draft legislation for tax reform (OECD, 1980: 25). Income policies in the form of restraints on union activities, collective agreement and wage freezes were also on the agenda (Hansen, 1991: 383). The task of overseeing this programme was given to the US-trained undersecretary for economic affairs in charge of planning, Turgut Özal (1927–93).

By the spring of 1980, it became apparent, however, that there was widespread opposition to what was depicted as the 'Chilean solution' – named after the policies General Pinochet had launched in Chile after the coup against President Allende. The inexhaustible activities of the left and the unions, particularly DİSK, made it impossible for Özal to execute the neoliberal economic package. As a result, the rulers of Turkey opted for the 'Chilean solution', as on 12 September 1980 the self-styled military guardians of the Republic staged a coup and took power again. The rising tides of political unrest in addition to the failure of Demirel's coalition to implement economic liberalisation policies were major factors in convincing the generals to act on 12 September 1980. The military regime that came to power endorsed the neoliberal economic policies and made a point of keeping Özal in the government, as the deputy prime minister in charge of economic affairs. Özal thereafter became a towering figure in Turkish politics. During 1983–7, he became the prime minister of Turkey and was later elected Turkey's eighth president (1989–93).

5.2 Authoritarian Neoliberal Restructuring of Turkey and the Emergence of the Armed Conflict between the PKK and the Turkish State

After the coup of 1980, the suppression of Kurdish identity intensified and the regional inequalities between the predominantly Kurdish ESA and the rest of Turkey persisted. Two interrelated issues that came to dominate Turkey's agenda as the years wore on were the rights of the Kurdish people and the massive underdevelopment of the overwhelmingly Kurdish ESA.

The authoritarian neoliberal restructuring of Turkey during the military regime (1980–3) and the transition period to multi-party politics under Özal's Motherland Party government (1983–7) put into place a stringent regime in the ESA provinces, revitalised the policy of denying the existence of the Kurds in Turkey and neglected the sector on which the predominantly rural Kurdish regions were heavily dependent: agriculture. The most detrimental change for the agricultural sector as a result of the neoliberal economic reforms was the virtual eradication of subsidies and price support programmes after 1980, which combined with the trends in the international market to create a severe deterioration in the sectoral terms of trade.

Inter-sectoral terms of trade turned against agriculture by more than 40 per cent until 1987, and the agricultural sector showed the lowest rates of output increase during the post-war era, averaging only 1 per cent per year from 1980 (Pamuk, 2008: 288). Moreover, Boratav, commenting on the fate of farmers growing crops that are found in the predominantly Kurdish south east, i.e. cotton and tobacco, points out that 'for these two commodities, the rapid depreciation of the Turkish lira during the 1980s has been beneficial to the exporters, but not to the farmer' (1990: 215). Consequently, peasant farmers were faced with 'increased and even extreme indebtedness to cover costs' (ibid.: 217). The conditions of the labourers employed in sectors other than agriculture were no better, as real wages during the same period dwindled by as much as 34 per cent (Pamuk, 2008: 288). Strikes were declared illegal, and the Supreme Arbitration Board was set up to settle all pending collective agreements and issued guidelines for future agreements – this Board was abolished only in April 1987 (Hansen, 1991: 386–7). This in part explains why Turkish capitalism as a whole was prepared and willing to trade off the economic and political problems of this period for restricted democracy, ideological hegemony and a disciplined labour force.

The reticence of the rulers of Turkey to leave behind policies of forcible assimilation based on a mono-ethnic conception of the nation-state compounded the problems the Kurds experienced, as well as sharpening the Kurdish question of Turkey. After the military intervention, two-thirds of the Turkish army were deployed in ESA (McDowall, 2000: 414). The authoritarian 1982 constitution did not only strengthen the power of the president – giving him the right to disband the Assembly and to rule by decree – and reduce the Assembly to a single chamber, but it also, under Article 14, restricted the freedoms of individuals and organisations and prohibited political struggles based on language, race, class and sect. Alongside targeting Marxists and Islamists, this provision was directed at the activities of the Kurdish nationalists.

More importantly, in October 1983, the military government introduced Law 2931 proscribing the use of Kurdish. By 1986, under Law 1587, 2,842 out of 3,542 villages in Adıyaman, Diyarbakır, Gaziantep, Urfa, Mardin and Siirt had been renamed in Turkish to obliterate their Kurdish identity (McDowall, 2000: 425). The PKK insurgency was one of the alleged causal factors stirring the reassertion of state authority in the 1980 coup, but it was not until 1984 that the PKK-armed struggle commenced in earnest.

In October 1984, the PKK followed up its initial August attack first by killing three members of a unit in charge of guarding President Kenan Evren at Yüksekova, and then ambuscading and killing eight soldiers in Çukurca, Hakkari. The PKK's methods were violent, and those perceived as cooperating with the state, including the government-sponsored village guard militia, *ağas* and civilian state employees such as teachers, were specifically targeted.

In April 1985, the Village Law was revised to allow for the maintenance of the state-sponsored militia employed to fight the PKK: village guards.[6]

[6] For detailed exploration of the village guards, see Aytar (1992).

The village guards were reminiscent of the Hamidiya Cavalry of the late nineteenth century analysed in Chapter 3. As with the Hamidiya, the Turkish state was quite willing to make use of Kurdish tribes and to work in close cooperation with its local intercessors, the *ağas*, to attain the manpower for the guards; individual village guards did not necessarily receive their salary since the *ağas* collected the wages of the guards on the state payroll.[7] Analogous to the Hamidiya chiefs, a section of the *ağas* manipulated their position to dispossess the weak or minority groups in ESA. Under the banner of Islam, the dominant tribal chieftains forcibly drove Assyrian and Yezidi villagers from their land in Mardin; others did the same to Alevi villagers near Maraş (ibid.: 422). In 1985, Turkey recruited 62,000 village guards to fight the PKK (Sarıhan, 2013: 94).

In juxtaposition to clans affiliated with the right or the far right or in conflict with the PKK voluntarily offering village guards to the state, the state also obliged the rural Kurdish communities to provide volunteers to prove their loyalty. If villages failed to come up with volunteers for the guards, they would risk being perceived as PKK adherents. Thus, the Kurdish villagers were stuck between a rock and a hard place since they could become village guards and chance being attacked by the PKK, or refuse and risk becoming victims of state security operations.

In July 1987, under Decree 285 (Olağanüstü Hal Bölge Valiliği İhdası Hakkında 285 Sayılı Kanun Hükmünde Kararname),[8] a governor-general was appointed over the eight overwhelmingly Kurdish provinces in ESA (Bingöl, Diyarbakır, Elazığ, Hakkari, Mardin, Siirt, Tunceli and Van) in which a state of emergency (Olağanüstü Hal, OHAL) was declared. Thereafter, the regime and the region came be identified as the OHAL, up until its annulment in November 2002. The governor-general was given the task of coordinating the different bodies fighting against the PKK guerrillas, the army, gendarmerie, police and village guards. He was equipped with a wide range of powers, including the forced evacuation of villages and pasturage where it was deemed necessary. By the end of 1989, the number of forcibly evacuated hamlets and villages had reached around 400 (McDowall, 2000: 426) and, as will be demonstrated, more followed the same in fate in the 1990s.

[7] As McDowall reported, 'in autumn 1992 Sadun Seylan, chief of the Alan tribe in Van, who owned 26 villages, fielded 500 village guards, a force he could increase six-fold if necessary. For these 500 men, Seylan received $115,000 monthly' (2000: 422).

[8] Decree 285 was published in *Resmi Gazete* on 14 July 1987, issue no. 19517, and came into force on 19 July 1987.

5.3 Gradual Democratisation Efforts and the Timid Politics of Recognition

After the referendum of 6 September 1987 on the question of whether to permit the old mainstream politicians/parties proscribed under the 1982 constitution to take part in politics, which resulted in the restoration of the political rights of the veteran politicians, the transition to a more open and competitive political system had begun. The seasoned leaders Demirel, Ecevit, Erbakan and Türkeş, and the representatives of the bourgeoning working-class movement outside of the Assembly, which culminated in 1989 'Spring Actions' in which around 1 million workers participated (Özuğurlu, 2009), albeit for dissimilar ends, instigated a vociferous criticism of the aforementioned repression of wages, deterioration of income distribution and significant rise in corruption and embezzlement, all of which came to be considered a direct legacy of the Özal era (Öniş, 2004).

In response, Özal reverted to the short-term deceptive populist policies of his predecessors (Boratav, 2003) at a time when the economy was sluggish with very low growth rates: the growth rates plummeted from 4.6 per cent between 1981 and 1985 (Hansen, 1991: 390) to 2.1 per cent in 1989 (Yeldan, 2006: 49). After 1987, public-sector wages, salaries and agricultural incomes saw an increase (ibid.: 49–50). Real wages almost doubled from their decade-low point in 1987 until 1990 (Pamuk, 2008: 289). In addition, as a result of the scheme of high support prices for agricultural producers, Özal poured around $2 billion into the countryside (Waldner, 1995: 39). Such policies sharply increased the budget deficit from 10.1 per cent of GDP in 1990 to 12.1 per cent in 1993 and renewed inflation, which jumped from 30 per cent in 1983 to 60 per cent in the years 1989–93 (Yeldan, 2006: 50). In 1989, in part to help finance the deficit and in part to attract short-term capital inflows or hot money, Özal fully liberalised the capital account and eradicated the obstacles to international capital inflows, which made the Turkish economy extremely vulnerable to sudden outflows of international capital and external shocks in the 1990s.

From 1989 onwards, the ANAP government in unison with President Özal embarked on further constitutional reforms. In April 1989, a number of amendments were announced, the most crucial being a decrease (from fifteen days to twenty-four hours) in the length of time individuals could remain in police custody without being charged. A year later, Özal gave hints of a new Kurdish policy at the meeting of the Turkish Industrialists and Businessmen's Association (Türk Sanayicileri ve İşadamları Derneği, TÜSİAD), which perhaps is indicative of the existing dissatisfaction and the influence TÜSİAD wielded over the Kurdish issue. In this meeting, he made public that the government was 'engaged in a quest for a serious model for solving the Kurdish problem in a manner that goes beyond the police measures' (Gunter, 2011a: 88). In early 1991, the cabinet introduced a package of constitutional restructurings which in part dealt with the political system (direct presidential elections, lowering the voting age to eighteen, enlargement of the Assembly), but partly dealt with human rights.

Pursuant to this, at the government's request, the Turkish Assembly revoked the 1983 ban on speaking Kurdish in public and annulled Articles 141, 142 and 163, which proscribed politics on the basis of class and/or religion as proscribed by the penal code. The latter amendment led to, among other things, the repealing of the ban on the DİSK trade union confederation after eleven years. The reforms undertaken in 1991 constituted a quintessential example of the inextricable link the Kurdish question has to the democratisation of Turkey.

Demirel, who became prime minister in the 1991 elections, extended the liberal dispensations in relation to the Kurdish issue of Turkey, as in a historic speech in Diyarbakır he declared that Turkey recognised 'the Kurdish reality'. In the meantime, President Özal was trying to sway the opinion of the bureaucrats and the public alike to support a PKK amnesty (Yeğen, 2011: 74). Overall, the early 1990s led to the abandonment of the hitherto dominant state discourse that the Kurdish question was devoid of an ethnic dimension.

The causality for the shift in the Turkish state's perception of the Kurdish issue and its methods of engaging with the question should be sought in the increasing discontent of the Turkish and Kurdish masses with the conventional nationalist arguments employed by the successive governments owing to damaging consequences of the clashes between the PKK and the armed forces. By the early 1990s, the militarised conflict not only attained a serious dimension as it claimed around 2,500 lives, but it also made it extremely difficult for the state to cling to denial politics in relation to Kurdish identity.

The first major blow to the orthodox Kemalist position came with the 1991 election results, which relayed the growing dissatisfaction of the masses in Turkey. In alliance with the SHP, the pro-Kurdish Peoples' Labour Party (Halkın Emek Partisi, HEP), founded in 1990, won twenty-two seats in Parliament. By 1990, a qualitative transformation had also taken place in the nature of the Kurdish discontent, as for the first time since 1984, families of the PKK martyrs dared to collect the corpses for burial from the Turkish authorities and organised public funerals in which popular resentment against the state's Kurdish policy was exhibited. On 20 March 1990, 10,000 Kurds took to the streets in Cizre (Siirt) and the state imposed a curfew on eleven towns in Mardin and Siirt (McDowall, 2000: 427).

In sum, the modification in the Kurdish policy of the Turkish state was necessitated by the untenable nature of the Turkish nationalist dogma on the Kurdish question. The politics of recognition was brief, though, as after the early 1990s, the Turkish state insisted on drawing the wrong conclusion from the right premises. In other words, the state acknowledged the existence of the Kurds, but reconceptualised the Kurdish question as a question of 'separatist terror'.

The Politics of Oppression and the Fourth Wave of Kurdish Deportations

The Turkish state revisited the politics of coercion with regard to the Kurdish question between 1993 and 1999. Having recognised the ethnic dimension of the Kurdish issue, the state now portrayed the conflict as an ethnic Kurdish rebellion with divisive aims that required military measures. As a result, during these years, the Kurdish issue sank increasingly into the grip of securitisation. A bloody and relentless war was waged against the PKK guerrillas and the public who were perceived to sympathise with them. According to Turkish official figures, out of 31,000 Turkish security forces members, civilians and PKK guerrillas who lost their lives during the first period of conflict between the PKK and the Turkish state (1984–99), 27,410 died between 1992 and 1999 (Sarıhan, 2013: 94).

Ostensibly as part of its bid to crush the PKK by routing its networks of support in the Kurdish countryside, the Turkish state forcibly evacuated more villages in ESA on a temporary and permanent basis. These deportations were outlined in a leaked February 1993 memo, which deals with the methods of solving the Kurdish issue, from President Özal to Prime Minister Demirel:

> Starting with the most troubled zones, village and hamlets in the mountains of the region should be gradually evacuated [and] resettled in the Western parts of the country according to a careful plan. . . . Security forces should immediately move in and establish complete control in such areas. . . . To prevent the locals' return to the region, the building of a large number of dams in appropriate places is an alternative. (K. Yıldız, 2005: 79)

Analogous to the preceding three waves of deportations, the state's alleged aim for mass forced evacuations – i.e. having overall control of 'troubled zones' – is only partially true because a closer inspection of the patterns of forced deportations or evacuation exhibits a multifarious collection of aims alongside confronting the PKK's support base in the Kurdish countryside. As observed by Kerim Yıldız, the executive director of the London-based Kurdish Human Rights Project (KHRP),[9] who has closely monitored the internal displacement policies of the Turkish state, '[v]illages and other settlements were routinely "cleansed" of their civilian Kurdish inhabitants, often as a form of collective punishment for refusal to join the state-sponsored civilian militia, the Village Guard' (2005: 77). In 1995, the Turkish Human Rights Association (İnsan Hakları Derneği, İHD) published an important survey in relation to those displaced by these evictions. Overall, more than 90 per cent of the evacuees confirmed they had come under direct pressure from the Turkish security forces to leave their homelands, and 88.7 per cent believed they were targeted solely because they were Kurds (İHD, 1995).

The mass internal displacement or forced deportation policies,[10] as Özal openly stated in his memo, were implemented in accordance with the long-term and wider strategy of banishing the Kurds from their ancestral homelands by the construction of dams, which is an integral part of GAP. A fact-finding mission by KHRP and the University of Galway, Ireland, in August 2004 found that this project would displace many thousands of local people; the pending İlusu Dam project alone would displace 78,000 individuals (KHRP, 2005).

Moreover, the security forces aimed to change the social and economic fabric of the predominantly Kurdish ESA by blazing houses, pastures and forests, slaughtering livestock and denying the villagers the opportunity to recover their possessions (Göç-Der, 2002). Hence, the wealth and lands the Kurds accumulated in these regions were directly targeted with tragic social and economic consequences. According to a report by the National Assembly, of 5,000 settlement units that existed prior to 1985, 3,848 were evacuated by 1999. It is estimated that around 3 million people were displaced during this period (K. Yıldız, 2005: 78). Disagreements exist with regard to the number of those displaced, however, as research findings by the Hacetepe University, Ankara, suggest that between 950,000 and 1,200,000 were deported (HÜNEE, 2006). Because of such

[9] The KHRP is an independent human rights organisation founded in London in 1992. It has been involved in influential fact-finding missions as well as publishing extensively on the issue of forced internal displacement in Turkey, see KHRP (1996, 2002 2004).

[10] For an overview, monitoring and specific case studies, other than the ones listed here, of this scheme, see Human Rights Watch (1994).

discrepancies, it is reasonable to assume that at least 1 million people were removed from their homelands.

Mass village evacuations were multifaceted processes and involved more than the professed aim of combatting the PKK. They formed part of the Turkish state's enduring desire to break up the Kurdish communities in the predominantly Kurdish ESA provinces and to consolidate control in Kurdish heartlands. In addition, disseminating the Kurdish population would not only advance the long-standing goal of assimilating Kurds into the dominant Turkish culture and attenuating the Kurdish identity, but it would also exasperate calls for autonomy. Political rights of Kurdish citizens were systematically violated. Two pro-Kurdish parties, HEP and the Democratic Party (Demokrasi Partisi, DEP) were banned by the Supreme Court in 1993 and 1994. In the latter year, parliamentary immunity for eight Kurdish deputies was revoked, four of whom, Leyla Zana, Hatip Dicle, Orhan Doğan and Selim Sadak, were arrested and sentenced to fifteen years' imprisonment. Other DEP leaders fled to Europe.

Another long-standing and preferred tool of assimilation employed by the Turkish state in the 1990s was state-funded boarding schools in the predominantly Kurdish regions. As before, these schools were set up in overwhelmingly Kurdish areas with the purpose of educating Kurdish pupils away from their families and outside of their normal cultural contexts. According to the figures provided by the Ministry of National Education, of 299 boarding schools, 155 are located in ESA provinces.

5.4 A New Phase in the Kurdish Questions Post-1999: The End of the First Period of Conflict

The late 1990s marked a shift in the Turkish state's Kurdish policies. A policy of recognition and engagement was substituted for that of securitisation and suppression on account of four pivotal developments: (a) the erosion of the hoary claims in relation to alleged separatist ideals of Kurds; (b) the growing frustration of the important institutions and circles in Turkey with both the prevailing perception of the Kurdish question and the methods of dealing with the issue; (c) the capture of the PKK leader Öcalan; and (d) Turkey's candidacy for European Union (EU) membership.

The 1990s were the most problematic period in the post–Second World War era for Turkey. Özal's decision to fully liberalise the capital account and abolish the barriers in the way of international capital inflows in 1989 exposed the country to sudden outflows of capital and external shocks, which led to the crises of 1991, 1994, 1998 and 2000–1. Concurrently, public-sector deficits widened in the 1990s and it was a period of very high inflation – jumping to 100 per cent in 1994 and remaining above 50 per cent each year through to 2001 (Pamuk, 2008: 289–90). In spite of the GDP per capita continuing to rise during the era of economic liberalisation, it was still at a lower rate than the former period: GDP per capita in the years 1980–2005 grew at a pace of 1.9 per cent whilst during 1950–80 it was 2.6 per cent (ibid.: 267).

There were two major factors for the persistence of public debt during the 1990s. The first was the deceptive populist policies Özal implemented after 1987. The second was the costly war waged against the PKK on which the Turkish state spent some $2 billion per annum during 1984–1999 (Faucompret and Konings, 2008: 168). In addition to the large fiscal burden of this conflict, the conventional methods of engaging with the Kurdish question were increasingly viewed as a barrier to Turkey flourishing economically and socially by the dominating classes in Turkey. Growing discomfort in Turkish business circles initiated gradual but adamant calls for alternative means of addressing the Kurdish question.

In 1995, the Union of Chambers and Commodity Exchanges of Turkey (Türkiye Odalar ve Borsalar Birliği, TOBB) published the results of a controversial survey[11] prepared by Professor Doğu Ergil, a political science professor at Ankara University, which exposed three principal factors regarding the Kurdish issue that were hidden from the public view. First, 61 per cent of those polled favoured amelioration of the cultural, political and economic rights of the Kurds (Ergil, 2009: 52) and only 9.4 per cent preferred secession (ibid.: 54), thus falsifying the state officials' hitherto propagated assessment that the conflict was motivated solely by secessionist or separatist objectives. Second, Kurdish identity was more widespread than the portrayal of the Turkish state officials, since 90.8 per cent of those surveyed identified themselves as Kurdish (ibid.: 38). Third, based on these and other findings, one important and uncomfortable conclusion of this survey was that the 'PKK was not the cause, but a product of the Eastern Question' (ibid.: 54). The publication of the findings and conclusions of this investigation caused uproar, and a court case was filed against Prof. Ergil from which he was later acquitted.

[11] The survey, titled *Doğu Sorunu: Teşhisler ve Tespitler*, consisted of interviews with 1,256 people in three predominantly Kurdish south eastern provinces (Batman, Diyarbakir and Mardin), and three provinces in various different of Turkey to which Kurds migrated (Adana, Antalya and Mersin). For the complete findings of this research, and other studies by Prof. Ergil on the Kurdish question, see Ergil (2009).

TOBB's research was followed by another contentious and influential report by TÜSİAD. In January 1997, TÜSİAD commissioned a report, authored by the prominent constitutional lawyer Bülent Tanor. It called for an end to the MGK in its present form as well as suggesting the removal of all barriers on the Kurdish language, for freedom of Kurdish expression – including the freedom to form political parties that could represent Kurdish concerns – and for cultural freedom in relation to the naming of places and persons (TÜSİAD, 1997). TÜSİAD's report indicated that the business circles in Turkey were growing ever warier of the mechanisms employed to resolve the conflict and thus demanded an alternative, liberal approach to the Kurdish question, the foundations for which were provided by the capture of Öcalan and the decision from the EU Summit in Helsinki in 1999.

PKK leader Öcalan was apprehended in Kenya in February 1999 and was flown to Turkey to stand trial, where he was convicted of treason and sentenced to death on 29 June 1999. The capture of Öcalan brought, albeit temporarily, the armed conflict between the PKK and the Turkish state to an end, since following his capture and imprisonment he declared a ceasefire, asked for the withdrawal of the PKK guerrillas from the bases in Turkey and reneged on the PKK's initial objective of establishing an independent Kurdistan.

In December of the same year, the European Council (EC) declared Turkey a candidate for membership in the EU. This decision was conditional on Turkey making satisfactory progress with meeting the EU's Copenhagen political criteria, which explicitly included: 'the stability of institutions guaranteeing democracy, the rule of law, human rights and respect for and protection of minorities' (EC, Conclusions of the Presidency, Copenhagen, 1993: para. 7 A (iii)). The pressures and prospects of EU conditionality spurred the existing coalition government – the constituent parties of which were the Democratic Left Party (Demokratik Sol Parti, DSP), MHP and ANAP – to implement immediate reforms in the field of minority rights. The Justice and Development Party (Adalet ve Kalkınma Partisi, AKP) that came to power in 2002, particularly, in its heyday of reforms from 2002 to 2004 continued these reforms.

On 3 October 2001, in accordance with the 'National Programme for Adopting the Acquis Communautaire,'[12] the coalition government

[12] Assistance for candidate countries is determined by the accession process and the need for candidate countries to harmonise with the EU. Their legislation needs to be aligned with the *acquis communautaire*, the substantial body of administrative, economic, environment and social EU law. The accession partnership has set out the road map for the

led by Ecevit adopted a series of thirty-four amendments to the 1982 constitution, which removed prohibitions on the use of languages other than Turkish. These amendments paved the way for the AKP government to introduce a sequence of harmonisation laws implemented in order to align the legal situation in Turkey with those of the EU standards. As a result, numerous restrictions on freedom of expression and association, which Kurds despised, were abolished. New legislations implemented by the AKP permitted limited broadcasting in Kurdish in 2002 – the state-run television channel TRT began broadcasting in Kurdish for thirty minutes per week – and in 2004 allowed private schools to offer Kurdish language courses. Moreover, yet again following the previous coalition government, the AKP government completed the gradual lifting of OHAL in November 2002. Within the same year, the National Assembly abolished capital punishment, sparing the life of Öcalan in the process. All of these important steps raised hopes that the protracted and brutal conflict with the PKK might at last be entering a more peaceful and productive phase.

5.5 The Second Period of Conflict and the AKP's Kurdish Overture

The hopes of a peaceful resolution to the Kurdish question in Turkey, however, came to an abrupt end in the first half of the 2000s. The formalisation of the hitherto de facto Kurdish polity in Iraq (established in 1991) after the collapse of the Saddam regime by the US-led invasion of 2003, the cessation of the reforms pertaining to the Kurds in Turkey and the PKK revoking the ceasefire observed since 1999 on grounds of ongoing state military operations against the guerrillas were all influential in preventing a peaceful conclusion to this long-simmering question of Turkey. These successive events reignited the tinderbox of nationalism.

Akin to the Kurds across the border, it was argued that Kurds in Turkey are preoccupied with secessionist aims harboured by the United States and the EU. In 2004, in response to European Commission President Jose Manuel Barroso's call 'to ensure both cultural and political rights for the Kurdish people of Turkey', General İlker Başbuğ, the commander of Turkish Land Forces, claimed the following: 'nobody can demand or expect Turkey to make collective arrangements for a certain ethnic group in the political arena, outside of the cultural arena, that would endanger

alignment process, and progress is monitored annually in the Regular Report, which reviews the process chapter by chapter.

the nation-state structure as well as the unitary state structure' (Yeğen, 2011: 77).

Başbuğ's statement in a sense signified the beginning of the end of the liberal overtures in relation to Kurds, as from 2004 up until late 2009, the politics of rapprochement and reform halted (Faucompret and Konings, 2009: 167–70; Bahcheli and Noel, 2011: 108–14). The politics of securitisation and discrimination was revisited.

One of the other influential reasons for the politics of reform losing ground is linked to the uncertainty concerning the EU's effectiveness as an instigator of reforms with regard to the Kurdish question in the years after the formal accession process in 2005. The EU made an important positive start in 1998 by amenably naming the Kurdish issue and citing its resolution as a requirement to Turkey's attainment of EU membership, as evinced in the European Commission's 1998 Regular Report on Turkey's Progress Towards Accession: 'A civil, non-military solution must be found to the situation in south-eastern Turkey, particularly since many of the violations of civil and political rights observed in the country are connected to in one way or other with this issue' (1998: 53).

As time has worn on, however, references to Kurds in EU documentation have become increasingly more subdued, and the European Commission has promoted the expansion of individual rights rather than collective rights for the Kurds and abstained from promoting an explicit political solution for the Kurdish question. This becomes evident when we compare the European Commission's analysis in relation to the Kurdish question cited earlier with those that are more recent. For example, in the 2005 Report on Turkey's Progress Towards Accession, the European Commission shares the following oblique observations with regard to the Kurdish question: 'Turkey continues to adopt a restrictive approach to minorities and cultural rights. Although there is a growing consensus on the need to address the economic, cultural and social development of the Southeast, little concrete progress has been made and the security situation has worsened' (ibid., 2005: 42).

A similar restrained tone and analysis are pursued in succeeding European Commission Reports (see ibid., 2006: 22–3; 2007: 23–4; 2008: 25–6; 2009: 30–1). As Nathalie Tocci noted, 'EU actors have paid only sporadic attention to the Kurdish question' and 'have become far less outspoken on Kurdish collective and territorial rights' (2011: 135).

However, by far the most important illustration of Turkey's shift in relation to the Kurdish question was the judgement that the foundation of a Kurdish political entity in the form of the Kurdish Regional Government (KRG) in Iraq would incite the perceived secessionist desires of the Kurds in Turkey, as Başbuğ unequivocally argued: '[the KRG] brought a political, legal, military and psychological power to the Kurds of the region . . . this situation may create a new model of belonging for a segment of our citizenry.'[13]

In a similar vein, on 2 November 2008, Prime Minister Tayyip Erdoğan, subsequent to refusing to shake the hands of elected deputies of the pro-Kurdish Democratic Society Party (Demokratik Toplum Partisi, DPT), declared in the predominantly Kurdish province of Hakkari that those who opposed the motto 'one nation, one flag, one motherland, one state' should leave the country.[14]

This hostile outburst by Erdoğan did not repress long-held collective sentiments of the Kurds; if anything, it prompted Kurds in ESA to support the pro-Kurdish Demokratik Toplum Partisi (DTP) in the local elections of 29 March 2009 and contributed to the AKP's poor performance among Kurdish electorates in the predominantly Kurdish regions. The victor in ESA was by a clear margin the DTP, which increased its share of votes and attained a majority of the mayoralties in these regions, whilst AKP support decreased by more than 15 per cent. The haemorrhaging of Kurdish votes in the local elections automatically raised grave doubts concerning whether the AKP could retain its 2007 electorate support among the Kurdish voters in the general election of 2011.

Such fears of the AKP as well as the relentless misgivings and resistance of the Kurds against the revisited politics of securitisation in relation to the Kurdish question led the governing party to devise judiciously a Kurdish reform agenda around the notion of individual rights and general minority rights instead of Kurdish collective rights. In the summer of 2009, Prime Minister Erdoğan unveiled a 'Kurdish Overture', which later came to be retitled the 'Democratisation Overture' and then re-designated as a 'National Unity Project', that heralded a new approach and process.[15] Henceforth, the AKP governments have been pursuing a political process with the alleged aim of resolving Turkey's long-standing Kurdish question, which in Turkey has commonly been titled 'the resolution process'.

Despite being devoid of a legal framework ratified by the Turkish Grand National Assembly and/or a mutually agreed and publicly

[13] *Today's Zaman*, 'Başbuğ Rules out any Ethnic Rights in the Political Field', 12 April 2008.
[14] *Today's Zaman*, 'Erdoğan Comment Rattles Kurds in Diyarbakir', 2 November 2008.
[15] For a comprehensive analysis of the causal factors generating this novel process, see the section titled 'The Kurdish Question in the Twenty-First Century'.

declared roadmap by relevant parties, based on all that has been undertaken in accord with 'the resolution process' since the summer of 2009, this political process appears to rely on two main pillars: first, the negotiations between state officials and the PKK; and, second, the implementations of reforms ensuring democratisation and recognition of the long-denied cultural and political rights of Turkey's Kurds. As such, 'the resolution process' seems actuated to attain the decommissioning of the PKK and the recognition of the Kurds' cultural and political rights.

Hitherto, both of these aims have yet to be materialised, and the prospect of this political process is unclear. These drawbacks are attributable to the differing contents imputed to 'the resolution process' by the ruling AKP and the pro-Kurdish political bloc, namely the PKK, the Peace and Democracy Party (Barış ve Demokrasi Partisi, BDP) and the Peoples' Democratic Party (Halkların Demokrasi Partisi, HDP), the successor of the BDP. The former conceives the process as, first and foremost, a mechanism for disarming and eventually liquidating the PKK, and it hopes to solve the Kurdish issue by means of extraction of discriminatory laws reviled by Turkey's Kurds as well as by granting certain limited and basic individual rights for Kurds. Whereas the latter regards the granting of the collective rights of Turkey's Kurds and adoption of a form of self-rule in Turkish Kurdistan as prerequisites for disarmament.

The divergence between the two parties was laid bare when, in juxtaposition to the PKK and the HDP linking disarmament and the resolution of the Kurdish question to the Öcalan-authored ten-article[16] draft for negotiations, the overarching leader of the AKP, President Erdoğan, in March 2015, vowed that there was no longer any such thing as the Kurdish question[17] by virtue of the reforms[18] implemented

[16] The ten articles were as follows: 1) the definition and content of democratic politics must be debated; 2) what needs to be done for the national and local dimensions of democratic settlement; 3) the legal and democratic assurances of free citizenship; 4) the relationship between democratic politics and the state and society and its institutionalisation; 5) the socioeconomic dimensions of the settlement process; 6) the new security structure that the settlement process will lead to; 7) the solving of problems and the legal assurances pertaining to women's rights, culture and ecology; 8) the concept, definition and development of pluralist, democratic and equal mechanisms to acknowledge identity; 9) the definition of the concepts of democratic state, common land and the nation by democratic means, their legal and constitutional rights enshrined in the pluralist democratic system; and 10) a new constitution aiming to internalise all of these democratic moves and transformations.

[17] 'Cumhurbaşkanı Erdoğan: Kardeşim ne Kürt Sorunu ya . . . ', in *Radikal*, 15 March 2015.

[18] The following are the reforms implemented by the AKP governments which Erdoğan was referring to: removal of the OHAL in the Kurdish region; assisting internally displaced Kurds to return to their former homes and properties; the launching of TRT6, the first

by AKP governments. These ten articles were announced to the public in a meeting attended by members of the AKP government and the HDP on 28 February 2015.

Representatives of the pro-Kurdish movement contend, rather compellingly, that the president's intervention into the process was owing to the fact that Erdoğan realised and convinced the AKP cabinet that 'the resolution process' was no longer operating to the interest of the AKP (Yeğen, 2015). Instead, it popularised the HDP, in that, as indicated by opinion polls, for the first time in the history of the Turkish Republic, a pro-Kurdish party might surpass the 10 per cent electoral threshold and enter the National Assembly. This could not only prevent the AKP from garnering a supermajority needed in the 7 June 2015 parliamentary elections to make the constitutional changes and thus realise Erdoğan's desire of a French-style Gaullist-inspired executive presidency in Turkey, but could also rekindle and substantially boost the pro-autonomy demands and bid of the mainstream Kurdish led by the HDP at a time when the autonomy-seeking PYD was making profound territorial gains along Turkey's southern border in Rojava.

Such fears were not in vain, as the HDP garnered an unexpectedly high 13.1 per cent of the vote, securing eighty members in the Turkish parliament, while the AKP, with 40.9 per cent of the vote and 258 MPs out of 550, was without a majority for the first time since 2002. When efforts to form a coalition government failed, Erdoğan called new elections for 1 November 2015. The inter-election period was one of the most violent periods in Turkey's history, dismantling the relative détente in Turkish–Kurdish relations during the two-and-a-half-year ceasefire (International Crisis Group, 2015). Thus, ever since its inception, 'the resolution process' has been squeezed between the differing conceptualisations of how to attain peace and the requirements of electoral success as well as the trepidations of Turkish statesmen concerning the attainments of the pro-autonomy PYD in Syria – in other words, countering the prospects of Rojava falling durably under autonomous rule by the PYD, which, they fear, could greatly enhance the pro-autonomy bid of the mainstream Kurdish movement in Turkey – which, in turn, explains the erratic and the fragile nature and evolution of this process.

official Kurdish TV channel; optional Kurdish courses in private schools; the right of villages to return to their original names; and the right of establishing institutions for living languages.

5.6 The Economic Balance Sheet of ESA in the Era of Neoliberalism

As the assessments in this study regarding the regional aspects of socioeconomic development have thus far demonstrated, the predominantly Kurdish ESA have been the least developed regions of the Turkish Republic. Neoliberal policies implemented since 1980 have not been able to overcome the persistent and large regional inequalities between these two regions and the rest of the country, as ESA continued to be the most disadvantaged areas of Turkey post-1980.

During 1993–2001, the average GNP per capita in these regions was about one-third of the country's average (TESEV, 2006: 14). A more comprehensive picture of regional disparities can be addressed by using the UNDP human development indicators of GDP per capita at PPP, life expectancy, adult literacy and combined school enrolment ratios for the year 2000, shown in Table 5.1. Out of the twenty least developed provinces, with the exclusion of Yozgat and Gümüşhane, eighteen were located in ESA. In other words, by 2000, unlike any other region of Turkey, 85 per cent of the ESA provinces constituted the most underdeveloped cities of Turkey. As a result, the two predominantly Kurdish regions were the only parts of the country which had an average HDI below that of Turkey's average.

The 'Emerging Euro Tiger' and the Perseverance of Regional Disparities

Following the 2001 crisis, Turkey enjoyed a period of rapid economic growth and increasing financial profits amidst the global upswing, which led World Bank Country Director Andrew Vorking in 2005 to euphemistically declare the country as an 'emerging Euro Tiger'. Turkey's rise to 'emerging Euro Tiger' status has not narrowed the persistent regional inequalities in the country, however. In 2005, as in 1995, out of the thirty-five OECD member countries, Turkey had the highest Gini index of GDP per capita or, put differently, it displayed the greatest regional disparities in GDP per capita (OECD, 2009: 91).

Before analysing the regional socioeconomic disparities in any further depth, a brief overview of the general economic development in the 2000s is apposite. On account of the 2000–1 crisis, Turkey for the eighteenth time sought the assistance of the IMF. In 2001, the DSP-MHP-ANAP coalition government invited Kemal Derviş to leave his post at the World Bank and take up the job of economy minister. Under IMF supervision, Derviş developed a programme centred on fiscal

Table 5.1 *Turkey's Human Development Index, 2000*

20 provinces with Lowest 20 Rankings in HDI	Life Expectancy at Birth (years)	Adult Literacy Rate 14+ (%)	Combined First-Second Gross Enrolment Ratio (%)	Real GDP Per Capita (PPP$)	Human Development Index (HDI) Value
Şırnak	57.7	62.3	70.6	1,816	0.56
Muş	62	67.3	58.3	1,587	0.57
Ağrı	60.4	67.4	57.6	1,803	0.57
Bitlis	59.9	71.8	53.1	1,932	0.58
Bingöl	59.5	72.4	65.5	2,331	0.60
Hakkari	60.7	67.5	75.8	2,445	0.61
Van	63.7	66.6	68.2	2,447	0.61
Şanlıurfa	64.0	65.7	63.2	2,847	0.61
Iğdır	60.3	73.2	83.7	2,556	0.63
Siirt	63.5	65.8	76.5	3,062	0.64
Mardin	66.2	67.6	70.4	2,519	0.64
Batman	63.1	67.4	77.3	3,410	0.64
Kars	60.3	81.2	80.4	2,882	0.64
Adıyaman	63.1	77.0	76.9	2,736	0.65
Erzincan	59.9	86.4	65.1	3,348	0.65
Ardahan	60.3	83	89.5	2,315	0.65
Erzurum	62.3	82.6	70.1	3,178	0.66
Yozgat	64.7	84.8	64.6	2,736	0.66
Diyarbakır	68.1	67.0	70.5	3,701	0.67
Gümüşhane	64.7	85.3	58.8	3,263	0.67
REGIONS					
Aegean-Marmara	70.4	89.9	92.2	7,820	0.79
Mediterranean	65.8	87.3	84.1	5,545	0.74
Central Anatolia	64.6	87.4	79.9	5,328	0.72
Black Sea	65.9	85.5	83.2	4,940	0.72
East-Southeast Anatolia	62.8	73.8	73.9	3,024	0.64
TURKEY	**65.8**	**83.5**	**82.2**	**5,194**	**0.72**

Source: UNDP Human Development Report of Turkey, 2004.

discipline and large budget surpluses. The Turkish economy has since witnessed a notable recovery. After falling by 9.5 per cent in 2001, Turkey's GDP increased by about 35 per cent during the next four years. By the end of 2005, annual inflation fell to less than 8 per cent, a level not seen since the 1960s (Pamuk, 2008: 291). Thus, the recovery that began under the fragile coalition government was continued by the

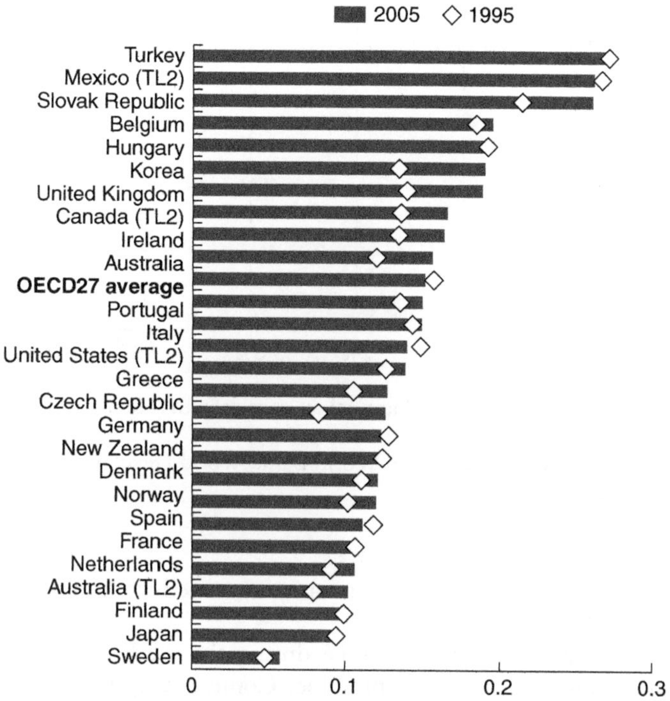

Figure 5.1 Comparison of regional disparities in OECD countries (Gini index for GDP per capita), 1995–2005
Note: The Gini index looks at not only the regions with the highest and the lowest values, but also at the differences among all regions. It ranges between 0 and 1; the higher the value, the larger the regional disparities.
Source: OECD, 2009: 91.

single-party majority government of the AKP from late 2002 onwards, as can be deduced when the figures tabulated for the compound annual average growth rate of GDP in the years 2002–11 (5%) are compared to that of the years 1989–95 (4%) and 1996–2001 (1%) (see Figure 5.2). Needless to say, the generally favourable international economic environment, with low interest rates for developing countries, also helped.

Turkey's public-sector debt decreased from 74 per cent of GDP in 2001 to 38 per cent of GDP in 2010. While the Turkish economy has been growing steadily, private debt and living standards have increased significantly: private-sector debt increased from 15.1 per cent of GDP in 2001 to 47.1 per cent of GDP in 2010 (World Bank, World Development

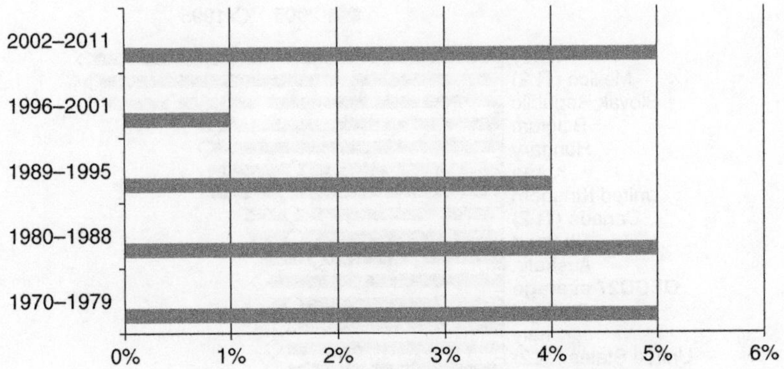

Figure 5.2 Compound annual average growth rate of GDP (%), 1970–2011[19]
Source: Calculated from World Bank, World Development Indicators: 2014a.

Indicators: 2014b). The GDP per capita increased from the level of US$ 7,834 in 2010 (see Figure 5.3).

Turkey's economic performance during the AKP period, however, does not constitute a monolithic bloc. Commencing from 2012, lower growth rates became the new normal for Turkey's economy. The Turkish economy recorded measly growth rates during 2012–14 with 2.1, 4.1 and 2.9 per cent real growth rates, respectively. Although Turkey's Tenth National Development Plan targets an annual average growth rate of 5.5 per cent between 2013 and 2018, the recent forecasts point to lower growth performances (Kutlay, 2015: 222).

Turkey's noteworthy economic performance in the 2000s was accompanied by a continuously mounting current account deficit (see Figure 5.4). As commented on by the OECD, Turkey's account deficit in this period reached 'unprecedented levels': in 2010, the country's deficit widened to just under 10 per cent of GDP (9.8 per cent), nearly 70 per cent more than what it had been in the 1990s (on average 3.10 per cent of GDP) (OECD, 2012: figure 1.1). By 2012, Turkey had

[19] In Figure 5.2, this book employed the compound annual average growth rate of GDP for the years 1970–2011 in order to enable a comparative understanding of annual average growth rates before and during the neoliberal era in Turkey. Moreover, the longitudinal data provided in this graph were preferred because they facilitate an understanding of the growth performance of the Turkish economy at economic turning points such as the structural adjustment programme in 1980, the liberalisation of capital accounts in 1989 and the post-2001 crisis restructuring.

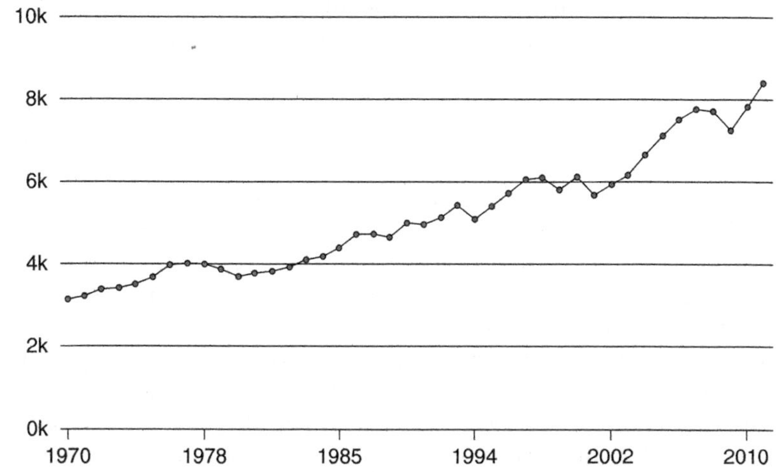

Figure 5.3 Turkey's GDP per capita (constant 2005 US$), 1970–2011
Source: World Bank, World Development Indicators: 2014c

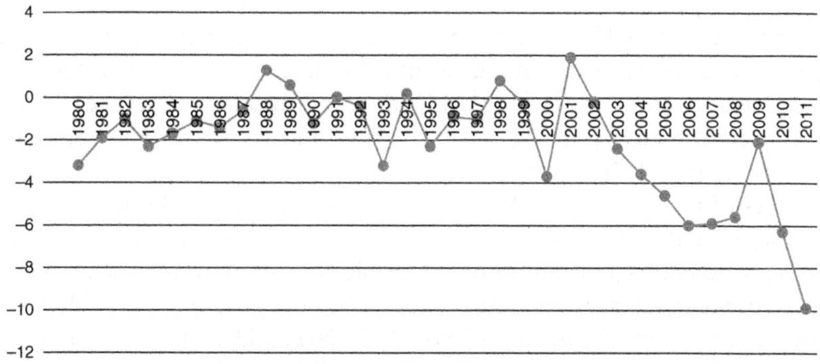

Figure 5.4 Turkey's current account balance as % of GDP, 1980–2011
Source: IMF, World Economic Outlook Database: 2014.

the world's third-largest current account deficit. Accordingly, the stupendous growth performance of the Turkish economy at the turn of the twenty-first century did not entail that Turkey overcame its perennial Achilles' heel: current account deficit. This weakness has been the integral aspect of Turkey's economic problem and has played a role in all the economic crises that it has experienced during the past half-century (Öniş and Rubin, 2003).

Before considering other features of the Turkish economy, owing to the fact that energy imports constitute the greater part of the current account deficit of Turkey, it is apt to elaborate on Turkey's energy woes. Energy-related issues have come to occupy increasingly the agenda of the Turkish Republic in the neoliberal phase of Turkish capitalism with the adoption of the export-oriented industrialisation strategy and the resultant ever-growing energy demands of Turkey.[20] So much so that, Turkey's rapprochement with the KRG governing the hydrocarbon-rich Iraqi Kurdistan[21] – alongside the traditional Turkish foreign policy of expanding its regional political influence, and America's encouragement of cordial relations between Turkey and Erbil – is based on Turkey's large energy demands and its need for the KRG's hydrocarbon reserves (Charountaki, 2012: 194–202). In 2010, Prime Minster Erdoğan validated this in a speech wherein he avowed that Turkey 'will build a very solid bridge in bilateral relations between Iraq and Turkey and between the Kurdistan Region and Turkey especially. We [Erdoğan and the president of the KRG, Masoud Barzani] will be in touch. The two countries also engage in economic cooperation. We will act together on energy and infrastructure' (ibid.: 199). Turkey sees the KRG and Iraq as an important part of the solution to its energy woes. Ankara wants to decrease its dependence on Russia and Iran, long unreliable energy suppliers that the US and EU sanctions are making more so. Iraq and its Kurdistan region are one way out of the bind.

According to a 2012 IEA report, Iraq will play a pivotal role in world oil markets in the coming decades and could produce up to 8.3 million barrels a day in 2035, but only if 'a resolution of differences over governance of the hydrocarbon sector . . . opens up the possibility for substantial growth also from the north of Iraq' (IEA, 2012: 83). The maps of oil and gas infrastructures that follow not only exhibit the pivotal role of the ESA regions for meeting Turkey's energy requirements, they also reveal the

[20] Turkey's oil demand rose from 447,000 barrels per day (kb/d) in 1990 to 670 (kb/d) in 2012, and its natural gas demand increased from 3.468 cubic meters per year (mcm/y) in 1990 to 45.254 in 2012 (mcm/y) (IEA, 2014: 447).

[21] With '23 rigs drilling exploration wells in mid-2012 (more than double the number from early 2011), the KRG area is now one of the most intensive areas for oil and gas exploration in the world, reflecting high expectations of significant discoveries in the heavily folded and faulted subsurface of the northern Zagros foldbelt. The regional government has awarded around 50 contracts with international companies to explore for and produce oil, and has stated its ambition to raise the region's production to 1 [million barrels per day] by 2015, based on existing discoveries, and to 2 [million barrels per day] by 2019, based on existing and expected discoveries' (IEA, 2012: 60).

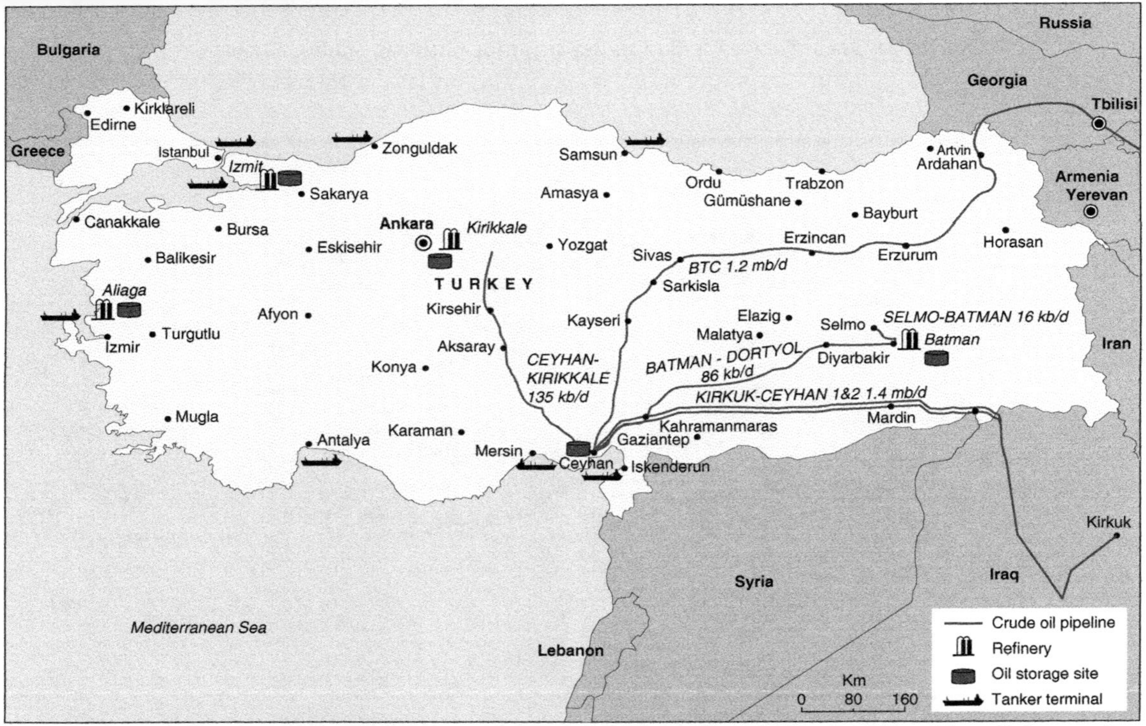

This map is without prejudice to the status of or sovereignty over any territory, to the delimitation of international frontiers and boundaries and to the name of any territory, city or area.

Map 8 Oil infrastructure of Turkey, 2013

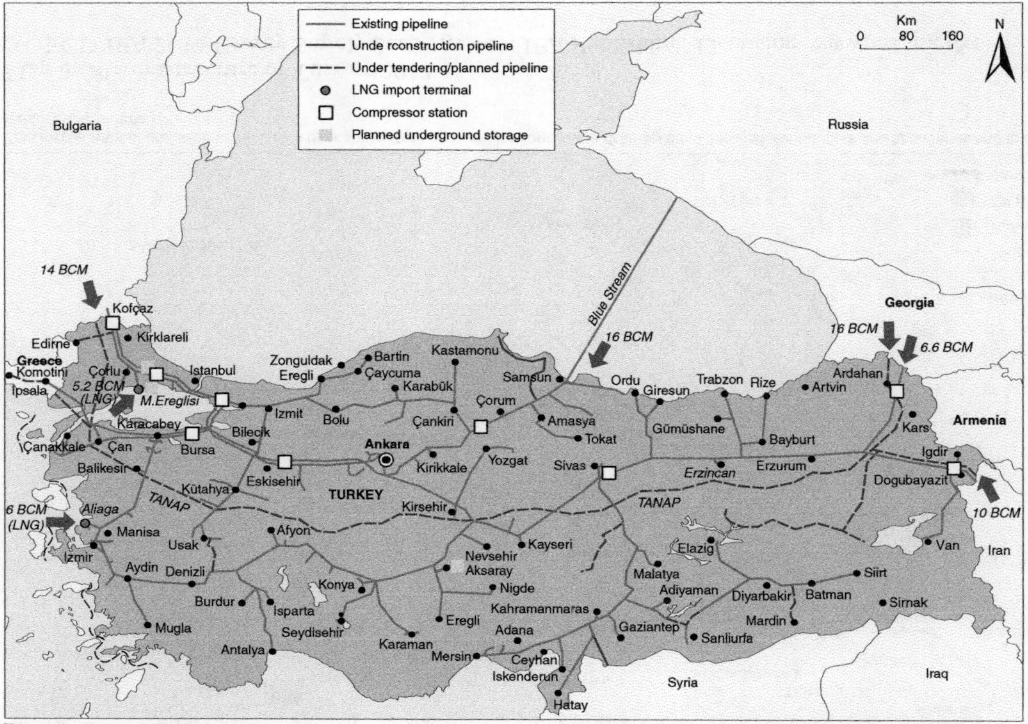

This map is without prejudice to the status of or sovereignty over any territory, to the delimitation of international frontiers and boundaries and to the name of any territory, city or area.

Map 9 Gas infrastructure of Turkey, 2013

importance of the Kirkuk-Ceyhan Crude Oil Pipeline[22] for satisfying this demand, which carries a total maximum annual capacity of 1.4 million barrels per day (IEA, 2014: 455).

As well as the current account deficit, unemployment remained high throughout the 2000s (Yeldan, 2009: 146–56). Unemployment in the country hailed as the 'emerging Euro Tiger' rose from 6.5 per cent in 2000 to 10.7 per cent by the end of 2010 (Eurostat, 2014). In 2010, Turkey's employment rate was 46.3 per cent, much lower than the crises-ridden euro-area average of 64.1 per cent (ibid.). In addition, despite the rise in the GDP per capita witnessed in the 2000s, the major income gap between the poor and rich persisted.

The income of the richest 10 per cent of people in the mid-2000s was, on average across the OECD countries, nearly nine times of the poorest 10% (OECD, 2008: 3). In Turkey, the richest 10 per cent in the mid-2000s had incomes of more than seventeen times those of the poorest 10 per cent, and, in Mexico, the ratio was 25:1 (ibid.). This trend appears to have continued in the latter part of the 2000s, since, according to the OECD data pertaining to the late 2000s, Turkey had the third highest Gini index for GDP per capita (see Table 5.2).

As briefly raised earlier, previously existing socioeconomic regional disparities persisted throughout the first decade of the twenty-first century, as exhibited by the persistence of the long-standing large discrepancies between the predominantly Kurdish ESA provinces and the rest of the country. In May 2003, the SPO published the results of a study, titled *Researching the Socio-economic Development Ranking of Provinces and Regions* (*İllerin ve Bölgelerin Sosyo-Ekonomik Sıralaması Araştıması*), shedding more factual and detailed light on the enduring regional divergences in Turkey pre- and post-2001 crisis.

In brief, this research, using the SPO's socioeconomic development index (SDI), ranked provinces and regions in accordance with their level of social and economic development from 1 to 5: 'first-level developed provinces' being the most developed and 'fifth-level developed provinces' being the least developed. The SDI is employed to measure the social and economic development level of provinces based on fifty-eight socioeconomic variables, including employment,

[22] The Kirkuk-Ceyhan Crude Oil Pipeline 'runs from Kirkuk, Iraq, to the Ceyhan Oil Terminal on the Mediterranean Sea and has been active since 1976. A second pipeline parallel to the first was commissioned in 1987. ... In September 2012, Iraq and Turkey agreed to extend the carriage of Iraqi crude oil import through the pipeline by 15 years. In 2011, this pipeline brought 163.3 mb of crude oil from Iraq to Turkey' (IEA, 2014: 455).

Table 5.2 *Income inequality league from low to high inequality in OECD countries, late 2000s*

Country	Gini Coefficient
Slovenia	0.24
Slovak Republic	0.25
Denmark	0.25
Norway	0.25
Czech Republic	0.26
Sweden	0.26
Finland	0.26
Austria	0.26
Belgium	0.27
Luxemburg	0.27
Switzerland	0.28
Iceland	0.28
France	0.29
Netherland	0.29
Germany	0.30
Ireland	0.30
Spain	0.31
OECD	0.31
Estonia	0.31
Poland	0.31
Korea	0.32
Canada	0.32
Greece	0.32
Japan	0.33
New Zealand	0.33
Austria	0.34
Italy	0.34
United Kingdom	0.34
Portugal	0.36
Israel	0.37
United States	0.38
Turkey	0.41
Mexico	0.48
Chile	0.50

Source: OECD, 2011: 67.

Table 5.3 *Socioeconomic development index in Turkey, 1996 and 2003*

	1996	1996
Region	SDI Index	SDI Index
Marmara	1.69	1.70
Aegean	0.50	0.48
Central Anatolia	0.46	0.48
Mediterranean Region	0.6	0.2
Black Sea Region	−0.54	−0.51
Southeastern Anatolia	−1.03	−1.01
Eastern Anatolia	−1.13	−1.16

Source: SPO, 2003: 78.

education, health, infrastructure, manufacturing and construction.[23] Unlike any other region in Turkey, all of the provinces in ESA, with the exclusion of Malatya and Elazığ, were ranked as fourth- or fifth-level developed provinces (see Map 10). In parallel with the latest country report for Turkey prepared by the UNDP quoted earlier, seventeen (out of the total twenty-one) provinces in ESA constituted the least developed domains in Turkey (SPO, 2003: 56).

With the country average at 0, the Marmara region at 1.7 was the most developed region. The Aegean and central Anatolia regions were the next developed regions at 0.48, followed by the Mediterranean region at 0.2. The Black Sea region was just below the national average at −0.51, while the south eastern Anatolia and eastern Anatolia regions fell far below the Turkey's average at −1.01 and −1.16, respectively (SPO, 2003: 78). Moreover, as the SPO pointed out, when the findings of this study are compared with that of 1996, it becomes apparent that virtually nothing had changed regarding the socioeconomic levels or rankings of the seven main regions in Turkey, as displayed in Table 5.3. Thus at the peak of the armed conflict in 1996 and four years into the ceasefire in 2003, the predominantly Kurdish ESA could not rid itself from the shackles of being one of the most underdeveloped regions of the country.

Between 2001 and 2010, the TÜİK, without any explanation, ceased to produce statistics pertaining to the regional distribution of the national income, thus the actual magnitude of spatial income disparities in the 2000s was not made public. In January 2010, however, it gave an end to

[23] For a full list of the variables, see SPO (2003: 45).

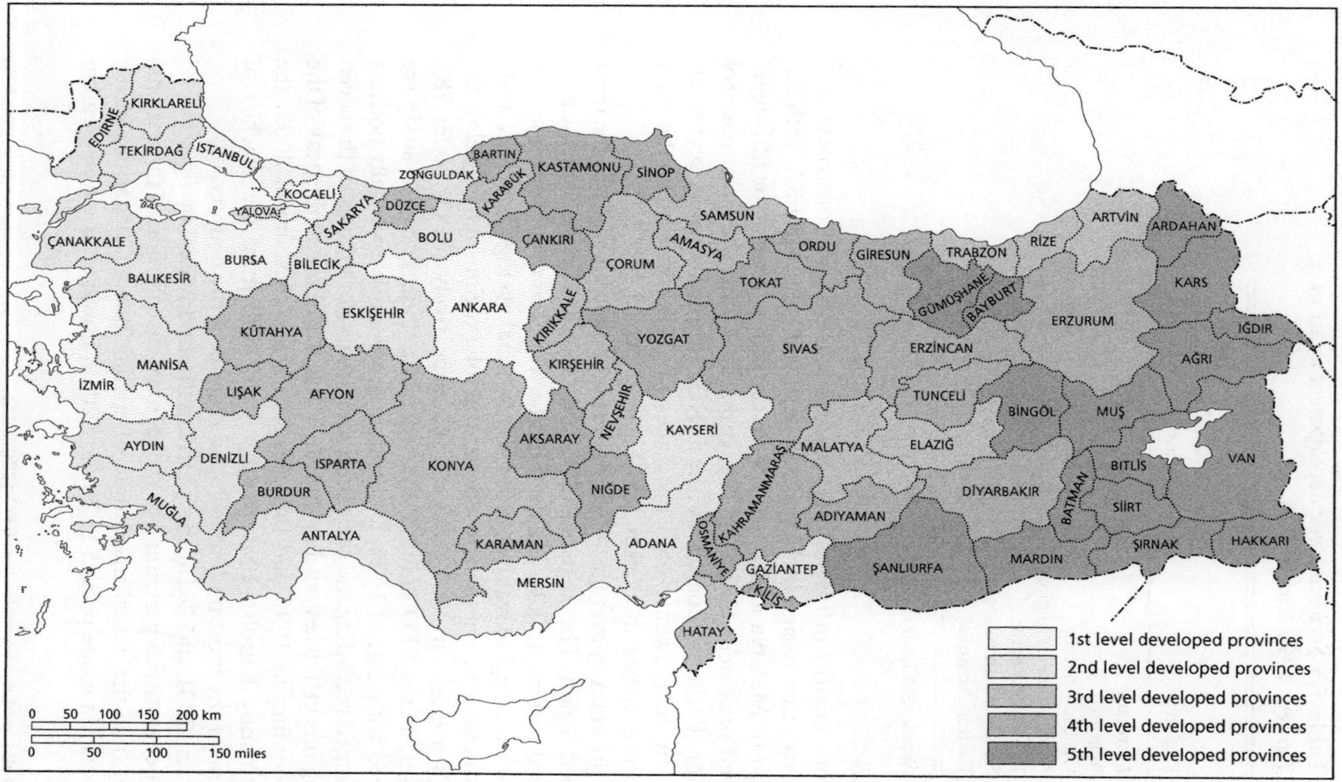

Map 10 Categorisation of provinces in Turkey, socioeconomic development index of SPO, 2003
Source: Based on SPO, 2003: 72.

Table 5.4 *Average per capita income, 2006*

Region	Average Income (US$)
Istanbul	10.352
Southeastern and Eastern Anatolia	3.017
Turkey	6.684

Source: TÜİK figures in Sönmez, 2012: 123.

this practice by only publishing the national income data for 2004–6. The long-awaited figures revealed that: (a) the national income share of the ESA regions which host 15 per cent of the total population of Turkey, typically decreased; and (b) the ESA had the lowest average per capita income in the country.

During the era of economic liberalisation in Turkey, analogous to the preceding ISI period, the predominantly Kurdish ESA witnessed an incessant decrease in their fraction of national income. In 1979, these regions accounted for 8.2 per cent of the national income, in 2001, this figure fell to 7.7 per cent, and by 2004–6, it further reduced to 6.9 per cent (Sönmez, 2012: 122). Consequently, by 2006, the national income shares of the twenty-one provinces located in this part of Turkey was less than half of their share of the total population. It is worth noting that this was at a time when Turkey's national income recorded a swift and remarkable growth from $181 billion in 2002 to $400 billion in 2006 (USARM, 2009: 13).

The ESA regions had the lowest per capita income in the country, as the average income in these regions was around 54 per cent less than Turkey's average and, more strikingly, approximately 70 per cent less than that of Istanbul's (see Table 5.4) (Sönmez, 2012: 123). It would be fair to say that neither the cessation of the militarised conflict between the PKK and the Turkish state between 1999 and 2004 nor the significant economic growth of the 'emerging Tiger' post-2001 crisis were efficiently utilised to remedy the economic underdevelopment of the ESA. As a result, Turkey could not shake off the notoriety of being the OECD member state with the highest level of regional income disparities in the mid-2000s (see Figure 5.1.)

Another indicator of the increasing poverty in the predominantly Kurdish provinces in the ESA, and the persistence of the regional income variations between the regions and the rest of the country, is the high rate of green card holders in these areas in the late 2000s. The Green Card (*Yeşil Kart*) Programme, initially set up in 1992 and replaced in 2011 with the General Health Insurance System, was

Table 5.5 *Green card holders in Turkey, 2008*

Region	Population	Green Card Holders	Average Green Card Holders%
21 Southeastern and Eastern Anatolia	11,186,951	4,290,996	38.4
60 Provinces	59,399,305	5,071,253	8.5
Turkey	70,586,256	9,362,249	13.3

Source: Ministry of Health figures cited in USARM, 2009: 27.

a non-contributory health programme that ensured the provision of health care services to individuals whose family earned less than one-third of the minimum wage. In 2008, according to the data the USARM obtained from the Health Ministry, the total number of green card holders in Turkey was 9,362,249, just under half of whom (4,290,996) lived in the ESA. While in the twenty-one ESA provinces green card holders accounted for 38.4 per cent of the regional population, in the remaining sixty provinces, this figure was 8.5 per cent, as demonstrated in Table 5.5.

The massive underdevelopment of ESA and the consequential persistence of regional disparities between these regions and the rest of the country are inextricably linked to three principal factors: first, the regression of agriculture in the predominantly agrarian ESA regions emanating from the negative repercussions of the armed conflict between the PKK and the Turkish state as well as the economic liberalisation policies implemented after 1980; second, the derisory and low level of public and private investments in ESA, which is nowhere near enough to counterbalance the long-standing underdevelopment and/or to minimise the destruction of the war in these domains. The third factor is the top-down developmental policies and vision of the Turkish state in relation to these regions that has thus far resulted in it paying minimal attention to the actual and urgent needs of the local populace in ESA.

Armed Conflict and Economic Liberalisation: Stunted Development

As discussed extensively in the preceding chapters, owing to the low level of industrialisation in ESA during the years after the proclamation of the Turkish Republic, these regions were heavily dependent on agriculture. For instance, by 1988, according to a survey by the SPO, there were only 41,411 workers in all of the manufacturing establishments in the two regions. Of these, 30,777 (74.32%) were in public manufacturing enterprises and only 10,634 (25.68%) in private establishments (Kutbay and Çınar, 1989: table 5).

It is apt to point out here that the previously cited workforce figures collated by the SPO, albeit demonstrating the very low level of industrialisation in ESA, does not account for informal employment in ESA, making it extremely difficult to ascertain the precise extent of employment in the non-agricultural sectors in these domains. This statistical lacuna was not unique to ESA: the TÜİK in the 1988 Household Labour Force Survey (HLFS) officially articulated the informal sector concept for the first time, and, as elaborated later, it was only after 2001 that the TÜİK defined and researched the informal sector in line with the internationally recognised standards (Bulutay and Taştı, 2004: 6–7; Kan and Tansel, 2014: 2–4). Thus, up until the 2000s, data limitations and heterogeneity have constituted major barriers to measuring informality (TÜSİAD, 2006: 44–53).

Keith Hart (1973) coined the term *informal sector* to designate self-employment, casual labour and small enterprise activities of the reserve army of urban unemployed and underemployed. The maiden internationally agreed definition was adopted at the Fifteenth International Conference of Labour Statisticians (ICLS) in 1993. According to this definition, the informal sector denotes employment and production that take place in unincorporated small or unregistered enterprises (e.g. fewer than five employees) (International Labour Organisation (ILO), 1993). In the ensuing years, this enterprise-based definition was criticised for failing to capture the increasing variety of informal employment forms, in particular marginal micro-scale informal activities, which are often unreported by individuals (Hussmanns, 2004). As a result, in 2003, a broader informality specification relating to an employment-based concept, namely, *informal employment*, was adopted at the Seventeenth ICLS. *Informal employment* referred to all employment arrangements that leave individuals without social protection through their work, whether or not the economic units they operate or work for are formal enterprises, informal enterprises or households (ILO, 2003). This study concurs with this broader definition and hence employs the notion of informality to refer to 'all forms of … employment without contracts (i.e. covered by labour legislation), worker benefits or social protection – both inside and outside informal enterprises' (Chen, 2005: 7).

In Turkey, although informality has been an issue for a long time, the size of the informal economy has grown rapidly since the 1980s.

The development paradigm centred on a state-led import substitution regime had reached its limits by the 1970s and was unable to engender sufficient regular employment (Pamuk, 2003). Additionally, the 1980 coup d'état dramatically shifted the balance between employers and employees (Öngen, 2003). Real wages declined by 40 per cent between 1980 and 1988 period (Özar and Ercan, 2004). As the economy was liberalised under a series of structural adjustment programmes, employers were able to informalise employment relations further (Boratav et al., 2000; Ercan, 2004). From 1990 to 2003, the share of informal employment in non-agricultural employment increased from 25 per cent to 31.5 per cent, accounting for 47 per cent of job growth outside of agriculture (Erdem, 2006 104). Informality is particularly widespread in small enterprises with low productivity and unqualified labour, but larger enterprises also engage in underreporting in order to save on labour costs and to avoid taxes and regulatory responsibilities (Peker, 1996).

Data on the unincorporated and tax-related characters of the informal sector are not included in any of the HLFSs in Turkey in the years prior to 2000 (Bulutay, 2004: 7). Relatedly, based on the findings of the HLFSs in Turkey after 2000 – which are employed by ILO[24] on informality – we are able to attain an approximate picture of this phenomenon. Based on the HLFSs for the years 2002–9, informal employment in Turkey is discerned to account 'for a little bit more than 50% of total employment during the years 2002–2005 and it went down to less than 50% in the period 2006–2009' (ILO, 2010: 9). During the years 2000–9, informality in the agricultural sector was around 90 per cent, while informal employment labour in the non-agricultural sector was around 30 per cent (ibid). These figures exhibit clearly the prevalence and persistence of the informal sector not only in Turkey, but also, more importantly for the purposes of this research, they highlight the importance of informality for the predominantly agrarian economy of the ESA regions.

The climate of violence, mass evacuations of villages and hamlets in ESA coupled with the aforementioned unfavourable conditions for the agricultural sector in Turkey in the neoliberal era – i.e. repression of agricultural incomes, decrease in agricultural subsidies and the sectoral terms of trade turning against agriculture – had detrimental results for the cultivation of crops and raising of livestock in these predominantly agrarian regions. In the first half of the twentieth century, agriculture

[24] The 2009 HLFS in Turkey is employed in one of the most detailed studies on informality in forty-seven countries; see ILO and WIEGO (2013).

accounted for just more than 80 per cent of employment and more than 50 per cent of the GDP in Turkey; in the early 2000s, this stood at 35 per cent and 10 per cent, respectively (Pamuk, 2008: 292). More specifically, in 1970, stock rearing, the single most important activity in ESA, accounted for 12.3 per cent of Turkey's GNP, whilst in 1997 it had dwindled to 2.2 per cent (McDowall, 2000: 448). Alongside the neglect of the agricultural sector by the successive governments of the 1980s and the 1990s, village evictions and the prohibitions on grazing in the summer pastures in the ESA, particularly in the 1990s, played a decisive role in the sharp decline of the agricultural output in these regions.

In 1994 alone, the agricultural loss of ESA, on account of the escalating violence, the mass evacuations of villages and hamlets, was estimated to be $350 million. In the province of Diyarbakir, it was estimated that livestock numbers were reduced by 50 per cent, stock rearing by 30 per cent and forested area by 60 per cent (ibid.: 440). In the 1990s, the contributions of the twenty-one ESA provinces to the national GDP continued to fall. In 1991, these areas accounted for around 6.40 per cent of Turkey's GDP and in 1995, this figure fell to 5.70 per cent, whilst by 2000 it dwindled to approximately 5.50 per cent (USARM, 2009: 18). Thus, the contributions of the two regions to the country's GDP diminished from 8.54 per cent at the dawn of the neoliberal era in Turkey in 1979 to 5.50 per cent two decades later. By the beginning of the twenty-first century, ESA, which accounted for 15 per cent of Turkey's population, contributed less than 6 per cent to the country's GDP.

According to the findings of a report published by the pro-Islamist Fazilet Party (Virtue Party) in June 1999, the armed conflict combined with the austerity policies of the consecutive governments after 1980 severely decreased the average income in ESA: 'in western regions of Turkey the per capita income is $4,000–$5,000, while in the east and south east it is only $600-$900.'[25] Concomitant to the low level of income, individuals in the eastern and south eastern provinces have very low levels of savings and credit use. In 2000, average per capita bank deposits in Turkey were around TRL[26] 200 (million), in eastern and south eastern Anatolia, it was approximately TRL 70 (million). Likewise, in the same year, average per capita bank credits in the country were about TL 400 (million), while in the south east they stood at TL 120 (million) (TESEV, 2006: 46).

[25] *Turkish Daily News*, 4 June 1999.

[26] The Old Turkish Lira (TRL) was replaced with the New Turkish Lira (TRY) on 1 January 2005. One TRY is equivalent to 1,000,000 TRL.

Table 5.6 *Bank deposits and credits, 2005*

Provinces	Per Capita Bank Deposits (YTL)	Per Capita Bank Credits (YTL)
Adıyaman	392	508
Ağrı	197	146
Bingöl	422	276
Bitlis	227	175
Diyarbakır	429	341
Elazığ	1.106	471
Erzincan	942	495
Erzurum	543	404
Hakkari	233	133
Kars	548	481
Malatya	764	495
Mardin	299	227
Muş	198	121
Siirt	294	241
Tunceli	1.485	508
Şanlıurfa	303	255
Van	296	301
TURKEY	**3.207**	**1.751**

Source: TBB figures in Sönmez, 2012: 218.

The remarkable economic growth witnessed in the post-2001 crisis years does not appear to have triggered an increase in personal savings and the availability of bank credit in these regions. In 2005, according to the figures of The Association of Banks of Turkey (Türkiye Bankalar Birliği, TBB), bank loans provided to individuals and enterprises in ESA constituted a mere 3.1 per cent of the total bank loans in Turkey, and per capita bank deposits in all twenty-one provinces in this quarter of Anatolia were far below the national average of TRY 3207 (Sönmez, 2012: 219). Although the volume of both deposits and credit is low in ESA compared to the rest of Turkey (see Table 5.6), the ratio of credit to deposit in certain provinces in these regions, such as Tunceli and Elazığ, is higher than the national average, which is an indication of a higher level of indebtedness in these areas.

Paltry Public and Private Investments

The insufficient and low public and private investment in ESA, far from minimising the negative repercussions of the armed conflict and the austerity measures of the IMF-inspired economic programmes, played

Table 5.7 *The regional breakdowns of subsidised investments in Turkey, 1995–2004*

Regions	Average Shares of Subsidised Investments %
Marmara	42
Central Anatolia	12.7
Aegean	11.8
Mediterranean	12.6
Southeastern Anatolia	8.9
Black Sea	5.3
Eastern Anatolia	2.4
Multiregional	4.4

Source: TESEV, 2006: 45.

a pivotal role in the persistence of the long-standing large socioeconomic disparities between these regions and the rest of country in the neoliberal era. In spite of the continuance of the state-sanctioned incentive scheme of Priority Development Regions (PDRs) Programmes introduced in 1968, discussed in Chapter 4, private investment in the predominantly Kurdish ESA provinces remained trivial in the years of high levels of armed conflict (1992–9), as well as in the period of relative tranquillity (1999–2004). In the years 1995–2004, ESA had the lowest and third bottommost average proportions of subsidised investments, respectively, as displayed in Table 5.7.

On 29 January 2004, Law 5068 was approved in order to augment private investment by offering additional financial incentives to employers and investors. The AKP government's aim to bolster investment from the private sector through a wide range of incentives, which includes, among other things, investment credits, tax relief, postponement of the value-added tax (VAT) and assistance with energy-related issues, appears to have primarily benefited the parts of the country that are more industrialised and better equipped with infrastructure facilities. In 2006, only 5.78 per cent of the subsidised investments went to ESA regions, and more strikingly, the combined subsidised investment in the years 2002–6 for the twenty-one ESA provinces was lower than that of the province of Bursa. Bursa' share of subsidised investment in 2002–6 stood at 4.45 per cent whilst the combined shares of the cities in eastern and south eastern Anatolia were 4.44 per cent (USARM, 2009: 35–6).

An important research commissioned by TESEV-UNDP-The Open Society Foundation (OSIAF) in the early 2000s explored, among other things, the reasons as to why entrepreneurs in Turkey were historically reluctant to invest in these regions. They found that along with the armed conflict, the inadequate public-sector investment in the south east played a decisive role in dissuading representatives of the private sector to invest in these regions. Members of TOBB who partook in this study stated that their enduring hesitance to invest in ESA was 'in part due to the security reasons' and partly because of 'problems pertaining to the recruitment of a well-equipped labour force as well as the lack of sufficient infrastructure in these regions' emanating from years of scarce state investment. Without the removal of these substantial obstacles, business executives argued that state-induced incentives would play a 'minimal role' in enthusing private sector investment in these lagging regions (TESEV, 2006: 19).

Indeed, public investments, or the lack thereof, have been a major problem in ESA, more noticeably in the 1990s. From 1990 to 2001, ESA received on average TRL 3,000 million public investment per capita, while the remaining five regions of Turkey attained TRL 8,000 million public investment per capita (ibid.: 28). Similarly, in the years 2002–7, the halcyon days of the Turkish economy following the 2001 crisis and prior to the global crisis of 2008 under the stewardship of AKP, the total amount of government expenditure in the ESA regions ranked the lowest among all seven regions of Turkey (see Table 5.9). In addition, unlike the other region that performed below Turkey's average in the SPO's SDI (i.e. the Black Sea region), in ESA public expenditure per person was below the national average, as demonstrated

Table 5.8 *The regional comparisons of public investments per capita, 2002–2007 (in%)*

Regions	%
Central Anatolia	1.83
Black Sea	1.73
Marmara	1.64
Mediterranean	1.57
TURKEY	1.57
Eastern Anatolia	1.50
Aegean	1.26
Southeastern Anatolia	1.23

Source: USARM, 2009: 65.

Table 5.9 *Sectoral distribution of public investment in ESA, 2002–2007 (in%)*

Sector	%
Energy	19
Agriculture	17
Health	14
Education	14
Communications	8
Housing	3
Mining	3
Tourism	0.9
Miscellaneous	22
Manufacturing	0.7

Source: USARM, 2009: 64.

in Table 5.9. In other words, with the exception of these predominantly Kurdish regions, other lagging regions received preferential treatment in the sphere of public investment, so much so that the Black Sea region had the second highest per capita public investment in the country (see Table 5.9).

In terms of the sectoral distribution of the public investment in these regions, we see that very little has changed from the ISI period. State expenditure in these regions continues to be driven by exogenous factors, and minimal financial attention is imputed to the exigent local needs of the populace in the ESA provinces. From 2002 to 2007, the biggest beneficiary of public investments in ESA was the energy sector (see Table 5.10), which, on account of the lack of industrialisation in these regions and the low level of employment opportunities generated, has nominal value or use to these regions. In 2006, 69 per cent of the electricity generated in ESA was used outside of these regions, yet, only 17 per cent of this energy was locally consumed (USARM, 2009: 43).

In spite of the infrastructural deficiencies in ESA, which prevent the local population enjoying the necessities of modern-day life and hinder private-sector investment in these regions, only 8 per cent of the state expenditure in these regions was spent on communication. In addition, the total public expenditure on health care and education (28 per cent) in these regions was not substantially different to that of the combined investments in the energy and mining sectors (22%), which to an extent explains the reason behind the large and persistent socioeconomic disparities between ESA and the rest of the country.

The lack of attention to the local needs of these regions is by no means unique to the five years covered here because state planning and investments in these regions in the neoliberal era, parallel to previous periods in Turkey, have largely been in disregard of the socioeconomic needs and demands of their people. The two operational codes of the state programmes and funds in these regions have thus far been political control as well as orientation towards meeting the requirements of the economic demands of the rest of Turkey, particularly the ever-growing energy needs of the country. Both of these conventional facets of the Turkish state policy in the predominantly Kurdish and naturally rich ESA are embedded in the socioeconomic engineering project born at around the same time as the arrival of neoliberal policies in Turkey: GAP.

GAP: A Paradigmatic Case of Developmentalism from Above

GAP at present comprises thirteen massive irrigation and energy projects and twenty-two dams, including the Atatürk Dam, the sixth largest of its kind in the world. It covers an area of about 75,358 square kilometres, which represents 9.7 per cent of the total area of Turkey, spread over nine south eastern provinces: Adıyaman, Batman, Diyarbakır, Gaziantep, Kilis, Mardin, Siirt, Şanlıurfa and Şırnak. The GAP region's total population is around 6.1 million, which constitutes just under 10 per cent of the total population.

The origins of GAP go back to a plan of the Directorate of State Hydraulic Works (Devlet Su İşleri, DSI) on hydraulic energy and irrigation, which was prepared in 1977. By the second half of the 1980s, the Kurdish insurgency, as well as the increasing regional disparities between the south east and the rest of Turkey, shifted the emphasis of GAP to 'integrated regional development' that aimed not only to efficiently utilise water and energy resources, but also to address the socioeconomic underdevelopment and poverty in this region. A new plan, the GAP Master Plan (1989), was prepared and a bureaucratic reorganisation was decreed which resulted in the establishment of the GAP Regional Development Administration (GAP-RDA). The GAP-RDA defined the objectives of GAP as: (a) generation of hydroelectric power; (b) developing regional agriculture through irrigation; (c) development of a regional agro-industrial base; and (d) providing better social services, education and employment to control migration and attract qualified individuals to the area (GAP, Master Plan, 1990).

The low financial realisation (40%) and the limited economic impact of GAP led to the 1998 decision of the Council of Ministers to revise the

Master Plan. GAP-RDA was assigned with the task and to ensure its completion by latest 2010. Accordingly, a new regional development plan was devised in cooperation with the UNDP. This novel plan incorporated the newly adopted principle of sustainable human development and resultantly pursued the following aims: (a) social sustainability and the development of social services; (b) optimum and sustainable utilisation of natural resources; (c) human settlements; (d) agricultural sustainability and development of agricultural productivity; and (e) local entrepreneurship and industrial development for economic viability.[27]

Owing to limited success in meeting these set targets, the completion date of GAP has constantly been revised. The current set date for completion, according to the present GAP administrator chairman, Sadrettin Karahocagil, 'of all main and sub-projects is the end of 2017'.[28] One of the factors, if not the main factor, for its continual postponement is the limited success in attaining the set objectives in areas other than the energy projects. That is to say, even after the systematic shift within GAP from dam-building or hydroelectric production project to a multi-sectoral and sustainable socioeconomic regional development programme, the overriding concern has been electricity production. The 'hydro-imperative' aspect (Kolars, 1986), as well as the enduring aim of controlling Kurdish heartlands, has thus far largely ignored the long-term and most beneficial facets crucial for the development of the south east: irrigation; agricultural training; crop breeding; industrial development; education; and improving health care services.

By the end of 2006, nearly two decades after the commencement of GAP, only 14 per cent of the projected irrigation investments materialised, while 74 per cent of the planned hydroelectric energy investments were realised. Eight hydroelectric power stations were in operation – in 2006, the GAP accounted for 48.5 per cent of Turkey's total hydroelectric electricity production (USARM, 2009: 42). As of 2007, the monetary value of the energy obtained from the GAP region, \$17.9 billion, was near equivalent to public investments made for the project up until that point, \$18.9 billion. The great majority of the electricity generated in the south east was, however, consumed outside of this region: in the mid-2000s, in spite of electricity consumption per capita in Turkey being 202 kilowatt-hours (kWh), electricity usage per capita in the GAP region was 78 kWh (ibid.: 66).

[27] For detailed and differing analyses of the evolution and objectives of GAP, see Kolars (1986), Mutlu (1996), Unver (1997) and Çarkoğlu and Mine (2005).

[28] *Today's Zaman*, 17 September 2013.

The large and persistent socioeconomic disparities, as exhibited by the UNDP HDI of 2000 as well as the SDI of the SPO in 1996 and 2003, confirm that GAP project objectives concerning sustainable regional development and minimising regional discrepancies between the ESA and the rest of the Turkey have largely stayed on paper. Likewise, there is a gap between the Turkish state's alleged aims of minimising migration and promoting human settlements in the region and what it applies on the ground in the Euphrates-Tigris basin.

As briefly alluded to previously, the construction of dams as part of GAP – Keban (1974), Ataturk (1992), Birecik (2000) and the pending Ilisu Dam – has resulted in the displacement of people and the evacuation of villages in ESA, augmenting the total number of migrations from the south east. Estimates in relation to the number of internally displaced peoples (IDPs) arising from the construction of the dams vary. The number of IDPs was 197,732, according to the DSI in 1999. Other sources do not authenticate official Turkish sources with regard to the number of deportations. Based on a report from a fact-finding mission in south eastern Anatolia, The Corner House in the UK in the year 2000 claimed that migrants ranged from 150,000 to 200,000 people (The Corner House, 2000). Comparatively, in 2004, individual resources reported that around 350,000 people had been displaced by the GAP project (Morvaridi, 2004: 729). Based on the different estimates, it is safe to suggest that the IDPs produced by GAP range from 200,000 to 350,000 people, which raises the total number of forced deportations in the late twentieth and early twenty-first centuries from ESA to around 1.5 million.

In light of the disclosure of the memorandum in 1993 from President Özal to Prime Minister Demirel advocating the construction of large dams in order to prevent the return of the local deportees back to the south east, dam-related displacements have naturally raised major doubts regarding the actual purpose of GAP from the local populations. In 1998, according to a poll conducted by the Union of Chambers of Turkish Engineers and Architects (Türk Mühendis ve Mimar Odaları, TMMOB), only 42 per cent of the local populations perceived GAP as a development project, and a mere 11 per cent had either short- or long-term expectations of GAP (McDowall, 2000: 448).

Other factors fuelling the suspicions of the largely Kurdish population in the south east with regard to GAP are closely associated with the shortcomings of the twenty-eight sub-projects launched in the third or sustainable development phase of GAP,[29] like the Multi-Purpose

[29] For a full list of these mentioned projects, see GAP (1997).

Community Centres (Çok Amaçlı Toplum Merkezleri, ÇATOM)[30] and the GAP Entrepreneur Support and Guidance Centres (GAP-Girişimci Destekleme Merkezi, GAP-GIDEM)[31]. By 2004, eight years after the inauguration of the GAP-UNDP sustainable development programme, only $1.3 million of the $5.2 million raised for this programme had been spent on the twenty-eight sub-projects. This low level of investment is not only indicative of the limitations of transforming GAP into a sustainable development project, but also lays bare the rationale for the Turkish state pursuing the fashionable sustainable development strategy advocated by prominent international developments agencies: to raise funds from a wide range of international institutions like the UNDP, UNICEF and the EU. In addition, the local inhabitants have questioned the motives of some sub-projects such as ÇATOM. The perception of some of ÇATOM's services – like the birth control training as an effort to 'contain' the rise of the Kurdish population[32] or the literacy courses in Turkish as an assimilation strategy (Çarkoğlu and Eder, 2005: 179) – is symptomatic of both the local populaces' estrangement from GAP and the immense influence the Kurdish question has over GAP.

Another issue closely connected with Turkey's Kurdish question as well as the socioeconomic development of the south east, which to date has largely been ignored by GAP, is the unequal distribution of landownership and the consequential perseverance of the traditional relations of production and social structure in the GAP region. Contrary to the avowed 'urgent' need of land reform in the GAP Master Plan (GAP, 1990: 23), the traditional land tenure system, as well as the disproportionate power of the co-opted Kurdish landed elite in the south eastern Anatolia region remained untouched by successive governments responsible for implementing GAP.

In 1990, within the GAP region, 8 per cent of farming families owned more than 50 per cent of all land, while 41 per cent held between 10 and 50 *dönüms* and another 38 per cent held no land at all. Of the large landowning families, significant portions were absentee, content to allow ineffective farming with the proviso that they attain a satisfactory

[30] ÇATOM started in 1995 and aims to ensure the participation of women in the following services: literacy courses in Turkish, health education, housekeeping courses, maternal education, knitting and weaving courses and poly-clinical services.

[31] GAP-GIDEM was founded in 1996 and is financed by EU grants aimed at providing consultancy services to businesses and promotion of private-sector investments in the GAP region.

[32] According to official statistics pertaining to the mid-1990s, average fertility in the east and south east is 4.37 per cent, while this figure is 2.65 per cent in other regions of Turkey. Relatedly, almost 35 per cent of the whole population in these regions is under fifteen years of age (GAP, 1998).

income from their lands (McDowall, 2000: 434). Relatedly, without a land reform, it was implausible that the majority of the agrarian population could benefit from GAP. The unequal distribution of the land ownership system inherited from the late Ottoman period and tenaciously preserved ever since the single-party period remained devoid of a fundamental reform, nonetheless.

According to the latest Agricultural Census of 2001, in the southeastern Anatolia region, there is in total 264.361 agricultural enterprises. Of these, 2.7 per cent is large-sized enterprises (i.e. farms over 500 hectares), owned by the wealthy landowning families that account for 33.2 per cent of all land, while 56 per cent is small-sized enterprises (i.e. holdings less than 50 hectares), and they only account for 9.7 per cent of all the land. In Diyarbakir, more strikingly, 3.3 per cent of the large-sized enterprises owned by the traditional landowning class accounts for 41.2 per cent of all land in the province. And in Şanlıurfa 1.5 per cent of the large-sized enterprises controlled by the wealthy landowning class, accounts for 28.7 per cent of all land (USARM, 2009: 33).

Despite such inequalities in landownership, the issue of land reform went unmentioned in the latest GAP Action Plan (2008–12) launched by Prime Minister Erdoğan in Diyarbakir in 2008 in order to 'complete' GAP (GAP, Eylem Planı, 2008). As a result, Erdogan, like his predecessors, indirectly assured the pro-government Kurdish landed elites that their wealth, and the immense political power yielding from it, will be conserved. Thus, yet again, the long-simmering issue of land reform, like other exigent prerequisites for the development of the region, has been substituted for political concerns of the ruling classes, in this context, the maintenance of the convenient alliance between the co-opted Kurdish landowning class and the governors.

Pursuing the goal of electoral gains as well as controlling Kurdish heartlands through the co-opted propertied Kurdish elite perpetuates the *status quo*, which hampers the necessary socioeconomic transformation and development of ESA. So long as the local intercessors of the Turkish state own most of the land in these regions, even the positive features of GAP, such as the much-needed irrigation projects, will only enhance the exploitation of the local peasantry and perhaps aggravate its mass resentment. This comes to show that the success of GAP as well as economic development in these regions hinges, above all, on a political resolution of the Kurdish question.

Conclusion

The evidence in the preceding chapters of this study on economic, political and social life in the predominantly Kurdish regions of ESA necessitates a reconsideration of the role and impact of economic development in ESA on the rise and evolution of the Kurdish question. An appropriate way of starting this reassessment, as well as summarising the findings of this study, can be by returning to one of the initial research questions set by this investigation: how economically developed or underdeveloped were the predominantly Kurdish domains of the Ottoman Empire?

At this point, it is worth recalling that, albeit on differing causal grounds, the development literature on the primarily Kurdish territories of ESA converges on the postulate that a unilinear continuum of underdevelopment has characterised the economic history of these regions, as outlined in Chapter 1. The findings of this study challenge this prevailing interpretation. The analysis of the vicissitudes in the primarily Kurdish provinces of ESA within the past four centuries, outlined in the previous sections of this study, paints a non-stagnant picture of economic life in these regions, which has important implications for the study of the link between economic development in these localities and Turkey's Kurdish question.

Hitherto, for manifold reasons expounded in Chapter 1, studies on the primarily Kurdish areas of ESA have either overlooked its Ottoman past or analysed Ottoman Kurdistan solely in terms of its political relations to the imperial capital. This resulted in the failure of a proper analysis of the historical antecedents of the principally Kurdish provinces of eastern Turkey. Such neglect was hazardous chiefly because it gave birth to a stationary understanding of economic (under)development in the predominantly Kurdish provinces of ESA. When the changes in Ottoman Kurdistan and its modern remnants in present-day Turkey are concurrently considered, a new periodisation for economic history of these regions emerges. The periodisation is no longer centred on a unilinear continuum of inadequate development. Rather, there are three distinct periods: the first of these begins from the early sixteenth century and ends with the arrival of the third decade of the nineteenth century, characterised by economic development. The second period commences ca. 1830 up until the first quarter of the twentieth century, and the major theme of this period is economic underdevelopment. The final period is an age of economic de-development, beginning from around the first quarter of the twentieth century, and continuing through the early 2010s.

As the data in Chapters 2 and 3 delineate, between the early sixteenth century and the early nineteenth century, the two paradigmatic Ottoman provinces predominantly inhabited by Kurds throughout the Ottoman period, Diyarbekir and Erzurum, were economically burgeoning areas, and constituted important sources of income for the Ottoman central treasury. The sheep breeding and sheep trade, textile production and trade and mining and mineral manufacturing and trade, as well as the international and interregional trade passing through Kurdistan, played an important role in the economic expansion of these regions. Up until the early nineteenth century, the revenues attained from these sectors of the local economy constituted the bulk of the provincial revenues of Diyarbekir and Erzurum. In the seventeenth and eighteenth centuries, the provincial revenues in these two provinces grew at a rate faster than those of the bordering Anatolian regions which modern-day Turkey comprises, and were among the principal revenues of the imperial treasury.

The exploration of the economic and political history of Ottoman Kurdistan outlined in Chapters 2 and 3, besides challenging the hypothesis of continual underdevelopment in this region, also oppugns the causal underpinnings proposed by scholarly studies for this postulate. The autonomous administrative structures founded in this region after 1514 are commonly thought to have occasioned the 'minimal implementation' of the governing *timar* or *dirlik* system and facilitated the 'centuries-long unbroken autonomy' of the 'economically disinterested' Kurdish rulers. The peculiar landholding regime put in place after the incorporation of the Kurdish principalities in the early sixteenth century is habitually seen as constituting a formidable and obstinate impediment to economic development in the predominantly Kurdish regions of ESA, by incessantly preserving the feudal relations of production in these domains after the nineteenth century. The findings of this study suggest quite the reverse.

The degree of autonomy the Kurdish rulers enjoyed was gradually eroded by the Ottoman state in the years following the incorporation of the Kurdish principalities into the Ottoman Empire. As charted in Chapter 2, in the period between the early sixteenth century and the late seventeenth century the degree of autonomy almost all of the Kurdish polities enjoyed was reduced to the extent that the majority became very responsive to Ottoman demands. Consequently, in almost all of these administrative structures, the *dirlik* or *timar* system was in operation. However, as explained in Chapter 3, during the eighteenth century, in virtue of the tax-farming policy in the Ottoman Empire, certain Kurdish notables, despite the Ottoman state overseeing the function of the Kurdish administrative units, gained immense fiscal and landed wealth. Indeed, some of these governors, such as Mir Muhammed of Rawanduz and Bedirkhan Bey of Botan, in the late eighteenth and early nineteenth centuries enjoyed de facto autonomy.

Nevertheless, because of the centralisation policies the Ottoman state implemented within the first half of the nineteenth century, long-standing Kurdish polities were eradicated and by 1847, not a single Kurdish administrative unit remained in existence. The fully fledged suppressive centralist reforms implemented in Ottoman Kurdistan after 1834, as revealed by the empirical evidence in Chapter 3, had severe economic and social ramifications. Ottoman state expropriation of land previously owned by Kurdish notables governing the Kurdish administrative units was an indispensable part of the centralisation process. During the late eighteenth century in Ottoman Kurdistan, as in other parts of the Empire, tax farming facilitated large-scale private ownership of land by the notables and engendered the gradual dissolution of the *dirlik* or *timar* system. This steady process enabled locally powerful groups, comparatively free from the supervision of the central authority, to respond to expanding opportunities of commodity production for long-distance markets during the late eighteenth and early nineteenth centuries through possessing private ownership of large estates and by escalating the exploitation of the dependent peasantry.

The domineering policies of the Ottoman state after the third decade of the nineteenth century instituted a major barrier to the expansion of commerce and export trade by inhibiting the development of export-oriented agricultural production in Ottoman Kurdistan. Put differently, economic underdevelopment in Ottoman Kurdistan after the 1830s was directly related to barriers to the penetration of market-induced commercialisation of agriculture in this region, which was closely connected to the negative repercussions of the centralisation policies of the Ottoman central authorities on regional agricultural production.

After the early 1830s, as the accounts of the contemporaries in Ottoman Kurdistan outlined in Chapter 3 emphasise, the central authorities seized almost all the lands previously owned and cultivated by the Kurdish notables, and, more importantly, large tracts of these repossessed lands remained uncultivated for a long period after their appropriation. Three decades after these lands were seized from the Kurdish notables, the greater part of the confiscated lands was either abandoned or was not resourcefully allocated to peasants by the Ottoman state. Such ill use of land, as well as the three decades of sporadic violence in this region, had inauspicious consequences for agricultural output and trade – as evinced by the relatively low-level cultivated land and production data in Ottoman Kurdistan in Chapter 3 – and augmented the pauperisation of agrarian labourers previously working in these lands.

The British and Russian consular reports from Ottoman Kurdistan referred to in Chapter 3 convey that after the 1830s the impecunious peasants in Ottoman Kurdistan, in the absence of state guidance and support, turned to usurers for financial support. Considering the very high rate of interest on loans during the nineteenth century in Ottoman Kurdistan, most peasants gave large sections of their agricultural yields to the moneylenders or ended up losing their lands on account of defaulting on their debts. Furthermore, unsurprisingly, after the third decade of the nineteenth century, commerce in this region also suffered a huge blow. During 1833–60, the trade of native products in Ottoman Kurdistan, as well as the transit trade passing through this region, which was an important source of provincial revenue and economic vibrancy, witnessed a steep drop. In sum, the destruction of autonomous Kurdish polities and the decline in economic development in this region went hand in glove.

The intrusive policies of the Ottoman state in Kurdistan after the 1830s triggered major social and political changes in this Ottoman borderland. A large section of the Ottoman Kurdish notable families and merchant elites both voluntarily and involuntarily resettled in western Anatolia, particularly in Constantinople, far from Kurdistan, during the time of the Tanzimat and the initials years of the twentieth century where they became increasingly integrated into the Ottoman state, language and discourse. This process is exhibited with the participation of émigré Kurds in the CUP and their support for the Young Turk Revolution of 1908.

Relatedly, the eradication of Kurdish administrative structures, by instigating a power vacuum in Kurdistan, created fertile conditions for the strengthening of tribal frameworks and deepened the feudalisation of Kurdish society. It is not a coincidence that with the obliteration of the Kurdish emirates, tribal confederacies occupied the central stage in Kurdish society and politics thereafter. Consequently, there was a significant rise in the number of tribal rifts, resulting in less law and order, particularly in the Kurdish countryside. Thus, the centralist modernisation policies implemented in Ottoman Kurdistan after the 1830s, on top of having damaging consequences for the means of production and relations of production in this region, paradoxically enhanced the feudalisation and fragmentation of society. The concurrence of these factors engendered socioeconomic underdevelopment in this region.

In light of what has been summarised thus far, it might seem plausible to explain the socioeconomic underdevelopment that befell Ottoman Kurdistan after the early 1830s through the binary and hierarchical state-versus-Kurdish-society model outlined in Chapter 1.

However, such an analysis does not enable us to attain an adequate understanding of the underlying causes of political change and economic underdevelopment in this period. The reforms during and after the early nineteenth century in the Ottoman Empire surfaced against the backdrop of the Ottoman leaders' increased awareness of the necessity for transformation and reform of the *ancient regime* to preserve the Empire, on the one hand. On the other, these reforms were shaped by the conflict among the Great Powers and their increased penetration into the Empire. Accordingly, the elimination of the Kurdish polities by the Ottoman state in the early nineteenth century was part of the general process of overthrowing semi-independent local potentates to enhance the efficacy and the centrality of the regime, as well as to extricate the Empire from the weaknesses that bogged it down since the eighteenth century. At the same time, though, as outlined in Chapters 1 and 3, this elimination process materialised as a result of the increasing incorporation of capitalism into the Empire and the imperialist conflict between Britain and Russia, against the background of the Ottoman defeats in wars against Russia, and the mounting tensions between the Muslims and the Christians in Ottoman Kurdistan.

The impact of political transformations on economic and social life in nineteenth-century Ottoman Kurdistan summarised earlier does also suggest that underdevelopment in this region cannot be adequately explained by the 'isolation' of Ottoman Kurdistan from the transformatory economic changes caused by the increasing incorporation of capitalism into the Ottoman Empire throughout the nineteenth and early twentieth centuries. Because of the absence of railroads and efficient transportation infrastructure in Ottoman Kurdistan, it is commonly hypothesised that this region, more than any other part of the Empire, was secluded from the changes invoked by the penetration of the capitalist system throughout the nineteenth and early twentieth centuries. The seclusion of Ottoman Kurdistan from the Ottoman and the European markets is often posited as a prime example of this phenomenon.

As the findings of Chapter 3 uncover, up until the early 1830s, commercial activity in Ottoman Kurdistan was as vibrant as it was in the late eighteenth century. In the years 1833–60, the commerce of this region witnessed a swift decline. From ca. 1860 up until the outbreak of the Turco-Russian War of 1877–8, even in the face of transportation barriers, with the arrival of relative stability to the region, commerce to and from Kurdistan did recover. Between 1890 and the outbreak of the First World War interregional and intraregional trade reached new and important heights.

These developments in the late nineteenth and early twentieth centuries coincided with the Hamidian Period (1876–1908). During this era, the politically co-opted (predominantly Sunni) Kurdish tribal elite, like Milli Ibrahim Pasha (chief of the Milan confederation), with economic and extra-economic means largely designated by the Ottoman state, accumulated immense landed wealth, reinvigorated the lord–peasant bonds and aimed to minimise the economic fortunes of the Christian community in Ottoman Kurdistan. Such factors did not only enable the aggrandisement of the politically receptive Kurdish elite, they also provided fertile conditions for commodity production and export orientation in the local economy by enabling the possession of private ownership of large estates and by accelerating the exploitation of the dependent peasantry.

As outlined in Chapter 3, the rise in urban population in most of the provinces in ESA in the late nineteenth and early twentieth centuries, coupled with the aforementioned favourable factors for commodity production and export orientation, was highly influential in the rise of intraregional and interregional trade in ESA during the latter part of the Hamidian era. Yet the growth in the local economy was not a harbinger of structural change, nor was it long term. In other words, the expansion in trade was not accompanied by a transformation of the relations of production, since it was based on usury and extraction of rent payments from direct producers. The combination of the outbreak of the First World War in addition to the destructive population policies had a deleterious impact on all of the previously recorded economic expansion in this region.

The politically integrated Kurdish rulers were neither autonomous nor did they request autonomy from the central state, because the nature and the maintenance of their power and wealth were grounded in the support provided by the Ottoman state. This helps explain why, in contrast to the Kurds in the Ottoman metropolis who were largely in support of the 1908 Revolution, the clientele Kurdish elite in Kurdistan vehemently opposed the notions of 'nation' and 'society' adopted by the Ittihadists Ottoman reformers in place of the *umma*, and were very hostile to the 1908 Revolution (McDowall, 2000: 96). Following the First World War, when the map of the Middle East was being redrawn, these schisms amidst Kurdish society played a pivotal role in the void of a leadership that could fill a role akin to that held by the Hashemite emirs in Hejaz in the emergence of the Arab national movement and the development of Arab nationalism during and after the Great War.

On the eve of the war, as explicated in Chapter 4, the Young Turk regime adopted ideological, political and economic programmes that were substantially different from those of previous Ottoman administrations. After the 1913 coup d'état, the late Ottoman rulers abandoned economic liberalism and, alternatively, embraced the economic model of *Milli İktisad* (National Economy), and concomitantly an ideological shift from pan-Islamism to pan-Turkism occurred among the political elite in the Empire. The economic development and ideological paradigms the Young Turk rulers espoused were inherited by their Kemalist heirs and formed the basis of the policies implemented in the Turkish Republic throughout the Republican era.

In the years 1913–50, the two operational codes of the state programmes in the residues of the Ottoman Empire were the construction and the preservation of the Turkish national economy. This entailed the protection and elevation of the Muslim/Turkish bourgeoisie and the Turkification of the ethnically heterogeneous demographic landscape. These objectives of the Turkist rulers after 1913, at a time when the Empire was largely reduced to its Anatolian heartlands, entailed policies of genocide, forced migration, confiscation of economic resources, and the suppression of all forms of non-Turkish identities and cultures in the ethnically mixed ESA provinces. These novel features of state policy persistently implemented in these regions during the first half of the twentieth century unleashed a unique and new economic process of de-development, proactively created by state policies geared towards precluding the possibility of an economic base to support independent indigenous existence. This process came to fruition in ESA by policies that not only hindered, but also deliberately and assiduously blocked internal economic development and the structural reforms on which it is based.

De-development in ESA commenced as a result of the state policies implemented by the Young Turks and their ideological heirs, the

Kemalist, centred on the objectives of nationalist demographic (i.e. turkification) and economic (i.e. Turkish National Economy) reorganisation. These state programmes differed greatly from those of the previous Ottoman regimes, which, albeit distorted, allowed for some form of indigenous economic development. Prior to the first decade of the twentieth century, at no point in history was ethnic nationalism a notion that struck a chord with the Ottoman political leaders. The Ottoman political establishment was above all occupied with preserving the territorial and political integrity of a multinational Empire. The heterogeneous character of the Ottoman Empire recurrently informed the policies of the Ottoman political leaders, and there was no predisposition towards formulating a nationalist agenda, which would have been antithetical to the prevalent aim of holding the multicultural domains together.

Turkish nationalism essentially emerged as a reaction to imperial disintegration, in a political milieu where imperial and multiethnic projects failed to stimulate a sense of Ottoman patriotism. The dismal image of the Ottoman Empire in the nineteenth century, powerless to reverse the secessionist dynamics and fighting for existence, weighed heavily in the minds of the Kemalist rulers, and it was the lessons drawn from this century that gave Turkish nationalism its most durable characteristics. For instance, the Kemalist tendency to analyse the Kurdish question along conspiratorial modes, with frequent reference to the 'Eastern Question' and the Sevres Treaty, is the prototypical illustration of this deeply rooted survivalist feature of Turkish nationalism.

Pursuant to what has been explained earlier and the findings of Chapters 4 and 5, it would be a mistake to confine Turkish nationalism exclusively to the post-Ottoman era, to trace the barriers to economic development stemming from the nationalist reorganisation of ESA only as far as 1923, and to perceive the obstacles to economic development in these regions as derivatives of the uneven development of capitalism in the Turkish Republic. Such inaccuracies result in the inability to identify the peculiar obstacles to economic development in ESA, as well as to detect the policy roots of the de-development programmes in ESA, and to discern the link between the Kurdish question and de-development in Turkey.

Existing development theories fail to account comprehensively for the deliberate economic and social extortion and destruction witnessed by the Kurdish and other autochthonic peoples of ESA, which this study argues is a constituent and indispensable feature of de-development in these Anatolian territories. The Turkist demographic engineering policies systematically implemented all over ESA during the CUP period and the

Republican era instigated de-development in these regions by, above all, mass murder, uprooting the indigenous populations from their ancestral habitat, confiscating their moveable and immovable properties and assimilating them into the Turkish nation and culture. Consequently, there was an indivisible and organic link between the economic and noneconomic aspects of dispossession or disarticulation in the state policies in these regions.

Between 1915 and 1950, in light of the figures given in Chapter 4, the non-existence of actual and definite statistics notwithstanding, ESA witnessed a depopulation of no fewer than 3 million, at least half of whom perished. Bearing in mind that the Armenian Genocide (1915) and the first wave of forced deportation of Ottoman Kurds in ESA (1916) accounted for around 2 million of the deported and massacred, the greater part of these killings and banishments occurred prior to 1923. Reducing the acts of the Young Turk government in ESA after the spring of 1915 to mere mass murder and deportation would curtail its complexity and downplay the long-term repercussions for these regions.

The Armenian Genocide and the ensuing mass expatriation of Kurds consisted of a set of coinciding processes that geared into each other and together engendered a deliberate and coherent system of destruction in ESA. As outlined in Chapter 4, these processes were expropriation, massacre, deportations, forced assimilation and construction of a destitute region. The overall aim of obstructing the possibility of autonomous existence of the indigenous populations in ESA within separate polities, which would have imperilled the Turkish nationalist reorganisation projects embarked on by the Young Turks, tied these processes together.

These atrocious engagements of the Young Turk government aimed to rescind the prospect of an independent Armenian state within the relics of the Ottoman Empire, which was ushered in by the reform agreement of February 1914. Besides, the CUP targeted the territorial and cultural unity of the Kurds, the other autochthonic community densely populated in ESA, through mass deportation to Turkish-populated regions to thwart them from 'preserving their nationality' and 'becoming harmful elements'. Heedless of the Ottoman Interior Ministry circular in November 1915 that accentuated the economic debilitation created in ESA by the clearance of the Armenian community, the Young Turk administration zealously continued with its nationalist demographic policies in these domains by evacuating the Kurds en masse in 1916. This disregard for economic life in ESA by the CUP government is a clear indication that the hegemonic forces conceived economic devastation as a means of inhibiting even the possibility of independent existence of the non-Turkish populaces in these regions, which with the exodus of Armenians was vastly inhabited by Kurds. As a result, by the end of 1917 ESA was a famine region.

Following the proclamation of the Turkish Republic, the Kemalist rulers unremittingly implemented nationalist population policies in ESA, reneged on their promise to recognise the collective rights of the Kurds, denied even the basic linguistic rights granted to them in the Lausanne Treaty and systematically hindered economic development in ESA. These concurrent decisions of the rulers of the Turkish Republic gave birth to the Kurdish question of Turkey and prolonged de-development in ESA. Thus, while the modernisation policies of the single-party regime integrated Turkey into the capitalist world economy and fostered remarkable economic development, the predominantly Kurdish regions of Turkey continued to endure economic de-development.

The nationalist demographic policies adroitly and meticulously implemented by the veteran Turkist demographic engineers during the Republican era constituted an important policy tool of protracting economic de-development in the predominantly Kurdish regions of ESA. These policies consisted of forced deportation of the Kurdish populace from its homelands and the dragooning of the Kurds into the dominant Turkish culture. The Kemalist rulers by means of these repressive social engineering objectives aimed to mutilate the territorial and cultural unity of the Kurds and exile the politically and economically prominent Kurdish families in line with the objective of obstructing the Kurdish elite 'from reviving as a ruling class', as instructed in the 1925 Report on the Reform of the East. Therefore, it was not by happenstance that by the late 1930s, at around the same time when Economic Minister Celal Bayar's report quoted in Chapter 4 testified both the collapse and the ensuing birth of a self-sufficient eastern economy, foreign observers in ESA reported that no wealthy Kurdish families were to be found in these regions. Policies directed against the wealth-owning Kurds prevented capital accumulation in these regions and played a key role in the creation of an ESA economy wherein production beyond that of personal use was non-existent. As a result, the state of the economy of ESA during the Republican era was inferior to what it was in the 1890s.

The other policy that nurtured economic de-development in this region is the paucity of state investments dispensed to the predominantly Kurdish ESA throughout the Republican period. According to Heper, a staunch defender of the Kemalist policies, 'in the early decades of the Republic, Chief of the General Staff Field Marshall Fevzi Çakmak had hampered investments in border areas ... because it would have been difficult to defend them' (2007: 6). The rationale Çakmak offered for the derisory state investments in ESA, delineated in Chapter 3, suggest that the state during the Republican era had allocated infinitesimal investments in the predominantly Kurdish regions in order to retard economic development. The seasoned politician posited that hastening the level of cognizance of the Kurds, economic development and wealth creation in ESA would endanger the policy of extinguishing the Kurdish identity and stimulate the development of Kurdish nationalism. Put differently, Kemalist officials conceived economic de-development in the early decades of the Republic as an indispensable means of foiling the possibility of autonomous existence of the Kurds and fostering the turkification of Kurdish lands. Such an outlook precipitated major social and economic divergences between the ESA and the rest of Turkey in the years 1923–50, as demonstrated in Chapter 4.

Relatedly, the peculiar policies of the Turkish state in the predominantly Kurdish ESA during the single-party period were not motivated by economic projects – like surplus appropriation and labour integration – per se as argued by Aydın and Boran, but by the political imperatives of assimilation, sovereignty and territorial unity of the Turkish Republic. In order to safeguard these interrelated political-national aims and to encumber Kurdish nationalism, economic development in the overwhelmingly Kurdish regions was deliberately blocked. Hence, the overriding political objectives of the Kemalist rulers in this dictatorial era played a determinate role in the minimal contact these regions had with capitalist development and the formation of the long-enduring features of the Kurdish question in Turkey. The systematic denial of the Kurdish identity and the negation of the collective rights of the Kurds, as well as the profound socioeconomic disparities between ESA and the rest of Turkey, were all corollaries of the tyrannical CHP rule in the remnants of Ottoman Kurdistan.

As the findings of Chapter 4 exhibit, in the years after the one-party dictatorship and before the outbreak of the armed conflict between the PKK and the Turkish state in 1984, the hegemonic forces in Turkey discarded the project of 'dismembering' the predominantly Kurdish ESA regions and instead opted to 'incorporate' these domains of Turkey. The increasing incorporation of the Turkish Republic into the liberal world order in the years after the Second World War initiated major readjustments in the Turkish political and economic system that resulted in the gradual erosion of the existing structure in the country. The other influential factor in this policy alteration with reference to ESA is the incessant rise of Kurdish radicalism from the 1960s onwards through multifarious means, among which were mass protests and electoral advances of pro-Kurdish candidates in ESA. The end of the 'period of silence' in Kurdish politics compelled the Turkish political elite to seek alternative modalities of suppressing Kurds. One of the underlying reasons for the institution and conservation of ties of all the post-single-party period administrations with the Kurdish clientele propertied class was to substitute and repress the radical Kurdish challenge against the Turkish state.

The policy oscillation from 'destruction' to 'incorporation' of the predominantly Kurdish regions did not implicate the recognition of the Kurdish identity and neither did it involve the modernisation of the ancient landownership and large-scale investment in land, human resources or physical equipment in ESA necessary for structural change. By hampering land reform and investments, the state facilitated the endurance of economic de-development because such negligence rid the ESA economy of its capacity and potential for structural transformation by engendering three inauspicious factors for development.

The first of these is the insufficiency of modern infrastructure and industry, both of which are necessary for capital accumulation and private investment. By 1988, despite the long period of planned import substitution industrialisation (1963–79), according to a survey by the SPO, there were merely 41,411 workers in all of the manufacturing establishments in ESA. Of these, 30,777 (74.3%) were in public manufacturing enterprises and the remaining 10,634 (25.7%) in private establishments (Kutbay and Çınar, 1989: table 5). As evinced with the composition of the four quinquennial plans in ESA during 1963–83, investments in modern infrastructure, particularly transport, were negligible. The premodern infrastructure in these regions played a pivotal role in the near absent private investment throughout 1968–80. Overall, despite the remarkable development in Turkey in those years, the predominantly Kurdish regions witnessed inhibited industrial development.

The second factor hindering development is the preservation of the landholding regime bequeathed from the Ottoman period devoid of land reform. In the second half of the twentieth century, the predominantly Kurdish regions were – and still are – the only domains in Turkey bereft of modernisation of the ancient land regime. After 1950, the banished Kurdish landed rural elites returned to their homelands, the lands they or their ancestors held from the Ottoman period were reimbursed and a sizeable section of them was politically incorporated into the political system. As demonstrated in Chapter 4, the inaction of the state over the much-needed land reform, besides occasioning the aggrandisement of the *ağas*, the pauperisation and the resultant emigration of the peasants, also played a pivotal factor in stunting agricultural development. The archaic landownership and relations of production in the predominantly Kurdish provinces inhibited agricultural productivity and the expansion of commodity production in agriculture.

The third factor that inhibited development is the occupational reorientation of the labour force away from the local economy mainly to the industrial metropolis of Turkey, which further weakened the local productive capacity and dependence on sources of income outside of the eastern economy. During 1960–90, the predominantly Kurdish regions had the highest rate of landless peasants in Turkey and, unsurprisingly, one of the uppermost mass migrations to the major cities mainly in western Turkey.

From the early 1980s through to the initial years of the 2000s, as the findings of Chapter 5 lay bare, the predominantly Kurdish provinces of ESA continued to endure stunted economic development, which, in turn, yet again, denied the economy of these territories the aptitude and prospect for structural transformation. The destruction wrought by the war between the PKK and the Turkish state, resulting in the forced displacement of large numbers of civilians and the destruction of Kurdish villages, along with adverse conditions for the agricultural sector created by the neoliberal policies, and the preservation of the antiquated land regime, played a vital role in the continuance of stunted development. Another important factor for arrested economic development is the failure of the GAP to fulfil promises of industrial development, irrigation, agricultural training, crop breeding, education and improving health services. Ever since its birth, GAP has been a strategic energy project. Despite official claims to the contrary, it has not promoted sustainable socioeconomic regional development in the GAP region.

As outlined in Chapters 4 and 5, ESA, alongside hosting vital international and national oil and natural gas pipelines, constitutes the most hydrocarbon-rich area of Turkey. As a result, its domains have unceasingly met the bulk of the energy demands of Turkey, particularly during the neoliberal era wherein persistent industrial development – almost all of which has occurred outside ESA – has engendered an ever-growing requirement for energy. The state-owned Turkish Petroleum Corporation (Türkiye Petrolleri Anonim Ortaklığı, TPAO), which regularly realises more than 70 per cent of the oil production in the country, relays the following illuminating datum pertinent to this phenomena: '72% of our [TPAO] total oil production is from Batman Region, 27% is from Adıyaman Region and 1% is from Thrace Region' (2014). In other words, ESA accounts for 99 per cent of crude extracted in Turkey. Concurrent to this extraction, the gargantuan twin Kirkuk–Ceyhan pipeline from Iraq to the Mediterranean snakes its way through the Kurdish mountains, transporting 1.6 million barrels of oil every day (see Map 8). Moreover, in late 2012, 'Royal Dutch Shell Plc and TPAO started exploring for shale gas in Diyarbakir's Saribugday-1 field … [t]here may be 13 trillion cubic meters of shale gas reserves [in Turkey], 1.8 trillion cubic meters of which is recoverable, Ismail Bahtiyar, chairman of the Turkish Association of Petroleum Geologists' (Ersoy, 2012).

However, the energy sources of ESA have functioned as a resource curse rather than as resource wealth, and thereby deepened and protracted the de-development of these regions. Specifically, as the findings of the two preceding chapters elucidate, the bulk of the public investments in ESA has chronically been energy-oriented and directed towards meeting the continually increasing energy demands of industrial Turkey. Put differently, the biggest recipient of the public investments in ESA, i.e. the energy sector, has nominal benefits or use to these predominantly agrarian domains and overshadows the exigent needs of the populace of these areas, e.g. transport infrastructure, which are essential for socioeconomic development. Additionally, demands for political pluralism, enhanced socioeconomic rights and/or autonomy by the Kurds were, and largely still are, unremittingly negated by the Turkish state because it has incessantly conceived these long-standing appeals as tantamount to or as a building block of secessionism and the resultant loss of these hydrocarbon-blessed ESA provinces.

Between the mid-1980s and the early years of the 2000s, socioeconomic divergences between the predominantly Kurdish regions and the rest of Turkey deepened, and the radical challenge of the Kurds against the exclusionary and assimilationist tendencies of the Turkish state entered its most vibrant and violent stage. As accentuated by the findings of Chapters 4 and 5, neither the Kurdish question nor the de-development in ESA owe their existence to the years of the armed conflict. The Kurdish question and the economic de-development in ESA predate the years of war and are corollaries of the denial, by the dominant state ideology, Turkish nationalism, of differences in general, and the Kurds' existence, issues and rights in particular. The monist and monolithic understanding of society and nation – invariably as Turkish – by the hegemonic forces in Turkey resulted in the economic de-development in ESA after 1913 and triggered the Kurdish question after the proclamation of the Turkish Republic.

Economic de-development policies in ESA after 1923 have become a means of protecting this monist and monolithic understanding of society and nation, as lucidly exhibited in the preamble of the current constitution of Turkey, which exemplifies much of the general tenor of the core ideology of the state: 'In line with the concept of nationalism and the reforms and principles introduced by the founder of the Republic of Turkey, Atatürk, the immortal leader and the unrivalled hero, this Constitution, which affirms the eternal existence of the *Turkish nation and motherland and the indivisible unity of the Turkish state, embodies . . . the principle of the indivisibility of the existence of Turkey with its state and territory, Turkish historical and moral values* or the nationalism, principle, reforms and modernism of Atatürk.'[1]

Hence, there is a symbiotic relationship between economic de-development and the Kurdish question and until the Kurdish question is resolved, the peculiar form of underdevelopment in ESA will endure.

The Kurdish Question in the Twenty-First Century

After the turn of this century, as discussed in Chapter 5, the intersection of five pivotal events within and outside of the border of Turkey necessitated all of the relevant stakeholders in the Kurdish question to re-evaluate their conceptualisation of and preoccupation with the issue. These were, first, the recognition of Turkey as a candidate for EU membership in 1999, conditional on its adequate progress in meeting the EU's Copenhagen political criteria, which specifically include democratisation and safeguarding of minority rights.[2] Second was the capture of Abdullah Öcalan in 1999 and his subsequent replacement of the project of establishing an 'independent Kurdish state' by means of a 'national liberation struggle' with that of 'democratisation of Turkey' and 'democratic self-government or autonomy' for Kurds.[3] Third was the invasion of Iraq in

[1] Emphasises added. The full text of the Turkish Constitution of 1982 is available at: www.anayasa.gov.tr/images/loadedpdf_dosyalari/the_constitution_of_the_republic_of_turkey.pdf.

[2] For a detailed exploration of the spill-over effects of Turkey's EU accession on Turkey's Kurdish question, see K. Yıldız (2005).

[3] In the political writings of Öcalan after his capture and imprisonment in Turkey, which set the ideological framework of the PKK after 2000, the project of democratisation of the Turkish Republic denotes the disassociation of citizenship in Turkey from Turkish nationalism. The idea of democratic autonomy for Kurds twinned to the idea of

2003 and the ensuing formalisation of the Kurdistan Regional Government (KRG) as well as the desire of the United States for Turkey to support the political stability of Iraq and patronise Iraq Kurds. Fourth was the rise and dominance of the majority government of the AKP in Turkey and its search for neoliberal pro-Islamic politics in the Middle East, the Balkans and Caucasia. The AKP's pursuit of such politics has necessitated the reorganisation and normalisation of the Turkish political system in accord with liberal democratic polity and attempts to eliminate long-simmering issues like the Kurdish question (Bahcheli and Noel, 2011; Çiçek, 2014). Last was the consolidation of pro-Kurdish politics in Turkey, and the recurrent electoral success of pro-Kurdish candidates and parties, particularly in ESA regions. The pro-Kurdish candidates from 1999 onwards have subsequently won the Municipality of Greater Diyarbakir, regarded as the Kurdish political and cultural centre by the pro-Kurdish political actors. In the 2003 municipal elections, the number of overall municipalities won by the DTP, sympathetic to the PKK, astonishingly rose to fifty-four. In 2009, it climbed to ninety-nine. More importantly, the general elections between 1991 and 2015 indicate that the electoral support given to the pro-Kurdish party in Turkey steadily increased from 4 per cent in 1991 to 13.1 per cent in 2015.

These manifestations engendered the re-evaluation of the Kurdish question by the two main adversaries on this issue, namely, the PKK and the Turkish state, and crystallised the limitations of their traditional approaches to the decades-long problem. That is to say, just as the latter recognised that it was unable to eliminate Kurdish identity and its political expressions through decades of negationist notions and brute force, the former realised it had been unable to materialise its project of overthrowing the 'colonial' state system by means of a 'national liberation movement'. Hence, both parties revised their default positions and presented differing 'democratisation initiatives/projects'.

The PKK and the legal political parties/actors sympathetic to it re-conceptualised the Kurdish question, as outlined in almost all of the 'defence texts' by Öcalan, which more than 3 million Kurds see as their

democratic confederalism refers to the right of Kurds to determine their own economic, cultural and social affairs (Öcalan, 2008). These projects are elaborated in the 'defence texts' submitted to the Turkish courts and to the European Courts – the European Court of Human Rights (ECtHR) Grand Chamber in 2001 and a court in Athens in 2003 concerning his expulsion from Greece. These 'defence texts' were translated and published in English under the titles *From Sumerian Clerical State towards People's Republic I-II* (2001), *The Defense of Free Man* (2003) and *Defending a People* (2004).

'political will',[4] in accordance with the two main democracy projects: democratisation of the Republic of Turkey and democratic autonomy for Kurds in Turkey. Essentially, as Öcalan announced in 2009, these projects entail the recognition by the Turkish state of the collective cultural rights of the Kurds, disassociation of citizenship in Turkey from the uniform Turkish national identity and regional self-governance for the Kurds.[5]

For the state authorities, as exhibited with the series of 'democratisation packages' proposed by the AKP government as of 2002, 'democratisation' entailed the removal of suppressive measures implemented during the 1980s and 1990s and the recognition of certain limited individual rights for Kurds. Thus far, the following steps have been implemented as a result of these 'democratisation packages': the removal of the OHAL in the Kurdish region; assisting internally displaced Kurds to return to their former homes and properties; the launch of TRT6, the first official Kurdish TV channel; optional Kurdish courses in private schools; the right of villages to return to their original names; and the right of establishing institutions for living languages. The leading actors and supporters of pro-Kurdish politics have seen these steps, as emphasised by Bahcheli and Noel (2011), Çandar (2013) and Çiçek (2014), as 'piecemeal and half-hearted' or 'too little, too late', and more importantly, falling short of their persistent demands for cultural recognition and some form of self-government.

As a prerequisite for the resolution of the Kurdish question, this study proposes the 'Democratic Autonomy Project', launched by the Democratic Society Congress, a broad platform that brought together Kurdish NGOs and intellectuals in Diyarbakir in December 2010. The 'Democratic Autonomy Project' set forth the restructuring of the Turkish political and administrative system as a precondition for the resolution of the Kurdish question. This restructuring involves the following pivotal eight elements:

(a) The drafting of a new constitution which would introduce a more pluralist concept of citizenship (one that is not based on an ethnocentric understanding of Turkishness);
(b) The removal of all barriers to cultural expression of diversity, including the use of languages other than Turkish, in the public sphere, education and politics;

[4] In a signature campaign, started on 18 August 2005 with the slogan of 'Öcalan is our political will,' the extended geography where Kurds live in the Middle East and Europe was ended on 20 October 2006 after the collection of 3,243,000 signatures. In Turkey, 2,243,000 were collected. Subsequent to the campaign, the sympathisers of the PKK branded Öcalan the 'Kurdish people's leader' (Çandar, 2012: 45).

[5] *Özgür Gündem*, 27 November 2010.

(c) Decentralisation and the institution of regional assemblies responsible for providing services in the areas of education, health care, culture, social services, agriculture and industry, among others, leaving the conduct of foreign affairs, the economy and defence to the central government, and assuming shared responsibility for judicial services;
(d) The allocation of part of local revenues to regional assemblies;
(e) Unconditional return to villages evacuated by the Turkish military during the fight against the PKK;
(f) Purging previously inhabited areas of land mines, and compensation to those affected by forced deportation;
(g) Removal of the Village Guard System;
(h) The creation of a peaceful atmosphere, which above all necessitates the cessation of hostilities, in the process that leads up to a new constitution.

A nationwide survey conducted after the declaration of the 'Democratic Autonomy Project' by the well-regarded public opinion research and consultancy company KONDA in fifty-nine provinces with 10,393 people confirms that the Kurdish population at large generally endorses this project. The result of this survey suggests that most respondents expressed their support for policies that entailed the constitutional recognition of Kurdish identity, education and broadcasting in the mother tongue, decentralisation and economic development of regions where the Kurds are concentrated and the abolition of the 10 per cent threshold for parliamentary representation (KONDA, 2011: 83–150).

The restructuring of the Turkish political and administrative system is an urgent and necessary step, but it is not sufficient for the resolution of the Kurdish question; it needs to be accompanied by a comprehensive regional development strategy that can remedy the long-standing socioeconomic issues in the regions. Both domestic (i.e. GAP) and international experiences (i.e. the EU, UNDP) prove that top-down development plans devoid of the participation of local actors are unlikely to be successful (TESEV, 2006). In order to identify accurately the needs of the ESA regions, the participation of the locally elected administrative bodies, like metropolitan municipalities, and the local NGOs in the preparatory phase is necessary. Moreover, regional development programmes should incorporate the economic, social, environmental and cultural aspects of development.

Investment policies are among the most important tools of development for regions that have witnessed decades-long neglect. The devastating result of neoliberalism in ESA, outlined in

Chapter 5, steers this book towards recommending a public-sector-led development policy. Employment-oriented investment should be the top priority of the public-sector-led development programme. Creation of long-term and unionised employment is vital in order to overcome the long-enduring problem of high unemployment in these regions and to increase the income of the local citizens. The creation of new and sustainable jobs is also necessary to prevent the occupational reorientation from these regions to other parts of Turkey and to prevent 'brain drain'.

In accordance with enhancing human development, investments in all sectors of education should be increased, and education should be free. These investments should not be seen as an instrument of cultural assimilation: education should be in both Kurdish and Turkish. Investments in the health care sector are also vital for human development, so health care investments should be multiplied, and health care should be free at the point of use. Investments in transportation and communications should also be enhanced and prioritised.

In order to be able to subsidise these investments, the income generated from local resources, such as the energy revenues from GAP, should be kept by the local administrative bodies, and, if need be, a diametric fund transfer from the developed regions to these regions could also be considered. These funds could partly be used to subsidise cooperatives that provide public credit support for the purchase of machinery and equipment for the peasants in the predominantly agrarian ESA, which will furnish the impecunious peasants with the necessary resources as well as enhance agricultural production in these domains.

Beside large-scale public investment, another important apparatus of development in ESA is root-and-branch land reform, without which the archaic relations of production and the resultant dependency of the landless peasants will persevere. In order to prevent additional inequitable landownership, small-sized family enterprises should be encouraged instead of larger agricultural enterprises, which conserve and promote concentration of land.

The irrigation projects of GAP need also to be concluded forthwith. Thus, all irrigation projects of GAP need to be prioritised, and the project should be completed by the newly set date of 2017. Alongside the execution of irrigation projects, GAP should train farmers to enrich their knowledge and skills in agricultural production. This training is also crucial to avoid ill use of irrigation and to prevent salinization.

Historically, the weakest link of the ESA economy has been the industrial sector. Growth of this sector is necessary for decreasing the dependence of these regions on other parts of Turkey and/or foreign dependency as well as for the complementation of the different sectors. Natural and mineral resources of ESA should not be processed outside, but within these regions. Large-scale investment in industry is critical for the expansion of industry in these regions.

The account of the Kurds in the Ottoman Empire and the Turkish Republic in this study underlined the linkages between the social, political, cultural and economic factors and life. The suppressive and/or negationist policies of the ruling elites in both of these polities regarding the Kurds have not only fettered economic development in ESA, but also targeted the cultural, political and social progression of the Kurds. Nevertheless, the inexhaustible struggle of the Kurds against oppression, assimilation and destruction has played a defining role in countering the domineering objectives of the dominant classes, in exhibiting the brute policies of the hegemonic elite in the Ottoman Empire and the Turkish Republic and in asserting the need for a peaceful resolution to Turkey's Kurdish question as well as for the thorough democratisation of the Turkish Republic in the twenty-first century.

Appendix I List of Interviews Undertaken in the Explanatory Phase of Fieldwork

1) Mr. Dirk Verbeken, European Commission, Lead Economist – Desk Officer for Turkey.
2) Mr. Özgür Altınoklar, Sector Manager for Infrastructure and Small and Medium Enterprises Programme, Delegation of the European Commission to Turkey.
3) Mr. Mesut Kamiloğlu: Head of the Department for the General Directorate of Regional Development and Structural Adjustment Department of EU Economic and Cohesion, State Planning Organisation (SPO), Republic of Turkey, Prime Ministry.
4) Mr. Mehmet Aydin: Head of Centre for Regional Competitiveness Programme Coordination and Implementation Centre, Ministry of Industry and Trade.
5) Mr. Yusuf İzzettin İymen, Deputy Secretary General of the Gaziantep Chamber of Industry.
6) Mr. Hasan Baran Uçaner, EU & Foreign Relations Representative of the Gaziantep Chamber of Commerce.
7) Mr. Mehmet Galip Ensarioğlu, former Head of Diyarbakır Chamber of Commerce, currently AKP Diyarbakır Member of Parliament.
8) Şahismail Bedirhanoğlu, President of Southeastern Industrialists and Businessmen Association (GUNSIAD).
9) Mr. Hasan Kılıç, GAP, Lead Economist for Regional Development.
10) Mr. Ahmet Türk, former Chairman of the Democratic Society Party (DTP), currently Mayor of Mardin.
11) Mr. Şeyhmus Diken, Advisor to the Diyarbekir Metropolitan Municipality.
12) Mrs. Nurcan Baysal, former member of the United Nations Development Programme, currently a social worker in Diyarbakır.
13) Mr. Hasan Maral, Development Specialist at the KARACADAĞ Development Agency in Diyarbakır.

14) Mr. Osman Baydemir, former Mayor of Diyarbakır and President of USARM.
15) Mr. Ahmet Çakır, Member of the Executive Committee of the Diyarbakır Branch of General Directorate of State Hydraulic Works (DSİ).

Appendix II Diyarbakir Commerce, 1863

Foreign Exports of Diyarbekir, 1863 (in pounds sterling)

Names of Articles	Value
Madder Roots	271
Cotton	92,916
Wool 1st Quality	64,090
Wool 2nd Quality	10,909
Mohair White	8,180
Mohair Red	1,970
Mohair Black	1,900
Polecat Fur	900
Buffalo Skins	6,337
(**Re-exported: from Baghdad**)	
Buffalo Skins	2,112
(**Re-exported: from Russia**)	
Cow Skins	492
Galls Best Blues	17,549
Galls White 1st Sort	5,991
Saltpetre	908
Orpiment in Leaves	491
Orpiment Red	67
Orpiment Lust	45
Wax	27
Gum	2,374
Total	**217,529**

Source: FO 195/799 Trade and Agriculture for Kurdistan for 1863, p. 63, enclosed in Taylor at Diarbekir, 13 July 1864.

Home Exports of Diyarbekir, 1863 (in pounds sterling)

Names of Articles	Value	Remarks
Madder Roots	542	Sent to Bitlis
Olive Oil	487	Sent to Sivas and Kharput
Olive Sesame	950	Sent to Sivas and Kharput
Manufactures	3,000	of Aleppo sent to Baghdad
Manufactures of Diyarbekir	71,511	Sent to Northern Turkey and Baghdad
Fox and Wolf Skins	638	600 pieces Fox, 200 Wolf sent to Aleppo
Leather dyed Red	5,813	Diabekir works sent to Aleppo
Leather dyed Yellow	1,093	Diabekir works sent to Erzurum and Treibizon
Leather dyed Red	786	Mardin works sent to Aleppo
Leather dyed Yellow	200	Mardin works sent to Erzurum and Treibizon
Leather dyed Red	786	Saert work sent to Aleppo
Leather dyed Yellow	200	Saert work sent to Erzurum and Treibizon
Galls White 1st Sort	2,770	Sent to Baghdad
Galls White 2nd Sort	8,583	Sent to Baghdad
Hantoof	966	Sent to Aleppo and Orfa
Orpiment in Leaves	491	Sent to Aleppo and Orfa
Orpiment Red	67	Sent to Aleppo and Orfa
Orpiment Lust	45	Sent to Aleppo and Orfa
Tallow	283	Sent to Aleppo and Orfa
Clarified Butter	4,500	Sent to Aleppo and Orfa
Dried Fruits	1,500	Sent to Baghdad
Pales and Rafters	2,000	Sent to Baghdad and Mosul
Sheep	11,000	4,000 in number, for Aleppo and Damascus
Camels	9,100	2,000 in number for Kaiserieh
Saltpetre	908	Sent to Aleppo and Orfa
Total	**128,174**	

Source: FO 195/799 Trade and Agriculture for Kurdistan for 1863, p. 77, enclosed in Taylor at Diyarbekir, 13 July 1864.

Foreign Imports into Diyarbekir, 1863 (in pounds sterling)

Names of Articles	Value	Remarks
Coffee via Aleppo	727	of the West Indies from England
Coffee via Baghdad	2,325	of the East Indies from Baghdad
Sugar Leaf	2,000	
Sugar Crushed	900	
Sugar Candy	1,625	
Pepper	408	
Sal Ammoniac	435	
Tea	306	
Zinc	66	
Tin Sheets in Boxes	727	
Window Glass in Boxes	1,090	

(cont.)

Names of Articles	Value	Remarks
Lead	812	
Iron English	68	
Iron Russian	812	
Steel	727	
Spelter	871	
Indigo	5,042	
Timbeki Isfahan [Tobacco]	681	
Timbeki Shiraz [Tobacco]	454	
Silk Persian	3,130	
Alum	1,530	
Cochineal	2,110	from France
Buffalo Skins Russian	4,116	via Erzeroom from Erivan
Spices	2,000	
Drugs	1,500	
Hardware	300	
Earthenware	1,325	
British Manufactures	75,000	via Aleppo
Sundries	2,500	from France and Switzerland
Total	**113,587**	

Source: FO 195/799 Trade and Agriculture for Kurdistan for 1863, p. 74, enclosed in Taylor at Diarbekir, 13 July 1864.

Home Imports of Diyarbekir, 1863 (in pounds sterling)

Names of Articles	Value	Remarks
Soap Aleppo	300	
Soap Orfa	90	
Lead	54	from Eggil in small pieces
Silk	10,338	from Amasia and Bursa
Buffalo Skins	6,300	from Baghdad
Cow	1,067	from Baghdad
Orpiment in Leaves	818	from Hakkari
Orpiment Red	90	from Hakkari
Orpiment Lust	59	from Hakkari
Manufactures	4,000	of Aleppo similar to those of Diabekir
Hanne	541	from Persian Coast via Baghdad
Specie	50,000	from Aleppo and Damascus
Total	**73,657**	

Source: FO 195/799 Trade and Agriculture for Kurdistan for 1863, p. 79, enclosed in Taylor at Diyarbekir, 13 July 1864.

Bibliography

Primary Sources

Archives

Unpublished British Archival Sources National Archives United Kingdom, Kew, London Foreign Office files:

FO 195: 799.

FO 371: 953; 4192; 7858; 12255; 11528; 13828; 14578; 14580.

FO 424: 265; 266.

Published British Archival Sources House of Commons Parliamentary Papers, *Parliamentary Papers, Account and Papers* (1857–98), ***'Commercial Reports'*** from consular offices in the Ottoman Empire for the following years:

(1857) Paper no. 2285, Vol. XXXVIII.
(1866) Paper no. 3582, Vol. LXIX.
(1867) Paper no. 3938–9, Vol. LXVIII.
(1871) Paper no. C.414, Vol. LXVIII.
(1872) Paper no. 110, Vol. XLVII
(1872) Paper no. C.530, Vol. LX.
(1872) Paper no. C.637, Vol. LVIII.
(1873) Paper no. C.824, Vol. LXVII.
(1873) Paper no. C.828, Vol. LXV.
(1884) Paper no. C.4106, Vol. LXXXI.
(1884–5) Paper no. C.4526, Vol. LXXIX.
(1886) Paper no. C.3582, Vol. LXXI.
(1890–1) Paper no. 6205, Vol. LXXXV.
(1893–4) Paper no. 6855–129, Vol. XCII.
(1895) Paper no. C.7581 C.7828, Vol. XCVI.
(1897) Paper no. C.8277, Vol. LXXXIX.

(1898) Paper no. C.8648, Vol. XCIV.

House of Commons Parliamentary Papers, *Parliamentary Papers, Account and Papers* ***'Diplomatic and Consular Reports Series. Annual Series'*** for Turkey for the following years:

(1911) Paper no. Cd.5465, Vol. XCVII.

(1914) Paper no. Cd.7048–187, Vol. XCV.

Other documents published in ***Parliamentary Papers, Account and Papers***:

(1870) *Reports from Her Majesty's Representatives Respecting the Tenure of Land in the Several Countries of Europe: 1869–70. Report by Consul Palgrave Respecting Land Tenure in Eastern Turkey*. Paper no. C.75, Vol. LXVII.

(1871) *Further Reports from Her Majesty's Diplomatic and Consular Agents of the Industrial Classes and the Purchasing Power of Money in Foreign Countries. Report by Consul Taylor for Kurdistan*. Paper no. C.414, Vol. LXVIII.

(1881) *Correspondence Respecting Kurdish Invasion of Persia*. Paper no. C.2851, Vol. 361.

(1886) *Depression of Trade and Industry. Second Report of the Royal Commission Appointed to Inquire into the Depression of Trade and Industry*. Paper no. C.4715, Vol. XIX.

Published Turkish/English-Language Primary Sources

Anter, Musa (1990). *Hatıralarım*. Istanbul: Doz Yayınlar.

Aşiret Raporları (2003). Istanbul: Kaynak Yayınlar.

Bayar, Celal (2006). *Şark Raporu*. Istanbul: Kaynak Yayınları.

Bayrak, Mehmet (ed.) (1993). *Kürtler ve Ulusal-Demokratik Mücadeleleri: Gizli Belgeler-Araştımalar-Notlar*. Ankara: Öz-Ge Yayınları.

Bayrak, Mehmet (ed.) (1994). *Açık-Gizli/Resmi-Gayriresmi Kürdoloji Belgeleri*. Istanbul: Öz-Ge Yayınları.

Behar, Cem (1996). *Osmanlı İmparatorluğu'nun ve Türkiye'nin Nüfüsü, 1500–1927. Tarihi İstatiskleri Dizisi Cilt 2*. Ankara: Türkiye Cumhuriyeti Başbakanlık İstatistik Ensitüsü.

Bilkur, Şefik (1949). *National Income of Turkey and Family Expenses in Country and Towns, Estimates 1927–1945, Forecasts 1948–1952*. Ankara: Türkiye Cumhuriyeti İstatistik Genel Müdürlüğü.

Bozarslan, Mehmet Emin (ed.) (1998). *Kürt Teavün ve Terraki Gazetesi: Kovara Kurdî-Tırkî 1908–1909*. Uppsala: Deng Yayınları.

Dankoff, Robert (trans. and ed.) (1990). *Evliya Çelebi in Bitlis*. Leiden and New York: Brill.

Dersimî, Nurî (1992). *Dersim ve Kürt Mücadelesine Dair Hatıratım*. Mehmet Bayrak (ed.). Ankara: Öz-Ge Yayınları.

Güran, Tevfik (1997). *Osmanlı Dönemi Tarım İstatistikleri 1909, 1913 ve 1914. Tarihi İstatiskleri Dizisi Cilt 3*. Ankara: Türkiye Cumhuriyeti Başbakanlık İstatistik Ensitüsü.

Hurewitz, J. C. (1956). *Diplomacy in the Near and Middle East: A Documentary Record, 1535–1914*. Princeton, NJ: Van Nostrand.

Kunt, Metin (ed.) (1981). *Bir Osmanlı Valisinin Yıllık Gelir ve Gideri: Diyarbekir, 1670–71*. İstanbul: Boğaziçi Üniversitesi Yayınları.

Perinçek, Doğu (ed. and pref.) (1993). *Mustafa Kemal Atatürk Eskişehir-İzmit Konuşmaları*. İstanbul: Kaynak Yayınları.

Turkey, SPO (1963). *Birinci Beş Yıllık Kalkınma Planı, 1963–1967*. Ankara: Devlet Planlama Teşkilatı.

Turkey, SPO (1965). *Genel Tarım Sayımı Örnekleme Sonuçları, 1963*. Ankara: Devlet İstatistik Ensitüsü.

Turkey, SPO (1968). *İkinci Beş Yıllık Kalkınma Planı, 1968–1972*. Ankara: Devlet Planlama Teşkilatı.

Turkey, SPO (1969). *İllerin ve Bölgelerin Sosyo-Ekonomık Sıralaması Araştırması*. Ankara: Devlet Planlama Teşkilatı.

Turkey, SPO (1973). *Üçüncü Beş Yıllık Kalkınma Planı, 1973–1977*. Ankara: Devlet Planlama Teşkilatı.

Turkey, SPO (1974). *National Income and Expenditure of Turkey, 1962–1973*. Ankara: Devlet Planlama Teşkilatı.

Turkey, SPO (1976). *Gelir Dağılımı, 1973*. Ankara: Devlet Planlama Teşkilatı.

Turkey, SPO (1977). *Summary of Agricultural Statistics, 1976*. Ankara: Devlet Planlama Teşkilatı.

Turkey, SPO (1979). *Dördüncü Beş Yıllık Kalkınma Planı, 1979–1983*. Ankara: Devlet Planlama Teşkilatı.

Turkey, SPO (2003). *İllerin ve Bölgelerin Sosyo-Ekonomık Sıralaması Araştırması*. Ankara: Devlet Planlama Teşkilatı.

Turkey, TCBIUM, *Annuaire Statisque (Istatistik Yıllığı)* from 1928 to 1950 (normally published biennially). Ankara: Türkiye Cumhuriyeti Başvekalet İstatistik Umum Müdürlüğü.

van Bruinessen, Martin and Hendrik Boescheten (trans. and ed.) (1988). *Evliya Çelebi in Diyarbekir: The Relevant Sections of the Seyahatname*. Leiden and New York: Brill.

Secondary Sources

Ahmad, Feroz (1969). *The Young Turks: The Committee of Union and Progress in Turkish Politics, 1908–1912*. Oxford: Clarendon Press.

Ahmad, Feroz (1977). *The Turkish Experiment in Democracy 1950–1975*. London: C. Hurst for the Royal Institute of International Affairs.

Ahmad, Feroz (1993). *The Making of Modern Turkey*. London and New York: Routledge.

Ahmad, Feroz (2008). 'Politics and Political Parties in Republican Turkey', in Reşat Kasaba (ed.) *The Cambridge History of Turkey, Volume 4: Turkey in the Modern World*. Cambridge: Cambridge University Press, pp. 226–65.

Ahmad, Kamal Madhar (1994). *Kurdistan During the First World War*. Translated by Ali Maher Ibrahim. London: Saqi.

Akçam, Taner (2012). *The Young Turks' Crime against Humanity: The Armenian Genocide and Ethnic Cleansing in the Ottoman Empire*. Princeton, NJ: Princeton University Press.

Aktan, Reşat (1966). 'Problems of Land Reform in Turkey'. *International Journal of Middle Eastern Studies*, 20(3), pp. 317–34.

Alakom, Rohat (1998). *Hoybûn Örgütü ve Ağrı Ayaklanması*. Istanbul: Avesta Yayınları.

Anderson, Benedict (1983). *Imagined Communities*. London: Verso.

Aras, İlhami (1992). *Adım Şeyh Said*. Istanbul: İlke Yayıncılık.

Arfa, Hasan (1966). *The Kurds: An Historical and Political Study*. London: Oxford University Press.

Armstrong, John (1982). *Nations before Nationalism*. Chapel Hill: University of North Carolina Press.

Arslan, Ali (2004). *Kısır Döngü-Türkiye'de Üniversite ve Siyaset*. Istanbul: Truva Yayınlar.

Arslan, Rıfkı (1992). *Diyarbakır'da Toprakta Mülkiyet Rejimleri ve Toplumsal Değişme*. Diyarbakır: Tanıtma Kültür ve Yardımlaşma Vakfı.

Aydın, Delal (2014). 'Mobilising the Kurds in Turkey: Newroz as a Myth', in Cengiz Gunes and Welat Zeydanlıoğlu (eds.) *The Kurdish Question in Turkey: New Perspectives on Violence, Representation, and Reconciliation*. New York and London: Routledge, pp. 69–88.

Aydın, Suavi and Jelle Verheij (2012). 'Confusion in the Cauldron: Some Notes on Ethno-religious Groups, Local Powers and the Ottoman State in Diyarbekir Province, 1800–1870', in Joost Jongerden and Jelle Verheij (eds.) *Social Relations in Ottoman Diyarbekir, 1870–1915*. Leiden: Brill, pp. 15–55.

Aydın, Zülküf (1986). *Underdevelopment and Rural Structures in Southeastern Anatolia: The Household Economy in Gisgis and Kalhana*. London: Ithaca Press & University of Durham.

Aydın, Zülküf (2005). *The Political Economy of Turkey*. London: Pluto Press.

Aytar, Osman (1991). *Kürdün 'Makus Talih'i ve 'Güneydoğu' Anadolu Projesi (Sorunlar ve Gerçekler)*. Istanbul: Medya Güneşi Yayınları.

Aytar, Osman (2000). *Hamidiye Alaylarından Köy Koruculuğuna*. Istanbul: Peri Yayınları.

Baer, Gabriel (1966). 'The Evolution of Private Landownership in Egypt and the Fertile Crescent', in Charles Issawi (ed.) *The Economic History of the Middle East, 1800–1914: A Book of Readings*. Chicago: Chicago University Press, pp. 80–90.

Bahcheli, Tozun and Sid Noel (2011). 'The Justice and Development Party and the Kurdish Question', in Marlies Casier and Joost Jongerden (eds.) *Nationalisms and Politics in Turkey: Political Islam, Kemalism, and the Kurdish Issue*. London and New York: Routledge, pp. 101–20.

Bajalan, Djene Rhys (2013). 'Early Kurdish "Nationalists" and The Emergence of Modern Kurdish Identity Politics: 1851 to 1908', in Fevzi Bilgin and Ali Sarıhan (eds.) *Understanding Turkey's Kurdish Question*. Plymouth: Lexington Books, pp. 3–28.

Banaji, Jairus (2010). *Theory as History: Essays on Modes of Production and Exploitation*. Leiden: Brill.

Barkan, Ömer Lütfi (1955–6). 'Osmanlı Bütçeleri'. *İktisat Fakültesi Mecmuası*, XVII, pp. 193–347.

Barkan, Ömer Lütfi (1957). 'Essai sur les données statistique des registres de recensement dans l'empire Ottoman au XVe et XVIe siécles'. *Journal of the Economic and Social History of the Orient*, 1(1), pp. 9–36.

Barkan, Ömer Lütfi (1970). 'Research on the Ottoman Fiscal Studies', in Michael Allen Cook (ed.), *Studies in the Economic History of the Middle East*. London: Oxford University Press, pp. 163–71.

Barkan, Ömer Lütfi (1975). 'The Price Revolution of the Sixteenth Century. A Turning Point in the History of the Near East'. *International Journal of Middle Eastern Studies*, 6(1), pp. 3–28.

Barkan, Ömer Lütfi (2000). *Osmanlı Devleti'nin Sosyal ve Ekonomik Tarihi: Osmanlı Devlet Arşivleri Üzerinde Tetkikler ve Makaleler*. 2 vols. Hüseyin Özdeğer (ed.). Istanbul: İstanbul Üniversitesi İktisat Fakültesi.

Barkey, Henri J. (1990). *The State and Industrialisation Crisis*. Boulder, CO: Westview Press.

Barkey, Henri J. and Graham E. Fuller (1998). *Turkey's Kurdish Question*. New York: Rowman and Littlefield Publishers.

Barlas, Dilek (1998). *Etatism and Diplomacy in Turkey: Economic and Foreign Policy Strategies in an Uncertain World, 1929*. Leiden: Brill.

Batatu, Hanna (1978). *The Old Social Classes and the Revolutionary Movements of Iraq: A Study of Iraq's Old Landed and Commercial Classes and of Communists, Ba'athists, and Free Officers*. Princeton, NJ: Princeton University Press.

Bauer, Martin (2000). 'Classical Content Analysis: A Review', in M. W. Bauer and G. Gaskell (eds.) *Qualitative Researching with Texts, Image, and Sound: A Practical Handbook* London: SAGE, pp. 131–51.

Baykara, Tuncer (1988). *Anadolu'nun Tarihi Çoğrafyasına Giriş*. Ankara: Türk Kültürünü Araştırma Ensitüsü.

Bayrak, Mehmet (1999). *Kürt Sorunu ve Demokratik Çözüm*. Wupertal: Öz-Ge Yayınları.

Bedirkhan, Kamuran Ali (1958). *La question Kurde*. Paris: np.

Beşikçi, İsmail ([1969] 1992). *Doğu Anadolu'nun Düzeni: Sosyo-Ekonomik ve Etnik Temelleri*. 2 vols. 3rd ed. Ankara: Yurt Kitap Yayınları.

Beşikçi, İsmail (1969). *Doğu'da Değişim ve Yapısal Sorunlar (Göçebe Alikan Aşireti)*. Ankara: Sevinç Matbası.

Beşikçi, İsmail (1977). *'Türk-tarih tezi', 'Güneş-dil teorisi' ve Kürt Sorunu*. Ankara: Komal Yayınları.

Beşikçi, İsmail ([1990] 2004). *International Colony Kurdistan*. London: Taderon Press.

Beşikçi, İsmail (1990). *Tunceli Kanunu (1935) ve Dersim Jenosidi*. Istanbul: Belge Yayınları.

Beşikçi, İsmail (1991). *Kürtlerin Mecburi İskânı*. Ankara: Yurt Kitap Yayınları.

Beşikçi, İsmail (1992). *Doğu Mitingleri'nin Analizi*. Ankara: Yurt Kitap Yayınları.

Bildirici, Melike and Fazıl Kayıkçı (2012). 'Global Imbalances in Current Account Balances'. *Journal of Applied Finance and Banking*, 2(6), pp. 83–93.

Bill, J. A. and Robert Springboard (1990). *Politics in the Middle East*. New York: Harper Collins Publishers.

Bloxham, Donald (2008). *Genocide, the World Wars and the Unweaving of Europe*. London: Vallentine Mitchell and Co.

Bois, Thomas (1966). *The Kurds*. Beirut: Khayats.

Bookman, Milicia Zarkovic (1997). *The Demographic Struggle for Power: The Political Economy of Demographic Engineering in the Modern World*. London: Frank Cass.

Boran, Behice (1974). *Türkiye ve Sosyalizm Sorunları*. Istanbul: Tekin Yayınevi.

Boratav, Korkut (1981). 'Kemalist Economic Policies and Etatism', in Ali Kazancıgil and Ergün Özbudun (eds.) *Atatürk: Founder of a Modern State*. London: Hurst and Company, pp. 165–90.

Boratav, Korkut (1982). *Türkiye'de Devletçilik*. Ankara: Savaş Yayınları.

Boratav, Korkut (1990). 'Inter-class and Intra-class Relations and Distribution under "Structural Adjustment": Turkey during the 1980s', in Torsun Aricanli and Dani Rodrik (eds.), *The Political Economy of Turkey. Debt, Adjustment and Sustainability*. London: Macmillan, pp. 199–229.

Boratav, Korkut (2003). *Türkiye İktisat Tarihi, 1908–2002*. Ankara: İmge Yayınevi.

Boratav, Korkut, A. E. Yeldan and A. H. Köse (2000). Globalization, Distribution and Social Policy: Turkey, 1980–1998, Centre for Economic Policy Analysis, Working Paper Series I, Working Paper No. 20.

Bozarslan, Hamit (1996). 'Political Crisis and the Kurdish Issue in Turkey', in Robert Olson (ed.) *The Kurdish Nationalist Movement in the 1990s: Its Impact on Turkey and the Middle East*. Lexington: The University Press of Kentucky, pp. 135–53.

Bozarslan, Hamit (2003a). 'Kurdish Nationalism in Turkey: From Tacit Contract to Rebellion (1919–1925)', in Abbas Vali (ed.) *Essays on the Origins of Kurdish Nationalism*. Costa Mesa, CA: Mazda Publishers, pp. 163–90.

Bozarslan, Hamit (2003b). 'Some Remarks on Kurdish Histiographical Discourse in Turkey (1919–1980)', in Abbas Vali (ed.) *Essays on the Origins of Kurdish Nationalism*. California: Mazda Publishers, pp. 14–39.

Bozarslan, Hamit (2006). 'Tribal Asabiya and Kurdish Politics: A Socio-historical Perspective', in Faleh A. Jabar and Hosham Dawod (eds.) *The Kurds: Nationalism and Politics*. London: Saqi, pp. 130–47.

Bozarslan, Hamit (2008). 'Kurds and the Turkish State', in Reşat Kasaba (ed.) *The Cambridge History of Turkey, Volume 4: Turkey in the Modern World*. Cambridge: Cambridge University Press, pp. 333–56.

Bozarslan, Mehmet Emin ([1966] 2002). *Doğu'nun Sorunları*. Istanbul: Avesta Yayınları.

Bozarslan, Mehmet Emin (1990). 'Foreword', in *Şerefname: Kürt Tarihi*. Istanbul: Hasat Yayınları.

Brant, James (1836). 'Journey through a Part of Armenia and Asia Minor in the Year 1835'. *The Journal of the Royal Geographical Society of London*, 6, pp. 187–223.

Brown, L. Carl (1996). 'The Background: An Introduction', in L. Carl Brown (ed.) *Imperial Legacy: The Ottoman Imprint on the Balkans and the Middle East*. New York: Columbia University Press, pp. xiii–16.

Bulut, Faik (1998). *Kürt Sorununda Çözüm Arayışları*. Istanbul: Ozan Yayınlar.

Bulutay, Tuncer and Enver Taştı (2004). 'Informal Sector in the Turkish Labour Market', Discussion Papers 2004/22. Ankara: Turkish Economic Association.

Burkay, Kemal ([1992] 2008). *Geçmişten Bügüne Kürtler ve Kürdistan: Coğrafya-Tarih-Edebiyat*, 4th ed. Diyarbakır: DENG Yayınları.

Burkay, Kemal (1995). *Seçme Yazılar-1*. Istanbul: DENG Yayınları.

Çağaptay, Soner (2006). 'Passage to Turkishness: Immigration and Religion in Modern Turkey', in Haldun Gülalp (ed.) *Citizenship and Ethnic Conflict: Challenging the Nation-State*. London: Routledge, pp. 61–151.

Çandar, Cengiz (2012). *'Leaving the Mountain': How May the PKK Lay Down Arms? Freeing the Kurdish Question from Violence*. Istanbul: TESEV Publications.

Çandar, Cengiz (2013). 'On Turkey's Kurdish Question: Its Roots, Present State, and Prospects', in Fevzi Bilgin and Ali Sarıhan (eds.) *Understanding Turkey's Kurdish Question*. Plymouth: Lexington Books, pp. 59–72.

Çarkoğlu, Ali and Mine Eder (2005). 'Developmentalism alla Turca: The Southeastern Anatolia Development Project (GAP)' in Fikret Adaman and Murat Arsel (eds.), *Environmentalism in Turkey: Between Democracy and Development?*. Aldershot: Ashgate Publishers. pp. 167–84.

Celil, Celilê (1992). *XIX. Osmanlı İmparatorluğu'nda Kürtler*. Translated by Mehmet Demir. Ankara: Öz-Ge Yayınları.

Cezar, Yavuz (1986). *Osmanlı Maliyesinde Bunalım ve Değisim Dönemi: XVIII.yy dan Tanzimat'a Mali Tarih*. İstanbul: Alan Yayıncılık.

Chaliand, Gerard (1993). *People without a Country: The Kurds and Kurdistan*. London: Zed Press.

Charountaki, Marianna (2012). 'Turkish Foreign Policy and the Kurdistan Regional Government'. *Perceptions*, 17(4), pp. 185–208.

Chen, Marther Alter (2005). 'Rethinking the Informal Economy'. Research Papers, 10. Helsinki: United Nations University-World Institute for Development Economic Research. 7.

Çiçek, Cuma (2014). 'Elimination or Integration of Pro-Kurdish Politics: Limits of the AKP's Democratic Initiative', in Cengiz Gunes and Welat Zeydanlıoğlu (eds.) *The Kurdish Question in Turkey: New Perspectives on Violence, Representation, and Reconciliation*. New York and London: Routledge, pp. 245–57.

Clark, Logan, C. Cooper, G. Gardner, E. Le Flore, J. Leguía, M. Marge, C. M. Padilla, G. Rosalsky, W. Umaira and C. Z. Lizama (2012). *The External Current Account in the Macroeconomic Adjustment Process in Turkey*. Princeton, NJ: Princeton University Woodrow Wilson School Policy Publication. Online: www.princeton.edu/sites/default/files/content/other/591b-Final_Report_PRINT_merged.pdf (Last accessed: 1 August 2016).

The Corner House (2000). *The Ilisu dam, the World Commission on Dams and Export Credit Reform: The Final Report of a Fact-Finding Mission to the Illsu Dam Region*. Online: http://www.thecornerhouse.org.uk/resource/ilisu-dam-world-commission-dams-and-export-credit-reform (Last accessed: 1 August 2016).

Cuinet, Vital (1890). *La Turquie d'Asie: Géographie Administrative, Statistique, Descriptive et raisonnée de chaque Province de l'Asie-Mineure*. 4 vols. Paris: Ernest Leroux.

Cumhuriyet. 23 June 1955.

D'Aramon, M. ([1555] 1864). *Le Voyage De M. D'Aramon*. Paris: Collectif.

Demirci, Süleyman (2009). *The Functioning of Ottoman Avarız Taxation: An Aspect of the Relationship between the Centre and Periphery: A Case Study of the Province of Karaman, 1621–1700*. Istanbul: Isis Press.

Dersimî, Nurî (1997). *Kürdistan Tarihinde Dersim*. Istanbul: Doz Yayınları.

Dündar, Can and Rıdvan Akar (2008). 'Tarihi Bir Raporun Kapısı Açılıyor: Ecevit'in Gizli Arşivindeki Belgeler'. Online: www.candundar.com.tr/ (Last accessed: 1 August 2016).

Dündar, Fuat (2002). *İttihat ve Terraki'nin Müslümanlar İskan Politikası (1913–1918)*. Istanbul: İletişim Yayınları.

Dündar, Fuat (2008). *Modern Türkiye'nin Şifresi: İttihat ve Terrakki'nin Etnisite Mühendisliği* (1913–18). Istanbul: İletişim Yayınları.

Dündar, Fuat (2012). 'Pouring a People into the Desert: The "Definitive Solution" of the Unionist to the Armenian Question', in Ronal Grigor Suny, Fatma Müğe Göçek and Norman M. Naimark (eds.) *A Question of Genocide: Armenians and Turks at the End of the Ottoman Empire*. Oxford: Oxford University Press, pp. 276–84.

Ekinci, Tarık Ziya (2011). *Kürt Siyasal Hareketlerinin Sınıfsal Analizi*. İstanbul: Sosyal Tarih Yayınları.

Eldem, Vedat (1970). *Osmanlı İmparatorluğunun İktisadi Şartları Hakkında bir Tetkik*. Ankara: Türkiye İş Bankası Kültür Yayınları.

Elphinston, William Graham (1946). 'The Kurdish Question'. *International Affairs*, 22(1), pp. 91–103.

Engin, Tandoğan, M. Balcı, Y. Sümer, Y. Z. Özkan (1981), 'General Geological Setting and the Structural Features of the Guleman Peridotite Unit and the Chromite Deposits (Elazig, Eastern Turkey)'. *Bulletin of the Mineral Research and Exploration of Turkey Institute of Turkey*, 95, pp. 34–56.

Entessar, Nader (1992). *Kurdish Ethnonationalism*. London: Lynne Rienner Publishing.

Entessar, Nader (2010). *Kurdish Politics in the Middle East*. Lanham, MD: Lexington Books.

Ercan, Fuat (2004). 'Sermaye Birikiminin Celişkili Sürekliliği: Türkiye'nin Küresel Kapitalizmle Bütünleşme Sürecine Eleştirel Bir Bakış', in Neşecan Balkan and Sungur Savran (eds.) *Neoliberalizmin Tahribatı: Turkiye'de Ekonomi, Toplum ve Cinsiyet*. Istanbul: Metis Yayınları, pp. 9–43.

Erdem, Esra (2006). 'Migrations from the "Global South" and Informal Economy in Turkey: Laissez Passer, Laisses Faire?'. *Revista de Economid Mundial*, 14, pp. 87–120.

Erder, Leila (1975). 'The Measurement of Pre-industrial Population Changes: The Ottoman Empire from the 15th to the 17th Century'. *Middle Eastern Studies*, 3(11), pp. 284–301.

Erder, Leila and Suraiya Faroqhi (1979). 'Population Rise and Fall in Anatolia, 1150–1620'. *Middle Eastern Studies*. 15(3), pp. 322–45.

Ergil, Doğu (2009). *Kürt Raporu: Güvenlik Politikalarından Kimlik Siyasetine*. Istanbul: Timaş Yayınları.

Eroğlu, Cem (1998). *Demokrat Parti: Tarihi ve Ideolojisi*. Ankara: İmge Yayınları.

Ersanlı-Behar, Büşra (1992). *İktidar ve Tarih. Türkiye'de 'Resmi Tarih' Tezinin Oluşumu (1929–1937)*. İstanbul: Arfa Yayınları.

Ersoy, Ercan (2012). 'Shell Starts Shale Gas Exploration in Southeast Turkey', Bloomberg, 5 September 2012. Online: www.bloomberg.com/news/2012–09-05/shell-starts-shale-gas-exploration-in-southeast-turkey.html (Last accessed: 1 August 2016).

Europa (2002). *Regional Surveys of the World: The Middle East and North Africa, 2003*. London: Routledge.

Europa (2003). *Regional Surveys of the World: The Middle East and North Africa, 2004*. London: Routledge.

European Commission (1993). Conclusions of the Presidency: European Council in Copenhagen, 21–22 June 1993. Online: www.consilium.europa.eu/ueDocs/cms_Data/docs/pressData/en/ec/72921.pdf (Last accessed: 1 August 2016).

European Commission (1998). Regular Report on Turkey's Progress towards Accession. Online: www.ec.europa.eu/enlargement/archives/pdf/key_documents/1998/turkey_en.pdf (Last accessed: 1 August 2016).

European Commission (2005). Regular Report on Turkey's Progress towards Accession. Online: http://ec.europa.eu/enlargement/archives/pdf/key_documents/2005/package/sec_1426_final_progress_report_tr_en.pdf (Last accessed: 1 August 2016).

European Commission (2006). Regular Report on Turkey's Progress towards Accession. Online: http://ec.europa.eu/enlargement/pdf/key_documents/2006/nov/tr_sec_1390_en.pdf (Last accessed: 1 August 2016).

European Commission (2007). Regular Report on Turkey's Progress towards Accession. Online: http://ec.europa.eu/enlargement/pdf/key_documents/2007/nov/turkey_progress_reports_en.pdf (Last accessed: 1 August 2016).

European Commission (2008). Regular Report on Turkey's Progress towards Accession. Online: http://ec.europa.eu/enlargement/pdf/press_corner/key-documents/reports_nov_2008/turkey_progress_report_en.pdf (Last accessed: 1 August 2016).

Eurostat (2014). Unemployment Statistics. Online: http://epp.eurostat.ec.europa.eu/statistics_explained/index.php/Unemployment_statistics> (Last accessed: 1 August 2016).

Faroqhi, Suraiya (1984). *Towns and Townsmen of Ottoman Anatolia: Trade, Crafts and Food Production in an Urban Setting, 1520–1650*. Cambridge: Cambridge University Press.

Faroqhi, Suraiya (1994). 'Crisis and Change, 1590–1699', in Halil İnalcık and Donald Quataert (eds.) *An Economic and Social History of the Ottoman Empire 1600–1914*. Cambridge: Cambridge University Press, pp. 413–636.

Faucompret, Eric and Jozef Konings (2008). *Turkish Accession to the EU: Satisfyng the Copenhagen Criteria*. London and New York: Routledge.

Fekete, Lajos (1947). 'Türk Vergi Tahrirleri'. *Belleten*, 11(42), pp. 299–328.

Fisher, N. Sydney (1959). *The Middle East: A History*. London: Routledge and Keegan Paul Ltd.

Frank, Andre Gunder (1966). *The Development of Underdevelopment*. Boston, MA: New England Free Press.

GAP (1990). *GAP Master Plan, Executive Summary*, 2nd ed. Ankara, Devlet Planlama Teşkilatı.

GAP (1997). *GAP-UNDP Sustainable Development Programme*. Ankara: GAP Publications.

GAP (1998). *GAP Social Policy Objectives*. Urfa: GAP Publications.

GAP (2008). *GAP Eylem Planı (2008–2012)*. Urfa: GAP Publications.

Gaunt, David (2006). *Massacres, Resistances, Protectors: Muslim–Christian Relations in Eastern Anatolia during World War I*. Piscataway, NJ: Gorgias Press.

Geertz, Clifford James (1973). *The Interpretation of Cultures: Selected Essays*. New York: Basic Books.

Gellner, Ernest (1992). *Nations and Nationalism*. Oxford: Basil Blackwell.

Gençkaya, Ömer Lütfü (1996). 'The Kurdish Issue in Turkish Politics: An Overview'. *Islamic World Report (London)*, 1(3), pp. 94–101.

Gill, Rosalind (2000). 'Discourse Analysis', in Bauer, Martin W. and Gaskell, George, (eds.) *Qualitative Researching With Image, Sound and Text*.Sage Publications, London, pp. 172–90.

Göç-Der (2002). *The Research and Solution Report on the Socio-Economic and Socio-Cultural Conditions of the Kurdish Citizens Living in the Turkish Republic Who Are Forcibly Displaced Due to Armed-Conflict and Tension Politics*. İstanbul: Göç-Der.

Gökalp, Ziya (1959). *Turkish Nationalism and Western Civilization: Selected Essays*. Translated by Niyazi Berkes. London: George Allen and Unwin Ltd.

Gökalp, Ziya (1968). *Principles of Turkism*. Translated by Robert Devereux. Leiden: Brill.

Gramsci, Antonio (1971). *Selections from the Prison Notebooks*. New York: International Publishers.

Griswold, W. J. (1993). 'Climatic Change: A Possible Factor in the Social Unrest of the Seventeenth Century Anatolia', in Heath W. Lowry and Donald Quataert (eds.) *Humanist and Scholar: Essays in Honor of Adreas Tietze*. Istanbul: Isis Press, pp. 36–57.

Gunes, Cengiz (2012). *The Kurdish National Movement: From Protest to Resistance*. New York and London: Routledge.

Gunes, Cengiz and Robert Lowe (2015). 'The Impact of the Syrian War on Kurdish Politics across the Middle East'. *Chatham House Research Paper*, July 2015 (London: Chatham House).

Gunes, Cengiz and Welat Zeydanlıoğlu (2014). 'Introduction: Turkey and the Kurds', in Cengiz Gunes and Welat Zeydanlıoğlu (eds.) *The Kurdish Question in Turkey: New Perspectives on Violence, Representation, and Reconciliation*. New York and London: Routledge, pp. 1–20.

Gunter, M. Michael (1990). *The Kurds in Turkey*. Oxford: Westview Press.

Gunter, M. Michael (2011a). 'Turgut Özal and the Kurdish Question', in Marlies Casier and Joost Jongerden (eds.) *Nationalisms and Politics in Turkey: Political Islam, Kemalism, and the Kurdish Issue*. London and New York: Routledge, pp. 85–100.

Gunter, M. Michael (2011b). *The Kurds Ascending: The Evolving Solution to the Kurdish Problem in Iraq and Turkey*. Basingstoke: Palgrave Macmillan.

Hale, William (1981). *The Political and Economic Development of Modern Turkey*. London: Croom Hell.

Halliday, Fred (2006). 'Can We Write a Modernist History of Kurdish Nationalism?', in Faleh A. Jabar and Hosham Dawod (eds.) *The Kurds: Nationalism and Politics*. London: Saqi, pp. 11–20.

Hanioğlu, M. Şükrü (1995). *The Young Turks in Opposition*. Oxford: Oxford University Press.

Hanioğlu, M. Şükrü (2001). *Preparation for a Revolution: the Young Turks, 1902–1908*. Oxford: Oxford University Press.

Hansen, Bent (1991). *Egypt and Turkey: The Political Economy of Poverty, Equity and Growth*. Oxford: Oxford University Press.

Hart, Keith (1973). 'Informal Income Opportunities and Urban Employment in Ghana'. *Journal of Modern African Studies*, 2 (1): 61–89.

Hassanpour, Amir (1992). *Nationalism and Language in Kurdistan, 1918–1985*. San Francisco, CA: Mellen Research University Press.

Hazar Strateji Ensitüsü (2013). *The Energy Bill of Turkey and Unsustainable Economic Growth*. Istanbul: Hazar Strateji Ensitüsü Publications.

Hechter, Michael (1975). *Internal Colonialism: The Celtic Fringe in British National Development, 1536–1966*. London: Routledge and Keegan Paul.

Heper, Metin (2007). *The State and the Kurds in Turkey: The Question of Assimilation*. Basingstoke: Palgrave Macmillan.

Herschlag, Zvi Yehuda (1958). *Turkey: An Economy in Transition*. Hague: Uitgevereij Van Keulen.

Herschlag, Zvi Yehuda (1968). *Turkey: The Challenge of Growth*. Leiden: Brill.

Hobsbawm, Eric (1990). *Nations and Nationalism since 1780*. Cambridge: Cambridge University Press.

Hobsbawm, Eric ([1997] 2004). *On History*. 2nd ed. London: Abacus.

Hovannisian, G. Richard (1999). 'Introduction: The Armenian Genocide, Remembrance and Denial', in Richard G. Hovannisian (ed.) *Remembrance and Denial: The Case of the Armenian Genocide*. Detroit, MI: Wayne State Press.

Hroch, Miroslav (1993). 'From National Movement to Fully-Formed Nation: The Nation-Building Process in Process in Europe'. *New Left Review*, 198, pp. 3–20.

Human Rights Watch (1994). *Turkey: Forced Displacement of Ethnic Kurds from South East Turkey*. New York and Washington, DC: Human Rights Watch.

HÜNEE (2006). *Türkiye'de Göç ve Yerinden Olmuş Nufüs Araştırması*. Ankara: Hacetepe Üniversitesi Nufüs Etütleri Ensitüsü Yayını.

Hürriyet. 8 September 1992.

Hussmanns, Ralf (2004). 'Measuring the Informal Sector: From Employment in the Informal Sector to Informal Employment'. *Working Paper* 53. Geneva: ILO Publication.

Hyed, Uriel (1979). *Foundations of Turkish Nationalism: The Life and Teaching of Ziya Gökalp*. Westport, CT: Hyperion Press.

Ibrahim, Farhad and Gülistan Gürbey, eds. (2000). *The Kurdish Conflict in Turkey: Obstacles and Chances for Peace and Democracy*. Germany: Lit Verlag.

IEA (2012). *Iraq Energy Outlook: World Energy Outlook Special Report*. Paris: IEA Publication.

IEA (2014). *Energy Supply Security 2014*. Paris: IEA Publications, pp. 446–61.

İHD (1995). *1995 Yılı İnsan Hakları İhlaleri Raporu*. Ankara: İHD Yayını.

ILO (1993). 'Resolution Concerning Statistics of Employment in the Informal Sector', in *Fifteenth International Conference of Labour Statisticians (Geneva 19–28 January 1993) Report of the Conference*. Geneva: ILO Publication.

ILO (2003). 'Guidelines Concerning a Statistical Definition of Informal Employment', in *Seventh International Conference of Labour Statisticians (Geneva 24 November–3 December 2003) Report of the Conference*. Geneva: ILO Publications.

ILO (2010). *Informal Economy and Labour Market Policies and Institutions in Selected Mediterranean Countries: Turkey, Syria, Jordan, Algeria and Morocco.* Geneva: ILO Publications.

ILO and WIEGO (2013). *Women and Men in the Informal Economy: A Statistical Picture* (Second Edition). Geneva: ILO Publications.

IMF (2004). *World Economic Outlook Database, Turkey: Current Account Balance, 1980–2011.* Online: www.imf.org/external/pubs/ft/weo/2014/02/weodata/weorept.aspx?pr.x=54&pr.y=16&sy=1980&ey=2011&scsm=1&ssd=1&sort=country&ds=.¦1&c=186&s=BCA_NGDPD&grp=0&a (Last accessed: 1 August 2016).

İnalcık, Halil (1970). 'The Ottoman Economic Mind and Aspects of the Ottoman Economy', in M. A. Cook (ed.) *Studies in the Economic History of the Middle East.* London: Oxford University Press, pp. 207–18.

İnalcık, Halil (1971). 'Imtiyazat', *Encyclopedia of Islam.* 2nd ed. Vol. 3, Leiden: E. J. Brill, pp. 1179–89.

İnalcık, Halil (1980). 'Military and Fiscal Transformations in the Ottoman Empire, 1600–1700'. *Archivum Ottomanicum,* 6 (1980), pp. 283–337.

İnalcık, Halil (1994). 'The Ottoman State: Economy and Society, 1300–1600', in Halil İnalcık and Donald Quataert (eds.) *An Economic and Social History of the Ottoman Empire 1600–1914.* Cambridge: Cambridge University Press, pp. 9–380.

İnan, Afet (1972). *Devletçilik İlkesi ve Türkiye Cumhuriyetinin Birinci Sanayi Planı.* Ankara: Türk Tarih Kurumu Basımevi.

International Crisis Group (2015). *A Sisyphean Task? Resuming Turkey–PKK Peace Talks. Crisis Group Europe Briefing No. 77 (17 December 2015).* Istanbul/Brussels: International Crisis Group.

Işıklı, Alpaslan (1987). 'Wage, Labour, Unionization', in Irvin Cemil Shick and Ertuğrul Ahmet Tonak (eds.) *Turkey in Transition: New Perspectives.* Oxford: Oxford University Press, pp. 309–32.

İslamoğlu-İnan, Huri (1994). *State and Peasant in the Ottoman Empire: Agrarian Power Relations and Regional Economic Development.* Leiden: Brill.

İstanbul İktisadi ve Ticari İlimler Akademisi (1973). *Türk Ekonomisinin 50 Yılı.* İstanbul: Fatih Yayınevi.

Issawi, Charles (1980). *The Economic History of Turkey 1800–1914.* Chicago; London: University of Chicago Press.

Izady, Mehrdad (1988). 'Kurdistan', in *The Encylopedia of Asian History.* New York: Charles Scribner's Sons, pp. 373–5.

Izady, Mehrdad (1992). *The Kurds: A Concise Handbook.* Washington, DC: Crane Russak.

Jafar, R. Madjid (1976). *Under-underdevelopment: A Regional Case Study of the Kurdish Areas in Turkey.* Helsinki: Social Policy Association.

Jennings, Ronald (1976). 'Urban Population in Anatolia in the Sixteenth Century: A Study of Kayseri, Karaman, Trabzon and Erzurum'. *International Journal of Middle Eastern Studies,* 1(7), pp. 21–57.

Jongerden, Joost (2007). *The Settlement Issue in Turkey and the Kurds: An Analysis of Spatial Policies, Modernity and War.* Brill: Leiden.

Jongerden, Joost (2012). 'Elite Encounters of a Violent Kind: Milli İbrahim Paşa, Ziya Gökalp and Political Struggle in Diyarbakır at the Turn of the 20th

Century', in Joost Jongerden and Jelle Verheij (eds.) *Social Relations in Ottoman Diyarbekir, 1870–1915*. Leiden: Brill, pp. 55–84.

Jongerden, Joost and Ahmet Hamdi Akkaya (2014). 'Confederalism and autonomy in Turkey: The Kurdistan Workers' Party and the Reinvention of Democracy', in Cengiz Gunes and Welat Zeydanlıoğlu (eds.) *The Kurdish Question in Turkey: New Perspectives on Violence, Representation, and Reconciliation*. New York and London: Routledge, pp. 186–204.

Jorgens, Denise (2000). 'A Comparative Examination of the Provisions of the Ottoman Land Code and Khedive Said's Law 1858', in Owen Roger (ed.) *New Perspectives on Property and Land in the Middle East*. Cambridge, MA: Harvard University Press, pp. 93–119.

Jung, Dietrich and Wolfgango Piccoli (2001). *Turkey at the Crossroads: Ottoman Legacies and the Greater Middle East*. London: Zed Books.

Jwaideh, Wadie (1961). *The Kurdish Nationalist Movement*. New York: Syracuse University Press.

Kaiser, Hilmar (1998). *Imperialism, Racism, and Development Theories: The Construction of a Dominant Paradigm*. Ann Arbor, MI: Gomidas Institute.

Kamenka, Eugene (1973). 'Political Nationalism – The Evolution of an Idea', in Eugene Kamenka, *Nationalism: The Nature and Evolution of an Idea*. Canberra: Australian University Press, pp. 4–20.

Kan, Elif Oznur and Aysit Tansel (2014). 'Defining and Measuring Informality in the Turkish Labor Market'. Discussion Paper Series, No. 8377. Bonn: Forschungsinstitut zur Zukunft der Arbeit-Institute for the Study of Labor Publication.

Karahan, Edip (2005). *Bir Kürt Devrimcisi. Edip Karahan'ın Anısına*. Istanbul: Elma Yayınları.

Karaman, Ismail (1986). *Gelir Dağılımı ve Türkiye'de Yapılan Gelir Dağılımı Çalışmaları, 1959–1986*. Ankara: Devlet Planlama Teşkilatı.

Karpat, Kemal H. (1959). *Turkey's Politics: The Transition to a Multi-party System*. Princeton, NJ: Princeton University Press.

Karpat, Kemal H. (1973). *Social Change and Politics in Turkey: A Structural-Historical Analysis*. Leiden: Brill.

Karpat, Kemal H. (1985). *Ottoman Population 1830–1914: Demographic and Social Characteristics*. Madison: University of Wisconsin Press.

Karpat, Kemal H. (2001). *The Politicization of Islam: Reconstructing Identity, State, Faith, and Community in the Late Ottoman State*. Oxford: Oxford University Press.

Kasaba, Reşat (1988). *The Ottoman Empire and the World Economy: The Nineteenth Century*. Albany: State University of New York Press.

Kaya, Ferzende (2005). *Mezopotamya Sürgünü: Abdülmelik Fırat'ın Yaşam Öyküsü*. Istanbul: Alfa Yayınları.

Keegan, John (1998). *The First World War*. New York: Vintage.

Keyder, Çağlar (1987) *State and Class in Turkey: A Study in Capitalist Development*. London: Verso.

KHRP (1996). *The Destruction of Villages South-East Turkey*. London: KHRP Publications.

KHRP (2002). *Internally Displaced Persons: The Kurds in Turkey*. London: KHRP Publications.

KHRP (2004). *Turkey's Implementation of Pro-EU Reforms: Fact-Finding Mission Report*. London: KHRP Publications.

Kılıç, Ayla H. (1998). 'Democratization, Human Rights, and Ethnic Policies in Turkey'. *Journal of Muslim-Minority Affairs*, 18(1), pp. 91–111.

Kılıç, Orhan (1999). 'Yurtluk-Ocaklık ve Hükümet Sancakları Üzerine Bazı Tesbitler'. *Osmanlı Tarihi Araştırma ve Uygulama Merkezi Dergisi*, 10, pp. 19–137.

Kirişçi, Kemal and Gareth M. Winrow (1997). *The Kurdish Question and Turkey: An Example of a Trans-state Ethnic Conflict*. London: Frank Cass Publishers.

Kırzıoğlu, Fahrettin M. (1963). *Kürtlerin Kökü*. Ankara: Ayyıldız Matbası.

Koçak, Cemil (2003). *Umûmi Müfettişlikler (1927–1952)*. İstanbul: İletişim Yayınları.

Kökdemir, Naci (1952). *Eski ve Yeni Toprak, İskan Hükümleri ve Uygulama Kılavuzu*. Ankara: Yeni Matbaa.

Kolars, John (1986). 'The Hydro-imperative of Turkey's Search for Energy'. *Middle East Journal*, 40(1), pp. 53–67.

KONDA ARAŞTIRMA (2011). *Kürt Meselesi'nde Algı ve Beklentiler*. İstanbul: İletişim Yayınları.

Koohi-Kamali, Farideh (2003). *The Political Development of the Kurds in Iran: Pastoral Nationalism*. Basingstoke and New York: Palgrave Macmillan.

Kreyenbroek, Philip G. (1992) 'On the Kurdish Language', in Philip G. Kreyenbroek and Stefan Sperl (eds.) *The Kurds: A Contemporary Overview*. London: Routledge, pp. 68–83.

Kreyenbroek, Philip G. (1996). 'Religion and Religions in Kurdistan', in Christine Allison and Philip G. Kreyenbroek (eds.), *Kurdish Culture and Identity*. London: Zed Books, pp. 85–110.

Kreyenbroek, Philip G. (1998). 'On the Study of Some Heterodox Sects in Kurdistan'. *Les Annales de l'autre Islam*, 5, pp. 163–84.

Kunt, Metin (1983). *The Sultan's Servants: The Transformation of Ottoman Regional Government, 1550–1650*. New York: Columbia University Press.

Kurdish Globe (2014). The Turkish Advocate of the Kurds – Dr. Ismail Beşikçi. Online: www.saradistribution.com/kurdish_globe.htm (Last accessed: 1 August 2016).

Küçük, Yalçın (1978). *Planlama, Kalkınma ve Türkiye*. Ankara: Tekin Yayınevi.

Kürdoloji Çalışmaları Grubu (2011). *Osmanlı Kürdistanı, Kürt Tarihi Araştırmaları-I*. Istanbul: Boğaziçi Gösteriler Sanatları Topluluğu Yayınları.

Kutbay, Cemil and Nihal Çınar (1989). *Kalkınma Öncelikli İllerin Sanayi Envanteri*. Ankara: Devlet Planlama Teşkilatı.

Kutlay, Mustafa (2015). 'The Turkish Economy at a Crossroads: Unpacking Turkey's Current Account Challenge', in Senem Aydın-Düzgit et al. (eds.) *Global Turkey in Europe III: Democracy, Trade, and the Kurdish Question in Turkey–EU Relations*. Roma: Istituto Affari Internazionali (IAI), pp. 219–40.

Landau, Jacob M. (1995). *Pan-Turkism: From Irredentism to Cooperation*. London: Hurst & Company.

Lerner, Daniel (1958). *The Passing of Traditional Society: Modernizing the Middle East*. Glencoe, IL: Free Press.

Lewis, Bernard (1968). *The Emergence of Modern Turkey*, 2nd ed. London: Oxford University Press.

Lewis, Bernard (1994). *The Shaping of the Modern Middle East*. Oxford: Oxford University Press.

List, Freidrich (1856). *National System of Political Economy*. Philadelphia, PA: J. B. Lippencott [republished by Michigan: University of Michigan Library (n.d.)].

Lutsky, Vladimir Borisovich (1969). *Modern History of the Arab Countries*. Translated by Lika Nasser. Moscow: Progress Publishers.

MacKenzie, D. N. (1961). 'The Origins of Kurdish', in *Transactions of the Philological Society*. Oxford: Basil Blackwell, pp. 68–86.

Mango, Andrew (1999). 'Atatürk and the Kurds'. *Middle Eastern Studies*, 35(4), pp. 1–25.

Marcus, Aliza (2007). *Blood and Belief: The PKK and the Kurdish Fight for Independence*. New York and London: New York University Press.

Margulies, Roni and Ergin Yıldızoğlu (1987). 'Agrarian Change: 1923–70', in Irvin Cemil Shick and Ertuğrul Ahmet Tonak (eds.) *Turkey in Transition: New Perspectives*. Oxford: Oxford University Press, pp. 269–92.

Marx, Karl ([1859] 1977). *A Contribution to the Critique of Political Economy*. Moscow: Progress Publishers.

Marx, Karl ([1867] 1982). *Capital: A Critique of Political Economy*. Moscow: Progress Publishers.

Marx, Karl ([1939] 1973) *Grundrisse: Outlines of the Critique of Political Economy*. London: Penguin.

Maunsell, F. R. (1894). 'Kurdistan'. *The Geographical Journal*, 3(2), pp. 81–92.

Maunsell, F.R. (1901). 'Central Kurdistan'. *The Geographical Journal*, 18(2), pp. 121–41.

McDowall, David (2000). *A Modern History of the Kurds*. London: I. B. Tauris.

McGowan, Bruce (1981). *Economic Life in Ottoman Europe: Taxation, Trade, and the Struggle for Land, 1600–1800*. Cambridge: Cambridge University Press.

McGowan, Bruce (1994). 'The Age of the Ayans, 1699–1812', in Halil İnalcık and Donald Quataert (eds.) *An Economic and Social History of the Ottoman Empire 1600–1914*. Cambridge: Cambridge University Press, pp. 639–758.

Meho, Lokman I. (2001). 'The Kurds, Kurdistan: A General Background', in Lokman I. Meho and Kelly L. Maglughlin (eds.). *Kurdish Culture and Society: An Annotated Bibliography*. Westport, CT: Greenwood Press, pp. 3–26.

Metz, Steven and Millen Raymond (2004). *Insurgency and Counterinsurgency in the 21st Century: Reconceptualising Threat and Response*. Carlisle: Strategic Studies Institute of the US Army War College Publication.

Minorsky, Vladimir F. (1927). 'The Kurdish Language', in *Encyclopaedia of Islam Vol. 2*, pp. 1151–5.

Moltke, Helmut Carl Bernhard von (1968). *Briefe aus der Türkei aus den Jahren 1835–1839*. Berlin Ernst Siegfreid Mittler und Suhn. Hofbuchhandlung.

Morvaridi, Behrooz (2004). 'Resettlement, Rights to Development and the Ilisu Dam, Turkey'. *Development and Change*, 35(4), pp. 719–41.

Muller, Mark (1996). 'Nationalism and the Rule of Law in Turkey: The Elimination of Kurdish Representation during the 1990s', in Robert Olson (ed.) *Kurdish Nationalist Movement in the 1990s*. Kentucky: University of Kentucky Press, pp. 173–99.

Murphey, Rhoads (1987). *Regional Structure in the Ottoman Economy: A Sultanic Memorandum of 1636 A.D. Concerning the Sources and Uses of Tax-Farms Revenues of Anatolia and the Coastal Northern Portions of Syria*. Wiesbaden: Otto Harrassowitz.

Mutlu, Servet (1996a). 'Ethnic Kurds in Turkey: A Demographic Study'. *International Journal of Middle East Studies*, 28(4), pp. 517–54.

Mutlu, Servet (1996b). 'GAP: Intentions, Hopes, Actions, and Results'. *Private View*, 6(2), pp. 38–44.

Mutlu, Servet (2002). *Doğu Sorunun Kökenleri: Ekonomik Açıdan*. Istanbul: Ötüken Nesriyat.

Nairn, Tom (1977). *The Break-up of Britain*. London: NLB.

Natali, Denise (2005). *The Kurds and the State: Evolving National Identity in Iraq, Turkey and Iran*. New York: Syracuse University Press.

Nezan, Kendal, (1993). 'Kurdistan in Turkey', in Gerard Chaliand (ed.) *A People Without Country: The Kurds and Kurdistan*. London: Zed Books, pp. 38–138.

Nezan, Kendal, (1996). 'The Current Position and Historical Background', in Philip G. Kreyenbroek and Christine Allison (eds.) *Kurdish Culture and Identity*. London and New York: Zed Books, pp. 7–19.

Niebuhr, Carsten ([1766] 1968). *Reisebeschreibung nach Arabien und Umliegenden Landern*. Austria: Dietmar Henze.

Öcalan, Abdullah (1992). *Kürdistan Devriminin Yolu (Manifesto)*, 4th ed. Köln: Weşanen Serxwebun.

Öcalan, Abdullah (2003). *War and Peace in Kurdistan*. Cologne: International Initiative Freedom for Öcalan.

Öcalan, Abdullah (2008). *War and Peace in Kurdistan: Perspectives for a Political Solution of the Kurdish Question*. Cologne: International Initiative.

OECD (1980). *Economic Survey: Turkey*. Paris: OECD Publishing.

OECD (2008). *Are we Growing Unequal?* Online: www.oecd.org/els/soc/41494435.pdf (Last accessed: 1 August 2016).

OECD (2009). 'Regional Disparities in GDP per capita', in *Regional Outlook at a Glance, 2009* Online: www.oecd-ilibrary.org/docserver/download/0409011ec019.pdf (Last accessed: 1 August 2016).

OECD (2011). 'Income Inequality' in *Society at a Glance 2011: OECD Social Indicators*. Online: www.keepeek.com/Digital-Asset-Management/oecd/social-issues-migration-health/society-at-a-glance-2011/income-inequality_soc_glance-2011-16-en (Last accessed: 1 August 2016).

OECD (2012). *Economic Surveys: Turkey 2012 (Overview)* Online: www.oecd.org/eco/surveys/OVERVIEW%20ENGLISH%20FINAL.pdf (Last accessed: 1 August 2016).

Öktem, Kerem (2004). 'Incorporating the Time and Space of the Ethnic "Other": Nationalism and Space in Southeast Turkey in the Nineteenth and Twentieth Centuries'. *Nations and Nationalism*, 10(4), pp. 559–78.

Olson, Robert (1989). *The Emergence of Kurdish Nationalism and the Sheikh Said Rebellion, 1880–1925*. Austin: University of Texas Press.

Öngen, Tulin (2003): '"Yeni Liberal" Dönüşüm Projesi ve Türkiye Deneyimi', in Ahmet H., Köse, Fikret Şenses and Erinç Yeldan (eds.) *Küresel Düzen: Birikim, Devlet ve Sınıflar*. Istanbul: İletişim Yayınları, pp. 161–90.

Öniş, Ziya (2004). 'Turgut Özal and His Economic Legacy: Turkish Neo-liberalism in Critical Perspective'. *Middle Eastern Studies*, 40(4), pp. 113–34.

Öniş, Ziya and Barry Rubin (eds.) (2003). *The Turkish Economy in Crisis*. London: Frank Cass.

O'Shea, T. Maria (2004). *Trapped between the Map and Reality: Geography and Perceptions of Kurdistan*. London and New York: Routledge.

Owen, Roger (1981). *The Middle East in the World Economy 1800–1914*. London: Methuen.

Öz, Mehmet (2003). 'Ottoman Provincial Administration in Eastern Southeastern Anatolia: The Case of Bidlis in the Sixteenth Century', in Kemal Karpat (ed.), *Ottoman Borderlands: Issues, Personalities and Political Changes*. Madison: University of Wisconsin Press, pp. 145–56.

Özar, Şemsa and Fuat Ercan (2004). 'Emek Piyasaları: Uyumsuzluk mu, Bütünleşme mi?', in Neşecan Balkan and Sungur Savran (eds.) *Neoliberalizmin Tahribatı: Turkiye'de Ekonomi, Toplum ve Cinsiyet*. Istanbul: Metis Yayınları, pp. 191–210.

Özcan, Ali Kemal (2006). *A Theoretical Analysis of the PKK and Abdullah Öcalan*. London and New York: Routledge.

Özer, Ahmet (1994). *GAP ve Sosyal Değişme*, Diyarbakır, Dicle Üniversitesi GAP Araştırma ve Uygulama Merkezi, No. 6. Diyarbakır: Dicle Üniversitesi Basımevi.

Özel, Oktay (2004). 'Population Changes in Ottoman Anatolia during the 16th and 17th Centuries: The "Demographic Crisis" Reconsidered. *International Journal of Middle East Studies*, 36(2), pp. 183–205.

Özgür Gündem. 27 October 2010.

Özoğlu, Hakan (2004). *Kurdish Notables and the Ottoman State: Evolving Identities, Competing Loyalties, and Shifting Boundaries*. Albany: State University of New York Press.

Özok-Gündoğan, Nilay (2005). '"Social Development" as Governmental Strategy in the Southeastern Anatolia Project'. *New Perspective on Turkey*, 32, pp. 93–111.

Özuğurlu, Sonay Bayramoğlu (2009). 'Türkiye'de Devletin Dönüşümü: Parlamenter Popülizmden Piyasa Despotizmine', in Nergiz Mütevellioğlu and Sinan Sönmez *Küreselleşme, Kriz ve Türkiye'de Neoliberal Dönüşüm*. Istanbul: İstanbul Bilgi Üniversitesi Yayını, pp. 261–302.

Pamuk, Şevket ([1987] 2010). *The Ottoman Empire and European Capitalism, 1820–1913: Trade, Investment and Production*. Cambridge: Cambridge University Press.

Pamuk, Şevket (1994). 'Money in the Ottoman Empire, 1326–1914', in Halil İnalcık and Donald Quataert (eds.) *An Economic and Social History of the Ottoman Empire 1600–1914*. Cambridge: Cambridge University Press, pp. 947–85.

Pamuk, Şevket (2003). 'Karşılaştırmalı Açıdan Türkiye'de İktisadi Büyüme, 1880–2000', in Ahmet H., Köse, Fikret Şenses and Erinç Yeldan (eds.) *Küresel Düzen: Birikim, Devlet ve Sınıflar*. Istanbul: İletişim Yayınları, pp. 383–98.

Pamuk, Şevket (2004). Coins and Currency of the Ottoman Empire. Online: www.pierre-marteau.com/currency/coins/turk.html (Last accessed: 1 August 2016).

Pamuk, Şevket (2008). 'Economic Change in Twentieth-Century Turkey: Is the Glass More Than Half Full?', in Reşat Kasaba (ed.) *The Cambridge History of Turkey, Volume 4: Turkey in the Modern World*. Cambridge: Cambridge University Press, pp. 266–300.

Peker, Mümtaz (1996). 'Internal Migration and the Marginal Sector', in Erol Kahveci, Nadir Sungur and Theo Nichols (eds.) *Work and Occupation in Modern Turkey*. London: Mansell Publishing, pp. 7–37.

Powers, Penny (2001). *The Methodology of Discourse Analysis*. New York: Jones and Bartlett.

Primary Documents, *Turco-German Alliance-2 August 1914*. Online: www.firstworldwar.com/source/turcogermanalliance.htm (Last accessed: 1 August 2016).

Quataert, Donald (1993). *Ottoman Manufacturing in the Age of the Industrial Revolution*. Cambridge: Cambridge University Press.

Quataert, Donald (1994). 'The Age of Reforms, 1812–1914', in Halil İnalcık and Donald Quataert (eds.) *An Economic and Social History of the Ottoman Empire 1600–1914*. Cambridge: Cambridge University Press, pp. 759–944.

Quataert, Donald (1996). 'The Social History of Labour in the Ottoman Empire: 1800–1914', in Ellis Jay Goldberg (ed.) *The Social History of the Middle East*. Oxford: Westview Publishers, pp. 19–36.

Quataert, Donald (2000). *The Ottoman Empire, 1700–1922*. Cambridge: Cambridge University Press.

Radikal, 15 March 2015.

Ralph, Davis (1970). 'English Imports from the Middle East, 1580–1780', in Michael Allen Cook (ed.) *Studies in the Economic History of the Middle East*. London: Oxford University Press, pp. 193–206.

Rambout, Lucien (1947). *Les Kurdes et le droit: Des textes, des faits*. Paris: Editions du Cerf.

Resmi Gazete. 21 June 1934. Issue No. 2733.

Resmi Gazete. 25 October 1960. Issue No. 10638.

Resmi Gazete. 23 October 1962. Issue No. 11239.

Resmi Gazete. 14 July 1987. Issue No. 19517.

Richards, Alan and John Waterbury (2008). *A Political Economy of the Middle East*. Boulder, CO: Westview Press.

Rışvanoğlu, Doğan (1975). *Doğu Aşiretleri ve Emperyalizm*, 2nd ed. Istanbul: Türk Kültür Yayınları.

Rivkin, Malcom David (1965). *Area Development for National Growth: The Turkish Precedent*. New York: Frederick A. Praeger.

Robinson, Richard D. (1963). *The First Republic: A Case Study in National Development*. Cambridge, MA: Harvard University Press.

Romano, David (2006). *The Kurdish Nationalist Movement: Opportunity, Mobilisation and Identity*. Cambridge: Cambridge University Press.

Roy, Sara (1995). *The Gaza Strip: The Political Economy of De-development*. Washington, DC: Institute for Palestinian Studies.

Rubin, Allen and Earl R. Babbie (2013). *Research Methods for Social Work*. Belmont, CA: Brooks/Cole.

Safrastian, Arshak (1948). *Kurds and Kurdistan*. London: Harvill Press.

Sahillioğlu, Halil (1970). 'Sıvış Year Crises in the Ottoman Empire', in Michael Allen Cook (ed.) *Studies in the Economic History of the Middle East*. London: Oxford University Press, pp. 230–53.

Salzman, Ariel (2003). *Tocqueville in the Ottoman Empire: Rival Paths to Modern State*. Leiden: Brill.

Sarıhan, Ali (2013). 'The Two Periods of the PKK Conflict: 1984–1990 and 2004–2010', in Fevzi Bilgin and Ali Sarıhan (eds.) *Understanding Turkey's Kurdish Question*. Plymouth: Lexington Books, pp. 89–102.

Saygılı, Şeref et al. (2010). 'Türkiye İmalat Sanayiin İthalat Yapısı', in Türkiye Cumhuriyet Merkez Bankası', Working Papers, No. 10/02.

Scalbert-Yücel, Clémence and Marie Le Ray (2006). 'Knowledge, Ideology and Power. Deconstructing Kurdish Studies', *European Journal of Turkish Studies*, 5. Online: http://ejts.revues.org/pdf/777 (Last accessed: 1 August 2016).

Schramm, Wilbur (1964). *Mass Media and National Development: The Role of Information in the Developing Countries*. Stanford, CA: Stanford University Press.

Serin, Necdet, (1963). *Türkiye'nin Sanayileşmesi*. Ankara: Sevinç Matbaa.

Shaw, J. S. (1969). 'Archival Sources for Ottoman History: The Archives of Turkey'. *Journal of American Oriental Society*, 80(1), pp. 1–12.

Sheyholislami, Jaffer (2011). *Kurdish Identity, Discourse, and New Media*. New York: Palgrave Macmillan.

Simeon, Polonyalı ([1612] 2013). *Polonyalı Simeon'un Seyahatnamesi*. İstanbul: Everest Yayınları.

Sinclair, Thomas Alexander (2003). 'The Ottoman Arrangements for the Tribal Principalities of the Lake Van Region of the Sixteenth Century'. *International Journal of Turkish Studies*, 9, pp. 119–43.

Sirkeci, Ibrahim (2000). 'Exploring the Kurdish population in the Turkish Context'. *Genus*, 56(1–2), pp. 149–75.

Smith, Anthony (1986). *The Ethnic Origins of Nations*. Oxford: Blackwell.

Sönmez, Mustafa ([1990] 1992). *Kürtler: Ekonomik ve Sosyal Tarih, Doğu Anadolu'nun Hikayesi*. Istanbul: Arkadaş Yayınevi.

Sönmez, Mustafa (2012). *Kürt Sorunu ve Demokratik Özerklik*. Istanbul: NotaBene Yayınları.

Spreen, Marinus (1992). 'Rare Populations, Hidden Populations and Link-Tracing Designs: What and Why?'. *Bulletin Methodologie Sociologique*, 1(36), pp. 34–58.

Sykes, Mark (1907). 'Journeys in the North Mesopotamia'. *The Geographical Journal*, 30(4), pp. 384–98.

Tabakoğlu, Ahmet (1985). *Gerileme Dönemine Girerken Osmanlı Maliyesi*. İstanbul: Dergâh Yayınları.

Tachjian, Vahe (2004). *La France en Cilicie et en Haute-Mesopotamie. Aux confins de la Turquie, de la Syrie et de l'Irak (1919–1933)*. Paris: Karthala.

Tan, Altan (2010). *Kürt Sorunu, Ya Tam Kardeşlik Ya Hep Birlikte Kölelik*, 6th ed. Istanbul: Timaş Yayınlar.

Tanin. 14 November 1914.

Taşpınar, Ömer (2005). *Kurdish Nationalism and Political Islam in Turkey: Kemalist Identity in Transition*. London and New York: Routledge.

Tavernier, Jean Baptiste ([1630] 1677). *Les six Voyages de Jean Baptiste Tavernier en Turquie en Perse at aux Indes*. Paris: Fricx.

TESEV (2006). *Doğu ve Güneydoğu Sosyal ve Ekonomik Öncelikleri*. Istanbul, TESEV Yayınları.

Tezel, Yahya S. (1982). *Cumhuriyet Dönemi İktisadi Tarihi (1923–1950)*. Ankara: Yurt Yayınları.

Thomson, Stephan K. (1997). 'Adaptive Sampling in Behavioural Surveys', *NIDA Research Monograph*, 296–319.

Thornburg, Max Weston (1949). *Turkey: An Economic Appraisal*. New York: Twentieth Century Fund.

Timur, Taner (1987). 'The Ottoman Heritage', in Irvin Cemil Shick and Ertuğrul Ahmet Tonak (eds.) *Turkey in Transition: New Perspectives*. Oxford: Oxford University Press, pp. 3–26.

Tocci, Nathalie (2011). *Turkey's European Future: Behind the Scenes of America's Influence on EU–Turkey Relations*. New York and London: New York University Press.

Today's Zaman. 12 April 2008.

Today's Zaman. 2 November 2008.

Today's Zaman. 17 September 2011.

Today's Zaman. 17 September 2013.

Toprak, Zafer (1982). *Türkiye'de 'Milli İktisat' (1908–1918)*. Ankara, Yurt Yayınları.

TPAO (2014). *Domestic Oil Production*. Online: www.tpao.gov.tr/eng/?tp=m&id=79 (Last accessed: 1 August 2016).

Türkdoğan, Orhan (1997). *Etnik Sosyoloji*. Istanbul: Timaş Yayınları.

Turkey, Constitutional Court of the Republic of Turkey, Constitution of the Republic of Turkey, 1982. Online: www.anayasa.gov.tr/images/loadedpdf_dosyalari/the_constitution_of_the_republic_of_turkey.pdf (Last accessed: 1 August 2016).

TÜSIAD (2006). *Kayıtdışı Ekonomi ve Sürdürülebilir Büyüme. AB Yolunda Değerlendirme ve Çözüm Önerileri*. Istanbul: Mikado Publishing.

TÜSIAD (1997). *Perspectives on Democratization in Turkey*. Istanbul: Lebib Yalkin Publishing.

Ülker, Erol (2005). 'Contextualising 'Turkification': Nation-Building in the Late Ottoman Empire, 1908–18'. *Nations and Nationalism*, 11(4), pp. 613–36.

UNDP (2004). *Human Development Report: Turkey 2004*. Ankara: UNDP Turkey.

Üngör, Uğur Umit (2011). *The Making of Modern Turkey: Nation and State in Eastern Anatolia, 1913–1950*. Oxford: Oxford University Press.

Üngör, Uğur Umit (2012). 'Disastrous Decade: Armenians and Kurds in the Young Turk Era, 1915–25', in Joost Jongerden and Jelle Verheij (eds.) *Social Relations in Ottoman Diyarbekir, 1870–1915*. Leiden and Boston: Brill, pp. 267–95.

Üngör, Uğur Umit and Mehmet Polatel (2011). *Confiscation and Destruction: The Young Turk Seizure of Armenian Property*. London; New York: Continuum.

Unver, I. H. Olcay (1997). 'South-Eastern Anatolia Integrated Development Project (GAP), Turkey: An Overview of Issues of Sustainability'. *International Journal of Water Resources Development*, 13(2), pp. 187–207.

USARM (2009). *Eastern and Southeastern Anatolia's Socio-economic Problems and Recommended Solutions*. Diyarbakır: Union of Eastern and Southeastern Anatolia Region Municipalities Publication.

Vali, Abbas (2003a). 'Introduction: Nationalism and the Question of Origins', in Abbas Vali (ed.) *Essays on the Origins of Kurdish Nationalism*. California: Mazda Publishers, pp. 1–13.

Vali, Abbas (2003b). 'Genealogies of the Kurds: Construction of Nation and National Identity in Kurdish Historical Writing', in Abbas Vali (ed.) *Essays on the Origins of Kurdish Nationalism*. California: Mazda Publishers, pp. 58–105.

Vali, Abbas (2006). 'The Kurds and Their "Others": Fragmented Identity and Fragmented Politics' in Faleh A. Jabar and Hosham Dawod (eds.) *The Kurds: Nationalism and Politics*. London: Saqi, pp. 49–78.

van Bruinessen, Martin (1988). 'The Ottoman Conquest of Diyarbekir', in Martin van Bruinessen and Hendrik Boescheten (trans. and eds.) *Evliya Çelebi in Diyarbekir: The Relevant Sections of the Seyahatname*. Leiden and New York: Brill, pp. 13–28.

van Bruinessen, Martin (1991). 'Religion in Kurdistan', *Kurdish Times*, 4, pp. 5–27.

van Bruinessen, Martin (1992). *Agha, Shaikh and State*. London: Zed Books.

van Bruinessen, Martin (2000). *Kurdish Ethno-nationalism versus Nation-Building States: Collected Articles*. Istanbul: Isis.

van Bruinessen, Martin (2003). 'Ehmedî Xanî's Mem û Zîn and Its Role in the Emergence of Kurdish National Awareness', in Abbas Vali (ed.) *Essays on the Origins of Kurdish Nationalism*. California: Mazda Publishers, pp. 40–57.

van Bruinessen, Martin (2003–4). 'İsmail Beşikçi: Turkish Sociologist, Critic of Kemalism, and Kurdologist'. *The Journal of Kurdish Studies*, 5, pp. 19–34.

van Bruinessen, Martin (2004). The Kurdish Question: Whose Question, Whose Answer? The Kurdish Movement Seen by the Kurds and Their Neighbours'. Online: www.let.uu.nl/~martin.vanbruinessen/personal/publications/Jwaideh_memorial_lecture.htm (Last accessed: 1 August 2016).

van Bruinessen, Martin (2006a). 'Can We Write a Modernist History of Kurdish Nationalism?', in Faleh A. Jabar and Hosham Dawod (eds.) *The Kurds: Nationalism and Politics*. London: Saqi, pp. 11–20.

van Bruinessen, Martin (2006b). 'Kurdish Paths to Nation', in Faleh A. Jabar and Hosham Dawod (eds.) *The Kurds: Nationalism and Politics*. London: Saqi, pp. 21–48.

Wahby, Taufiq (1982). *The Origins of the Kurds and Their Language*. Sweden: K.K.S.E.

Waldner, David (1995). 'Avoiding the Inevitable Pain. The Politics of Turkish Economic Reform', *Middle East Insight*, 11(3), pp. 39–41.

Waldner, David (1999). *State Building and Late Development*. Ithaca, NY, and London: Cornell University Press.

WEIGO (2014). 'Statistics on the Informal Economy: Definitions, Regional Estimates & Challenges', *WIEGO Working Paper 2. Cambridge*, MA:WIEGO Publication.

White, Paul (2000). *Primitive Rebels or Revolutionary Modernizers: The Kurdish National Movement in Turkey*. London and New York: Zed Books.

White, Paul (2015). *The PKK: Coming Down from the Mountains*. London: Zed Books.

Williams, Collins (1988). 'Minority Nationalist Historiography', in R. J. Johnston, David B. Knight and Eleonore Kofman (eds.), *Nationalism, Self-Determination and Political Geography*. London: Croom Helm, pp. 203–22.

Woodhead, Christine (ed.) (2012). *The Ottoman World*. Oxon: Routledge.

World Bank (1980). *Turkey: Policies and Prospects for Growth, Country Study*. Washington, DC: World Bank Publications.

World Bank (2014a). World Development Indicators, Turkey: Annual Growth of Rate GDP, 1970–2011. Online: http://data.worldbank.org/country/turkey (Last accessed: 1 August 2016).

World Bank (2014b). World Development Indicators, Domestic Credit to Private Sector (% of GDP), 2001–2010. Online: http://data.worldbank.org/indicator/FS.AST.PRVT.GD.ZS/countries (Last accessed: 1 August 2016).

World Bank (2014c). World Development Indicators, Turkey: GDP per capita, 1970–2011. Online: http://data.worldbank.org/country/turkey (Last accessed: 1 August 2016).

Yalçın, Heckman, Lale (1991). *Tribe and Kingship among the Kurds*. Frankfurt: Peter Lang.

Yalman, Galip (2009). *Transition to Neoliberalism: The Case of Turkey in the 1980s*. Istanbul: Istanbul Bilgi University.

Yavuz, Hakan M. (2007). 'Five Stages of the Construction of Kurdish Nationalism in Turkey', in Charles G. Macdonald and Carole A. O'Leary (eds.) *Kurdish Identity: Human Rights and Political Status*. Florida: The University of Florida Press, pp. 56–76.

Yaycıoğlu, Ali (2012). 'Provincial Power-Holders and the Empire in the Late Ottoman World: Conflict or Partnership?', in Christine Woodhead (ed.) *The Ottoman World*. Oxon: Routledge, pp. 436–52.

Yeğen, Mesut (1999). *Devlet Söyleminde Kürt Sorunu*. Istanbul: İletişim Yayınları.

Yeğen, Mesut (2007). 'Türkiye Solu ve Kürt Sorunu', in Murat Gültenkingil (ed.) *Modern Türkiye'de Siyasal Düşünce Cilt 8: Sol*. Istanbul: İletişim Yayınları, pp. 1208–36.

Yeğen, Mesut (2011). 'The Kurdish Issue in Turkey: Denial to Recognition', in Marlies Casier and Joost Jongerden (eds.) *Nationalisms and Politics in Turkey: Political Islam, Kemalism, and the Kurdish Issue*. London and New York: Routledge, pp. 67–84.

Yeğen, Mesut (2015). 'The Kurdish Peace Process in Turkey: Genesis, Evolution and Prospects', in Senem Aydın-Düzgit et al. (eds.) *Global Turkey in Europe III: Democracy, Trade, and the Kurdish Question in Turkey–EU Relations*. Roma: Istituto Affari Internazionali (IAI), pp. 157–84.

Yeldan, Erinç (2006). *Küreselleşme Sürecinde Türkiye Ekonomisi: Bölüşüm, Birikim ve Büyüme*. Istanbul: İletişim Yayınları.

Yerasimos, Stefanos (1987). 'The Mono-Party Period', in Irvin Cemil Shick and Ertuğrul Ahmet Tonak (eds.) *Turkey in Transition: New Perspectives*. Oxford: Oxford University Press, pp. 66–100.

Yıldırım, Kadir (2013). *Osmanlı'da İşçi Grevleri (1870–1922)*. Istanbul: İletişim Yayınları.

Yıldız, Hasan (1989). *Aşiretten Ulusallığa Doğru Kürtler. Politik Felsefe Açısından Kürt Toplumunun Bir Kritiği*. Istanbul: Fırat-Dicle Yayınları.

Yıldız, Kerim (2005). *The Kurds in Turkey: EU Accession and Human Rights*. London and Ann Arbor, MI: Pluto Press.

Yılmazçelik, İbrahim (1995). *XIX. Yüzyılın İlk Yarısında Diyarbakır*. Ankara: Türk Tarih Kurumu.

Zeki, Muhhamed Emin ([1947] 2005). *Kürd ve Kürdistan Ünlüleri (Meşahire Kürd u Kürdistan)*. Ankara: Özge Yayınları.

Zürcher, Erik-Jan (1994). *Turkey: A Modern History*. London: I. B. Tauris.

Zürcher, Erik-Jan (2000). 'Young Turks, Ottoman Muslims and Turkish Nationalists: Identity Politics 1908–1938', in Kemal H. Karpat (ed.), *Ottoman Past and Today's Turkey* Leiden: Brill, pp. 150–79.

Zürcher, Erik-Jan and Donald Quataert (eds.) (1995). *Workers and the Working Class in the Ottoman Empire and the Turkish Republic*. London: I. B Tauris.

Index